As press secretary and close friend to John F. Kennedy, from the early days of the Democratic primary through the Presidential years, Pierre Salinger offers an expert and warmly human perspective on the founding and forging of the New Frontier, and the fantastic complexities and pressures that go with being press secretary to the President of the United States.

Salinger, a master of the fast-paced and colorful anecdote, brings to light many previously unknown facts. In addition to his capacities as press secretary, Salinger served as a vital diplomatic liaison between Kennedy and Khrushchev, especially when the more orthodox channels of diplomacy seemed too cumbersome: a task which caused more than just a little friction with the State Department.

On the mournful day of November 22, 1963, aboard Air Force One, Pierre Salinger and five members of the Cabinet, all bound for Tokyo, were flashed in code that tragic message: "Lancer is dead."

But the scenes shift quickly to lighter and often hugely amusing events: J.F.K.'s whirlwind Presidential campaign; Salinger's dogged insistence—despite an outraged press corps—on live TV coverage of Presidential face-to- _ Khrushchev _ endeavor _ Russia _ demanding effort to compete with his capacity for food and vodka; J.F.K.'s secret correspondence with Khrushchev (for which Salinger was a diplomatic courier); the author's TV debate with his Russian news media counterparts; the fantastic problem of arranging for Presidential trips, called "advancing the President"; the peril of the Cuban missile crisis and the stunning story of the Scali memorandum in which a seasoned Washington correspondent puts the well-being of his country before his personal ambition; the hilarious account of Salinger's Folly—the 50 Mile Hike That Almost Was, and many other incidents that this dedicated and fascinating man relates without fear or favor in the lively, controversial, and distinctive style with which he handled his job as "Mr. Secretary."

**Pierre Salinger** was born in San Francisco, where he began his career as a reporter and night city editor of the *Chronicle* from 1946-55. Following a two year stint with Collier's magazine, he became investigator for the U.S. Senate Select Committee on Improper Activities in the Labor and Management Field—and a friend of Senator John Kennedy of the Senate Labor Relations Committee. Named the Senator's press secretary in 1959, Salinger's public milestones since then are well known. He is now the Vice President of International Affairs for Continental Airlines.

WITH KENNEDY

# WITH
# KENNEDY

## PIERRE SALINGER

1966

DOUBLEDAY & COMPANY, INC., GARDEN CITY, NEW YORK

To Nicole
and to Marc, Suzanne,
Stephen, and Gregory

# ACKNOWLEDGMENTS

The author is deeply indebted to a number of people for their assistance in the preparation of this book. I will try to name as many of them here as possible in the hope that I will not omit anyone who helped me during the many months it took me to write it.

I wish to thank Mr. Robert F. Six, president of Continental Airlines, where I am currently employed as vice-president of International Affairs, and Mr. Eugene V. Klein, president of National General Corporation, where I was formerly a vice-president and now a consultant, both of whom patiently allowed me to spend time on my book while in their employ. I am grateful to the former archivist of the United States, Dr. Wayne C. Grover, and to the members of his staff, particularly Mr. Harold Elliott, the director of the General Services Administration Record Center in Bell, California, for their help in making my records available to me. I have had the constant encouragement and support of Mrs. John F. Kennedy and Senator Robert F. Kennedy. I have also profited from the help of Miss Pamela Turnure, former Press Secretary to Mrs. Kennedy.

The writing of the book would not have been possible without the help of Mr. Roy Ringer who edited my writing and who constantly prodded my memory to make the book as complete as possible. Miss Joan Miller, my very efficient and lovely secretary, has typed the manuscript with the assistance of Mrs. Betty Duffy, another member of my staff at Continental Airlines. Miss Christine Camp, my former executive secretary at the White House, and now a member of the State Department's public affairs division, has helped me immensely in research.

My wife, Nicole, has assisted me tremendously with her advice and counsel, based on her former career as a magazine writer.

viii ACKNOWLEDGMENTS

I will always owe a debt of gratitude to my co-workers in the press office in the White House for their loyalty and effective work. These include Associate White House Press Secretary Andrew T. Hatcher, Assistant White House Press Secretaries Jay Gildner and Malcolm Kilduff; my secretaries, Chris Camp, Sue Vogelsinger, Barbara Coleman, Barbara Gamarekian, Helen Ganss, Nancy Larson, and Jill Cowan; and the key members of the White House Transportation Office and Records Division—Wayne Hawks, Dewey Long, Edwin (Jiggs) Fauver, Ray Zook, and Bob Manning.

But, most of all, I owe my thanks to John F. Kennedy, who provided me with the opportunity to live through and participate in these exciting events.

# CONTENTS

# LIST OF ILLUSTRATIONS

# CAST OF CHARACTERS

## THE AMERICANS

| NAME | CHRONOLOGY | NOW |
|------|-----------|-----|
| BUNDY, McGEORGE | Special Assistant to the President for National Security Affairs | President, Ford Foundation, New York, New York |
| CLIFTON, CHESTER (Ted) V. | Military Aide to the President (1961 rank was Brigadier General but raised under JFK to Major General, now retired) | President, Thomas J. Deegan Co., public relations, Washington, D.C. |
| DUNGAN, RALPH A. | Special Assistant to the President | U.S. ambassador to Chile (appointed by LBJ) |
| FELDMAN, MYER | Deputy Special Counsel to the President | Ginsberg & Feldman, law firm, Washington, D.C. |
| GOODWIN, RICHARD N. | Assistant Special Counsel to the President | Professor, Wesleyan University, Middletown, Connecticut |
| HATCHER, ANDREW T. | Associate Press Secretary to the President | Market promotion manager, Ballantine Brewery, Newark, New Jersey |

| | | |
|---|---|---|
| KILDUFF, MALCOLM | Assistant Press Secretary to the President | Horton and Kilduff Associates, public relations, Washington, D.C. |
| LAWRENCE, WILLIAM H. | New York *Times* correspondent (1943–61) White House correspondent, American Broadcasting Company (1961– ) | Same position |
| McHUGH, GODFREY T. | Air Force Aide to the President (1961 rank was Colonel but raised under JFK to Brigadier General, now retired) | Vice-president of Magnavox Corporation, Paris, France |
| MANNING, ROBERT J. | Assistant Secretary of State for Public Affairs (1962–64) | Executive editor, *Atlantic Monthly* |
| MURROW, EDWARD R. | Director, United States Information Agency (1961–64) | Deceased |
| O'BRIEN, LAWRENCE F. | Special Assistant to the President | Postmaster General of the United States, Washington, D.C. |
| O'DONNELL, KENNETH P. | Special Assistant to the President | Gubernatorial candidate, state of Massachusetts |
| POWERS, DAVID | Special Assistant in the White House Office | Assistant to the U.S. archivist for Presidential Libraries, The Archives, Washington, D.C. |
| REARDON, JR., TIMOTHY J. | Special Assistant to the President for Cabinet Affairs | Executive assistant to the board of directors, Federal Deposit Insurance Corporation, Washington, D.C. |
| SCALI, JOHN A. | Diplomatic correspondent for Associated Press (1943–61) Diplomatic correspondent for American Broadcasting Company (1961– ) | Same position |

| | | |
|---|---|---|
| SCHLESINGER, JR., ARTHUR M. | Special Assistant | Professor, New York University, New York, New York |
| SHEPARD, TAZEWELL T. | Naval aide to the President (1961 rank was Commander but raised under JFK to Captain, his present rank) | Military Retention Task Force, Office of the Secretary of the Navy, The Pentagon, Washington, D.C. |
| SMITH, MERRIMAN | Chief White House correspondent, United Press International | Same position |
| SORENSEN, THEODORE C. | Special Counsel to the President | Paul, Weiss, Rifkind, Wharton & Garrison, law firm, New York, New York |
| SORENSEN, THOMAS C. | Deputy director, United States Information Agency (1961–64) | Vice-president for public relations, University of California |
| SYLVESTER, ARTHUR | Assistant Secretary of Defense for Public Affairs (1961– ) | Same position |
| TUBBY, ROGER W. | Assistant Secretary of State for Public Affairs (1961–62) | U.S. representative to the European Office of the United Nations and other international organizations in Geneva, with ambassadorial rank |
| WHITE, LEE C. | Assistant Special Counsel to the President | Chairman, Federal Power Commission, Washington, D.C. |
| WILSON, DONALD M. | Deputy director, United States Information Agency (1961–64) | General manager, Time-Life International |

## THE RUSSIANS

| | | |
|---|---|---|
| ADZHUBEI, ALEKSEY I. | Editor of *Izvestia* from 1959 to October 1964; son-in-law of Nikita Khrushchev | On board of magazine, *Soviet Union*, writes articles for magazine under assumed name |

| | | |
|---|---|---|
| BOLSHAKOV, GEORGI N. | At Embassy in Washington as acting editor-in-chief, *USSR* magazine (September 1959–December 1962) | Director of radio and television for the Novosty News Agency |
| BARSUKOV, YURI V. | *Izvestia* correspondent in Washington (November 1961–December 1963) | Not known |
| DOBRYNIN, ANATOLY F. | Chief, American Countries Division, Ministry of Foreign Affairs (1960–62) | Ambassador to United States, since March 1962 |
| FOMIN, ALEKSANDR S. | Counselor of Soviet Embassy (September 1960–February 22, 1964) | Not known |
| GROMYKO, ANDREY A. | Minister of Foreign Affairs (February 1957–  ) | Same position |
| KHARLAMOV, MIKHAIL A. | Chief, Press Section, Ministry of Foreign Affairs (1958–62) | Deputy chief of the Soviet State Printing Office |
| | Chairman, U.S.S.R. State Committee for Radio Broadcasting and Television (February 1962–October 1964) | |
| MALINOVSKY, RODION Y. | Minister of Defense (October 1957–  ) | Same position |
| MENSHIKOV, MIKHAIL A. | Ambassador to United States (December 1957–March 1962) | Minister of Foreign Affairs of the Russian Soviet Federated Socialist Republic |

| | | |
|---|---|---|
| SUKHODREV, VIKTOR M. | Member of Bureau of Translations, Ministry of Foreign Affairs since 1958 (rank of First Secretary since 1963)<br><br>Official interpreter for Khrushchev, Gromyko, and other Soviet leaders. | Still acts as interpreter for top Soviet officials |
| ZAMYATIN, LEONID M. | Deputy chief, American Countries Division, Ministry of Foreign Affairs (1960–62) | Chief, Press Division, Ministry of Foreign Affairs, since June 1962 |
| ZHUKOV, YURI G. | Chairman, State Committee for Cultural Relations with Foreign Countries until April 1962 | "Observer" (columnist) for *Pravda* |

# I

## LANCER TO WAYSIDE

On the morning of November 19, 1963, I received a letter from a woman in Dallas, Texas.

She wrote: *Don't let the President come down here. I'm worried about him. I think something terrible will happen to him.*

I answered her letter that day. "I appreciate your concern for the President," I wrote, "but it would be a sad day for this country if there were any city in the United States he could not visit without fear of violence. I am confident the people of Dallas will greet him warmly."

I never showed the letter to the President, or spoke to him about it, but November 19, 1963, was the last day I was to see him alive.

It was a busy day, but nothing happened to distinguish it from other days John F. Kennedy had spent in the White House.

There had been some concern about the President's upcoming trip to Texas because of incidents involving Chief Justice Earl Warren and UN Ambassador Adlai Stevenson. The President, however, was the last person in the world to be concerned about his personal safety. On the several occasions the subject had come up in discussions with him, he always replied: "If anyone is crazy enough to want to kill a President of the United States, he can do it. All he must be prepared to do is give his life for the President's."

The President had flown back from a speech in Miami Beach to the Inter-American Press Association the night before, and we had landed at Andrews Air Force Base outside Washington around one-thirty in the morning of November 19.

The helicopters whisked us to the south lawn of the White House, where I said good night to the President and stepped into a waiting car for the twenty-minute drive to my home in suburban Virginia.

I was up at 7 A.M. because I had a long day in front of me. I packed for a ten-day trip to Hawaii and Japan. I was going to Hawaii to attend another of the regular meetings on the situation in Vietnam. This one was to be attended by Secretary of State Dean Rusk, Secretary of Defense Robert S. McNamara, Ambassador Henry Cabot Lodge, General Maxwell D. Taylor, chief of the Joint Chiefs of Staff, McGeorge Bundy of the White House staff, and others. From there, I was going on to Japan as part of a delegation headed by Secretary Rusk for a five-day economic conference with the Japanese Cabinet. While my announced role was to act as one of the spokesmen for the delegation, the President had asked me to make some first soundings for a possible trip to Japan he had envisaged for early in 1964.

It was 8:30 A.M. when I got to my White House office. The day went by quickly and routinely with most of the time spent on briefings for Honolulu and Tokyo. A State Department courier arrived in my office with a black, classified book about three inches thick on U.S.-Japanese economic relations. I glanced through it, resolving to read it at length on the long, over-the-ocean flight from Honolulu to Tokyo.

I held two press conferences that day, one at eleven in the morning, and the second shortly before 4:30 P.M.

The prime subject was the President's upcoming trip to Texas. The reporters were particularly rough in the afternoon session because we had been less than precise in putting out the exact routes of the motorcades through the various Texas cities the President was going to visit. This imprecision was deliberate on orders of Ken O'Donnell, the President's Appointments Secretary, who was working closely with the Secret Service on the security arrangements for the trip.

In the afternoon session, however, I did spell out the actual itinerary of the trip for the first time, with arrival and departure times at San Antonio, Houston, Fort Worth, Dallas, Austin, and finally the LBJ Ranch, the Vice-President's Texas home, where the President and Mrs. Kennedy were going to spend the last night of the trip.

The rest of the press conferences dealt with such routine subjects as appointments to the Federal Water Pollution Control Advisory Board, the release of the second annual report of the Peace Corps, and some questioning about the purposes of my trip to Honolulu and the Far East. The afternoon briefing was the 1323rd held by my office since John F. Kennedy had become President.

Around seven-thirty that night, I walked into President Kennedy's office to say goodbye.

The President, looking tired, was sitting behind his desk signing letters, his glasses perched precariously on his nose. He wore those glasses in the privacy of his office, but carefully tucked them into his pocket when appearing in public.

"I'm off tonight and just wanted to say goodbye," I told the President. He looked up from his desk.

"The Texas trip is all set as far as my office is concerned," I continued. "Mac Kilduff will be going down there with you. Andy Hatcher will be staying in Washington. I'll be back in ten days, just before Thanksgiving and in time to go to the Army-Navy game with you."

"Who is going to handle Chancellor Erhard's visit here?" the President asked.

"Andy will handle it."

"OK, that will be fine."

The President paused, then pulled the glasses off his nose.

I was reminded at that instant of the first impressions of tiredness I had seen written on the President's face when I walked into the office.

"I wish I weren't going to Texas," he said. As I look back on that remark, he did not say it in any sense of uneasiness about the trip or fear for his life. He said it with an air of fatigue. We had traveled a great deal in the few preceding months.

I reassured him. "Don't worry about it. It's going to be a great trip and you're going to draw the biggest crowds ever. Going with Mrs. Kennedy will be terrific."

The President smiled again. "Well, hurry back."

I shook hands with him, turned my back, and walked out of the office.

On November 22, 1963, I rose at 6 A.M. The Hawaiian sun was pouring into the officers' quarters which had been assigned to us for the Vietnam meeting. The conferences had gone on for two days and there had been a sense of optimism in the reports from Ambassador Lodge and General Paul D. Harkins about the progress of the war. The meeting was held soon after the overthrow of President Ngo Dinh Diem, and the feeling was that the military officers who had taken over the government were doing a good job. One ominous note crept into the proceedings—a report that the Viet Cong had made some important advances during the period of confusion which followed the overthrow of Diem.

The night before (November 21), the five members of the Cabinet who were joining Secretary Rusk for the trip to Japan arrived in Hawaii. All were accompanied by their wives, and my wife, Nancy, arrived with them. Secretary McNamara and Bundy had taken a jet plane back to the United States.

By 7 A.M., our sleek blue and white presidential Boeing 707 jet was lifting off Hickam Field, headed for Wake Island and Tokyo.

We were served a quick breakfast and I reached into the briefcase I was carrying and pulled out the book on U.S.-Japanese economic relations. I found the book particularly heavy going. Economics has never been my strong point, and the intricacies of economic cooperation between the

United States and Japan were not easy reading. I looked around the plane and found that most of my colleagues were involved in the same task.

I was immersed in my reading sometime later when I felt a tap on my shoulder and looked up. It was Robert Manning, the Assistant Secretary of State for Public Affairs. "The Secretary wants to see you up forward," he said. Up forward was the private cabin reserved for the President, but used on this trip by the Secretary of State as the senior officer aboard.

I found the Secretary, grave-faced, holding a yellow piece of paper in his hand. I recognized it instantly as coming from the plane's teletype machine. Because this plane was used a great deal by the President, it carried sophisticated communications equipment not usually carried on commercial airliners. One of these extra communications items was a newspaper teletype. The other members of the Cabinet on the trip were already in the cabin. There was Secretary of the Treasury Douglas Dillon, Secretary of Interior Stewart Udall, Secretary of Commerce Luther Hodges, Secretary of Agriculture Orville Freeman, and Secretary of Labor Willard Wirtz.

As we waited for Myer Feldman of the White House staff and Walter Heller, the chairman of the President's Council of Economic Advisers, I looked over Secretary Rusk's shoulder.

The words on the page were badly scrambled—but what I managed to read was unbelievable.

UPI–207
     HANNOVER, GERMANY. NOV. WW (UPI)—THE STATE
     PROSECUTOR

BUST

     BUST

QMVVV

UPI–207
     BULLET NSSS

PRECEDE KENNEDY
X DALLAS. NTEXAS, NOV. 22 (.708LASTHREE SHOTS WERE FIRED AT
PRESIXENT KENNEDY'S MOTORCADE TODAY IN DOWNTOWN DALLAS.
                                     HSQETPEST

VVUPLF208
     HANNOVER. GERMANY. NOV WWKVUPI) –.THE STATE
PROSECUTOR TODAY DEMANDEJ AN QIAMONTH PRISON TERM FOR
WEST GERMANYSJS ZSTZRILIZATION DOCTOR."
X.X.X.X X,XNXLKDN, VOGEL TOLD THE THREEJU
THAT HANDSOME DR. AXEL DOHRN. %%. WAS AN IDEALIST BUT
BROKE THE LAW IN AT LEAST IP OF THE QNEPP STERILIZATION
OPERATIONS HE HAS PERFORME ON LOCAL WOMEN
    MORE
        HS 137PEST

RV
SSSSSSSSS
FLASH
          KENNEDY SERIOSTY WOUNDED.
                                        HS 138PESTSSSSSSSSSSSSSSSSSSSS

MAKE THAT PERHAPS PERHAPS SERIOUSLY WOUNDED.
                                        HSQEOPEST

SSSSSSSSSSSSSS
SL GJ OWHL W WOUNDED BY
               HQ139PESTXXXXXXXXXXXXXXXXXXXXXXXX

P
KENNEDY WOUNDED PERHAPS FATALLY BY VASSASSINS BULLET.
                                        HS139PEST'SSSSSSSSSSSSSSS

SSSSSSSSSSSSSSSSSSSSSSSSSSSS

I kept reading it over and over again as Feldman and Heller pushed their way into the cabin. The words stayed on the paper. They would not go away.

Secretary Rusk read us the last brief bulletin.

"My God!" gasped Orville Freeman. Luther Hodges started to sag toward the floor; he gripped a table with his hands and several of us eased him into one of the chairs.

Then there was an interminable silence as each man became lost in his private sorrow.

"We've got to turn back right now," I said to Secretary Rusk.

"That's right, but we have to verify this somehow. Get us in communication with the White House and see if you can get Admiral Felt at CINCPAC [Commander-in-Chief, Pacific]."

I pushed my way through the forward door of the cabin into the communications section of the plane. "Get the White House and Admiral Felt," I ordered the communicators, Sergeants Walter C. Baughman and Darrel Skinner.

In less than a minute, from almost 6000 miles away, I was talking to the White House Situation Room, the operating nerve center of the nation.

"Situation Room, this is Wayside [my code name]. Can you give me latest situation on Lancer [the President's code name]?"

The answer came right back: "He and Governor Connally have been hit in car in which they were riding."

I replied: "Please keep us advised. Secretary Rusk is on this plane headed for Japan. We are returning to Honolulu. Will be there in about two hours. We will need to be advised to determine whether some members should go direct to Dallas."

I put the microphone down and told Sergeant Baughman to keep the line open and working on our call to Admiral Felt and stepped back into the cabin to report to Secretary Rusk. He promptly ordered the plane turned around.

The radio operator called me forward almost immediately to take a call from the Situation Room:

"AP bulletin is just coming out. President hit in the head. That just came in."

"Understand. President hit in the head," I replied, heading back to Secretary Rusk's cabin.

We were then 1200 miles from Wake Island and 800 miles from Hawaii.

Secretary Rusk had swiftly taken control of the situation. If the President lived, he felt it was essential that certain members of the party on the plane go immediately to Dallas, to his side. Others should get back to Washington as soon as possible. The Secretary decided that he, Bob Manning, and I should go to Dallas, and that the others on the plane should go back to the Capital.

Communications were established with Admiral Harry D. Felt. His information on the President's condition was the same we had received from the White House. The Secretary instructed him to have a fully fueled Boeing 707 standing by on the runway at Honolulu to take Manning, himself, and me to Dallas. The plane we were on was to refuel in Hawaii as quickly as possible and head back to Washington.

And then the radio was crackling again.

Situation Room: ". . . where are you, sir?"

Radio operator: "Wayside has gone in the back. We are two hours out of Honolulu."

Situation Room: ". . . hold Wayside on the line. More information coming up . . . I read from AP bulletin: 'Kennedy apparently shot in the head, fell face down, blood on his head, Mrs. Kennedy cried out . . . Connally half-seated slumped to the left, blood on face and forehead.'— Nothing further." Then a pause. "President and Governor Connally were rushed to Parkland Hospital near Dallas Trademart . . . will contact you if we get more."

The radio operator brought the report back to the private cabin and read it in clipped tones to the hushed room. Secretary Dillon just shook his head back and forth in disbelief.

In the front cabin there was more radio traffic.

Andrews Air Force Base tower: "869.72 [the number of our plane]. Mr. Murray Jackson [special assistant to Secretary of State Rusk] would like to talk to Colonel [Lieutenant Colonel James] Toomey [the pilot], and Colonel [Clare T.] Ireland [the co-pilot]."

Mr. Jackson: "Colonel Toomey, the President of the United States has been shot and seriously wounded in Dallas, Texas. Also, Governor Connally was shot at the same time."

Colonel Toomey: "We have already received that information on the UPI ticker, have turned around, and are one hour twenty minutes out of Honolulu."

The plane roared through the early morning skies. We were informed that a jet had been set up for a trip to Dallas, if necessary. I got two more messages.

The first was from "Stranger." He said our plane was to turn around and go back to Washington. I informed him we were already on our way back to Honolulu.

The second was from Mac Kilduff. "Wayside, Kilduff requests all Cabinet members to return to Washington immediately. We do not have any further word . . . stand by for Situation Room."

Situation Room: "Latest bulletin: 'President Kennedy has been given blood transfusions in efforts to save his life after being shot . . . President is still in emergency room, Connally moved to operating room.' Are you getting press coverage or do you want us to relay? We will have information on whether to proceed to Dallas upon your arrival in Honolulu."

My report of these messages seriously troubled Secretary Rusk. He wanted to know who Stranger was.

Aboard every presidential jet there is usually a White House codebook. We searched for it for about five minutes, but there was none abroad this plane.

"We have to know who Stranger is," Secretary Rusk said. "We don't know what is happening in Dallas. Who is the government now?"

And certainly this was a question running through everybody's mind. We had no further word on President Kennedy. Was his shooting an isolated event or part of a national or international conspiracy? Certainly, if the latter were true, our own plane was not immune to attack because any foreign power which had planned the shooting of the President would certainly not be unaware of the fact that six of his ten Cabinet members were in an airplane high over the Pacific.

The decision was made that I was to break the code and find out the identity of Stranger.

In a minute, I got the answer back. Stranger was Major Harold R. Patterson, a high-ranking officer in the White House Communications Agency. He was, at the time of his transmission to our plane, in Washington, D.C. I knew Patterson well. He was one of the most trusted members of the White House staff and he would not have sent us the message without very clear instructions.

I was just going back to the cabin to give Secretary Rusk this information when the Situation Room called again.

"Stand by for a moment. Waiting for confirmation of something . . . Hear you loud and clear . . . nothing further for you."

I stood by the radio. Thirty seconds passed. A minute. Then again:

"Wayside, this is Situation Room. We have conflicting reports now, getting no confirmation, will call you again. Your office has the information. We'll call you again when we get confirmation."

It was an agonizing message. I hoped for the best, but I suspected the worst. The next message did nothing to alleviate my fears.

"This is Murray Jackson. Can we get Secretary Rusk again. We want to tell the plane that Acting Secretary Ball wants all to return to Washington instead of going to Dallas. Have Secretary call Mr. Ball when he gets on the ground in Honolulu."

It was only seconds to the next message.

"Situation Room relays following to Wayside. Have report quoting Kilduff in Dallas that the President is dead. That he died about thirty-five minutes ago. New subject. Front office desires plane return to Washington with no stop in Dallas."

*The President is dead.* The words were unreal. The microphone dropped out of my hands.

I walked slowly back to Rusk's cabin. Tears were already streaking down my face.

"The President is dead," I told the Cabinet officers. Without another word being said, everyone bent his head and said his private prayer.

Secretary Rusk then walked to the microphone in the front of the plane and announced the President's death to the twenty-eight passengers.

"Ladies and gentlemen, this is the Secretary of State speaking. We have received official confirmation that President Kennedy is dead. I am saddened to have to tell you this grievous news. We have a new President. May God bless our new President and our nation."

There was a cumulative cry of anguish from the passengers. I was standing at the front of the aisle, sobbing. My wife, Nancy, came up and held me, tears rushing down her face. Other wives reached for their husbands and the aisle was clogged.

Slowly the sobbing subsided, and those aboard returned to their seats and sat in stunned silence.

One thought kept going through my mind. I had been everywhere in the world with the President, from the small towns of America to Paris, and Rome, and Caracas, and Bogotá. I had been with him in the difficult campaign days when we were lucky to get twenty people in one group, to the tumultuous welcome he had received from two million in Mexico City. I wished I had been with him in Dallas.

In the forward cabin, Secretary Rusk took out a yellow pad of paper and slowly started to write out a joint statement from the Cabinet to be issued when we landed in Hawaii. He drafted a message of condolence to Mrs. Kennedy and a message of hope and support to the new President of the United States, Lyndon B. Johnson.

We kept our radio channels open to both Washington and Hawaii. It soon became apparent that the new President was flying back to Washington from Dallas immediately, and we eliminated the requirement for the extra jet to go to Dallas. Instead, arrangements were made for the speediest possible refueling of the presidential jet and then a non-stop dash from Hawaii to Washington. The Cabinet delegation and their wives were ordered to stay on the plane in Honolulu when the plane landed so that there would be no impediment to speedy refueling.

We touched down at Hickam Field, one hour and fifty-five minutes after the original bulletin. Secretary Rusk and I hurried off the plane to contact Washington, and Bob Manning got off to give the press the Cabinet statement. There was a large crowd of press at the airport, but the Secretary and I walked by them without a word to a waiting car, and sped to the headquarters of the Pacific Command of the U. S. Air Force. There on different phones, I contacted the White House and the Secretary called the State Department.

I talked to Bromley Smith, the executive secretary of the National Security Council. His information matched that which we had already received. The new President was on his way to Washington. The same plane bore the President's casket and his widow.

We were to come to Washington immediately. It was possible President Johnson would call a Cabinet meeting as soon as we landed—if not then, at ten o'clock the next morning.

Secretary Rusk talked to Under Secretary of State George W. Ball. He ordered an immediate study, country by country, to see what foreign policy problems might be triggered by the assassination of the President.

Our work was over in less than ten minutes and we raced back to the plane.

The refueling took only fourteen minutes and we were airborne again in twenty-two minutes. Now a fitful silence developed. Occasionally, someone would start to cry again.

Somebody, I don't know who, suggested we have a poker game to pass the time. It was certainly the most bizarre poker game I have ever been in. We played for table stakes. People threw money around as if it were worth nothing. There was none of the joking and asides that one usually finds in a poker game. There was only dead-serious betting in hushed voices.

It seems now, looking back, almost sacrilegious to have played poker at such a time. But if there had not been that game, it is hard to tell what would have happened on that plane, so high were the emotions.

After a while, however, the poker game could not keep our attention, and some of us slowly drifted forward to Secretary Rusk's cabin.

There, the topic of conversation was what kind of a man would kill President Kennedy. I remember now that there was almost unanimous opinion at the time that it would have to be a militant right-winger from the lunatic fringe of Dallas.

The messages kept coming off the wire service machine and finally one started grinding out the story of Lee Harvey Oswald and his previous life in Russia and his membership in the Fair Play for Cuba Committee.

This went against all the preconceived theories we had established.

"If this is true," Secretary Rusk said, "this is going to have repercussions around the world for years to come." His words were prophetic because even today, only in the United States is the report of the Warren Commission, fixing the sole responsibility on Oswald, widely believed.

It took us only eight hours and thirty-one minutes to make the nonstop flight from Honolulu to Andrews Air Force Base. We arrived there at 12:31 A.M., Washington time, and stepped out of the plane into a barrage of lights from television cameras.

Secretary Rusk made a brief statement on behalf of the Cabinet. Then I started wandering out of the lights and into the darkness of the airfield. I heard my White House driver calling, "Mr. Salinger," and I tumbled into the car for the drive back to the White House.

The lobby was crowded with reporters, the way it had been during the Cuban missile crisis and at the time of the release of Francis Gary Powers, the U-2 pilot shot down over Russia in 1960.

I avoided the newsmen by coming in the west basement entrance of the White House and slipping in the back door of my office. My two principal secretaries, Chris Camp and Sue Mortensen Vogelsinger, were sitting in the office, weeping. Andy Hatcher and Mac Kilduff were there awaiting my arrival, and Paul Southwick, another member of the staff, was at Bethesda Naval Hospital with Mrs. Kennedy.

Thought of rest was impossible. Weariness was replaced by numbness, and I plunged into work, almost like a sleepwalker. I talked to Ken O'Donnell and Dave Powers at the hospital, and learned that the President's body would be brought back to the White House sometime after 4 A.M. I walked over to the East Room of the White House where the body was to lie in state to check the arrangements and then out to the north driveway, where a military honor guard was already forming.

At four twenty-five in the morning, a black hearse drove through the northwest gate and past the squad of Marines standing at attention.

Another honor guard stood at attention inside the north portico of the White House and lined the corridors to the East Room. The casket of President Kennedy was carried by a group of men representing all of our military services.

Following the casket came Mrs. Kennedy, Attorney General Robert F. Kennedy, other members of the family, and some of the President's close associates—Ken O'Donnell, Larry O'Brien, and Arthur Schlesinger, Jr.

The casket was placed on a black-draped catafalque in the center of the room while four guards took their places at the corners.

Mrs. Kennedy walked forward slowly and knelt by the casket in silent prayer. She then leaned forward and kissed the casket and slowly walked out of the door of the East Room.

Our chief was home. And for the first time since I had stared incredulously at the piece of yellow paper in the hands of the Secretary of State, I began to believe he was really dead.

The rest of the night is a blur. I went back to my office for several hours. Mrs. Kennedy had invited O'Brien, O'Donnell, and me to spend the night sleeping at the White House in the quarters on the third floor, over the rooms where she and the President had lived.

We sat on the edge of the bed talking for a half hour or so, trying to piece together and relive the events of the day—as if our sharing them might make them more bearable.

George Thomas was there, too. George had been the President's butler for almost twenty years. He had laid out the President's clothes, drawn his baths, fixed him a highball before supper. He had traveled throughout the world with him. And now here he was with no President, with no one to take care of. In that moment, when the major human bond he had known in his life had been torn from him, he needed someone to take care of. He occupied himself by making drinks for Ken, Larry, and me, by turning down our beds, and by laying out our clothes for the following morning.

Finally, about 7 A.M., we went to sleep.

At 8 A.M., the phone by my bed rang. I picked it up.

The operator said, "Mr. Salinger, the President is calling." And for that instantaneous second, I thought to myself, it was all a dream, he wasn't really dead.

And then another voice came on the phone. "Pierre, this is Lyndon Johnson."

# II

## CHASING RACKETEERS

The road that took me from my native San Francisco to Washington, D.C., and service to two Presidents was a most unlikely one.

In fact, it was the political career of Adlai E. Stevenson, not of John F. Kennedy, that led me directly to the White House.

The sequence of luck and coincidence began in June 1956 with a call from Ken McArdle, the editor of *Collier's* magazine, for which I was then West Coast editor. Governor Stevenson had just won his second Democratic nomination for President, and one of his first recruits was John Bartlow Martin, the nationally prominent magazine writer who had also been on his staff for his first go at Dwight D. Eisenhower four years earlier.

McArdle told me Martin had been assigned by *Collier's* to write an exposé of the Teamsters Union, but would have to postpone it because of his full-time duties with Stevenson. The magazine didn't want to wait. Would I be willing to take over the assignment and with it a transfer from San Francisco to *Collier's* New York office as a contributing editor?

I quickly agreed. The reporter in me couldn't resist a crack at what I knew was an important and potentially sensational story. I was aware, through my Teamster contacts in California, of a growing rebellion against International President Dave Beck of Seattle. The principal grievance against him was his bullying of officers and locals who wouldn't go along with his dictatorial control of the union. But there were also persistent rumbles that he had his hand in the till to maintain a standard of living far beyond his union salary. Even from the fragmentary evidence then available, it was clear that Beck and his sidekicks were violating not only the law but the democratic processes of their own union.

The Teamsters Union is the largest and most powerful labor organization in America, if not the world. Other great unions in steel, mining, or shipping can paralyze a single industry and disrupt a vast sector of the economy by strike action. But the products of *all* industries—food, milk, medicine, clothing, steel, lumber, gasoline—move on wheels. And the wheels are on trucks driven by Teamsters. One high official of the union told me:

"When a woman takes a cab to the hospital to have a baby, the cab is driven by a Teamster. When the baby grows old and dies, the hearse is driven by a Teamster. And in between we supply him with a lot of groceries."

A national strike by the union could strangle the nation's economy within hours. The union itself and the entire nation have a right to demand that such fantastic power should not fall into the wrong hands. My assignment for *Collier's* was to find out if Beck and his heir apparent—James Riddle Hoffa—were worthy of the power they held.

I was not new to investigative reporting. In fact, it had been my forte during my later years on the staff of the San Francisco *Chronicle*. One of my first assignments for the *Chronicle* after leaving the Navy in the summer of 1946 was on the police beat. I found that a police reporter had hours of free time on slow nights. He could either spend it playing poker or trying to dig up a feature story.

Leafing through old court and arrest records, I came across unmistakable evidence of a highly lucrative bail bond racket, involving dishonest judges and many of San Francisco's most active bail bondsmen. The purpose of bail is to insure a suspect's appearance in court. If he flees the court's jurisdiction before his arraignment or trial, the bondsman must forfeit the guarantee, which might run from $50 for a misdemeanor to $10,000 for a felony. I found many cases in which the judges, through a highly suspect legal technicality, were returning the money to the bondsmen after their clients became fugitives. The effect of this, of course, was to rob the city treasury. My exposé of the racket stimulated a state investigation and brought about a tightening of bail bond regulations.

A short time later, Robert DeRoos, one of the ablest reporters on the *Chronicle*, said he was working on a case that might interest me—the New Amsterdam Hotel fire in 1944. I went to the files to read up on the disaster, which had occurred while I was still with the Navy in the Pacific.

Twenty-two denizens of skid row had lost their lives in the pre-dawn fire—an apparent case of arson—and there was a tremendous hue and cry for the arrest of the person responsible. Finally, a Negro, George Holman, was convicted of the crime and sentenced to twenty-two consecutive life terms in San Quentin.

It struck me, as it had DeRoos, that the evidence against Holman was of the flimsiest nature. In fact, the key prosecution witness against him was a known narcotics peddler and Holman's rival for the affections of a prostitute who lived in the New Amsterdam.

The witness testified that he saw the defendant run out the back door of the hotel with a gas can in his hand seconds before the building broke into flames. His intention, it was testified, was to murder the faithless prostitute. I doubted the testimony for two reasons. First, the dope pusher was hardly an unprejudiced witness, and second, the prostitute had a first-floor room. All she would have to do to escape the fire was to open her window and drop three feet to the sidewalk—and that's exactly what she had done.

When I went to San Quentin to interview Holman, Warden Clinton Duffy said that "every man in San Quentin claims to be innocent, but if there is an innocent man here, it's George Holman." Despite the severity of his sentence, the Negro was one of the hardest-working and most popular inmates of the prison. Until his conviction for mass murder, he had never received so much as a traffic ticket.

Working with DeRoos, I finally traced the dope peddler to Los Angeles, only to learn he had died just two weeks earlier. I found the prostitute living in the little town of Hazlehurst, Mississippi, where the editor of the Copiah County News met me at the airport with the comment, "Why would a white man come two thousand miles to try and get a nigger out of jail?" My interview with the prostitute was a total failure. She would tell me nothing because she was afraid she might have to come back to California, and that she would not do.

But we were able to dig up two witnesses who had also seen Holman flee the hotel, but without a gas can. We also came up with evidence that the fire was caused not by arson but by spontaneous combustion, resulting from years of spraying kerosene on the walls to combat cockroaches.

But despite the new facts, Governor Earl Warren (now Chief Justice of the Supreme Court) would not free Holman from prison. DeRoos and I finally enlisted the help of mystery writer Erle Stanley Gardner and his Court of Last Resort. Gardner assigned a young investigator, Bob Rhay (later warden of Washington State Prison at Walla Walla), to work with us, and he eventually wrote a series of articles for *Argosy* magazine exposing the unjust conviction. In 1956, ten years after we began working on the case, Governor Warren's successor, Goodwin J. Knight, finally granted a parole to Holman.

My last exposé for the *Chronicle* began in April 1953 with a routine assignment to cover a meeting of the American Friends Service Committee, which was demanding more humane treatment of prisoners in county jails throughout California. I was so appalled by what I heard that I decided to do more than merely report on the meeting. It seemed to me the only way to tell the ugly story with absolute accuracy was to become a prisoner myself.

Attorney General (now Governor) Pat Brown agreed to help me by informing local judges—but not the jailers—that I would provoke my arrest as a vagrant in Stockton and Bakersfield. Under the alias Peter Emil Flick, I spent four days in the Stockton jail—the worst in the state—and three in the lockup in Bakersfield. In Stockton, I spent the first night in a cell with eighty other prisoners, sleeping on a dirty, slatted floor.

My subsequent seventeen-part series triggered a statewide demand for jail reform and Governor Warren took personal charge of the investigation. New jails were built in both Stockton and Bakersfield but, still more important, the series forced a new approach toward local penology, with the emphasis on rehabilitation, not punishment.

The opportunity to investigate the Teamsters Union for *Collier's* was even more challenging, however, because it had national, not merely local, significance.

I spent the next three months researching my articles, first in Seattle, Beck's headquarters, and then in Detroit, where Hoffa ran the affairs of the Central States Conference of Teamsters. The picture that began to emerge was one of almost unbelievable corruption and brutality. While Beck was lining his pockets with union funds, Hoffa was brazenly recruiting a rogue's gallery of ex-convicts and racketeers to do his bidding in the union. There was also evidence of "sweetheart" contracts with a number of employers, an obvious betrayal of the drivers the union was paid to represent. Gangsters were given charters in New York for non-existent locals to insure the "ins" against losing union elections.

It was a hell of a story and I began writing it for *Collier's* in mid-October. But one morning I came across three paragraphs in the New York *Times* that were to influence the future course of my life. Senator John L. McClellan, the Arkansas Democrat, was preparing to convene a Select Committee on Improper Activities in the Labor or Management Field, the precise area in which I had been working. He already had chosen his chief counsel—Robert F. Kennedy, the younger brother of Senator John F. Kennedy of Massachusetts.

I had never met Bob or his brother, who was a member of the committee. But the same week I read the announcement in the *Times* I flew from New York to Washington to confer with the young chief counsel. My primary purpose was to find out when the new committee would start rolling. Obviously, it would boost the sale of *Collier's* if my articles hit the newsstands at the same time the committee was holding its first public hearings.

I will never forget my first meeting with Bob—a two-hour lunch in the Senate dining room. Although I was there as a reporter to interview him, I spent most of the time answering his questions on Beck and Hoffa. It wasn't until we were ready to leave that I was able to elicit from him the information that the committee would hold its first hearings in

February—a date that would fit perfectly with *Collier's* publication plans for my series.

Bob and I hit it off from the very beginning. He was a man who wasted neither time nor words and was determined to pursue the investigation no matter where it led. Over the next two and a half years, he was as rough on dishonest employers as he was on the labor leaders to whom they paid tribute.

Bob was impressed with the information I had been able to gather on the Teamster leadership, and I agreed to keep him up to date on new reports of corruption that I was still trying to document.

On my return to New York, I wrote the Teamster series and then was sent to Pittsburgh to do an article on a community of Hungarian Freedom Fighters who had settled there after the abortive revolution of 1956. On the night I got back to New York, the first week in December, I was awakened from a sound sleep by a telephone call from John G. (Dick) Trezevant, the managing editor of *Collier's*.

"Don't bother finishing the Hungarian article," he said. "If it ever sees print, it won't be in *Collier's*. The owners are going to fold it."

The entire staff knew that *Collier's* was in bad shape financially, but we were all hopeful that its aggressive new editorial policy might keep it alive by attracting new investors. We were wrong. The principal employees, led by Theodore H. White (*The Making of the President, 1960, 1964*), spent the next week trying to save the magazine. But ten days before Christmas we were notified that it was out of business.

I had two significant telephone calls within the next forty-eight hours. The first was from Paul Smith, editor-in-chief of *Collier's*. If I was looking for a job, he knew where I could find one. Einar Mohn, then executive vice-president of the Teamsters, had told him the union would like to hire me as its public relations director. Mohn, whom I had known in San Francisco, was an honest Teamster. Nothing in the subsequent investigation of the union would cast the slightest doubt on his integrity. In this case, he was obviously acting on orders from higher-ups in the union who would prefer to have me working with the Teamsters instead of against them. I was out of a job but I wasn't that hungry.

The second call was from Bob Kennedy. What was I going to do with my Teamster evidence? I said it was available to him to use as he saw fit, although I was still determined to see it in print. (The series ran the next year in another magazine, but under a pseudonym, because I was then working for the rackets committee.)

Bob took me up on my offer. A day or two later, Carmine Bellino, the brilliant chief accountant for the McClellan committee, and investigator Paul S. Tierney came to New York and we spent many hours going over my dossier on both the union and its dealings with "respectable" trucking industry officials. Bellino told me I could expect to hear further from Bob Kennedy.

Santa Claus came that Christmas in the person of Gurney Brecken-feld, editor of Henry Luce's *House and Home* magazine. He had a spot open as assistant news editor. Was I available? I went to work December 29, 1956. Although I was grateful to Breckenfeld, I found my principal assignment—articles on the GI mortgage market—much too dull to hold my interest.

Bob Kennedy came to my rescue the first week in February 1957 with an offer to join his staff as an investigator. I took no more than three seconds on the telephone to think it over before I said "yes." It proved to be the most important decision of my life.

Bob introduced me to Senator McClellan my first day in Washington, and it was obvious the senator took a dim view of hiring a reporter as an investigator. Traditionally, congressional investigators have come from the FBI or other law-enforcement agencies.

I remember the senator peering intently at me across his desk. "All right, you can come to work," he said. "But if I ever hear of you talking to the press, I will deal with you in the harshest manner possible."

(McClellan was chairman of both the Permanent Investigating Sub-Committee on Government Operations and its Select Committee on Improper Activities in the Labor or Management Field. Slightly more than eight years after joining the select committee as an investigator, I was a member, as a senator myself, of the parent committee, and Mc-Clellan was still its chairman. Although I disagree absolutely with his illiberal position on civil rights, I cannot fault his handling of the rackets committee. He was tough but fair and he gave Bob Kennedy a free rein even when the evidence was likely to incriminate management executives of his own conservative leaning.)

My first day on the rackets committee payroll, I was Bob's guest for dinner at his home in McLean, Virginia. On our drive across the Potomac, he said frankly that he was beginning to have his own misgivings about hiring me. Although his original intention had been to send me into the field immediately, he now thought it would be safer for me to stay in Washington for a time and study the committee process. I was disap-pointed and argued that a good reporter could hold his own with any in-vestigator. But Bob still had his doubts.

On entering his home, he asked me what I would like to drink. I told him nothing until dinner and then I would enjoy a glass of wine. Bob confessed that he didn't have a drop in the house. He was more than a little surprised when I went out to my car and came back with a bottle of premium California red I had in reserve for just such emergencies.

We had a most cordial dinner and talked until midnight. I don't know what caused Bob's change of plans for me, but he telephoned at seven-thirty the next morning, a Saturday, and instructed me to catch a plane that same day to Seattle and join forces with Bellino, who was looking into Beck's labyrinthine financial affairs.

I had my first exposure to the workings of the rackets committee when I arrived in Seattle at midnight. I assumed that we would have a quiet Sunday and turn to on Monday morning. But when I got to the hotel, there was a message waiting from Bellino.

"Welcome to Seattle. See you at eight in the morning."

We spent sixteen hours on Sunday interviewing dissident Teamsters and compiling leads from other sources on Beck's highly questionable use of Teamster funds. It was to be that way for the next two and a half years—sixteen to twenty hours a day, seven days a week. But there were no complaints from the staff, which eventually grew to more than one hundred investigators, accountants, and secretaries. We all knew that Bob was working just a little harder than we were.

One night Bob and I left our offices in the Senate Office Building after one o'clock in the morning. He offered to drive me home, but as we passed the Teamsters' Washington headquarters, which is just across the street from the SOB, he saw a light burning in Jimmy Hoffa's office.

"If he's still at work, we ought to be," said Bob. And we went back for another two hours.

On another occasion, I threw a party at my home for more than seventy-five members of the committee staff. Bob and Ethel Kennedy didn't leave until 2:30 A.M. Two and a half hours later, the telephone woke me from a sound sleep. It was Bob. "I'll be by to pick you up in twenty-five minutes," he said. "We've got a big day coming up."

I was lucky on my first assignment in Seattle. One of the missing elements in the case against Beck was the source of $20,000 that had been spent on construction of a bar in Seattle in which Beck had a direct financial interest. We had a suspicion the Teamster president had taken union funds for this obviously non-union purpose, but we couldn't prove it. The key to the riddle was a high-ranking Teamster official in Spokane. Prior to my arrival, two committee investigators had questioned him but he wouldn't give them the time of day. Bellino sent me to Spokane for another try.

I went to the union leader's home early in the evening and found him carving his way through a huge steak. I don't know whether it was the sumptuousness of his dinner or our discovery that we had mutual Teamster friends in San Francisco, but he decided to confide in me. "It's just a question of time until you dig up the truth anyway," he said. His own local, he admitted, had "lent" the $20,000 to build the bar. The Teamster official then drove me to his office and showed me how he had concealed the transaction in his books.

I telephoned Bob in Washington from the union office. He spoke briefly to the official and persuaded him to fly back to the Capital with his records. It was Bob's policy to have the investigator in each case work with him in organizing the evidence and preparing the interrogation of witnesses. On the morning the $20,000 "loan" evidence was to be heard, I was sitting next to Bob at the counsel table as the committee members filed in to take their places before the TV cameras and a capacity crowd of spectators. Bob tapped me on the shoulder. "Pierre, I want you to meet my brother Jack."

That was my first meeting with the future President. I recall only two impressions. He was taller than I thought he would be and his hair wasn't half as bushy as it was in the cartoon caricatures of him.

Not all of my investigations were as productive as the Spokane case. An Army intelligence officer from Fort Lewis came to our Seattle office one day. He had read in the newspapers that many Teamsters records of interest to me and other investigators were mysteriously missing from union headquarters.

"I have a hunch where you can find those records," he said.

His story was that a sergeant under his command at Fort Lewis had a girl friend who was a maid in the home of a Teamster official. The maid had told her Army lover that there were boxes full of union records hidden under her employer's bed.

The intelligence officer gave me the address of the employer, a known intimate of Beck's who would have access to his most secret records. I reported to Bob, who told me it was vital that we have a look under the bed. He left it to my discretion to find a way.

I called Fort Lewis, asked for the sergeant and was dismayed to learn that he had been mustered out of the Army the day before, after thirty-eight years' service, and was driving to Florida to retire. It would take him at least six days to reach there!

Did he have relatives on the way he might visit? Only one, I was told—a brother in Vancouver, Washington. I put in a call to the brother.

"Haven't seen the sergeant in fifteen years," he said, "and don't expect to." But just as I was ready to hang up, he shouted: "Wait a minute. There's somebody coming up the driveway now."

It was the sergeant. After a ten-minute appeal to his patriotism, he agreed to return to Seattle to help me.

The maid, it should be understood, was not one of the great beauties of the Pacific Northwest and the sergeant was most reluctant to resume their relationship. But he agreed to ask her on a double-date with me and a girl I knew in Seattle. We met in a bar and, after a massive transfusion of martinis, the maid gave me a description of the records. My hopes rose even further. They just could be the ledgers and checkbooks we had been trying to track down for weeks.

The maid begged off at three o'clock in the morning, insisting that she had to have a little sleep before reporting to work. We all agreed the party was too good to stop and that after her employer left for work, we would show up with a couple of cases of beer.

All that day and night, a team of committee investigators had the official under surveillance from a motel across a small lake from the home to be certain that the records weren't removed. My colleagues, watching with binoculars, notified me the next morning of the maid's arrival and her employer's departure for work. Still another investigator, watching Beck's office, let me know when the official got there.

The coast clear, the sergeant and I drove to the house and the maid was waiting for us, bottle-opener in hand. While he kept her otherwise occupied in the parlor—an act clearly above and beyond the call of duty—I squirmed under the official's bed. There were Teamster records there all right but they weren't the ones we were looking for. All our efforts, gin, and beer had gone for naught.

One of the most shocking phases of the Beck investigation was the discovery that one of his closest friends—Nathan W. Shefferman of Chicago—was a professional union-buster. Shefferman was paid extravagant fees by major corporations to advise them on how to defeat organizing drives. He had two favorite tactics for keeping the unions out: unfairly accusing labor leaders of being Communists and forming captive company unions. Yet Shefferman was a confidant and business associate of Beck's, whose sworn duty as a union president was to oppose all that Shefferman stood for in labor-management relations.

Bob Kennedy sent me and other investigators to Chicago to nail down the evidence of Beck's collusion with the management consultant. We were able to discover that Beck had given Shefferman $85,000 in union funds to buy articles for the personal use of Beck and his family. Among his wholesale purchases were golf balls, football tickets, nylons, a deep-freeze, two boats—and even diapers. Bob later summed up the extent of Shefferman's shopping spree for Beck with the classic comment:

"Wonder no longer who the 'I' is in 'I can get it for you wholesale.' It's Nathan W. Shefferman."

The management consultant denied, of course, that he knew Beck had stolen the $85,000 from the union. He was, he said, just doing a favor for a friend. It must have been quite a friendship because Shefferman later testified before the committee that he had given Beck $24,000 over a short span of years because he was "grateful" to him.

The Shefferman investigation was to be our most revealing inquiry into questionable management practices in the labor relations field. Bob Kennedy, Bellino, and I interviewed the profusely sweating Shefferman for two hours in his lavish Chicago offices, but he would tell us nothing. We subpoenaed his records before leaving and carried them out of the office ourselves.

We found in his files copies of letters advising clients how to deal with union leaders trying to organize their plants: "Don't dignify them. Call them bums and hoodlums. Cheap common bum. Material to use: Communism, un-Americanism, destroying our country . . ."

One of Shefferman's major clients, Sears Roebuck & Company, had paid him $250,000 for such statesmanlike advice from 1953 to 1956 alone. I tried to question Wallace Tudor, the labor relations director of the company. He admitted knowing Shefferman and retaining his services, but generally refused to answer other questions. Tudor had a change of heart, however, when Bob put him under oath before the committee.

"I want to state with the utmost candor and conviction," he testified, "that many of the activities engaged in by Labor Relations Associates [Shefferman's firm] and certain company personnel acting with them were inexcusable, unnecessary and disgraceful . . . a repetition of these mistakes will not be tolerated by this company."

Nothing in the Beck investigation, however, prepared us for the infinitely more corrupt and dangerous administration of Jimmy Hoffa, who became the international president of the Teamsters in 1957. In early July of that year, Bob sent me to Hoffa's headquarters city of Detroit to open a committee office and undertake a thorough investigation of Hoffa's activities, which already were creating a storm of protest within the union.

I promptly served subpoenas on the officers of five Detroit locals. The next morning I got a call from Frank Fitzsimmons, the president of Hoffa's own Local 299:

"Jimmy wants to see you."

I immediately called Bellino, who was in Chicago, and he flew to Detroit that afternoon to go to Hoffa's office with me.

Hoffa, a very short man, had his desk on a raised platform. The low chairs on which we sat allowed him to tower over us, and it was not hard to conjure up a picture of him tongue-lashing underlings from his Olympian heights.

All five union officers I had served were with Hoffa when we arrived. They stood, subpoenas in hand, looking like little boys who had been caught with their fingers in the cookie jar.

Hoffa was in a rage and shouted, "What are you trying to do to me?"

Bellino and I explained that we had been investigating the Teamsters before he became president, and that unless he had something to hide there was no reason he shouldn't cooperate with us.

Hoffa sneered. "You tell Bobby Kennedy for me that he's not going to make his brother President over Hoffa's dead body."

With that, he stood up and went around the office snatching the subpoenas out of the hands of his fellow officers. But he was too shrewd to tear them up. His contempt for the committee would come later.

When Bellino and I left, we saw a fleet of identical black Cadillacs in the union parking lot. One could always tell exactly how many of his lieutenants Hoffa had in his office by counting the Cadillacs in the lot. Each top official got a brand new one every year, complete with radio-telephone—and paid for by the membership.

Much already has been written on Hoffa's record as a union leader, and the definitive history can be found in Bob Kennedy's own book, *The Enemy Within*. I will not attempt to tell the whole sordid story but three incidents illustrate the fear he was able to instill not only within the union but among employers.

Acting on a tip, I went to Iron City, Michigan, in July 1958 to question a former Detroit laundry owner on reports of a huge cash payoff to Hoffa by the Detroit Institute of Laundering in return for a "sweetheart" contract. He gave me a sworn affidavit admitting the bribe to Hoffa. But when he flew to Washington to testify publicly, Hoffa was on the same plane. The launderer repudiated much of his affidavit when he took the stand.

That same year, I kept an appointment in Los Angeles with a Teamster friend of mine who was in Hoffa's inner council but who had nothing but contempt for him. Although he was generally sympathetic with the work I was doing, he would not cooperate for fear of reprisals and because he thought the reform of his union would have to come from the inside.

His fear was such that he would speak to me only if there were absolute guarantees that we could not be seen or overheard. We met close to midnight and walked more than eight miles along darkened city streets. He spent most of the time trying to convince me that "public persecution" of Hoffa would only strengthen his position in the union. "Leave him to us. We'll run him out eventually."

I replied that there weren't many indications of effective revolt against Hoffa.

"Let me tell you something," he said. "My boy comes home from school a couple of times a week with a bloody nose from fighting other kids who yell at him that his father's nothing but a gangster because he works for the Teamsters. I'm ashamed, and there are a lot of other Teamsters who feel the same way. That's why we've got to bounce Hoffa—and we will."

On another occasion, I found a Midwestern trucking company executive who was willing to confess to almost every felony but murder to conceal what we had reason to believe was another payoff to Hoffa. With the assistance of committee auditors, I had spent weeks examining the company's books for evidence of the bribe, but without success. Then, late one afternoon, we found a mysterious account for "labor expenses," on which checks totaling $30,000 had been written. I felt we were on the verge of a major discovery.

That night, while I was having a nightcap, the son of the company's owner came up to me in the hotel bar in a state of near panic. He was aware of my discovery of the missing $30,000 and had a ready explanation for it.

"I've been keeping a woman for years," he said. "The money went to pay her rent and to buy her clothes and gifts."

He admitted it was illegal to write off his amours as a tax-deductible business expense, but what was a young man in love to do? I thanked him for the information but was back at his office again the next morning with my crew of accountants. He was amazed that his story hadn't ended my investigation. But when he saw that I was determined to examine every last ledger and checkbook, he took me into a private office and said that his earlier confession was incomplete. He said he had bought, through proxies, a second trucking company which ran over the same routes as his older fleet. He told me he knew this was illegal under the regulations of the Interstate Commerce Commission, and that's why it was necessary for him to conceal the transaction.

The next day, he took me back into the private office for still another codicil to his confession.

"I might as well level with you," he said. "Part of that thirty grand went to pay my monthly charge account at a local house of prostitution. I take clients of the company there when they come to town."

He then produced a series of checks written to a madame named Julie.

"I think you'll have to admit that entertaining customers is a legitimate business expense," he said. "But how would Julie's name look in our books? Maybe now you'll understand why I had this special labor account."

I told him I didn't think the Internal Revenue Service would regard a madame as a proper deduction, and went back to the books.

We completed our investigation a day or two later and all of his stories proved to be true. He was keeping a mistress. He was the owner of an illegal truck company. He was a client of Julie's. But the expenses for all three ran far short of $30,000.

When I went back for one final look at the books, the young man was desperate and again led me into his confessional.

"I might as well tell you where the rest of the money went," he said. "I've been seeing another young lady besides my mistress, and let's just say that I got her into a little trouble and had to pay for an abortion."

At this point, I threw up my hands. It was evident he would go to any lengths to explain the thousands that were still missing from company funds. I got him to sign an affidavit confessing his many crimes and left town. We never used it.

As for Jimmy Hoffa, he has been convicted of only one major crime growing out of his union activities, that of tampering with a jury that was trying him in Chattanooga on charges of accepting kickbacks from an employer. At this writing, he is appealing the case to the U. S. Supreme Court.

Hoffa's principal weapon is his knowledge of the cupidity of man. He once told Clark Mollenhoff, a reporter for the Minneapolis *Star and Tribune:* "Every man has his price. What's yours?"

When Hoffa can't buy what he wants, his weapons become fear and intimidation. The day before the first public hearing into his affairs by the rackets committee, Bellino and I went to the Teamsters building in Washington for a final interview with him. He glared across his desk at us for a long moment, and then said:

"Someday, somewhere, I'm going to get you."

But the most frightening moment I ever had as a Senate investigator was in the process of exposing a corrupt official in the South. I went to his office one day and told him we had overwhelming evidence that he was stealing union funds, but there was one $240 check he had written that was still a mystery to us.

He reached into the drawer of his desk, pulled out a .45 automatic and pointed it at my head.

"I used the money to buy this," he said.

I asked him to hand me the gun and he finally did—muzzle-first and his finger still on the trigger. I unloaded it with a pounding heart and went on with my questions.

Over the three years of its life, the hearings of the Senate Select Committee on Improper Activities in the Labor or Management Field were held in the caucus room of the old Senate Office Building—the same chamber where the investigation of the late Senator Joseph McCarthy's charges against the Army led to his Senate censure and decline from power.

The committee heard more than fifteen hundred witnesses at more than five hundred public hearings. The testimony of witnesses ranging from corporation presidents to gangsters ran to fourteen million words and was heard by millions of Americans on live television.

The statutory function of a congressional investigating committee is to develop the case for new legislation in important areas of our national life, or to demonstrate that present laws are abusive and require amendment or repeal. But the criticism persists that certain committees, principally the House Committee on Un-American Activities, ignore their statutory purpose in favor of witch-hunting and in flagrant disregard of the constitutional rights of those who appear before them.

Although much of the testimony before the McClellan committee was of a sensational character, it was rarely the target of such criticism.

Intensive investigation went into every case. Bob Kennedy had a firm rule that he would introduce no evidence before the committee that was not provable in a court of law. Nor did he resort to character assassination for the sake of sensation. For instance, he did not subpoena the amorous young trucking executive because he had no direct evidence linking the $30,000 to Hoffa. Even when we had solid information that a West Coast union leader was robbing the treasury to support his mistress, Bob never put the lady in question on the stand. All such embezzlements were referred to merely as expenditures "on behalf of himself or friends." One emotional Teamster official, desperately afraid the committee was going to call a girl friend with whom he had been cavorting adulterously in Hawaii at union expense, tried to kiss Senator McClellan when he heard she would not have to testify before the nation—and his wife.

The most vocal critic of the committee, of course, was Hoffa. He tried to hide his own misdeeds behind a smoke screen of charges that John F. Kennedy, with brother Bob's connivance, was using the committee to advance his presidential ambitions. He was 180 degrees off course.

JFK knew from the outset that service on the committee would be a political liability. It would jeopardize his relations with labor and with Democratic leaders in certain cities who were accepting payoffs to look the other way. Two other presidential hopefuls—Senators Stuart Symington of Missouri and Henry M. Jackson of Washington—had refused to sit on the committee. JFK knew that if he also declined, South Carolina's reactionary Strom Thurmond was next in line.

Through the life of the committee, John F. Kennedy was relentless in pursuing the facts, no matter where they led. One of our best investigators, LaVern Duffy, had been looking into labor racketeering in Gary, Indiana. He flew to Washington one night and told the Kennedy brothers that the evidence led directly to the mayor of the city, the most powerful Democrat in the state.

"Go back and build the best case against him you can," the senator told Duffy. "We have only one rule around here. If they're crooks, we don't wound 'em, we kill 'em." As a result of the investigation, the mayor of Gary was later indicted and convicted.

JFK not only won the enduring enmity of influential, if corrupt, labor leaders, he also was criticized by business leaders for revealing management collusion with the hoodlums.

The one political advantage to Senator Kennedy was his exposure on national TV, but the disadvantages were much greater. He told me during the presidential campaign of 1960 that "even people I thought were my friends in labor are still suspicious of me, or pretend to be. I tell them the Republicans on the committee would have beaten their brains out if there hadn't been some of us to keep things on the track. But all I hear is how tough it is to sell me to their memberships."

The one attempt to pervert the committee for political purposes did, in fact, come from Republican members. Senators Barry M. Goldwater,

Karl E. Mundt, and Carl T. Curtis saw the hearings as a chance to smear Walter P. Reuther, president of the United Auto Workers. They spread the story around Washington that Bob Kennedy was "afraid" to look into Reuther's affairs because it might cost his brother the UAW leader's support for President. But Bob had a devastating answer. The one political appointee among our investigators was Jack McGovern, a hell-bent-for-leather Republican who had been hired at the urging of Senator Goldwater. Bob gave McGovern a free hand to delve into Reuther's affairs, but he came up with absolutely nothing.

It should be said that Reuther was among the handful of top labor leaders who recognized the importance of the committee's work and Chairman McClellan's determination to be both fair and relentless in exposing illegalities in both labor and management. Others who took this same view were David Dubinsky, president of the International Ladies Garment Workers Union, and David McDonald, president of the United Steelworkers. Arthur J. Goldberg, who was then chief counsel for the Steelworkers, was a behind-the-scenes force in organizing responsible labor support for the committee.

Despite the personal danger to themselves and their families, many important Teamster officials were helpful to the committee in preparing the case against Hoffa, and certain of our informants were in Hoffa's own headquarters.

Senator Kennedy was not happy with all the new legislation resulting from the committee's activities. But he was able to water down or defeat many of the repressive proposals of the anti-labor senators and to support laws to protect the union member against corrupt leadership. Labor chieftains may no longer conceal their financial and administrative affairs from the rank-and-file. They may no longer enter into secret deals with management to sell out their own union. And management must now report all funds spent for anti-union purposes, including fees to "labor consultants" such as Nathan W. Shefferman.

Union members are now guaranteed a secret ballot and fair election procedures. Still another law requires that ex-convicts cannot serve as union officers until five years after their release from the penitentiary—a death blow to Hoffa's palace guard. A $2000 limitation on the amount of money a union may lend to one of its officials has put an end to the manipulations of a Dave Beck, for instance, whose "loans" ran up to more than $300,000.

In May 1959—twenty-seven months after joining the committee staff— I had a call from Democratic National Chairman Paul Butler. He said the party already was planning strategy for the 1960 elections and he had an assignment that might interest me. I went to see Butler in his Washington office. With him was Charles S. Murphy, who had been an adviser to President Harry Truman, became Under Secretary of Agriculture under President Kennedy, and is now chairman of the Civil Aeronautics Board.

The national chairman was trying to beef up the Democratic Advisory Council, whose purpose was to launch an all-out attack on the Republican record and to develop Democratic alternatives in both foreign and domestic fields.

"We want you to take over as publicity director of the council," said Butler, "and do the same kind of job on the present administration that Charley Michelson did on Hoover." Michelson, a one-time Washington correspondent for the New York *World*, was publicity director for the national committee in the early 1930s, and was the architect of the early strategy against the Hoover administration. He later became one of Franklin D. Roosevelt's closest advisers.

I told Butler I was interested but there was one important drawback. Working for the national committee, I would have to serve all the potential Democratic nominees for President.

"I can't do that because I've already made my own choice for President."

"Who's that?" Butler asked.

"John F. Kennedy."

The national chairman smiled. "That will present no problem."

After leaving Butler's office, I telephoned Bob Kennedy and told him of the offer. "Hold off on your answer for twenty-four hours," he said.

The next morning I had a call from John F. Kennedy, inviting me to his office. He stood up from behind his desk, shook my hand, and came right to the point.

"Pierre, I'm going to run for President next year and I want you with me in the campaign."

Although there was no mention of duties, salary, or when I would report to work, I didn't hesitate.

"Senator, you've got yourself a man."

# III

## FROM NEW HAMPSHIRE TO
## WASHINGTON, D.C.

John F. Kennedy's race for the presidency started in a modest set of offices located over a garage in downtown Washington.

American politics still require the quaint fiction that a man is not really running for President until the day he declares his candidacy. In the case of John F. Kennedy this was more ludicrous than usual. Any person with a modest amount of political antennae would have known the senator was running early in 1959 (and some might say, without malice, from the day he lost the vice-presidential nomination to Senator Estes Kefauver in Chicago in 1956).

To play out this charade the Kennedy forces leased offices over the Esso Garage on Constitution Avenue. The door merely carried the inscription—STEPHEN E. SMITH—the name of JFK's brother-in-law who was in charge of this pre-announcement operation.

I reported for work on September 1, 1959. Senator Kennedy had given me a broad directive to "set up a press operation," but no specifics. "If I have any objections about what you are doing, you'll hear from me," he said.

I quickly hired two girls, Lenore Ostrow (now Jacobson) who had been my secretary in San Francisco when I worked in Adlai Stevenson's campaign for President in 1952; and Barbara Coleman, a young reporter for the Washington *Post*, who walked into Senator Kennedy's office one day looking for a new job.

We immediately started the massive task of accumulating lists of key newsmen around the country who would be involved in covering a presidential campaign. I also started circulating around the Washington political reporters to get to know them better, because most of them were completely unknown to me. I also accompanied Senator Kennedy on several trips out of Washington to test the political waters.

My first several months in the Kennedy for President campaign were awkward. Over thirty-one months of service with Robert F. Kennedy, I had gotten to know him well and considered him a friend. But John F. Kennedy was an unknown quantity to me and I was an unknown quantity to him. He had hired me on the say-so of his brother and he had not developed the confidence in me that he had in many members of his staff whom he had known for years.

I felt very much like an outsider during those first months. Men like Ken O'Donnell and Larry O'Brien, who had worked with the senator in his 1952 and 1958 senatorial campaigns, had an easy relationship with him, born of long acquaintance.

I also made some mistakes. The key one was to think that if Bob Kennedy said to do something, it was necessarily John F. Kennedy's desire that I do it. On one occasion Bob called and dictated a news release to me. I dutifully put it out. The next day John Kennedy called me in anger: "Who authorized you to put out that release?" I told him it was his brother. "Well, check those things with me. You're working for me, not for Bob, now." I never made that error again.

In looking back on those early months, I guess it was another mistake (not *my* responsibility this time) that finally brought me to a closer relationship with the candidate.

JFK had planned to announce his candidacy for President on January 2, 1960. On December 17, 1959, however, an enterprising reporter for United Press International was wandering through the Senate Office Building when he noticed an extraordinary amount of activity in the "robotype" room of Senator Kennedy. A robotype room is operated by each of the one hundred senators and permits literally thousands of letters to be mailed to constituents, each looking like an original. The massive robotypers operate mechanically, not only typing the letters, but picking up from punched tapes the addresses of the recipients, and even the information whether to address them by the first or last name. The reporter picked up one of the letters in the Kennedy robotype room and immediately knew he had a story. The letter started out: "*I am announcing on January 2 my candidacy for the Democratic Presidential nomination.*"

The letter was one of thousands being prepared for mailing to Kennedy supporters throughout the nation to give them a little advance notice on the senator's decision to run. With the publication of the UPI story the press came running to me for confirmation.

My explanation was not very convincing: "Senator Kennedy has not yet made a decision as to whether or not he will seek the Democratic nomination in 1960. The unsigned draft published by the United Press

International is but one of a number of drafts being prepared by his staff covering all possible eventualities concerning the senator's decision."

Then I added: "I have grave doubts the senator has even seen it." Which caused at least one newspaper, editorializing on the situation, to say it had "grave doubts about the future of Mr. Salinger's job."

Senator Kennedy, after a moment of anger, took the incident with great humor. In the conversations which ensued, I began to feel more and more like a member of the team.

On New Year's Eve the senator called me from Nassau where he had gone for a short vacation with Mrs. Kennedy and talked to me for more than a half hour. When I hung up the phone I recall feeling that the trial period was over and I had been fully accepted.

Despite the difficulties of those early months, I never had the slightest doubt that John F. Kennedy would be the next President of the United States, particularly after my first trip to Wisconsin with him in September 1959. We toured four or five cities in the family Convair airplane, the *Caroline*. Senator Kennedy had spoken at each stop with a clarity and persuasiveness that won his audiences over completely. I remember getting back to Washington and calling a number of my friends around the country to tell them of my great discovery. A number of these friends— many with long political experience—accused me of temporary insanity.

Looking at it from their viewpoint, the candidate was too young, a Catholic, with only a modest record in the Senate. But looking at it from mine, I had heard a fresh voice in American politics—a voice that cut through much of the political polemics of our time, and got down to discussion of the problems of living in an atomic world.

Two things won the primaries, nomination, and election for John F. Kennedy.

The most important factor was John F. Kennedy himself.

The second was the kind of organizational skill which marshaled forces across the country in the candidate's behalf.

Much has been written about the campaign of 1960, and I will not attempt to repeat it. I will concern myself, rather, with the critical press phase of the operation.

While Senator Kennedy had given me no direct orders on how to run the press aspects of the campaign, I did discuss with him my philosophy on the matter. That philosophy was grounded in one principle: to make the campaign as easy for the press to cover as possible.

From the beginning, we attempted to create a climate in the campaign entourage that would make the reporters' work agreeable. Covering a political campaign is usually one continuing set of inconveniences and annoyances for the newsmen traveling with a candidate. The days are long, travel is swift, and working conditions are not always the best. Over-zealous police in town after town attempt to guard the candidate from surging crowds—and usually end up assaulting a few newspapermen while they are at it. I remember a little town in Pennsylvania where I went to the rescue of two photographers who were in trouble with the police and got myself knocked to the pavement in the process. I was about to be struck a second time when Governor David L. Lawrence of Pennsylvania happened to recognize me and called to the policeman to leave me alone.

Some things are standard in national political campaigns—chartering planes for the press, making hotel reservations, and making sure that each reporter's baggage finds its way to his hotel room. Buses were provided for motorcades so that the candidate could be followed by the press. Press rooms were set up in hotels with extra telegraphic and telephonic communications. As we progressed from New Hampshire through Wisconsin, West Virginia, Oregon, and the other primaries, these arrangements became more and more complicated as the size of the press party grew.

The day Senator Kennedy started campaigning in New Hampshire in January 1960, we had about twenty newsmen with us. The night of the election in Hyannis, Massachusetts, there were almost four hundred. At first we had been able to take all the press who wanted to follow us in one plane, but as the campaign heated up from the primaries into the main event, we added a second, and then a third, press plane.

While some of the things we did were considered standard operating procedure by the press, we also brought two innovations to the business of presidential campaigning. Starting in the New Hampshire primary, with the help of Jim Williams, a vice-president of the New England Bell Telephone Company, we arranged for a two-channel telephone car to be placed in all motorcades directly behind the candidate. This permitted the wire service reporters riding in the car to file running accounts to their offices of the receptions the candidate was receiving while the parades were actually in progress.

The most important innovation, however, was the introduction of the instant transcript. Following John Kennedy's nomination at the Democratic Convention in Los Angeles, I met with Hal Alderson, the president of a Washington firm of stenographic reporters. Alderson had previously told me he wanted to help Senator Kennedy. I asked him how difficult it would be to set up a twenty-four-hour reporting service that would turn out instant transcripts of everything John Kennedy said on the campaign trail. Alderson assured me it could be done.

We put the system into effect on the first campaign trip after the convention and it proved an instantaneous success. This was due in great measure to the ability of Chick Reynolds, the stenotypist assigned to us by Alderson. Reynolds took down the candidate's speeches under the most difficult circumstances possible. One often found him perched on top of the hood of a parked car, straining to hear every word of a speech, and methodically tapping out the words on his machine. Chick always had a transcriber with him, usually Ken Bowers, who would take the stenotype tape from him and run to the press plane where we had special typewriters and a mimeograph installed. Within fifteen minutes of the end of any speech the press had full copies of what the senator had said. Sometimes the work was even harder—on the days when the senator campaigned by car. On these occasions, Bowers would work on a typewriter in the back of a rocking bus. My secretaries also worked under the toughest conditions possible. I remember listening to JFK address a rally in a small town in Connecticut around two o'clock in the morning. I walked around the fringes of the crowd to see if I could pick up reactions and stumbled into two of my girls, with a portable mimeograph machine set up on the roof of an automobile, turning out, by flashlight, a press release on a future speech by the senator.

The key to the whole press operation, however, was the availability of John Kennedy. He made himself accessible to the reporters as often as they needed to see him, and by so doing gave the press a real feeling of being on the inside of the campaign, which they never felt with Vice-President Richard M. Nixon. In fact, more than one reporter, switching back to the Kennedy camp after traveling for a while with the Vice-President's party, told me they felt like they were "coming home" when they rejoined us.

The primaries were crucial for Senator Kennedy. He had to demonstrate his vote-getting ability in order to win the 1960 nomination.

After an easy victory in the New Hampshire primary over California ball-point pen manufacturer Paul Fisher, Kennedy moved into Wisconsin, his toughest test of the primary season.

Wisconsin was in the back yard of then Senator (now Vice-President) Hubert H. Humphrey. For an Eastern senator, with little or no background in agriculture, to win this state from Humphrey, the acknowledged farm expert of the Democratic party, was a tough task indeed. The press, pouring into Wisconsin to cover the race, invariably called on Edwin Bayley, Press Secretary of Wisconsin's Governor (now Senator) Gaylord A. Nelson. For each reporter Bayley saw, he had the same story. There were ten districts in Wisconsin and Kennedy should win all ten. This information was sent back by many reporters to their newspapers.

Thus, on election night, when Kennedy finally won the state by six districts to four, what should have been considered by all accounts a major victory for the Massachusetts senator was portrayed in some parts of the press as a defeat, because of what they considered the narrowness of the margin. The candidate was very angry at these reports. He considered any victory in Wisconsin a great victory, under the circumstances. He asked John Bailey, then the Connecticut State Democratic Party chairman (now chairman of the Democratic National Committee) and

me to stay in Milwaukee an extra day and call in the reporters who were
cleaning up the story, and try to convince them that Kennedy had indeed defied all odds by winning in Wisconsin. We had some success
in this endeavor, but the impression lingered that, somehow, Kennedy
had not done as well as he should have in Wisconsin.

This is what convinced Hubert Humphrey that he should not throw
in the towel after Wisconsin, but rather that he should challenge JFK
in West Virginia. And it was in West Virginia, with his stunning 60–40
triumph, that Kennedy really sewed up the Democratic nomination for
President.

One other historical note is in order. One small error by Senator
Kennedy's personal pollster, Louis Harris, also played a role in the events
of Wisconsin and West Virginia. Several days before the election, Harris
submitted a poll to Kennedy which showed he had a small chance of
winning the Ninth and Tenth congressional districts on the northern
fringe of Wisconsin near the Minnesota border. The same poll showed
Kennedy had no chance of winning the important Second District, which
included the capital of Wisconsin, Madison.

Acting on this information, Senator Kennedy spent his last campaign
day in Superior, Wisconsin, in the frosty Tenth District, futilely attempting to win that region. When the returns came in Kennedy lost
both the Ninth and Tenth by wide margins (showing he never really had
a chance there), but lost the Second by less than 1000 votes. Kennedy
always felt that if he had spent that last day campaigning in Madison,
he might have won the Second, and therefore won the state, seven districts
to three.

Here is where fate intervened. Vice-President Humphrey has confided
to me since that if Kennedy had won Wisconsin by seven districts to
three, he would have given up the campaign then and there and would
not have run in West Virginia. If Kennedy had not had a Humphrey
campaign in West Virginia, he might never have been able to demonstrate that he could overcome the Catholic issue. In this case, the pollster's
error worked to his advantage.

The flare-up of the Catholic issue during the West Virginia primary
resulted in an effort by top Kennedy aides to obtain support for a statement by leading Protestant ministers throughout the country calling for
tolerance in the election.

While this effort was in progress I had to make a trip from Bluefield,
West Virginia, to Indianapolis, Indiana, and while breakfasting on the
train I saw evangelist Billy Graham sitting two tables away. Acting on an
impulse, I walked up to him, introduced myself, and asked if I could join
him. During our breakfast discussion I told him of the ministers' statement that was being drafted and asked him if he'd be willing to sign
it. He said he would. I then arranged to have Ted Sorensen call him the

next day to clear the wording of the statement with him. Sorensen tried for two days to get the reverend on the phone, and when he finally reached him Graham flatly refused to sign the statement on the grounds that he should not interfere in the election. Later in the campaign, however, he participated in rallies on behalf of Vice-President Nixon.

The primaries produced a presidential campaign first—voiceless press conferences. First in Indiana, and later in Oregon, the overworked candidate lost his voice. In both cases he went through with previously scheduled press conferences. Instead of responding to the questions orally, which he could not do, Kennedy wrote his answers out on long sheets of yellow paper, and I read them to the press.

With the primaries behind him, the next to the last hurdle between John F. Kennedy and the presidency was the Democratic National Convention of 1960. Although he was confident he would win his party's nomination on the first ballot, he left nothing to chance. The staff spent as much time and energy preparing for the convention as we did for the toughest of the primaries.

I flew to Los Angeles to launch our press operation three weeks before the opening of the convention on July 11. JFK was keenly aware of the importance of swift and effective communication with the news media, whose representatives would outnumber delegates and alternates, 4750 to 4509. A party convention is a highly volatile affair. The defection of one or two delegates or a dramatic demonstration on the floor has been known to defeat a candidate who went into a convention an odds-on choice to win. Two other front-runners for the Democratic nomination—Champ Clark in 1912 and William Gibbs McAdoo in 1924—had come into their conventions with clear majorities and had lost. Although JFK would have to win only a simple majority, not the two-thirds majority that threw the 1912 and 1924 conventions into deadlock, we knew that his chances would diminish with each succeeding ballot. It was critical that he reach the magic number of 761 votes on the first ballot.

Our first requirement was communication with the delegations—directly through our headquarters and indirectly through the press.

Waiting for me in Los Angeles was Robert B. Troutman, Jr., an Atlanta attorney and Harvard classmate of Senator Kennedy's older brother, Joe, who died in World War II. Troutman, a tremendously imaginative man, had been given two important assignments: to set up our central command post in the headquarters hotel—the Biltmore—and to organize the floor demonstration when John F. Kennedy's name was placed in nomination.

Troutman knew nothing about showmanship and turned to an old friend in Hollywood to help him buy banners and noisemakers and form the line of march for the "spontaneous" demonstration. His friend agreed to help him, but with one stipulation. "You must tell no one except the candidate—and tell him only if he wins." The irony of the matter is that Troutman's show business friend was actor George Murphy—who four years later was to take his first plunge into elective politics and defeat my bid for return to the United States Senate.

The most ingenious feature of the Biltmore command post was the telephone system—the joint creation of Troutman and Lyle Moore, a representative of the Pacific Telephone & Telegraph Company. There were direct lines to the rooms of every Kennedy staff member staying at the Biltmore, to JFK's hideaway in Hollywood, and to a model home just outside the Sports Arena, where we would transfer our central operation the night of the balloting. A Home Show was to close on the eve of the convention and Troutman had persuaded a builder to leave his exhibit behind for our candidate's use.

The model home was also converted into a prime communications center. Lines from its switchboard ran to key telephones on the convention floor, enabling our strategists to communicate with the chairmen of delegations even while voting was in progress. But we also knew that telephone communication might be impossible during the frenzy of demonstrations on the floor, and developed a network of two-way walkie-talkies that would link the model home with our roving managers inside the Sports Arena.

In addition to our two systems of almost instantaneous communications with staff and delegation leaders, we put together our own telephone directory—an alphabetical listing of all delegates, their hotels, the times and places of their caucuses, and the numbers of restaurants, bars, and tourist attractions where we might find them in an emergency.

We also had a master card file on every delegate and alternate, showing if he or she was pro- or anti-Kennedy and if his or her commitment was firm. Also on the card were his profession, his religion, the party offices he had held, and even his nickname and hobby. The cards also showed whether Senator Kennedy had met the delegate or alternate and whether he called him or her by first name, nickname, or last name. This file was extremely useful in wooing delegates.

It took only one glimpse at a map of Los Angeles to convince us that communications with the press would be more critical than in any other convention city the party might have chosen. In Chicago or Philadelphia or Atlantic City, all the delegates stay in downtown hotels within minutes' walk of each other. This centralization keeps a candidate close to his delegate strength, and permits swift responses to the maneuvering of other candidates.

But Los Angeles has always had a shortage of downtown hostelries. The delegations were spread out in hotels and motels ranging from Pasadena in the foothills to Santa Monica at the sea—a distance of thirty miles as the rumor flies. In the strategically important days before the opening of the convention, delegates would be racing all over the landscape to take in the sights—Disneyland, the Hollywood studios, the homes of the movie stars, the beaches, and even a cemetery, Forest Lawn.

All of this would weaken our communications with major delegations and their communications with each other, and we knew they would rely heavily on the newspapers, radio, and television for reports of what was happening in the pre-convention skirmishing. It was decided that our press headquarters in the Biltmore should be open twenty-four hours a day to enable JFK to respond immediately to the charges of his opponents and to launch counterattacks of his own, if necessary. To accomplish this, I would have to beef up my staff considerably. Going into the convention, I had only two assistants—Charley Roche and Ron Linton, former newspapermen from Boston and Michigan, respectively. Both were with us in the primaries and had shown themselves to be coolly efficient under fire.

The first addition to the convention staff was Roger Tubby, who had been Press Secretary to President Truman in the last months of his administration. He was at that time the owner of a small newspaper, in Saranac Lake, New York, the *Adirondack Daily Enterprise,* but Senator Kennedy was eager to have the benefit of his long experience in politics. Tubby, who was already wearying of the sedentary life of a small-town publisher, immediately agreed to come to Los Angeles.

Roger was kept on the staff after the convention, manning our Washington headquarters at the Democratic National Committee as I moved around the country with the candidate. He later became Assistant Secretary of State for Public Affairs—an appointment that caused one of the rare disputes I had with Secretary of State Dean Rusk.

After Rusk's appointment as Secretary of State, I told him I felt we had a moral commitment to give Tubby the job as his top press officer. But the Secretary had a number of other newsmen in mind, including Elie Abel, the erudite Washington correspondent of the Detroit *News* (now London bureau chief for NBC), and Douglass Cater, Jr., of *Reporter* magazine (now a special assistant to President Johnson). I had the highest respect for both men but I felt that Tubby's willingness to leave his newspaper and join forces with JFK at the convention entitled him to first consideration. But Rusk wouldn't go along with my argument and I finally asked the President-elect to intervene. He did and Tubby got the job. This proved to be a mistake on my part, however.

Although Roger was an extremely able man, he never had Rusk's full confidence. This, in turn, kept him from having the full confidence of the press. After serving in the State Department for a year, he accepted an ambassadorship—our representative to the United Nations agencies in Geneva—where he serves with distinction. Tubby was replaced at the State Department by Robert J. Manning, formerly of *Time* magazine and more recently Sunday editor of the New York *Herald Tribune*. Manning built up the most efficient press operation the State Department has ever known. (He is now editor of *The Atlantic Monthly*.)

The second old pro I brought onto the staff before the convention was Andrew T. Hatcher, the former managing editor of *The Sun Reporter*, a Negro newspaper in San Francisco. Andy and I were old friends. We had gone through many political wars in California together, including the 1952 and 1956 Stevenson for President campaigns. After I went East to work as an investigator for the Senate labor rackets committee, Andy was appointed by Governor Brown as an assistant labor commissioner. As he always did, Andy quickly responded to my appeal for help and agreed to resign from his state office to join the convention staff. Through that hectic week in Los Angeles and the long, arduous campaign to follow, he was the spark plug of our operation. There was no job, big or small, for which Andy was not the first volunteer, and he handled every assignment with competence and imagination. He later became Associate White House Press Secretary, the highest position a Negro had ever held in Washington until that time. When I resigned from President Johnson's staff on three-hours' notice to run for the Democratic nomination for senator in California, Andy came West with me to help manage my campaign. He is now market promotion manager for the Ballantine Brewery in Newark, New Jersey.

My team at Los Angeles was rounded out by Chris Camp, Barbara Coleman, Sue Vogelsinger, and Lenore Jacobson, four of the most efficient, amiable, and attractive girls in Washington. From then until Election Day, they kept going night and day, stenciling speeches and press releases, answering telephones, delivering coffee and hamburgers, and shooing the kooks out of headquarters.

One of my first tasks in Los Angeles was to prepare a press kit for the horde of American and overseas reporters who would soon be descending on the city. It included a full biography of the senator, a collection of pictures of him in action, information on the primaries he had won, quotes from his most important speeches, the backgrounds of important staff members, and the night and day telephone numbers of the press staff.

The kits had a twofold purpose: to make it easier for newsmen to pound out feature stories on JFK and to reduce the number of purely routine questions a busy staff would have to answer on the candidate and his personal and political history.

Senator Kennedy was easily the most newsworthy figure at the convention. Our press office was sheer bedlam from early morning until late at night. But in addition to the reporters jamming the office for statements and schedules, another contingent of newsmen followed the candidate wherever he went. He left a caucus at the Statler Hotel one morning and dashed into a side room. The reporters thronged in after him—only to discover it was the men's john.

Ron Linton was put in charge of one of our major press projects—the publication of a daily convention newspaper. This had never been done before and was to prove highly effective in our direct communication with the delegates.

The paper had a very professional look. Ron was assisted by Stan Weber, a former Oregon newsman, as managing editor, and Fred Forbes, a former newspaperman from Boston and Philadelphia, as city editor. The reporters were my brother, Herbert, then a high school principal in Napa, California, and two graduating seniors from Goucher College in Baltimore— Phyllis Wear and Jill Cowan, better known to the press corps as Fiddle and Faddle. Their enthusiasm for JFK's candidacy was so great they flew to Los Angeles at their own expense and would accept no salary for their work.

Although the newspaper emphasized what Senator Kennedy was doing, we also covered the activities of other candidates to give the publication an aura of impartiality. The copy would go to the printers early in the evening and the edition would roll off the presses shortly after midnight. At that point, circulation manager Jack McNally, a Webster, Massachusetts, real estate appraiser, took over. Jack, who had been on the Kennedy team since the New Hampshire primary, had recruited a volunteer crew that slipped a copy of the paper under the door of every delegate and alternate between the hours of midnight and 6 A.M.—a staggering task in a convention city as sprawling as Los Angeles.

The total press run was 12,000 papers daily, 3000 of which were distributed from a newsstand near the Biltmore Hotel. Within twenty-four hours of the establishment of the project, the newspaper had its own city room, an Associated Press ticker, and a photographic dark room in a closet. When I told Senator Kennedy about the operation of the paper, he became very concerned about the potential high price of this journalistic enterprise. He was amazed when I told him we would be able to put out seven issues of the paper for $6000, including printing costs. The senator's query about the newspaper's price was symptomatic, however, of his whole attitude toward the campaign from a financial standpoint. He was always cautioning his aides to hold down costs of the campaign, and he remained, in the White House, a very cost-conscious person.

Troutman also put in one additional innovation of great value to our convention operation—the "locator" system. Key Kennedy aides carried a small telephone company gadget in their pockets. When they were needed at headquarters a prearranged telephone number would be dialed and the gadget in the pocket would emit a sound. The recipient would then know that he was to call in to the "locator's" office to find out who was looking for him.

All of our pre-convention planning—the telephone and walkie-talkie systems, the twenty-four-hour press operation and the newspaper—had but two purposes: to hold our own delegates in line and to counteract moves from the opposition that might turn the uncommitted delegates against us.

But the senator took out one final insurance policy against delegate panic. We had counted the votes very carefully and there was little doubt that he would make it on the first ballot. But we also knew that many of the speculative articles giving JFK a first ballot victory had included states of which we were uncertain. If even a handful of such delegates were to come out for another candidate, it would appear that our man was slipping.

California was a prime example. The tally in the national magazines and wire services had given us up to sixty-five votes in the Golden State's delegation. But it was the opinion of Larry O'Brien and Jesse Unruh, the powerful speaker of the California State Assembly, that our total would not go much over thirty-five.

For that reason, we did not include California and other doubtful states in our tally showing a first ballot JFK victory. Thus, when all or part of their delegations did come over to us, they were reported in the press as a net plus in our total, not as an indication that Senator Kennedy was losing ground.

Our conservative count was to stand us in good stead on the second day of the convention when the California caucus announced only thirty-seven votes for JFK. Because we had never claimed as much as one vote in California, our behind-the-scenes defeat in the California delegation actually appeared as a victory.

The convention itself produced only two crises we had not anticipated. The first was a press conference held on the first day of the convention by John B. Connally, now Governor of Texas, and Mrs. India Edwards, former chairman of the Women's Division of the Democratic National Committee. They announced to an incredulous press corps that John F. Kennedy had Addison's disease and might prove physically unfit for the ardors of the presidency. This was one of the last gasps of the sputtering drive in behalf of Lyndon B. Johnson.

It must be said at the outset that the press shared my view that the accusation went far beyond the latitude of fair play, even in the rough and tumble of convention politics. I met with the senator and Bob Kennedy and it was their inclination to ignore the charge as being unworthy of a reply. Johnson himself had issued a statement denying advance knowledge of the Connally-Edwards charge and repudiating it in the strongest possible language. But despite this, I felt we must respond, and quickly, to quash the possibility that the Republicans might repeat the unanswered allegation after the convention. The senator's physicians were contacted and we agreed on a medical statement conceding that he had an adrenal insufficiency which had been under control for many years but which none of his doctors considered to be Addison's disease. With this prompt response, the story became a one-day affair and did not come back to haunt us until the last forty-eight hours of the presidential campaign. The Republicans chose Congressman Walter H. Judd, a physician in private life, to raise the issue. But it was too little and too late. It's an ironic footnote to history that Connally, who was co-author of the charge that JFK might prove physically unequal to the presidency, was riding in the same car with him the day he was shot to death.

From my first intimate contact with President Kennedy, it was obvious he was a man who lived with pain. His back, injured in World War II, was the source of his problem. Even a serious operation in 1954 (from which he almost did not recover) failed to adequately cure his condition. He was forced to wear a canvas back support, about eight inches wide, strapped around his waist. The support sought to minimize strain on the back, particularly on days the President was unusually active.

Such things as long motorcades during the campaign and after he was President were most painful to him. The smiling candidate or smiling President would arrive in his hotel room, shuck off his support, and ease into a warm bath with a sigh of relief—the closest he ever came to complaining about his ailment.

The President rarely talked about his back—even with his closest friends and aides. They knew he was in pain and would sometimes try to offer comfort. He would usually smile them off with an assurance that everything was well. Occasionally, he would direct a bit of profanity toward his back, and then the subject would be forgotten for weeks.

The closest he came to permanent relief resulted from the work of Dr. Hans Kraus of New York. Dr. Kraus, who has specialized in therapy for ailing backs, put the President on an exercise schedule and gradually built up his back to the point where he could play golf and do other physical activity with a minimum of reaction.

Our second tense moment at the convention came after the senator accepted a routine invitation to address the Texas delegation. A number of newsmen confided to me that Lyndon Johnson was planning to show up at the same time and challenge JFK to a debate before the television cameras. We had nothing to win and much to lose by such a confrontation, and were looking for a way out of it.

Then we got word from friends in the Texas delegation that LBJ would not attend the caucus. I and other staff members took this as an indication that Johnson had had a change of heart, and was backing out of the debate. I spent a half hour on the telephone planting this story with reporters before I got a call from Phil Graham, publisher of the Washington *Post*.

"Young man," he said, "I want to give you a little advice. Never tear something down in such a way that you can't put it back together again." With that, he hung up.

I was mystified. I had never met Graham but I knew he was a personal friend of LBJ's and had probably caught wind of the story I was spreading. After a moment, it hit me. Graham was telling me that if JFK won the nomination he might want LBJ as his running mate. My "plant" that the senator from Texas was afraid to debate the senator from Massachusetts could only create bad blood between them.

The debate did take place, but before a joint caucus of the Massachusetts and Texas delegations. It did not produce many fireworks, however, and reporters wrote it off as a draw.

I should add that the call from Graham was my first real clue that Lyndon Johnson was in line for the vice-presidential nomination if JFK carried the convention, as he certainly would. Speaking strictly on a hunch a month before the convention, I had told Earl Mazo of the New York *Herald Tribune* that the ticket would be Kennedy-Johnson. When that's the way it worked out, Mazo credited me with inside information that the deal was made long before the balloting in Los Angeles. I was never able to convince him my off-the-record comment was a lucky guess. By the time the convention came around, my guess would have been Senator Stuart Symington.

The big story the first day of the convention was the tumultuous demonstration when Adlai Stevenson took his seat with the Illinois delegation—contrary to the rigid tradition that an aspirant for the nomination never enters the convention hall until it's all over but the shouting—or pouting.

Our switchboard was jumping with calls from newsmen and friendly delegates that Governor Stevenson's dramatic appearance was stampeding the convention. But we knew differently. The demonstration was the climax of long planning by Stevenson's Southern California supporters. They had gotten hold of every ticket they could beg, borrow (or print) to pack the house. Only a handful of the wildly enthusiastic demonstrators had a vote, and they weren't likely to sway many others.

We also knew that Governor Stevenson had been told that very morning by Illinois political leaders that he couldn't count even on his own state. He knew it was all over when he came to the Sports Arena. But the demonstration—Adlai Stevenson's last curtain call on the stage of presidential politics—will stand witness to the tremendous emotion and faith this remarkable man was able to inspire among his adherents. I was on his staff in the campaigns against Eisenhower in both 1952 and 1956—and never worked harder or with greater conviction. But I was convinced in 1960 that even if he could win the nomination, he could not defeat

Nixon. I think he knew it, too, which in my opinion was the reason he never put up an all-out fight for the nomination.

The night of the balloting was one of the most exciting of my life.

Bob Kennedy, Larry O'Brien, Ken O'Donnell, Steve Smith, the Senator's brother-in-law, and I took up stations in the model home outside the Sports Arena. (It was the first time I had been within a mile of the actual convention. Since my arrival in Los Angeles almost a month earlier, the work load in the press office had kept me at the Biltmore twenty-four hours a day.)

O'Brien had a state-by-state delegate list in front of him and his prediction of how the vote for JFK would go on the first ballot. He turned out to be a half vote off, a remarkable tribute to his ability as a vote-counter—a skill he was to employ later as the President's liaison officer with Congress.

As the voting got under way, Bob Kennedy placed a call to one of our floor men:

"Go tell Bob Meyner [the Governor of New Jersey] that we're going to win this thing on the first ballot, and this is his last chance. He either switches his delegation to us or he's going to be rolled over."

The word came back in moments.

"Meyner's going to stand pat on the first ballot. He doesn't think we can make it the first time around and will take the votes himself as a favorite son." It was a classical political error.

As the voting ran deeper into the alphabetical list of states, it was clear that Wyoming's fifteen votes could put JFK over the top. Bob Kennedy picked up the telephone and spoke to his brother Teddy, who was with the Wyoming delegation.

"Tell them if we have all fifteen, Wyoming will cinch the nomination of the next President."

Wyoming got the message. Its national committeeman, Tracy F. Mc-Craken, stood before the microphone, savoring the drama of the moment, and announced:

"Wyoming casts all fifteen votes for the next President of the United States."

The bedlam that broke out on the convention floor was nothing compared to the riot in our model home. Bob and I leaped to our feet shouting. We danced around the room, hugging everybody in sight. It had been a long and difficult road but there were many miles to go.

The remaining act of the convention was the selection of the candidate for Vice-President. That which already has been written on the subject is either contradictory or the product of hindsight. I offer here a memorandum I wrote the week after the convention when the matter was still fresh in my mind.

Following the nomination and selection of Johnson as the vice-presidential candidate Thursday night, I returned to the office and was immediately called by a number of newspaper men who were checking on a story by John S. Knight, publisher of the Knight Newspapers, which purported that Johnson had forced Kennedy to select him as the vice-presidential candidate.

Earlier that day I had gone to Bob Kennedy's room which was across from mine in the Biltmore Hotel. Ken O'Donnell was there and after I came in they were discussing the possibilities for Vice-President. Bob Kennedy asked me to compute the number of electoral votes in New England and in the "solid South." I asked him if he was seriously thinking of Johnson and he said he was. He said Senator Kennedy was going over to see Johnson at 10 A.M. Ken O'Donnell violently protested about Johnson's being on the ticket and I joined Ken in this argument. Both of us felt that Senator Stuart Symington would make a better candidate but Senator Johnson seemed to be on Bob's mind. I remembered all of this later that night when I saw the news report about Johnson forcing himself on the ticket.

I called Bob Kennedy that night to check the Knight story. Bob said it was absolutely untrue. From my conversation with him, however, I gathered that the selection of Johnson had not been accomplished in the manner that the papers had reported it had. I got the distinct feeling that, at best, Senator Kennedy had been surprised when he asked Senator Johnson to run for Vice-President and Johnson accepted.

Following my conversation with Bob Kennedy, I put out a denial of the Knight story under my own name and went to bed. I was awakened an hour later by a phone call from Bill Moyers of Senator Johnson's staff. He said the speaker, Mr. Rayburn, wanted to speak to me, Mr. Rayburn got on the phone and it was evident that he was highly agitated. He wanted, first, a complete denial of the story under Senator Kennedy's name and, second, he wanted me to awaken Senator Kennedy and have him call John S. Knight and tell the latter of the story's falsity. Mr. Rayburn said Senator Johnson was extremely disturbed about the story and wanted it nipped in the bud before it got wide circulation. George Reedy, who was Senator Johnson's Press Secretary, had located Knight and told me where Knight could be reached.

I told the speaker I would go to work on this project and would call Bob Kennedy who was also asleep by then. Bob was extremely loath to call Senator Kennedy as the senator had had a particularly tough day. We worked out a statement together to issue in the senator's name and Bob said he would call Knight, since part of the story related to a conversation between Bob and Senator Johnson before Senator Kennedy saw Johnson. This, Bob said, was completely untrue.

We also tried to find out who the source for the Knight story might be. Since Knight is a reputable newspaperman it appeared he had gotten the story from someone high in the party. We finally narrowed the list down to Clark Clifford who had been Senator Symington's campaign manager.

When Senator Kennedy had informed Clifford that Johnson was going to be the vice-presidential candidate (around three on the afternoon of July 14) he had told Clifford that he was surprised that Johnson was willing to make a fight for the second spot nomination. Bob Kennedy felt that perhaps Clifford had interpreted this remark to mean that Johnson had "forced" his way on the ticket.

The fact of the matter was that after Walter Reuther, Governor G. Mennen Williams, and others had protested to Senator Kennedy about putting Johnson on the ticket, Bob had gone to Johnson and told him of these objections. Senator Johnson had said that if Senator Kennedy wanted him to run for the vice-presidency he was willing to make a fight for it. It was to this that Senator Kennedy alluded in talking to Clark Clifford.

After his talk with John Knight, Bob Kennedy called me back. He told me that after their conversation, Knight's confidence in the story was shaken; that he was going back to his source and check further on the matter.

(We later learned that the source was not Clark Clifford but Governor James T. Blair of Missouri, to whom Clifford had confided his conversation with Senator Kennedy.)

I called Moyers back and read him a statement which he read to the speaker. I also told him that Knight had been contacted. I did not tell him that Knight had been contacted by Bob Kennedy rather than by Senator Kennedy, nor did they ask me. Through this vigorous action that night, we were able to prevent further spread of the story and I spent most of Friday (the 15th) backgrounding newspapermen on the facts of the vice-presidential nomination as they had been outlined by Bob Kennedy.

The most authoritative story appeared Saturday morning (July 16) in the New York *Herald Tribune*, written by Earl Mazo. Mazo had obtained some of the facts on his own. For instance, he knew that Bob Kennedy had not seen Senator Johnson before Senator Kennedy saw him because Mazo had visited Bob's room shortly after I left it on Thursday morning, and had been told that the senator was going to see Johnson at 10 A.M.

I believe that much of the controversy and confusion over LBJ's selection is the result of a semantic misunderstanding. When Bob Kennedy told the Johnson forces that certain labor leaders and northern politicians were against his nomination for Vice-President, Bob's prime reason was to ascertain if LBJ was willing to put up a fight for it. But Johnson's people interpreted this as an effort to talk him out of the race. This was not Bob's intention and he certainly was not acting on his own, as some accounts have intimated. He would never have undertaken a mission of this kind without the direct concurrence and direction of his brother.

Senator Kennedy was an admirer of LBJ's. He commented more than once that if he didn't win the nomination, he thought Senator Johnson was the best equipped Democrat to serve as President. His choice certainly was vindicated by events immediately after the assassination and since.

But at least one element of mystery over his selection will always remain: That is the question whether Senator Kennedy actually expected Lyndon Johnson to accept second position on the ticket or whether his offer was merely a pro forma gesture. A day or two after the convention, I asked JFK for the answer to that question. He gave me many of the facts in the foregoing memo, then suddenly stopped and said:

"The whole story will never be known. And it's just as well that it won't be."

I cannot explain the cryptic remark. I can only report that JFK made it.

In analyzing the role of the press in the general election, I cannot help but feel that Senator Kennedy—on balance—got the best of the coverage. Certainly his more cordial handling of the press was the primary factor. I think it can be said that the majority of the reporters wanted to see Senator Kennedy win the election. This contrasted to their newspapers, which were approximately 4 to 1 for the election of Vice-President Nixon. On a post-election program, where I appeared with Herbert Klein, the Press Secretary to the Vice-President, I voiced the feeling of the senator and the members of the staff when I said that I thought we were by and large treated fairly by the press. There has been a general, and I believe a favorable, trend by the press to give two-sided coverage to presidential campaigns. This has not always been true in this country, but I believe it was more true in Senator Kennedy's case than in that of any Democratic candidate in the twentieth century. It is also true that the reports from the press covering Nixon's campaign indicated that he often worked against his best interests. He was considered by the press to be aloof and inaccessible. Reporters, being human, can only reflect these attitudes from time to time in their copy. It was to Senator Kennedy's credit that he understood the massive importance of the press and treated the reporters as his equals. In general, he trusted the American press as an institution and respected its power. This came through in his everyday dealings with the press and was felt keenly by the reporters.

Much has been written about the television debates. I know that when Senator Kennedy received the first offer to debate Vice-President Nixon from NBC, he accepted it on the spot. In my view his election would have been impossible without the debates—really, when you analyze it, without the first debate. The majority of the American people made up their minds on the basis of this debate and merely reinforced their views by watching the other three. The first debate was a debacle for the Vice-President, particularly because of his appearance on the television screen. Mrs. Rose Kennedy characteristically stated after the first debate: "I felt so sorry for Nixon's mother tonight."

The day after the first debate, we hit Cleveland, Ohio, and you could feel, in the crowd reaction, that JFK had scored heavily the night before. There were repeated shouts from the crowd, such as: "Keep after him, Jack." "You really got him last night, Jack." The impact of the debate was everywhere.

And so it came to election night. The shouting and the speeches were over. The Hyannis Armory had been converted into a press room by two advance men I had sent there two weeks before the election. One was Cornelius Ryan, author of *The Longest Day* and *The Last Battle* (Simon and Schuster), with whom I had worked at *Collier's* magazine, and the other was Charles W. Henderson, an old San Francisco friend, who was administrative assistant to the then Congressman John F. Shelley of San Francisco (now mayor of that city).

The returns from Connecticut, the first state to report, showed a Kennedy sweep, and the early returns from other states indicated Kennedy was going to win by a landslide. As the evening wore on, however, the margin narrowed dangerously. Even with the small margin, President Eisenhower's Press Secretary, Jim Hagerty, called me shortly after midnight to tell me that Nixon was going to concede and that a congratulatory telegram was on the way from President Eisenhower. A half hour later he called me back and told me Nixon had changed his mind about conceding. He asked me to forget about the premature Eisenhower telegram. I told Jim I would say nothing about any message from the President until I heard from him again.

Shortly before 4 A.M., a tired Vice-President appeared on the television screen. His statement fell short of an outright concession, although he conceded that if "present trends" continued, Kennedy would be elected.

The calmest man in the room was the candidate himself. He quietly turned off the television set. We were all angry with Nixon for not conceding, but Kennedy shut off the conversation. "If I were he, I would have done the same thing." With that, he walked out of Ambassador Joseph Kennedy's home where we had been watching the returns and went back to his own home several hundred yards away and went to bed—not yet knowing whether he was President of the United States.

# IV

## THE LONG WAIT

The phone in my room at the Yachtsman Hotel in Hyannis jangled me awake at eight-thirty in the morning, November 9, 1960. The call was from a desk man at the local Associated Press bureau.

"It's all over," he said. "Your man has carried Minnesota and is elected. How fast will you have a statement from him?"

Still half asleep, I mumbled an answer and hung up. Then it hit me. *We had won!* I sprang out of bed shouting like a wild man.

Five minutes later, unshaven and wearing the rumpled suit I had taken off only an hour earlier, I was racing along the low dunes toward Hyannis Port. It was a golden Cape Cod morning. At that early hour, the sun already was warm and Nantucket Sound was as calm as a lake. A block from the Kennedy compound, a young man standing in the center of the street waved my car to a stop.

"Oh, good morning, Mr. Salinger. You can go ahead."

I had never met him before in my life, yet he recognized me instantly. Urbanus E. Baughman, chief of the Secret Service, had also heard the returns from Minnesota. The stranger in the street was one of sixteen Secret Service agents he had assigned to protect the next President. Another sixteen had been standing by in Los Angeles in the event Nixon had been the winner. I was to learn later that every Secret Service agent assigned to the White House had studied the pictures, habits, and background of every member of Senator Kennedy's staff, and knew who should be given unquestioned access to him.

Ted Sorensen was the first to reach JFK with the news. I found them in an upstairs bathroom. The President-elect was sudsing himself in the tub and Sorensen was perched on the edge of it, reading him the late returns.

The senator waved a dripping hand in greeting.

"Any word from Nixon yet?"

I told him no. It was only six in the morning on the West Coast. We agreed that he should not claim victory until Nixon had formally conceded on television from Los Angeles. After that, he would go in a motorcade to the Hyannis Armory, where almost four hundred haggard newsmen had been standing by through the night. JFK climbed out of the tub and I threw him a towel. Even in his first exuberance, he was shaken by the narrowness of his victory.

"I still don't know how we did it without California," he said. "I was counting on that. Losing out there made it too close."

He blamed Carmine DeSapio and Bill Prendergast for the loss of California, which had the greatest number of electoral votes after New York.

"If they hadn't panicked and talked me into running all around New York in the rain for an extra day last week, I would have spent it in California. I had New York won and one more day in California would have given me that, too. It was a stupid mistake."

The Kennedy strategists had never fully understood California. Although it had a 3 to 2 edge in Democratic registration, it also had a perverse tradition of voting for the man, not the party. The Eisenhower ticket had carried the state by huge majorities in 1952 and 1956. Yet Pat Brown, a Democrat, had won the governorship in 1958 by more than a million votes. This pattern was completely mystifying to Democratic politicians from patronage-rich Eastern states who could forecast precinct results in their own bailiwick within one or two votes. JFK's instincts had been right. Despite its preponderance of Democratic voters, he did need at least one more day in California. He lost Nixon's native state and mine by a fraction of one percentage point.

I drove back to Hyannis for a shave and a change of clothes. Shortly before noon, I got a call from Jim Hagerty. He thanked me again for not releasing the premature wire from President Eisenhower, and said another would be on its way immediately after Nixon's concession. He had learned from Herb Klein, Nixon's Press Secretary, that Nixon would concede at the Ambassador Hotel in Los Angeles at 1 P.M. our time.

At that hour, the entire Kennedy family, and most of the staff, were waiting in front of the TV set in Ambassador Kennedy's home. We were all surprised when Klein, not Nixon, pushed his way toward the microphones through a dispirited crowd of Republicans, many of whom were weeping.

Noting Klein's sharp tailoring and trim waistline, JFK said to me over his shoulder: "He looks more like a New Frontiersman than you do."

After Klein read the cold, brief statement of concession, someone remarked that Nixon should have had the grace to go before the cameras himself, if only to thank personally his tens of thousands of campaigners who were watching. JFK agreed.

"He went out the way he came in—no class."

There was a slight delay before our motorcade left for the armory. Jacqueline Kennedy had slipped out of the house to walk alone on the beach. JFK went after her and they came back down the dunes together, arm-in-arm, and laughing.

She stood at his side before the television lights in the armory as he promised to commit all his energies to "the long-range interests of the United States and the cause of freedom around the world . . . So now my wife and I prepare for a new administration and a new baby." John, Jr., was born three weeks later.

The President-elect spent the rest of the afternoon walking alone on the beach, skittering stones in the surf, and playing a knock-down game of touch football in the compound with his brothers and sisters, their wives and husbands, and the more athletic members of the staff. I shrewdly went back to bed.

The work of taking over the presidency began in earnest the next morning when JFK summoned the entire staff to a meeting in his father's home. I was walking over with him from his own cottage when he suddenly broke into a report I was giving him on editorial reaction to his election.

"Pierre, I want you to stay on as my Press Secretary. All right?"

*All right?* It was exactly the assignment I had been hoping for since the day we first met in his Senate office.

"I would like that," I said. "I would like that very much."

"It's yours then. I'll let you pick your own second in command."

I told him my choice would be Andy Hatcher, who had been with us ever since the convention in Los Angeles—a man of great ability and deep loyalty.

"You've got him then," JFK replied.

Not once through the long campaign, or the months before, had we ever discussed what I would be doing after the election—win or lose. But it was settled that morning in a space of no more than thirty seconds— a half minute that would influence every future moment of my life. Yet we didn't even break stride in our brief walk across the compound.

It was completely reminiscent of the way I had gone to work for JFK in the first place.

Among those waiting for us at Ambassador Kennedy's was Clark Clifford, the brilliant Washington lawyer whom JFK had appointed weeks before to direct the presidential transition, if there should be one. He came armed with copies of a thick handbook that would serve as a guide through this twilight zone when a man knows he is going to be President but is not

President yet. We all left with our assignments—and they were formidable.

The Inauguration was only ten weeks away. In that time, JFK would have to select his White House staff; form a new government which would direct the activities of fifty separate departments and agencies, employing more than 2,300,000 persons; reappraise the policies of his predecessor in light of highly secret information that would now become available to him; and launch sixteen task forces to explore new alternatives in foreign and domestic policy. He would have to prepare a new budget— itself an enterprise of massive proportions; develop his legislative proposals to the new Congress, and start work on his Inaugural and State of the Union messages. In addition to all this, there was a mountain of congratulatory mail. Whether it came from premiers or precinct captains, an answer had to be written.

Yet, through a strange omission in the law, a President-elect could not call on the vast resources of the government he would soon be leading for either staff or financial assistance through the critical weeks of transition. He was on his own. One of JFK's first actions as President, however, was to win congressional approval of a $250,000 appropriation for future Presidents-elect who would find themselves in the same spot.

We broke camp at Hyannis Port two days after the election. From then until the Inauguration, we would operate from three headquarters—Ambassador Kennedy's sprawling white stucco mansion at Palm Beach, the two-story penthouse of the Carlyle Hotel in New York, and the senator's own red-brick residence in Washington's Georgetown. He flew more than 15,000 miles over the next two and a half months, and held eighteen news conferences. But by the end of the year, the new Cabinet had been chosen, many of his legislative proposals were in draft form, and he was beginning to sense the full round of the presidency.

I now had an entirely new relationship with the press. I was no longer speaking for a political candidate but for a man who would shortly become the leader of the free world. At a time when adversaries at home and abroad were analyzing his every word for clues to his intentions, it was crucial that he not be misunderstood. I was working not only in an entirely new atmosphere but with a greatly expanded group of reporters, some of whom I knew only slightly or not at all. Many of the correspondents who had been with us on the campaign trail were now back at their former desks in newspaper offices and TV and radio newsrooms across the country. Their replacements, who took over the day after the election, were the White House regulars—the presidential experts. They were led by Merriman Smith, senior White House correspondent of United Press International and a White House fixture. It was Smith who would close most of the presidential news conferences with a curt, "Thank you, Mr. President," and who had written a successful book of Washington reminiscences with that title.

When JFK saw him in the throng of reporters waiting at the Hyannis Armory, he smiled and shook his hand. "If you're here, Smitty, I guess I've really been elected." The President-elect introduced his wife to the veteran correspondent with the comment: "This is Merriman Smith. He goes with the White House."

After Hyannis Port, I took a vacation at Montego Bay, Jamaica— the first I had had in fifteen months. It was also my first awakening to the fact that a presidential Press Secretary cannot afford the luxury of loose conversation.

I had dinner one night with Bill vanden Heuvel, a young lawyer who had been an unsuccessful Democratic candidate for Congress in New York. Also present was a top editorial official of *Time* magazine. It was a relaxed evening and I let my hair down a little on certain unpublished aspects of the campaign. The next day I learned that the *Time* executive had wired more than a thousand words of what I considered a social conversation to his office in New York. I confronted him angrily and demanded that he kill the story. He did.

My run-in with the representative of *Time* was only a preliminary for the main event that was waiting for me in Palm Beach when I flew there to join the President-elect. One of the first decisions JFK made on my advice was to provoke a storm of historic proportions. Many old-timers in the press corps still regard it as an administration disaster second only to the Bay of Pigs.

My advice was that JFK, the third White House occupant of the television age, be the first to open his press conferences to live coverage by the TV networks. Today, no one blinks at the prospect of the most powerful head of state in the world exposing himself to free and often hostile questions before an audience of many millions and with no possibility of censorship. But in 1960 my proposal was a radical departure from tradition, and the reaction was swift and violent. I had to contend with strong disagreement among JFK's closest advisers, much head-shaking in the State Department, and a near riot among the White House correspondents.

Those first days in Palm Beach were rough on all of us. Except for a swim or an occasional round of golf, JFK was at his desk in his father's den most of his waking hours. The largest part of his time was taken up with appointments to the Cabinet and other high-ranking government positions. In charge of this national talent search was his brother-in-law, Sargent Shriver, who previously had been assistant general manager of the Chicago Merchandise Mart, owned by Ambassador Kennedy. But in addition to the top-level offices, JFK also had 1200 other appointive positions to fill. He threw up his hands at a staff meeting one day.

"Where am I going to find that many good people? Are there that many in the country?"

He was also host to scores of important visitors. Among them were
Allen Dulles, director of the Central Intelligence Agency, and Richard
Bissell, the deputy director. They told the President-elect for the first time
on November 17 that the Eisenhower administration was training a Cuban
exile force on a coffee plantation on the Pacific coast of Guatemala for
possible use against Castro.

I was staying in the Palm Beach Towers Hotel—headquarters for the
press—but drove the two miles to Ambassador Kennedy's twice a day to
clear the latest batch of appointments with JFK and to get his guidance
on questions I would be asked at my next press conference. I said to him
one morning: "What do you think of opening up your press conferences
to live television? I don't think there's any doubt that you can handle it.
You proved that against Nixon in the debates."

Without television, JFK could not have won the election, and the
debates certainly were the turning point. He came across on TV as a
mature, knowledgeable, attractive man. Nixon came across with all the
sincerity of an actor reading a toothpaste commercial.

"We wouldn't have had a prayer without that gadget," the candidate
told me one night after watching a replay of one of the TV debates.

But he had reservations that morning in Palm Beach. Wasn't there a
danger of overexposure? Would the networks be willing to give us the
time if there was no certainty of a major news break? How would the
pencil and paper reporters react to the obvious competitive advantage we
would be giving TV?

I replied that if the audience fell off, or if the networks became unwilling to televise them all, we could always take a second look at it. As
for the reporters, their reaction had to be negative, but they would learn
to live with it. I also made the point that presidential press conferences
were not given verbatim coverage by a majority of the newspapers. In
fact, only six ran the full transcripts of Eisenhower's conferences: the
New York *Times*, the *Wall Street Journal*, the Washington *Post* and
*Star*, the Denver *Post*, and the St. Louis *Post Dispatch*.

"Start it moving with the networks," he finally told me. "But let's hold
off on the announcement until we know they'll buy it."

The strongest and most persistent argument against live TV press conferences was that a single slip of the lip by an American President could
push an already jittery world a little closer to disaster. The prospects for
peace in the winter of 1960 were not very promising. There were shooting
wars in Africa and Southeast Asia, and the fuse was burning short in
Cuba, West Berlin, and the China Sea.

It was against this backdrop of crisis that John F. Kennedy would have
to decide whether to take his chances in a free-for-all with the press,
including at least six Communists representing newspapers and wire
services in the Soviet bloc.

Certainly no other major world leader was willing to risk it—then or now. De Gaulle's press conferences have always been carefully staged. He has a "direct confrontation" with the press only once or twice a year, when it serves *his* purposes. His aides plant every question in advance with pro-administration reporters, and *Le Président* carefully rehearses the answers.

The British parliamentary system precludes the Prime Minister from holding press conferences and announcing important changes in policy before making these announcements to the House of Commons. Rather than the U.S. system of the press conference, the British Prime Minister accounts to the people through the parliamentary question period. Minority members of Parliament are often used by the press to put questions to the Prime Minister.

There are those who hold that the presidential press conference system is a substitute for the parliamentary question period. Nothing could be further from the truth. A Prime Minister *must* answer questions from the House of Commons. The President, however, has the complete discretion whether to hold press conferences or not, and a President who decided to completely refuse to hold press conferences (while subject to attack from the press) would be well within his rights.

In the Soviet Union, there's not even a pretense of free inquiry into public policy. The government owns and edits both the newspapers and wire services and the Soviet citizen reads only what the Kremlin wants him to read. On his visit to America in 1959, Chairman Khrushchev held a press conference at the National Press Club in Washington, D.C. But except for that, no Soviet head of state, to my knowledge, holds still for public questioning by reporters of his own country, much less those from foreign nations, except at infrequent social gatherings.

Modern American Presidents of course, have been more available to the fourth estate. But until John F. Kennedy, all were insistent on at least minimum censorship of their press conferences. Franklin D. Roosevelt, despite his flair for turning a phrase, would never, except by specific permission, permit the press to quote him directly. In fact, he would often insist that newsmen attribute even the paraphrase of his direct remarks to "a White House spokesman."

Harry S. Truman was more willing to speak for the record, although many of his comments were too salty for newspapers of family circulation. Television came into its own during the Truman administration but he wouldn't permit TV or even newsreel cameras at his press conferences.

Dwight D. Eisenhower and his Press Secretary, Jim Hagerty, made a major breakthrough when they permitted the press to do two things: first to film and tape the presidential press conference and second to permit the press to use exact quotes from a transcript of the conference. Hagerty maintained one thin hold over the presidential words—the right to edit the transcript if he so desired—and also to edit film and tapes if the transcript was altered. Thus the transcript, film, and tape were held up by the press for a short period while the wording was being checked. Hagerty infrequently used this power, however, and the American people read and saw actual press conferences for the first time. In a way, the result was not helpful to President Eisenhower, whose shattered syntax was the subject of much humor in the country. Any verbatim press conference suffers from the same problems, however.

JFK would not even have the temporary protections of a transcript check. He would be communicating instantaneously with tens of millions of Americans in their homes—and watchful Communist diplomats in their embassies. He could not go off the record. He could accuse no one of misquoting him.

The question of live TV came up frequently at staff conferences over the next week. McGeorge Bundy and Ted Sorensen thought it was too hazardous. Dean Rusk was not yet Secretary of State but he, too, argued against the new format after his appointment. JFK, however, gave no weight at all to the possibility that he might be caught off-guard on a foreign policy question. He was absolutely confident of his ability to handle himself. Further, he agreed with me that even if he did blow a question—TV or no TV—it would be impossible to suppress it for very long.

A more important factor, in his opinion and mine, was the editorial opposition we were certain to encounter from a majority of the newspapers on domestic policy. Although no Democratic candidate for President had ever been given fairer treatment by a predominantly Republican press, the honeymoon couldn't last. The publishers of seven out of ten dailies had come out for Nixon. We could expect them to hold their fire for a time, at least, on foreign policy. But we could also expect immediate and powerful opposition, both in the press and in Congress, to his early plans for stimulating the economy and resolving the volatile civil rights issue.

FDR, when he was under strongest attack, took his case directly to the people with his "fireside chats" on radio. I felt JFK would have to do the same eventually—and live TV was the way to do it. After several weeks of discussion he finally agreed, on December 27, 1960.

"This is the right thing," he told me. "We should be able to go around the newspapers if that becomes necessary. But, beyond that, I don't know how we can justify keeping TV out if it wants in."

There was now no question that TV was willing to pre-empt millions of dollars in commercial time to carry the press conferences. I had met for five hours that day with the top news executives of the networks. All were enthusiastic.

My next chore was to tell the newspapermen. JFK was puffing on a cigar when I stood up to leave.

"Let me know what happens," he said. He was smiling when I shut the door behind me. I wasn't.

The press already was suspicious. They knew the network VIPs had been in town, and every hour on the hour a reporter would bug me with the line that Hagerty had run the best presidential press shop in history, and that I would be wise to change nothing. They were half right. Hagerty was the best. But Dwight D. Eisenhower and John F. Kennedy were totally different personalities. My President would have to project himself and his thinking in his own way.

I could anticipate the objections of the senior correspondents. They had been raising them for years. Live TV would turn the press conference into amateur night in Dixie, with the extroverts hamming it up for the cameras. (This did occur but no more often than under the Eisenhower rules.) There was also the argument that there could be no questioning in depth in such an atmosphere. (That, too, was specious. In-depth questioning, strangely, hadn't been a characteristic of the presidential press conference since Herbert Hoover's day.) Finally, there was the objection that the President might duck a tough question he would answer if he had time to think it over—time he would not take with the cameras pointing at him. (That didn't prove out, either. JFK's press conferences were extremely candid.)

Although they didn't emphasize it, the newspaper reporters' prime reason for opposing live TV was that it would put them at a competitive disadvantage. Under Eisenhower, the afternoon newspapers could be on the streets hours before the evening newscasts. Now the break would go to TV. But even this objection was largely invalid. Most of the major newspapers in the country now operate their own television stations and the new format would strengthen their total news operation. It was the reporters on the White House beat, not their publishers at home, who were to give us the most static.

H-hour had come. I held my press conference at the Palm Beach Towers just after lunch. Most of the reporters were lounging around in swim trunks or Bermuda shorts. (I had worn Bermudas, too, until JFK saw me on television one day. "Get back into long pants," he said. "You haven't got the legs for shorts.")

I shall never forget this press conference. I went right into the announcement of the live TV decision and said that the President's first press conference would be held on January 25—five days after the Inaugural. As I explained the new ground rules, a storm of protest came from the assembled reporters.

Not only was the decision to televise the press conferences live abhorrent to many of them—but some of the technical details did not suit them. For example, I explained that reporters attending the press conference would, as in the past, have to stay until the end of the conference.

The reporters wanted to know how I could keep them in the room for the press conference if the public at large was seeing the conference on the TV screen. I told them we could not have the question-and-answer period interrupted by reporters walking in and out.

As the details of the ground rules got more and more complicated, I heard the gravelly voice of Bill Lawrence, then the White House correspondent of the New York *Times*. I do not remember his question, but the introductory phrase is sufficient:

"Mr. Salinger, as you plunge deeper and deeper into matters about which you know absolutely nothing . . ." he asked with a voice dipped in sarcasm.

That did it. I didn't wait for the rest of the sentence. Now I was shouting back. It was the President's press conference—not theirs—and he would run it his own way. The decision was final. They could take it or leave it.

I went to my office and put in a call to JFK. He was laughing. "Don't tell me," he said. "I already know. I could hear it clear across town."

That's where it stood when the whole entourage went back to Washington the week after New Year's. But the press still wasn't through with me. I got an invitation from a group of correspondents to join them for lunch at the Sheraton Park Hotel. Waiting for me, among others, were Merriman Smith, Ed Folliard of the Washington *Post*, Robert Donovan of the New York *Herald Tribune* (now with the Los Angeles *Times*), and Raymond (Pete) Brandt of the St. Louis *Post Dispatch*. Lawrence wasn't there—probably a break for me. I had sent him a transcript of the tumultuous Palm Beach press conference, underlining his words, "*As you plunge deeper and deeper into matters about which you know absolutely nothing . . .*" and predicting that he would one day admit he was wrong. He did.

Even without Lawrence, however, the Sheraton Park luncheon had all the cordiality of a drumhead court-martial. Folliard, who had been around Washington since Woodrow Wilson's day, told me flatly that "You're turning the presidential press conferences into a sideshow." Others said the press conferences would become a propaganda tool for the President and would cease to be newsworthy. How either could happen when the press itself was asking the questions, I didn't know, and they were in no mood to explain it to the new boy.

I was also told that day that I must always inform the correspondents when the President left the White House, where he was going, and with whom.

"I don't have to at all," I replied. "Obviously you'll be told if he's leaving town or attending an official affair. But he has a right to his privacy. I don't intend to tell you where he spends his evenings or release the guest list when he entertains his friends."

"In that case," one of my hosts shot back, "we'll have to post a twenty-four-hour guard around his office."

"That's your privilege," I said.

We also disagreed on another tradition that went back to President Truman's day—the requirement that a reporter must identify himself and his affiliation when he stood up to ask a question at a news conference. It was Truman's counterattack on anonymous reporters who would fire a hot question at him from the back of the room and then duck out of sight.

My hosts at luncheon thought it was a good practice and should be continued. I said it would not be. There was no good reason for permitting reporters to advertise their affiliation on television.

The identification of reporters had brought some abuses during the Eisenhower administration. For example, Sarah McClendon, a Washington correspondent who represents a number of Texas newspapers, would get up at consecutive Eisenhower press conferences and announce herself from different newspapers, knowing that the names of her papers would be advertised in the official transcript. I felt that the lure of coast-to-coast television would be too much of a temptation for this kind of advertising.

We did reach agreement on press arrangements for the Inaugural, and the organization of the press pool that would accompany the President when he left Washington. But that was all. I finally left after three hours of bombast and bourbon.

But I was to have still another invitation to lunch—from James (Scotty) Reston of the New York *Times*. I found him a far more amicable host. But we did disagree on the attitude the President should adopt toward old friends and confidants in the press corps.

Reston felt he should stop seeing them socially because it would give them a clear advantage over the outsiders. JFK knew such criticism was coming and already had told me: "I'm going to keep my old friends and the presidency is not a good place to make new ones."

I argued with Reston that a friend actually would be at a disadvantage because he would lean over backward to avoid violating a presidential confidence.

I told Scotty that the President's newspaper friends posed a problem which could be faced in two ways. One way was to tell the President that he had to channel these contacts through me or he was going to cut off my effectiveness with the rest of the press. The other approach was to say to the press: "Look, these guys were friends of his long before I met him, and I'm not going to stick my nose into who his friends are." I had chosen the latter course—and I still believe it was the right course. Reston felt the friends would have an advantage over other reporters. I will say that none of these friends—with one exception—ever took advantage of him. For example, the copy of Charles Bartlett of the Chattanooga *Times* (now a syndicated columnist) became particularly dull during the Kennedy administration because he did not want to give the outside world the appearance he was trading on his friendship with the President.

Scotty was also very concerned about my decision, announced at the Sheraton Park luncheon, not to tell the press every time the President left the White House. He argued that a President had no privacy and asked what would happen if the President had an automobile accident, for example, while out of the White House on one of these unannounced visits. Reston said it was the responsibility of the press to be with the President all the time. I disagreed with him and told him that under the circumstances he described the press would find out soon enough anyway. I think I left him largely unconvinced by my argument, but I knew that I was not going to be able to change President Kennedy's habits—and there was no use in trying.

We left Washington Thanksgiving Day on the *Caroline* for the warmer weather in Palm Beach. Mrs. Kennedy was expecting her baby the following week and didn't join us. But when I stepped from the plane in Palm Beach, a messenger told me I had an urgent call from Washington waiting on an open line. It was the Georgetown University Hospital. Mrs. Kennedy had been rushed there and was giving birth to her child.

JFK spoke briefly to the doctor, John Walsh, and then ordered the press plane back to Washington. Halfway there, the radio operator on our American Airlines charter told the President-elect that a son had been born. The announcement was then made to the cheering press over the intercom system. American Airlines later had the intercom microphone mounted and presented it to JFK as a memorial of the event.

One of my most frustrating problems during this period was the constant leaking of prospective presidential appointments to the press. I hardly ever made an announcement that had not already broken in one or more newspapers.

The President-elect didn't like it and was impatient with my failure to track down the culprits in the administration responsible for the leaks. But the angriest he ever became with me—that first year, at least—was when the Washington *Post* prematurely broke the story under a page-one banner that Dean Rusk would be the new Secretary of State. It was true but only a handful of JFK's closest advisers knew it.

"Stop everything else you're doing," he told me. "I want the name of the person responsible for this and I want it today. This has got to stop."

I spoke to Bundy, Sorensen, Shriver, O'Brien, and O'Donnell. No one had a clue. Then I decided to conduct an independent investigation. Two hours later, I called the President-elect.

"I have caught the leaker," I said.

"All right, who is it?"

"You."

"What do you mean, me?"

I asked him if he hadn't discussed the appointment the night before by telephone with Phil Graham, publisher of the *Post*.

"I did talk to Graham about it last night."

"Did you tell him he couldn't use the story?"

There was a long silence, then a low chuckle.

"No, I guess I didn't."

On another occasion, JFK told me to announce the appointment of Boisfeuillet Jones as Special Assistant to the Secretary of Health, Education and Welfare for Health and Medical Affairs. I had never heard of Boisfeuillet Jones before and I was certain the press hadn't either. This was my story—all mine—and no one was going to steal it from me.

I spent half the morning furtively digging up every last fact I could find on the career of Boisfeuillet Jones, then locked myself in a room and wrote the story myself.

An hour before my next press briefing I ran into Bill Lawrence in the lobby. "I've got an appointment you never heard of today," I told him.

"Don't bet on it," he answered.

Finally, the great moment had come. I stood before the mike in the press room and said, "Gentlemen, I have an announcement of great . . ."

Lawrence interrupted me. "Before you start, Pierre, what can you tell us about the appointment of one Boisfeuillet Jones as Special Assistant to the Secretary of Health, Education and Welfare?"

I had been beaten again.

Lawrence told me later that my crack to him in the lobby was a challenge he couldn't resist. He ran over the recent sequence of appointments and figured out that the next one would be in HEW. He then placed a long-distance call to Abraham Ribicoff, Secretary-designate of Health, Education and Welfare, who was playing golf at the Diplomat Country Club in Fort Lauderdale.

When Lawrence told him of his little plot against me, the Secretary-designate became a willing co-conspirator and gave him Jones' name.

My son, Marc, was a leading character on New Year's Eve in a comedy of confusion that would have done justice to the Marx Brothers. I was at a party at the Palm Beach Country Club when the telephone rang in my suite at the Palm Beach Towers. Marc, who was alone, answered it.

"This is the Soviet Embassy in Washington. I want to dictate to Mr. Salinger a New Year's greeting to the President-elect from Chairman Nikita Khrushchev."

My twelve-year-old son was only half awake and couldn't remember where I had gone.

"Hold the phone a minute," he said, and ran down the hall to confer with Tim Smith, the son of UPI correspondent Merriman Smith. The two sleepy boys agreed that Smitty, who was celebrating in the bar downstairs, was the man to take over, and Tim went down after him.

"I'll take this call," Smitty told the embassy attaché.

"Are you a member of Mr. Kennedy's staff?"

Smitty answered, quite honestly, "Yes, I am with the presidential party." He then scrawled the message on a piece of paper.

Smith and Marvin Arrowsmith, the White House correspondent of the Associated Press, then drove to the Palm Beach Country Club and delivered the message to me at about 2 A.M. New Year's morning. I decided not to bother the President at that time, but delivered it to him the next morning—still in Smith's handwriting.

I can thank Jim Hagerty for the warmest memories I have of the days just before the Inauguration. Following my appointment, he invited me to the White House for a visit. I had been a great admirer of Hagerty's integrity and ability, and now we were to become close friends.

I had never been inside the White House before when I walked into his office in late November. The photographers took our picture together and then he sat me down in a chair next to his desk.

"I want to make one thing clear at the outset," he said. "I won't tell you how to run things. I'll just show you what you have to work with here —and then you're on your own."

That was but the first of four visits in which he briefed me on the high-speed world-wide communications equipment in the White House; the travel organization procedure; and the highly secret plan that would allow the press and the President to function in the event of nuclear attack.

The last day I saw him in his office, just a week before the Inauguration, he said to me: "I want you to know that Dwight D. Eisenhower has been *my* President. More than that, he's been almost a father to me. But John F. Kennedy will be my President, too. If I can ever help you, or him, just pick up the phone."

Shortly after he left the White House, Jim became vice-president and director of News Operations for the American Broadcasting Company, a tough, demanding assignment. But he was as good as his word. I went to him many times for advice and he would often call me with suggestions he thought might be useful. They always were. And during the Cuban missile crisis of 1962 he was to respond immediately to a call to serve his government once again. In contrast to certain members of the Eisenhower administration who were quick to find fault with their successors, Hagerty never criticized my operation.

The interim weeks sped toward their end—the Inauguration—the first of 1000 fantastic days of hope and disappointment, joy and sadness. But one thing those days never were was dull.

# V

## THE YOUNG MEN TAKE OVER

President John F. Kennedy's personal staff was an unlikely mixture. We were Catholics, Protestants, and Jews. We came from the East, the Midwest, and the Far West, and from backgrounds of poverty and wealth. Among us were visionary intellectuals and rock-hard political pros—historians and football players—Americans for Democratic Action and an Eisenhower Republican.

What we had in common, however, was our salary, which was $21,000 a year, and our commitment to the President, which was total.

There wasn't one of us who couldn't have made more at his former calling, and under far better working conditions. We spent twelve to fourteen hours a day at our desks but were on call around the clock, seven days a week, 365 days a year. The work load at the White House was enormous and the deadline was always *yesterday*. Many of us spent months of every year on the road, flying in hazardous weather, living out of overnight bags, and gulping our meals on the run. We worked under constant pressure and for an employer who was never satisfied—with his efforts or ours.

But none of us will ever have a better job as long as we live. There was no overtime, no expense account, no health or retirement plan. But the big *plus*—the fringe benefit that made it all worthwhile—was JFK himself.

Our faith in him and in what he was trying to do was absolute, and he could impart to our work together a sense of challenge and adventure—a feeling that he was moving, and the world with him, toward a better time. We could accept without complaint his bristling temper, his cold sarcasm, and his demands for always higher standards of excellence because we knew he was driving himself harder than he was driving us—despite great and persistent physical pain and personal tragedy.

The White House staff, however, was not one big, happy family. Strong and even angry disagreements among us were common and certain staffers simply didn't like others personally. This didn't concern the President. "The last thing I want around here is a mutual admiration society," he told me one day after a hostile exchange between two staffers in his presence. "When you people stop arguing, I'll start worrying."

There was, however, no basis for reports early in the administration of a power struggle on the staff between the "eggheads" and the "Irish Mafia" —descriptions that would arouse JFK to profane anger. He had chosen the bulk of his staff from two principal milieus—the academic community at Harvard University and the Irish-Catholic sector of Massachusetts politics. But there was never a split along such lines. Ted Sorensen, one of the President's key advisers, came from neither camp, nor did I. Yet Ken O'Donnell, the most powerful member of the staff, was both a Harvard graduate and an Irish-Catholic politician from Massachusetts. The reports of such dissension came from unsuccessful applicants for White House positions or lightweights who didn't last long on the staff, many of whom found "blackballing" by one element or the other a handy alibi for their rejection or dismissal.

From my viewpoint, O'Donnell had the greatest responsibility, influence, and accessibility to the President. Ken is a slight man but tough and wiry with black hair and a disposition to match it when he thought someone was working against JFK's best interests. His father, Cleo O'Donnell, was a legendary football coach at Holy Cross. But Ken chose to pass up the Catholic institution for Harvard, which was the other side of the tracks for an Irishman from Worcester. He was first string quarterback, captain of the Harvard football team, and an honorable mention All American. One of his favorite passing targets on the same team was an end by the name of Robert F. Kennedy. The two became close friends despite their great difference in backgrounds. After graduation, when Ken was considering an offer to play professional football with the old Buffalo Bills of the All American Conference, Bob persuaded him to go into government and politics instead.

O'Donnell worked on precinct organization for John F. Kennedy's winning Senate campaign against Henry Cabot Lodge in 1952. I first met Ken when he came to Washington in 1957 as administrative assistant to Bob Kennedy on the Senate labor rackets committee, for which I was then an investigator. I found him to be one of the most candid and direct men I have ever met. He would never use five words if one would do, and that word was very often a flat "no." One could admire him immediately but it took a little longer to like him. It was obvious to me, even in 1957, that Ken was merely marking time for the "big game," and in 1959 he left the rackets committee to join the Kennedy for President staff.

Once the campaign was under way, he was constantly at JFK's side. He took his orders directly from the candidate and saw to it that the rest of us carried them out—and to the letter. The senator had absolute confidence in O'Donnell, and after we were in the White House the rapport between them grew even stronger. In moments of high exhilaration or deep depression, the President would most often reveal his innermost thoughts to O'Donnell. The two men were different yet very much alike. Both were Irish, but the President had grown up rich and O'Donnell poor. Both had valorous war records—Ken as a bombardier-navigator on B-17s in the European theater. Both had come up through the jungles of Massachusetts politics—and both had the instinct for the jugular necessary to survive in that jungle. Yet both saw politics as an honorable calling—one that could place a man or a party in a position to change the world for the better.

Ken had many duties at the White House. One of them was Appointments Secretary. Except for members of the official family and state visitors, no one could see the President without first clearing with O'Donnell—and he could say no to a corporation president trying to promote an ambassadorship as readily as he could to a ward politician trying to influence the award of a contract. Ken was also the liaison between the White House and the Secret Service and FBI. Their highly confidential reports came across his desk before reaching JFK's. One of his most important duties was arranging the President's travels. Whether it was a flight to Chicago to speak to a political rally or a state visit to Europe to confer with de Gaulle, Khrushchev, or Macmillan, O'Donnell was the chief planner. He also had an amazing knowledge of Democratic politics and personalities in every one of the states, and would referee many of the disputes among warring factions. When the word came down from O'Donnell, that was it!

It was my impression that O'Donnell had the greatest influence in shaping the President's most important decisions. He was able to set aside his own prejudices against individuals and his own ideological commitments (I would rate him a moderate Democrat) and appraise the alternatives with total objectivity. It was impossible to categorize O'Donnell, as White House observers did with other staff members, as either a "hawk" or a "dove" on foreign policy, or a Stevenson liberal or Truman conservative on civil rights. JFK gave extra weight to O'Donnell's opinions because he knew he had no personal cause to argue. Ken had only one criterion: Will this action help or hurt the President? And that, for O'Donnell, was another way of asking: Will it help or hurt the country?

To emphasize Ken's role is not to diminish the performance or importance of other White House staffers. This, simply, is how I saw it from the Press Secretary's office. Next to him, I would rank Theodore C. Sorensen and McGeorge Bundy as the advisers who left the greatest imprint on the Thousand Days.

Ted, a Unitarian from Lincoln, Nebraska, is the son of a former Republican attorney general of that state, but an heir to the progressive tradition of Senator George W. Norris (and organizer of the Lincoln chapter of Americans for Democratic Action). Sorensen was first in his class at the University of Nebraska Law School and came to Washington to work for the Federal Security Agency. He left there in 1953 to join JFK's staff after his election to the Senate. They hit it off magnificently. Sorensen not only had strong social convictions echoing those of the young senator, but a genius for translating them into eloquent and persuasive language. During the Kennedy for President campaign, Ted was in charge of the special task force that developed policy positions and speech drafts for JFK. I must add that nothing eats up material faster than a presidential campaign in which a candidate speaks three or four times a day on subjects ranging from nuclear armaments to conservation. The voters expect not only that he be knowledgeable but that he have new and positive alternatives to present policy. Ted somehow was able to keep up with the demand and to maintain a high level of creativity.

Like O'Donnell, Sorensen wore more than one hat at the White House. He was the coordinator of planning for domestic policy and had a key role in formulating JFK's recommendations to Congress. But he also continued to serve as the principal speech writer. Actually, speeches were not written *for* the President but *with* him. He knew what he wanted to say and how he wanted to say it. The role of the speech writer was to organize JFK's thoughts into a rough draft, on which he himself would put the final touches. His revisions would often change it dramatically.

Ted, who did all his writing in longhand on yellow legal pads, had been grinding out words for JFK for eight years and knew his style best. As one reporter wrote, "Sorensen had the glory of words." But he was also widely read and could always find exactly the right classical reference to bring a major point into critical focus.

In advance of his most important addresses, the President would summon his top advisers for a conference on content. For instance, if the speech was on foreign policy, McGeorge Bundy, the ranking White House adviser on foreign affairs, Secretary of State Dean Rusk, and the appropriate specialists in State would listen to JFK's views on what he planned to say and contribute thoughts of their own. Ted would then prepare a first draft. The President, Rusk, and Bundy would all have a look at it, come up with new suggestions, and Sorensen would blend them into a second draft. (His TV report to the nation announcing the Cuban missile blockade in 1962 went to five drafts before it was acceptable to the President.) Finally, when there was agreement on content and emphasis, JFK would go to work on the text with his own pencil. Ted had an excellent ear for the President's speech rhythm and almost never wrote a phrase he might stumble over. But when he did, JFK would discover it while practicing the speech aloud and would substitute a phrase with which he felt more comfortable.

Among others who would contribute speech drafts if the subject fell within their provinces were Arthur M. Schlesinger, Jr., the Pulitzer Prize-winning historian; Ralph A. Dungan, one of the most versatile members of the staff; Assistant Special Counsel Richard N. Goodwin, who later became President Johnson's chief speech writer, and myself.

I must note, however, that the President was a text deviate. Depending on his mood, his confidence in his text, the lateness of the hour, or the reaction (or lack of it) from his audience, he might throw away most or all of his address and speak extemporaneously. The exceptions were major TV addresses to the nation and his appearances before the UN or joint sessions of Congress, when every word had been carefully chosen for its impact both on the nation and on foreign governments. But his frequent deviations from the text in less significant forums were frustrating not only to the speech writers but to the correspondents whose quotes from the text were in print or on the air before he even spoke.

When I came to him with complaints from the press, he would shrug me off.

"Tell them I stand by every word in the text, whether I read it or not."

I told him that wouldn't do. "Your audience will pick up the morning paper, read quotes you never said, and decide that the reporter was either too drunk to take notes or didn't show up for the speech. Unless you stick to the text, the reporters won't file until after you're through speaking and you'll miss most of their editions."

The only concession he ever made to me was to read the advance stories on the AP and UPI wires, and read verbatim those quotes they were playing as the lead. I was willing to settle for that, inasmuch as the two wires were responsible for at least ninety per cent of the coverage.

McGeorge Bundy was one of the ablest, and least understood, members of John F. Kennedy's staff. On the surface he was cold and austere. But if he took you into his circle of friends and confidants you found behind the computer-quick brain and haughty appearance a man of great charm and wit.

Bundy was the only Republican on the staff and the only one of us who was not in the campaign. He took a leave of absence as dean of Harvard's Faculty of Arts and Sciences to join JFK after the election as his specialist on foreign policy. He was a member in good standing, for many years, of the Eastern Establishment that had controlled American foreign policy under both Democratic and Republican Presidents. His brother, William, is married to the daughter of former Secretary of State Dean Acheson. Bundy himself was the editor of the Henry L. Stimson papers, an account of our diplomatic history from Theodore Roosevelt through Harry S. Truman.

Bundy had the largest support staff in the White House—ten or more assistants to whom he assigned specific world areas for study and recommendation. JFK spoke of this operation as his "little State Department," but there was no truth to speculation that Bundy's expansion of the White House foreign affairs section led to friction with Secretary Rusk. Bundy had great respect for Rusk personally and for his judgment, and Rusk had respect for Bundy.

The same was true of the President. Not once did I ever hear JFK express a lack of confidence in Rusk, much less a desire to remove him from the Cabinet. He did, on occasion, express the wish that Rusk would be more forceful in presenting his own views, but the criticism was not quantitive. JFK was frequently upset with many of his appointees, including me, but his anger of the moment did not reflect his total opinion of us.

Because of Bundy's personal abilities and his White House staff of specialists on the Near East, Middle East, Far East, *ad infinitum*, JFK had more effective liaison with the State Department than any President in history. The staff itself was also kept up to date on what was happening around the world. Bundy held a briefing for key White House personnel every morning on significant overnight developments.

Bundy had a number of brilliant men working for him. At the top of the list was Dr. Carl Kaysen, recently named head of the School for Advanced Studies at Princeton, New Jersey. Kaysen was a specialist in nuclear disarmament and European policy. Bundy's assistant for Far Eastern affairs was Mike Forrestal, the son of the late Secretary of Defense James V. Forrestal. The specialist on Near Eastern affairs was Robert Komer, a former employee of the Central Intelligence Agency. Komer has now become President Johnson's key specialist on matters affecting Vietnam and Southeast Asia policy.

Burly, crewcut Larry O'Brien was another staffer in whom the President placed great confidence and responsibility. A tough but amiable Irishman from Springfield, Massachusetts, Larry was in advertising and public relations before joining the Kennedy team in 1951. A former administrative assistant to Massachusetts Congressman (later Governor) Foster Furcolo, Larry knew the politics of the Bay State inside out. His specialties, like O'Donnell's, were voter registration and precinct organization. John F. Kennedy's success in the presidential primaries in 1960 was due in large part to O'Brien's application of the precinct strategy he conceived in JFK's first race for the Senate in 1952, and refined even further for the senatorial landslide victory in 1958.

O'Brien continued to be one of the President's most influential political advisers after the Inauguration, dealing directly with Democratic governors and mayors. But his specific duty at the White House was congressional liaison. He was JFK's contact with the Democratic leadership in both houses, and was on a first-name basis with almost every legislator of both parties. He was the trail boss, as it were, of the President's legislative program. Obviously, it was left to the Democratic leadership to move the bills on the floor. But O'Brien met with them constantly on strategy. He was the man to see to find out if the President would accept an amendment. If the administration didn't have the votes, it was Larry who would arrange for the President to speak directly to recalcitrant Democrats. I still marvel at O'Brien's ability as a vote-counter. Even before legislation went to the Hill, he could tell you almost exactly who would be for it, who would be against it, whose vote could be changed, and whose could not.

He dealt with hundreds of legislators—ultraliberals and ultraconservatives, statesmen and hacks. They came from farm country and major urban areas and their ideological and geographical interests were almost always in direct conflict. But O'Brien and the Democratic leadership somehow were able to bring them together into a voting majority on many of the President's prime legislative goals. Larry has since been appointed Postmaster General of the United States by President Johnson.

Schlesinger, the brilliant Harvard historian, held a unique position at the White House. Unlike O'Donnell, Sorensen, or Bundy, he was not a policy maker. His official role was that of White House liaison with United Nations Ambassador Adlai Stevenson. Schlesinger had been a speech writer and consultant to Stevenson on both foreign and domestic policy in the campaigns of 1952 and 1956, and the two were still close friends. JFK never had a warm personal relationship with Stevenson and Schlesinger was the ideal choice to serve as their go-between.

The President and Schlesinger were also strong friends. JFK was intrigued both by his wit and intelligence and he was a frequent guest at intimate White House dinners. Schlesinger had the ability to discard conventional approaches and to think creatively on all manner of questions, ranging from containment of Castro to White House incentives to culture. His suggestions would reach the President's desk in a constant stream of memoranda. Although many of Schlesinger's recommendations were put to use, JFK occasionally was impatient with their length and frequency, and felt that many of the memos should have gone to staff specialists, not directly to him.

Myer (Mike) Feldman, the deputy to Sorensen, was the best lawyer in the White House and held one of the most sensitive positions. He gave up careers as a practicing attorney and owner of radio stations in Rhode Island, Oklahoma, California, and Oregon to serve JFK with intense loyalty and integrity.

Mike spoke for the White House on all matters that came before the regulatory agencies. As liaison with these agencies, he dealt in tariff and trade matters, advised on international air routes, oil import quotas and licenses, and special industry problems concerning the textile, shoe, and lumbering interests. He supervised the drafting of presidential proclamations and executive orders. One of his most important responsibilities was to advise the President on what action to take on all bills passed by Congress—whether to veto them or sign them into law.

He had advance knowledge of the granting of government leases and many other transactions from which a dishonest man could have made millions for himself and his friends through hidden investments. The President often said that "if Mike Feldman ever sold out, we could all go to jail." But Feldman was scrupulously honest and there was never the slightest hint of indiscretion on his part.

Special Assistant Ralph Dungan had the most diverse range of duties at the White House. JFK first became aware of his talents and enterprise when Ralph became his legislative assistant in 1956. He later served as consultant to the Senate Labor and Public Welfare Committee and advised JFK on labor legislation and labor politics. Dungan had impressive contacts with labor leaders across the country and was an effective speech writer. This combination served candidate Kennedy well in the campaign of 1960.

After coming to the White House, Ralph continued his liaison with labor but also became an authority on Latin American affairs. He was held in high regard by the Roman Catholic hierarchy and JFK, determined to lean over backward to disprove the suspicion that he would be a *Catholic* President, often used Ralph to explain his positions to the bishops.

Dungan was also the chief talent scout for the New Frontier. It was his responsibility to come up with the names of men and women for the highest appointive positions in government, and to work with the FBI on an investigation into their backgrounds. (This security check was unbelievably thorough. In my own case, more than seventy-five of my friends, former schoolteachers, and newspaper colleagues were interviewed in depth. JFK was more than a little shaken when the FBI came up with the information that I had an arrest record in California under the alias Peter Emil Flick—a matter for which I had a ready explanation and the clippings from the *Chronicle* to back me up.)

Other staffers who had direct access to the President were Timothy J. Reardon, Jr., and Lee C. White. Reardon became administrative assistant to JFK when he was first elected to the House of Representatives in 1946, a position he still held when John F. Kennedy resigned from the Senate to enter the White House. Reardon was the President's Assistant for Cabinet Affairs and was responsible for preparing the agenda of Cabinet sessions and coordinating White House relations with the many departments of the executive branch.

White, a law school classmate of Sorensen's, spent a great deal of his time on civil rights matters. He was also responsible for legal work involving presidential pardons, appeals for clemency, liaison with the Commonwealth of Puerto Rico, and with housing and power matters. One of his assignments was liaison with the Better Business Bureau on commercialization of President Kennedy and his family. He later became special counsel to President Johnson and is now chairman of the Federal Power Commission.

The President also had a close working relationship with his three White House military advisers—Army Major General Chester V. Clifton, Navy Captain Tazewell T. Shepard, and Air Force Brigadier General Godfrey T. McHugh. Although they were chosen by the President, and were accountable only to him, the three were under constant pressure from their respective services to "lobby" JFK for appropriations or to win his support in the unending Pentagon feud among the Army, Navy, and Air Force.

Ted Clifton, the most influential of the three, was brought to the President's attention by his brother, Bob, on the recommendation of Charles Bartlett, a columnist and close friend of JFK. Clifton gave the President his daily intelligence briefing, both in the White House and on the road. Prior to his appointment, Clifton had been in charge of public information for the Army—a background that brought him into some conflict with me. It became obvious to me early in the administration that he was trespassing in my area and I wrote him a hot memo suggesting that he tend to his own affairs. After that we had an excellent relationship, and I developed a great respect for him and his abilities.

Captain Shepard, the son-in-law of Senator John J. Sparkman of Alabama, was also highly capable and intensely loyal to the President. The most flamboyant of the military aides was Godfrey McHugh, a handsome officer who was said to be the most eligible bachelor in Washington. He was in constant demand in Washington social circles yet found the time and energy to handle his White House chores with a high degree of efficiency. Shepard, McHugh, and I almost had to take a fifty-mile hike together, a harrowing episode in our White House careers that I will describe in a later chapter.

The most gregarious and popular member of the staff was Dave Powers, the official White House greeter. Dave would escort prominent visitors from their cars into the President's office and could rarely resist testing their sense of humor. When the Shah of Iran came to call, Dave put a friendly hand on his shoulder and said, "I want you to know you're my kind of Shah." He was even more direct with Soviet First Deputy Premier Anastas Mikoyan. "Tell me," he said, "are you the real Mikoyan?"

Powers was an unemployed veteran just returned from the China-Burma-India theater of operations when a young man campaigning for Congress knocked on his door and asked for his help. Powers agreed and was with John F. Kennedy more than any other man from that time until the assassination. Dave was the first staffer to see the President up in the morning and the last person to see him at night. He flew with him wherever he traveled, always making certain that a clean shirt and a cool drink were waiting for him in his hotel room.

Although Powers was somewhat older, and didn't pretend to be an expert on anything but baseball, JFK always enjoyed being in his company. Dave had more success than all the rest of us put together in raising the President's spirits when he was low.

Dave's knowledge of baseball was fantastic. I never knew anyone who could stump him with a question. He could not only recite the batting averages of obscure players of half a century ago but tell you how they did against right- and left-hand pitchers and whether they were faithful to their wives. His own favorite question was, "Whose record did Babe Ruth break when he hit sixty home runs?" When his victim couldn't remember such an obvious landmark in baseball history, Dave would shake his head in disgust. "He broke his own record of fifty-nine. What kind of an American wouldn't know that?"

My own duties at the White House were explicit. I was responsible for the flow of news not only from the President's office but from the entire executive branch of government. JFK held me as accountable for an error in fact in a press release from Agriculture or Interior as for one written in my own office. And there wasn't much that got by him. I recall a two-paragraph story, buried deep in the encyclopedic Sunday edition of the New York *Times*, reporting the award of a minor federal highway contract. He had torn the clipping from the paper and shoved it across his desk to me on Monday morning.

"The amount of that contract is wrong," he said. "It's only a third of what the paper says it is. You'd better check Commerce and find out if they had the figure wrong in their release."

I was back ten minutes later and told him it was just a typographical error in the *Times*. The department had sent out the correct figure.

"All right then, have Commerce call it to their attention," he replied.

JFK was determined that the New Frontier should speak with one voice. He was willing to listen long and patiently to conflicting views on policy, but once a decision was reached he expected his own appointees in the Cabinet and other high administration posts to support it. One of my responsibilities was to see to it that his appointees and their public information officers were aware of White House policy and did not, unwittingly or intentionally, issue press releases or statements in conflict with it. This, of course, led to charges of censorship and news management. But JFK was right. If officials serving at his pleasure, and sworn to support his administration, could not go along with him, they should resign, not use the position he had given them to attack his policies.

This was not at all a new attitude. All Presidents expect loyalty and support from their official family, and Jim Hagerty enforced the dictum as vigorously as I did. There was, however, a major difference in Hagerty's White House role and mine. In addition to running the press shop, he was one of President Eisenhower's advisers on foreign and domestic policy. My only policy duties were in the information field. While Jim had a voice in deciding *what* the administration would do, I was responsible only for presenting that decision to the public in a way and at a time that would generate the best possible reception.

For example, when I went to the Soviet Union, and spent two days with Chairman Khrushchev, I had specific instructions to discuss only a freer exchange of information between our two countries, not the policies over which there was a misunderstanding. When Khrushchev, who was always full of surprises, chose to make his views known to me on a broad range of critical issues, I told him my only role would be to relay his views to the President.

One reason that Hagerty, and other Eisenhower staffers, had wider responsibilities than their counterparts on the Kennedy staff was a difference in operating concept between the two Presidents. JFK gave each of us exact duties and held us individually responsible for carrying them out. President Eisenhower would disperse the authority for a single project among a number of staff members, probably the result of a military background in which many general officers would participate in top-level decisions. In both cases, of course, the final decision was the President's. The difference was in the way the recommendations came up to them from the staff level. I should add that Hagerty, probably the most influential Press Secretary in history, had knowledge in foreign and domestic fields that was superior to many of his colleagues on the Eisenhower staff, and it was, properly, put to use.

Except for Franklin D. Roosevelt, no President of the modern era has been more expert in public relations than JFK. I have said many times, and I still believe, that he could have gotten along without a Press Secretary if he had had time to handle the day-to-day routine of my office.

The President, a former newspaperman himself, was neither in awe of the press corps nor intimidated by it, as many of his predecessors had been. They had their job to do and he had his, and he knew there was very little he could do to influence either the reporters or the editorial policies of their newspapers. Early in 1962, after he had been in office slightly more than a year, he was asked at his press conference to comment on his treatment by the mass media. He replied:

"Well, I am reading more and enjoying it less [Laughter] and so on, but I have not complained nor do I plan to make any general complaints. I read and talk to myself about it, but I don't plan to issue any general statement to the press. I think that they are doing their task, as a critical branch, the fourth estate. And I am attempting to do mine. And we are going to live together for a period, and then go our separate ways [Laughter]."

President Kennedy saw the members of his White House staff as equals. In order that we should see it that way, too, he decreed that all of us would receive the same salary—$21,000 a year. Under Eisenhower, Hagerty and Special Assistant Sherman Adams were paid $22,500, with the rest of the staff ranging down from that in ratio to the importance assigned to their work. It is said that FDR thought he got the most out of his staff by playing one off against the other. JFK insisted on teamwork, not intramural competition. He would not tolerate staff politicking for his favor, and minor White House aides who tried it early in the administration either were transferred to other departments or told to knock it off.

In all the time President Kennedy was in the White House, he never once met with the full staff. He held to the belief that the productivity of all meetings is in direct inverse ratio to the number of participants. He had given each of us precise duties to carry out, and when there was an overlap he felt we ought to have the good sense to work together without instructions from him. Nor did he feel that it was necessary for him to be present when two or more staff members put their heads together. If we had something to tell him or ask him, the door to his office was always open. We were not to waste his time, and ours, with formal meetings.

The entire staff was sworn into office in a single ceremony the morning after the Inauguration. The language of our commissions, signed by the President and the Secretary of State, was impressive:

*JOHN F. KENNEDY, PRESIDENT OF THE UNITED STATES OF AMERICA, To PIERRE E. G. SALINGER of California, Greeting: REPOSING special trust and confidence in your Integrity, Prudence, and Ability I do appoint you Press Secretary to the President of the United States of America, authorizing you, hereby, to do and perform all such matters and things as to the said place or office do appertain, or as may be duly given you in charge hereafter, and the said office to hold and exercise during the pleasure of the President of the United States for the time being. IN TESTIMONY WHEREOF, I have caused the Seal of the United States to be hereunto affixed. DONE at the City of Washington this twenty-first day of January, in the year of our Lord One Thousand Nine Hundred and Sixty-One, and of the Independence of the United States of America the one hundred and eighty-fifth.*

All of us promptly had the commissions framed and hung in our offices —and, I am certain, they will continue to hang in a prominent position in whatever offices we may occupy the rest of our lives.

Unlike most other presidential appointments, members of the President's personal staff are not subject to confirmation by the United States Senate. They serve completely at the pleasure of the President and he can hire and fire them as he sees fit.

The working quarters of the White House are in the West Wing, built by Teddy Roosevelt when there was no longer space for both his family and his staff in the White House itself. An East Wing was added later and now accommodates, among other presidential employees, the personal staff of the First Lady. O'Donnell, who was given the chore of assigning offices in the West Wing, discovered that we were far short of space. Schlesinger readily agreed to move into the East Wing, whose calmer atmosphere he must have found more congenial to his cerebrations. He was joined there by the three military aides.

The President's oval office was in the southeast corner of the West Wing and had a dramatic view of the rolling south lawn of the White House and the Capital's most impressive landmark, the Washington Monument. Immediately outside his office was the Rose Garden, a huge expanse of hedge-lined walkways and occasional rose bushes that were in bloom only a small part of the year. JFK, who saw the garden as an ideal place to entertain visitors, took personal charge of redesigning it. Huge magnolias were planted in the four corners, with connecting beds of flowers that were in color from spring until winter. The central expanse was sown with grass but it was slow coming up. I went into the President's office one day and found him staring gloomily out the window. "Isn't that damned lawn ever going to grow?" he said. When it did come up, the lawn was blighted with disease and JFK had the bare spots sprayed with green paint when he was expecting important visitors.

He had a look at the crazy-quilt of browns and greens on the lawn one day when we were coming in for a landing in a helicopter. "Remind me," he said, "to bring my own gardener down from Hyannis Port."

JFK had a running feud with the White House gardener. He was convinced his crew was twice as large as necessary and that the budget for maintenance of the grounds could be cut in half. Finally, he did bring his own gardener down from Hyannis Port, who agreed the operation was wasteful. JFK confronted the head gardener with this information and they had a wild argument. But no one was ever fired.

The President stuck his head into his office for the first time in late afternoon on Inauguration Day. His office, like all others in the West Wing, had been freshly painted in melancholy "government green." He promptly ordered it repainted in a shade of off-white. President Eisenhower's desk didn't remain long, either. Mrs. Kennedy, rummaging through the basement of the White House, came across a sturdy old desk that had been given to President Rutherford B. Hayes by Queen Victoria. It was made of timbers from the famous frigate *HMS Resolute*, and was in use as a sawhorse when Mrs. Kennedy found it. The desk had last been used by FDR for his "fireside chats." Mrs. Kennedy had it sanded down to the bare wood and refinished, and JFK sat behind it until the day before his death.

Like FDR's, his entire office had a nautical motif. The mantels were covered with his collection of ship models, including a scale miniature of his own *PT 109* and a full-rigger that was a gift from Chairman Khrushchev. Pictures of naval battles hung on the walls with a plaque given to him by Admiral Hyman G. Rickover: *"Oh, Lord, Thy Sea is so great and my Life is so short."*

Behind his desk were the American and presidential flags and the colors of the Army, Navy, Air Force, and Marine Corps with their battle streamers. There was a fireplace in the wall opposite his desk and in front of it a conversational unit of white sofas and his rocking chair.

On his desk were pictures of Caroline and John as toddlers, leather-bound copies of the books he had written, a handsome black alligator desk set given to him by General de Gaulle, and the coconut shell on which he had scratched an SOS when his crew was stranded after the sinking of *PT 109*. The shell, delivered to an Australian shore-watcher by a Solomon Islands native, eventually led to their rescue.

Also on the desk were three decorated whale teeth (scrimshaw) given to the President by his friend K. LeMoyne Billings of New York. There was the Inaugural medal given to the President by the Inaugural committee, and a large cut-glass ashtray made in Ireland with the Kennedy crest—a gift from Mrs. Ethel Kennedy's friend, Dot Tubridy of Dublin, Ireland. The bookends were replicas of twelve-pound secondary battery-type cannons used on the old U.S. naval ships *Constitution* and *Bon Homme Richard*. They were made for the President by Lieutenant Commander Rutledge B. Barry, USNR (Ret.).

There had been certain similarities in JFK's war service and mine. We were both in the Pacific Theater, both skippers of small craft, and had both won the same decoration—the Navy and Marine Corps Medal. He received his, of course, for the wartime exploit of saving ten of his crew on the *PT 109* after it was cut in half by a Japanese destroyer. The war was over in October 1945 when I was cited for helping to swim a line to fourteen sailors who were stranded on a sandspit when their patrol craft went down in Buckner Bay, Okinawa, during a typhoon.

The President often joked with me about it. "I'll never figure out how you got the same medal I did. After all, I was in action against the enemy when I had to swim for it. All you had to contend with was a little peacetime typhoon."

My pat answer was that "You saved only ten but I had to worry about fourteen. Also, you were commanding a piddling little 65-footer but I had a real warship." Actually, I did not take command of my ship until after the typhoon, and it was only a 110-foot submarine-chaser, the SC 1368.

There were three ways into the President's office—through the central door and through the flanking offices of O'Donnell and Mrs. Evelyn Lincoln, his personal secretary. He had to pass through her office to reach the Cabinet Room, where the major meetings of the administration were held. It was here also where he met with EXCOM (the Executive Committee of the National Security Council) to hammer out strategy for the Cuban missile crisis and other fateful decisions. Dominating the Cabinet Room was a massive table given to FDR by his Secretary of Commerce, Jesse Jones. Around it were heavy black leather chairs for each Cabinet member, with his name on the back on a shiny brass plate. When a man left the Cabinet, he could take his chair with him by paying its $240 replacement cost. The President sat at the center of the table with the Secretary of State on his right and the Secretary of the Treasury on his left. The wall facing the President was lined with shelves of current reference books and behind him were the doors leading out to the Rose Garden.

The several entrances caused some problems for Ken O'Donnell. This was particularly true of the door through Mrs. Lincoln's office which was often used by staffers who did not want to go through the formality of asking Ken's permission to see the President. In the door that went into the President's office from Mrs. Lincoln's office there was a small peephole. Looking through the hole, a person could see if the President was occupied. Often, finding him alone, staffers would walk into the office with their problems. There were periodic efforts by the President to tighten up entry of staff and others through Mrs. Lincoln's office. He would sternly instruct Mrs. Lincoln to send all visitors to Ken O'Donnell's office for permission to enter. But his admonitions would be forgotten within several days and the stream of visitors was again getting in the back way.

My office was directly across the hall from the Cabinet Room. Although the White House is the most important news center in the world, the quarters from which my staff and I would direct the flow of news to tens of thousands of newspapers, magazines, and TV and radio stations around the world was not much larger than a double garage. Originally, I had a staff of six: Associate Press Secretary Andy Hatcher and his secretary, Barbara Gamarekian; Sue Mortensen Vogelsinger, who was my correspondence secretary; Barbara Coleman, who was in charge of photo coverage; Helen Ganss, indexer of the President's press conferences and my press briefings; and Christine Camp, my personal secretary. All except Mrs. Ganss, who had been in the White House since the days of Truman, had been members of JFK's election staff. And all except Miss Camp, whose desk was in my office, were jammed into a small cubicle. To add to the congestion, the wire service teletypes—which ran twenty-four hours a day—

were stuck between the plumbing in the bathroom, whose door was practically next to my desk. We began with two—AP and UPI—and I later put in tickers for Agence France Presse, which was strong on African and Latin American coverage, and Reuters, which was frequently first with the news from European capitals. A visit to the john could be most traumatic with all four teletypes rattling away simultaneously.

Twice daily, at 11 A.M. and 4 P.M., I would call the correspondents into my office to release the White House news of the day and to answer questions. As many as a hundred would wedge themselves into the narrow spaces between desks, filing cabinets, and bookcases. Commuters on a New York subway at the height of the evening rush had more elbow room.

The lobby outside the press offices was a lounging place for reporters and photographers, who were there to catch important visitors as they left the President's office, just seventy-five feet down the hall from mine. Directly across the lobby were the working quarters for the White House correspondents who were in regular attendance. The place was a disgrace. The desks were a litter of old newspapers, playing cards, and medicine bottles. A heady odor rose from the dank spittoons. And, despite an abundance of wastebaskets, the floor always had the appearance of Broadway after a ticker-tape parade.

One of my first official acts was to instruct the White House carpenters to divide the large, open room into small compartments. I thought the reporters would appreciate the order and privacy. I was wrong. The press quarters are still known as the Salinger Loan Company. (At a later date, George Reedy, my successor as Press Secretary to President Johnson, hung new pictures in the lobby and replaced the old black sofas with new green leather armchairs. The press had an indignant description for both the lobby itself—the LBJ Hilton—and for the new furniture—Dallas Modern.)

The door to my private office opened on the hall but I kept it locked. My visitors always came through the reception area. There was, however, a buzzer concealed in the paneling that could open the door from the outside. On many occasions this door would fly open and my callers would be startled to find themselves in the presence of the President.

O'Brien, Feldman, and Reardon had their offices on the second floor of the West Wing. The only staff occupant of the basement was Bundy, who needed a lot of space for his "little State Department." One of Bundy's major facilities in the basement was the Situation Room—the intelligence and communications center of the White House. It was under military guard twenty-four hours a day and was manned around the clock by Bundy's staff. Actually, it was two rooms. The walls of the larger one were covered with charts containing important intelligence information, including the exact whereabouts of our own important diplomatic and military officials and all major foreign heads of state. If it were necessary, for instance, for the President to communicate with Prime Minister Macmillan, the chart would tell exactly where he could be found on any given day. It was on another chart that the hour-by-hour course of the Soviet freighters was plotted during the Cuban missile crisis. This room was also used for conferences on classified matters such as the planning of presidential visits overseas.

The smaller room was the domain of the White House Communications Agency. All diplomatic cables for the President and the staff were sent here for distribution. There was also a battery of teletypes to receive tens of thousands of words daily from the Foreign Broadcast Information Service. The FBIS monitors all radio broadcasts in both hostile and friendly nations and transmits an almost instantaneous translation of important announcements.

Also in the basement was a small restaurant, where most of us ate lunch. It was manned by Navy stewards and we became eligible to eat there by paying a $25 deposit against our tabs and buying a silver napkin ring, which bore the inscription, "White House Staff Mess," and the member's name. No drinks were served but the quality of food and service was excellent and the prices were unbelievable. My favorite meal was the luncheon steak. It came with soup, salad, coffee, and dessert and the cost was $1.25. Other full lunches, with a meat entrée, ran as low as 78 cents. Although it didn't appear on the menu, the pièce de résistance of the White House Mess was the parade of Washington beauties the dashing General Godfrey McHugh brought to lunch. When I was too busy to leave my office, an attendant would bring my meal to my desk. The President almost always had lunch in the Mansion.

The Situation Room and the President's office had the highest security priority. The hallway around JFK's office was guarded at all times by the Secret Service and White House police. No one could enter when he was not there except by special permission. Although there was a central door opening into the hallway, it was used only when the press was ushered into his office for a statement or pictures. When this door was left open, it signified that JFK was not in his office. If I had to see him, I would open my door, glance down the hall and tell in an instant whether he was in or out.

The President himself used this main door only to walk across the hall to the Fish Room, which received its name during FDR's administration because of his penchant for hanging stuffed fish on the walls. President Kennedy carried on this tradition with a large sailfish he caught at Acapulco on his honeymoon. The Fish Room was used for many purposes, including major presidential announcements to the press. I held my own briefings for the correspondents there after JFK's assassination because the crowd was too large to accommodate in my own office. It was also the location of the weekly press conferences by the Democratic leadership of the House and Senate after their Tuesday morning breakfasts with the President.

A large number of presidential aides and assistants had their offices in the rococo Executive Office Building, which was across an alley from the West Wing. This ancient structure, once headquarters for the State Department, has survived all the assaults of those who would tear it down in favor of a more modern building—a victory of sentiment over practicality because the EOB is at least a quarter of a century past its time in utility. Budget Director David Bell and later Kermit Gordon had their offices here, as did Walter Heller, chairman of the Council of Economic Advisers. The Indian Treaty Room, where Presidents Truman and Eisenhower held their press conferences, also was in the EOB.

In too many countries around the world, a change in national leadership occurs in an atmosphere of hostility and crisis. New governments often fall within weeks of taking office because the outgoing administration covertly, or openly, sabotages all attempts at peaceful transition. This, fortunately, has never been the case in our own and most other democracies. Although certain outgoing Presidents, still simmering over defeat at the polls, have been disdainful of their successors, they have been able to place the national interest above their own personal feelings. The exchange of presidential power between Dwight D. Eisenhower and John F. Kennedy, however, was notable for its total absence of rancor. The two men had deep respect for each other. This cordiality between the two principals was the cue for their respective staffs. Just as Jim Hagerty had been more than generous in explaining the options and facilities available to me in the press office, every other member of Eisenhower's staff was determined that there would be an effective continuity in the executive offices. As a result of their cooperation, we were a fully operating White House by the end of JFK's first day in office. General Eisenhower himself, and many members of his staff, continued to be available for advice and counsel to the New Frontier long after they had left Washington for other pursuits. One key member of the Eisenhower staff stayed on for six months, however. He was Major General Andrew J. Goodpaster, the outgoing President's Assistant for National Security Affairs.

Historically, the casualty rate on presidential staffs has been high. Many advisers in past administrations have left the White House for higher-paying positions in private enterprise, because of disagreements on policy, conflicts of interest, or even personal corruption. But every principal member of JFK's staff who took the oath of office the day after his Inauguration was still working for him on the day of his death.

# VI

## LIFE IN THE WHITE HOUSE

Imagine that you live in an old but reasonably well-equipped sixteen-room house in the center of a big city. It is three stories high, but for at least half of every day you cannot visit two of the floors because they are full of tourists, peering at your furniture and dropping litter on your floor.

You have to entertain a lot. In fact, in the course of a year you may give as many as ten parties for 2000 persons and many, many "little" parties for 150. Your employer picks up the better part of the tab for these parties, but if you want to do them well, you have to reach into your pocket for a substantial contribution, also.

There are expansive grounds around the house, surrounded by high and impenetrable fences. The grounds are also protected by guard gates, and everyone who walks in and out of your house has to be identified. If you want to take advantage of these spacious grounds and go outside for a walk, you will notice literally hundreds of people hanging on the fence looking at you. There is a nice play area in the back yard for your two children, but every time they go out to play there are strangers there with cameras and telescopic lenses, shooting through the fence, trying to record everything they do. If you want to leave the house and go to visit someone, a whole group of outsiders goes with you, some riding in your own car and some in a strange-looking car which follows you everywhere.

If your wife or children want to take a walk, go down to the corner for an ice cream cone, or visit a carnival, strange men go everywhere with them, too. From many standpoints, it's not a bad place to live. You have your own swimming pool and your own movie theater. You can see any movie which has ever been produced—even the ones which the general public has not seen yet. The phone system is excellent. You can pick up the phone and call anywhere in the world just for the asking. Unfortunately, phones work both ways. You can rarely eat a meal or pass a complete evening of sleep without interruption. Getting to work is no problem. There is no morning traffic to worry about. It is a fifty-yard walk from your house to your office. But once there, some one hundred newspapermen regularly watch everything you do, and if you make a mistake they tell the whole country about it. If you want to make a trip somewhere, a helicopter lands on the lawn behind your house and takes you to the airport. If you want to go to the country for a vacation, you have the best transportation—including jet planes—at your disposal. But you also have to take key members of your staff with you, as well as a minimum of fifty newspapermen. And those same phones go with you, too. And finally, even though the house is rent free, the people who give it to you can take it away every four years, and then you have to find another place to live.

If you can imagine all this, then you have a small idea what it is to live in the White House.

The Kennedys were lively, interesting people who had some definite ideas on how they wanted to live their lives—even under the scrutiny of the hundreds of reporters who covered the White House on a daily basis.

The Kennedys had an important desire to separate their public and private lives—a desire with which I fully sympathized. There are those who hold that everything that a President does should be known. President Kennedy did not agree. He shuddered at some of the information given out in previous administrations—what the President ate for breakfast, when he went to bed, what he wore in bed, and so on. I noted early in the administration, in a speech I delivered to a newspaper group in Pittsburgh, that if the press devoted as much time to some of the important stories of the day as they did in an attempt to find what I considered "trivialities," their readers would be well rewarded. Nevertheless, in most cases, members of the press were trying to find out things they thought their readers wanted to hear about.

In attempting to divide between the Kennedys' public and private life I stepped into a major trap early in 1961—and committed one of the worst blunders I was to be involved in.

The President reprimanded me more seriously than he did at any other time I served him as Press Secretary.

There had been a short (and totally untrue) flap about the efforts of the White House to steal the Vietnamese chef of the French Embassy in London. It was true at this time that the White House was looking for a new chef, but there was never any truth to the story the White House tried to proselyte another nation's chef.

The flap had almost died down when at one of my daily briefings a member of the press expressed some interest in the name of the then current chef of the White House. I replied that the White House policy was not to identify domestics working for the President. This was an old policy, and was mainly for security purposes. Most of the domestic help at the White House lived in private homes in the Washington, D.C., area, and the Secret Service did not want them identified so they could be approached by unscrupulous people. The questioning reporter was not satisfied with the answer, however, and retorted: "It won't do you any good to keep their names secret. They'll all go out and write their memoirs after the President has left office, anyway."

It was true in the past that domestic help in the White House, in the Roosevelt, Truman, and Eisenhower eras, had written "inside stories" on life in the White House. But I happened to know that all the domestic help at the White House had been asked by the Kennedys to sign pledges that they would not write books about what went on in the private areas of the White House. The reporter's taunt was too much for me, and I replied rather heatedly that this "wouldn't happen in this administration."

When reporters pressed me as to how I could be so sure, I told them of the signed pledges. Then we got into a big hassle over whether this pledge included White House staffers like Arthur Schlesinger, Ted Sorensen, or myself. (It didn't.)

When the President read a copy of my press briefing he hit the roof. Grabbing a phone, he called for me only to find I had gone to lunch. Then he asked for Andy Hatcher to be sent in. Hatcher had also gone to lunch. Finally, the only person he could find was my executive secretary, Chris Camp.

Chris was ushered into the President's office to find him pacing the floor swearing at a totally flabbergasted Ken O'Donnell. Then he turned on Chris.

"Am I to believe by reading the tickers that Pierre's briefing solely concerned my domestic staff and my cook? Where does he get off volunteering this stuff? Would Jim Hagerty have conducted a press conference this way? And furthermore, didn't anyone ask a question about Laos or Berlin?" The President kept on for several minutes before perceiving that he did not have the real culprit in his grasp.

By the time I arrived he had cooled down somewhat. It seemed that there had been no pledge at large for the servants as I had described. The only servants asked to sign such pledges had been personal employees of the Kennedys, brought to the White House. And in one instance, even one of these, Maud Shaw, the nurse who took care of Caroline and John, had not been asked to sign a pledge. (She is the only personal servant of the Kennedys who has written a book to date.)

It took the President several days to finally cool down completely, but I had seen that when he was mad, he was effectively mad.

The efforts to insure privacy involved us in a more lasting conflict with the press—and particularly the press photographers.

This question revolved around the right of the press to attempt to get off-guard, candid pictures of the children and Mrs. Kennedy. The problem grew out of the very location of the White House. Situated as it is, in the middle of busy Washington, D.C., there was no real problem in getting pictures through the fences with telescopic lenses. The streets which surround the White House are public streets, and my authority to prevent cameramen from going on a public street and shooting through the fence was nil. Persuasion, therefore, was my only weapon, and it was a weak weapon at best. I cannot tell you the number of times I called in the press cameramen, and asked them to desist. On some occasions they agreed, but always with the request that they be protected from competition.

That was easier said than done, however. Not all the photographers in the world are professional. In fact, a very small minority are. And the tourists who hung on the fences around the White House also included a number of excellent photographers, who had highly sophisticated camera equipment, including telescopic lenses. On more than one occasion, during the period that the White House photographers had agreed to stop taking pictures of Caroline and John, some tourist would get a priceless set of pictures through the fence, run down to a newspaper or wire service office, and sell the pictures to them. These pictures would then appear in the press.

Three things would happen predictably. I would get a memorandum from Mrs. Kennedy, asking me what I was spending my time doing as Press Secretary. Obviously, I was not doing my job in protecting the children. The White House photographers would get calls from their offices asking them how they were earning their pay. Obviously, they weren't doing their job if some casual tourist could get these great pictures and they couldn't get them. And the White House photographers, stung by the criticism from their home offices, would be back at the fences in the next hour trying to take their own pictures, starting the whole cycle over again. Nor was the problem confined to the White House. When the President and his family went to Hyannis Port or Newport, and Palm Beach, they particularly enjoyed going to sea in one of the presidential powerboats, especially the *Honey Fitz.* Whenever they put to sea, however, they were followed by an armada of press boats, filled with photographers with telescopic lenses trying to record their oceanic adventures.

Again, the press argument was the same. If the press did not follow the President, tourists would follow him in their own boats and get the same pictures. This became particularly sticky after Ambassador Joseph P. Kennedy's paralytic stroke. The President and Mrs. Kennedy liked to take the ambassador out on the boat for an afternoon of sun. They particularly resented the pictures which appeared in the press of the paralyzed patriarch of the Kennedy family, sitting in his wheel chair on the fantail of the boat. The same problem occurred at Glen Ora, the Virginia farm residence of the Kennedys, some thirty-five miles from Washington. Running alongside the house was a public road, and more often than not it was the hunting ground for groups of photographers with telescopic lenses. In all my time at the White House we never did satisfactorily solve this problem, running through phases of press cooperation, and press non-cooperation, of relative stoic quiet on the part of the Kennedys followed by periods of high agitation about this invasion of their privacy.

About the only place the President and his family were totally safe was at the mountain retreat run by the Navy, Camp David, named after President Eisenhower's grandson. Because it was a military reservation, the press was never permitted on the premises and the family was left completely alone. In the latter days of his administration, when he was in Washington, the President tended more and more to go to Camp David, which had been Shangri-la during the administration of Franklin D. Roosevelt, and where he could do what he wanted to do without the peering eyes of the press. I made one concession to the press when the President went to Camp David. I allowed the photographers into the preserve as far as the helicopter landing pad, so they could personally observe that the President and his family had arrived safely. They were then ushered off the premises. I also allowed them to come to the pad to see the President take off on Monday mornings, again to assure them that the take-off had been made safely.

Camp David was actually the perfect place for the President. He had a beautiful house there, with all his necessary communications equipment built in. Next to the house was a one-hole golf course, but actually it was two-hole because you could play it in both directions. There was a swimming pool, a bowling alley, a basketball court, a skeet shooting range, and ample grounds for horses to romp. There were Catholic services in the enlisted men's mess hall on Sundays which the President and his family could attend in privacy. The view from the house of the surrounding Catoctin Mountains of Maryland was breathtaking, particularly in the spring and fall. And, of course, you could be sure that no photographers were hiding in the trees.

Bob Kennedy was just as insistent as his sister-in-law that his children be kept out of the glare of publicity. He took his family to the compound in Hyannis Port in the summer of 1961 for a brief vacation. His son, Bob, had a broken arm and his daughter, Courtney, a broken leg. Both were wearing casts.

Bob gave firm instructions to the Secret Service that no press pictures were to be taken of the children. But the day after their arrival, UPI clients all over the country ran front-page shots of Bob and Courtney, taken from the *inside* of the compound.

The Attorney General was furious. He got hold of me at the motel where I was staying with my family in Hyannis and told me to find out how Stan Tretick, the UPI photographer, had been able to penetrate the rigid security around the compound. When I braced Stan, he looked me squarely in the eye.

"I swear to you, Pierre, I did not take those pictures," he said.

I reported back to Bob.

"Well, if you can't find out, I will," he said.

He was back on the line minutes later.

"Pierre, I'll give you one guess who took those pictures."

"I haven't the foggiest notion."

"Your own son, Marc!"

Tretick, who is now with *Look* magazine and who is one of the most enterprising photographers I have ever met, had been giving my son secret lessons with a Nikon camera for weeks. Marc had free run of the compound and his mentor simply told him to go inside, shoot a roll of film, and return the camera to him out of sight of the Secret Service.

Even Bob had to admire Tretick's ingenuity.

Actual living space in the White House was not much larger than that in the average suburban home.

The private living quarters were on the second floor and were accessible either by a stairway from the main entrance hallway of the White House or by a small elevator. In the southwestern corner was Mrs. Kennedy's bedroom and sitting room, which had doors opening east to the President's bedroom and north into another spacious and comfortable living room. The west window of the living room had an excellent view of the West Wing and the Executive Office Building. The living room was furnished with brightly colored overstuffed chairs and sofas. In the middle was a large table, on which were arranged collections of art books and current magazines. The walls were lined with bookcases, one of which was filled with phonograph records. In the center of the living room on the north side was the door which leads to the President's dining room (not to be confused with the family dining room which was on the first floor). The President's dining room was really the Kennedy's private dining quarters and it was here they sometimes ate lunch and here that they entertained at their small dinners in the evening. There was a small kitchen off the dining room. Both the little dining room and the kitchen were put in by the Kennedys.

As I have related before, the acquisition of a new White House cook caused several flaps around the White House, not the least of which was the so-called plan to abduct the French Embassy's Vietnamese cook in London. Then, with the help of Ambassador Joseph P. Kennedy, the President and Mrs. Kennedy finally settled on René Verdon as the White House chef. Verdon, a French citizen, had been a guest chef at the Caravelle Restaurant in New York City where he came to the attention of one of the restaurant's most enthusiastic patrons—Ambassador Kennedy. The ambassador passed the word, and René was hired. Only American citizens can work in the Executive Mansion so, at the start, JFK had to pay Verdon out of his own pocket until arrangements could be made for his naturalization. One of my unofficial duties at the White House was to administer to René's homesickness for Paris. New York hadn't been too lonely because of its large French-American community, but in Washington Verdon had no contact at all with La Belle France. At the request of the Kennedys, I would wander into the kitchen two or three times a week and spend a half hour speaking French to him. Verdon's mood—and my waistline—immediately became more expansive. He would give me a taste from every pot on the stove and a tray of French pastries to take back to my office.

Verdon quit the White House late in 1965 after a donnybrook with Lady Bird Johnson's kitchen coordinator and was, apparently, difficult to replace. The Christmas card my wife, Nicole, and I sent out a day or two after his fiery departure was a miniature cookbook with recipes for Filet de boeuf Rossini, Farce aux marrons, and Bûche de Noel. On receiving hers, Liz Carpenter, Press Secretary to Mrs. Johnson, sent me the following telegram:

IF YOU CAN COOK ANY OF THE THREE RECIPES, YOU'RE HIRED.

Chef Verdon was not the total master of the White House food situation. He had someone looking over his shoulder from time to time checking the cost of food—the President. Despite his great wealth and his generosity in contributing all of his salaries as congressman, senator, and President to charities, the President was not a man to waste pennies. Because the government allowance for operation of the White House (including state dinners and big receptions) was never sufficient to cover actual expenses, the President had to make up the difference out of his own pocket. He would occasionally go on rampages against the high cost of groceries and suggest to Mrs. Kennedy or to Verdon that they buy from another vendor whose prices were more reasonable. At one point, the President had an entire cost study on the household expenses of the White House made by Carmine Bellino. Bellino, whose accounting genius had thrown fear into labor racketeers all over America, was injected into the struggle to find out why it cost so much to live around the White House. After one of the dinner dances at the White House, the President found a number of half-full champagne bottles. He immediately summoned J. Bernard West, the chief usher, and told him in the future that no waiter was to be given a full bottle of champagne until he turned in an empty one.

Members of Mrs. Kennedy's staff who ran the social and household functions of the White House noticed that the more serious the crisis in the world, the more President Kennedy would get involved in the details of how they ran their business. He seemed to get relaxation and a little respite by quarreling over food prices rather than atom bombs.

As you walked east out of the living room, you found yourself in a large hallway. The first room on the right was the President's bedroom. The President slept in an antique four-poster bed and his bedroom was always littered with papers, reports, newspapers, and magazines to fill his insatiable desire for reading. The next room east along the corridor was the Oval Room, another room where the Kennedys could relax with guests at state dinners or where the President could, on occasion, hold staff meetings or meetings with guests when he wanted less formality than was offered by his own office or the Cabinet Room. On the other side of the hallway were the bedrooms of Caroline and John. Next to the Oval Room was the Treaty Room, once used as a Cabinet room by President Andrew Johnson. Mrs. Kennedy's sense of history made her ask the President if he would sign the U.S.-Soviet Nuclear Test Ban Treaty there. He agreed. Next to the Treaty Room was the more austere Lincoln Room, the site of many of the Cabinet meetings of President Lincoln. The room had a large black bed in the center and the Kennedys allowed many of their house guests to sleep in the room, an event they would never forget. After the 1963 salute to JFK's birthday, the President brought Carol Channing (the star of *Hello, Dolly!*) to the White House with the other entertainers. He was giving them a private tour around the White House and started to show them the Lincoln Room. As he opened the door, he exclaimed: "Oops, Mother's asleep in there." The second floor was rounded out by the Rose Guest Room (also known as the Queen's Room because no less that five reigning queens had slept there at one time or another) and the East Sitting Room, which was next to the Rose Guest Room. The Rose Guest Room was also frequently used for friends when the Kennedys entertained.

The White House came with a Civil Service domestic staff, but President and Mrs. Kennedy brought two personal servants and a jack-of-all-trades to the White House with them. The first was the President's butler and manservant, George Thomas. A Negro of unfailing humor, he was in charge of laying out the President's clothes in the morning and, in general, of taking care of the President's personal needs. Mrs. Kennedy's maid, Providencia Paredes, was a native of the Dominican Republic. She was a woman of high intelligence and native beauty. She and George fought like cats and dogs, but always in good humor. The third integral party of the team was John (Muggsy) O'Leary, an old Boston retainer of the Kennedys who ran errands for them. Muggsy had been around the President as long as I had known him. He worked part time as a chauffeur for the President when he was senator, which was always a kind of inside joke because the senator liked to drive his own car and Muggsy sat in the right-hand seat in regal splendor, being driven around by a future President of the United States.

In order to work at the White House, Muggsy was put on the payroll of the United States Secret Service, and he proudly carried his Secret Service badge although he did none of the work normally associated with the service.

George was in charge of waking up the President, although his lack of reliability in this department was legendary. I remember one time on a trip to Duluth when the President asked George to wake him at 7 A.M. He was outraged when George woke him up an hour early. George, it seemed, had forgotten to change his watch to conform with Central Standard Time. But most of the time George made it, and the President got up between seven-thirty and eight in the morning. He was immediately handed the morning papers which he scanned rapidly, often pausing to call aides to demand if they had seen this or that item in the paper and to ask what they were doing about it. I was the recipient of a number of these calls, and rarely had gotten as far in my newspaper reading as the President when the call came.

Some mornings General Clifton or McGeorge Bundy would come over early and give the President the Intelligence Check List, a highly confidential memorandum for the President's eyes only, prepared by the Central Intelligence Agency on information they had picked up of interest in the previous twenty-four hours. Reading this list, the President would give a series of orders—to get more information on this item, to remind him to talk to this or that official in the State or Defense Department on that item. It was the responsibility of Clifton or Bundy to follow up on the orders. The President normally had his breakfast in bed. He would sit propped up, drinking a glass of fresh orange juice, eating two soft boiled eggs and some toast, and then a cup of coffee, heavily laced with sugar and cream. While eating, he might read further newspapers or memoranda, or entertain his children, who by that time had come into the room to say good morning. Then he got up and eased into a hot tub, drawn for him by George Thomas. President Kennedy liked hot baths, particularly because they soothed his usually aching back. He was also an avid reader in the bathtub, and would sometimes stay in the tub for twenty minutes or a half hour. Memoranda sent to the President would sometimes come back slightly moist with notes penned on them. The memos had simply fallen into the tub while he read them. By nine o'clock he was dressed and on his way to the office. Usually he walked over with Caroline and John, always in animated conversation as they made the short stroll to the office. As he passed the guard in the basement, heading to the office, the guard would press a button, which would activate a bell in the West Wing, notifying everyone there that the President was on his way to work.

The President would usually leave his office at 1 or 1:15 P.M., going first to the White House pool for a swim. Located between his office and the Mansion, it was built during Franklin Delano Roosevelt's administration with public donations raised by the New York *Daily News*. Swimming was the major therapy for FDR, a polio victim, and it also gave JFK relief from the almost constant pain in his back.

Midway in the administration, Ambassador Kennedy commissioned a huge mural on all four walls surrounding the pool. It was a re-creation of the harbor at Saint Croix in the Virgin Islands. The swimmer had the impression of being in the lagoon and the feeling was the more realistic because of an ingenious lighting system. When the President swam at noon, the waterfront and the landscape beyond were lit with bright sunlight. When he swam after dark, there were lights twinkling around the harbor and a moon and stars in the sky.

The mural was painted by French artist Bernard Lamotte. He had to work from a scaffolding which was placed over the pool, but the water was kept in the pool because the President wanted to keep swimming. On one occasion Lamotte dumped a pot of paint in the pool by accident and the water had to be drained and the pool cleaned before the President arrived for his daily swim. Being a Frenchman, Lamotte liked his wine and cheese for lunch. Every day he would go into the flower room, situated next to the White House gymnasium (which was next to the pool), and sit among the potted plants with fellow Frenchman Verdon and have a leisurely meal. Sometimes they were joined by Pam Turnure, Mrs. Kennedy's Press Secretary. Finally, Mrs. Kennedy heard about the meals herself—and the day Lamotte finished the mural she invited him for a sumptuous meal in the State Dining Room.

At lunchtime, the President would swim slowly back and forth for twenty minutes or a half hour, usually in the company of Dave Powers, who would regale him with the latest jokes he had heard. If there was a pressing matter, however, White House aides were permitted to come to the pool and take it up with the President while he was swimming. Following his swim, he would go into the adjoining room, the White House gymnasium, where he would go through a set of exercises prescribed by Dr. Hans Kraus, a New York back expert. Presiding over the exercises was one of three Navy chief pharmacist mates assigned to the White House dispensary, all of whom had been trained in how to administer Dr. Kraus' exercises. They were simple, and all aimed at strengthening the President's back. They would include movements like lifting your legs off the table while lying flat on your back, bringing one knee then another to the chest, pushups, knee bends, and finally exercises to touch the floor with your hands while standing up. There was an exact number of each exercise prescribed and the chiefs saw to it that the President did them all.

Following the exercises and a shower, the President would go to the

White House for lunch. Mrs. Kennedy was usually lunching with the children—starting much earlier than he normally got back from the White House at the noon period. The President would drop in on this lunch and then go off to a business lunch of his own. On the rare days that he had no business lunch (and they were rare) he took his meal with Mrs. Kennedy in the family dining room. Following lunch, the President went to his bedroom and took a nap of forty-five minutes or an hour. He had a facility for going to sleep immediately and was not to be disturbed during this rest except for reasons of high emergency. Following his nap, he would take a short bath, dress, and return to the office, often staying as late as 8 P.M. The evenings at the White House were usually private and consisted of small dinners, arranged by the President or Mrs. Kennedy and including persons who would stimulate or amuse the President. Dinner might be followed by a movie, or a lengthy session of reading papers accumulated during the day. The President had a short attention span as far as movies were concerned, unless they were particularly good. More often than not, he would walk out on the showing with the movie barely started and go upstairs for some night reading. The movie theater was set up with a particularly comfortable chair for the President so he could practically lie down and watch the film, giving his back a rest from the day's activities.

Life away from the White House was somewhat different. Of all the places the President went to rest, his favorite was his home at Hyannis Port. By almost any standard, it was a modest home, furnished with the simplicity but beauty of taste of Mrs. Kennedy. It was somewhat rustic, with a great deal of white-painted rattan furniture, but there were also flower-patterned sofas and chairs. The main floor was made up largely of a living room, with a big fireplace which crackled with a warm wood fire during the winter months. Off the living room was a closed-in porch, where there were often easels for Mrs. Kennedy's painting in the quiet moments. A small dining room (which seated no more than twelve) and a kitchen rounded out the main floor. Upstairs were the President's, Mrs. Kennedy's, and the children's bedrooms, as well as a couple of servants' rooms. Off the living room was a beautiful patio, bathed in sunlight during most of the day, where the President liked to sit and read his newspapers. The Hyannis Port house was surrounded by a high wooden fence (installed after JFK became President) and behind the house sat a trailer which was the headquarters for the Secret Service men assigned to protect the President. From the President's house to Robert F. Kennedy's house was a hundred-yard walk and to Ambassador Joseph P. Kennedy's house it was another hundred yards. The compound, as it was known, was always full of children—Kennedy children and their friends, cycling, running, playing. The President had a special love for children, and would often go into the back yard and throw a football around with some of the boys, or wrestle on the lawn with Caroline and John.

The President's arrival at the compound was greeted by whoops of joy from the children who knew that "Uncle Jack," as they called him, would have invented some new games for them to play. The President had a genius for thinking up games for the children that resulted, in the end, with all of them winning a prize of some kind. With his own children in the games, he showed absolutely no favoritism toward them.

When in Hyannis Port (and this was true also of Palm Beach), the President liked to keep his contacts with the staff down to a minimum. I would usually see him around ten-thirty in the morning, in company of the military aide who had the duty on that particular weekend. The purpose of my visit was to go over subjects that might come up at my noon press briefings, which went on even when we were away from the White House proper. The military aide was in charge of giving the President the daily intelligence briefing and any other messages which may have come in to our message center. In Hyannis, the message center was located in the basement of the Yachtsman Hotel, about two miles from the presidential home, which was also the headquarters for the fifty or more press that followed President Kennedy on his weekend visits. The President usually spent the early part of the afternoon aboard the *Honey Fitz*, or *Marlin*, taking a cruise on Nantucket Sound, and then would turn up at the Hyannis Port Club, located about 300 yards up the hill from his house, for an afternoon nine holes of golf.

In the last year of his administration, the President moved out of his own house into a leased house on Squaw Island about a mile and a half from the compound. The number of tourists coming by his own house had by this time become too great and the President had to retreat for privacy and quiet. In his new rented home there were no tourists, because the Secret Service set up a check point at the bottom of the road which led up to his house, and would pass only bonafide residents of the area and members of his staff.

In Palm Beach, the President stayed at his father's oceanfront house during the period between the election and the Inauguration, but following his father's stroke in December 1961, he was forced to find other quarters. A beautiful oceanfront house was loaned to the Kennedys by Colonel C. M. Paul, a New York and Palm Beach businessman. About two miles closer to the center of Palm Beach, this house, too, was on the ocean. The President had the choice of swimming in the ocean or in a large heated pool in front of the house, off an extensive patio. The patio was so large that while the Kennedys were staying in Palm Beach they were able to set a movie screen outdoors on the patio and watch movies there at night, in the balmy evening air of south Florida. In Palm Beach the President's habits were pretty much the same as at Hyannis Port. We had our morning meetings and some at the end of the afternoon. The President spent the rest of the day reading, swimming, going out on the *Honey Fitz* or playing golf at the Palm Beach Country Club.

Where the Hyannis Port Club was a very tough, par 72 layout with a wealth of traps and water hazards (there were a number of holes where your ball had to carry some 175 yards over watery marshes from which balls were rarely recovered if lost), the Palm Beach Country Club was a comparatively short, par 69 course, tailored for good scores. The President was welcomed there warmly by the members, who would invariably give him the right-of-way on the tees when he appeared to play.

When President Kennedy showed up to play golf at Palm Beach following his election, a major secret was broken. President Eisenhower was known as an inveterate golfer, but President Kennedy had never been associated with golf. The extent to which President Eisenhower concentrated on his golf did not become clear to President Kennedy until he moved into his office and found a track between the Presidential desk and the door leading out to the south grounds, made by Ike's golf cleats. It seemed the former President put on his shoes at his desk and then went out to the putting green on the south lawn for practice, leaving his permanent imprint in the presidential office. But President Kennedy by all comparisons was a better golfer than President Eisenhower. (It was once suggested that they have a match to prove the point, but President Kennedy declined on the ground the idea was frivolous.)

President Kennedy was able to play golf only fifteen or twenty times a year but was consistently in the high 70s and low 80s. Although he was erratic with his long irons, his strong tee shots and deftness around the greens always kept him within range of par. The smoothest part of his game, however, was not his swing but the "con" he gave his fellow players on the first tee. Through a complex system of betting, which only he understood fully, JFK won most of his matches before the first ball was even hit. There were bets not only on who won the hole, but for the longest drive, first on the green, closest to the pin, and first in the hole. In addition, there were automatic press bets whenever one team fell two holes behind and bonus points for birdies and tee shots holding the green on par 3s.

Just keeping track of the bets gave his opponents little time to concentrate on their game. But the President was also a master psychologist. Just before his opponents were ready to hit, he would call their attention to out-of-bounds markers, sand traps, and other hazards—a "courtesy" that would have taken the confidence out of a Ben Hogan.

Never more than four or five dollars would change hands in a match, but JFK would play for it as if it were the national debt.

The President's most frequent golfing partners were his brother-in-law Stephen Smith (almost a par shooter) and British Ambassador David

Ormsby-Gore, now Lord Harlech. But he also played frequently with his brother Robert, with actor Peter Lawford, New York banker Charles Spalding, Under Secretary of the Navy Paul Fay, Baltimore Colts' owner Carroll Rosenbloom, and Chris Dunphy, a retired businessman who had made a specialty of advising on the construction of golf courses. From time to time he played with members of the press, his favorite partner being Bill Lawrence, the White House correspondent of ABC. All of these men were excellent golfers, but, because of JFK's gamesmanship, I have seen them walk off the eighteenth green as if they had spent the afternoon in a disaster area.

On one of the rare days the President lost all bets, his playing partner was his military aide, General Chester V. Clifton. They came to the eighteenth green, trailing by one stroke. All Clifton had to do was sink a straight four-foot putt to even the match. The general took long minutes to line it up, and then left the ball a full two feet short of the hole.

JFK shook his head and said, "Nice putt, *Sergeant.*"

While we were in Palm Beach in the interim between JFK's election and Inauguration, the photographers were insistent on a picture of him on the golf course. He was reluctant because he thought there had been too great an emphasis on President Eisenhower's linksmanship. But I finally persuaded him to let the photographers take just one picture of him driving off the first tee at the Palm Beach Country Club. His 200-yard shot was in the fairway but struck a Secret Service agent who was surveying the terrain ahead and whose back was to the tee. Except for a slight bruise, the agent wasn't hurt. But that was the first and last time the President knowingly held still for cameras on the golf course.

JFK was witness to the worst golf shot in the history of the Hyannis Port Country Club.

Very often, when we were at Cape Cod or in Florida, I would play in a foursome just behind the President, and he had ample opportunity to observe my game. I couldn't hit a wood, not even off the tee, and it often took me more shots to putt out than it did to reach the green. The goal of most duffers is to break 100. I was still trying to break 120.

JFK, of course, would not play with me. I didn't mind that too much because I knew I wasn't in his class. But I thought his comments on my form were rather unnecessary, and decided to take the game up seriously. Tom Niblet, the pro at Hyannis Port, gave me a number of lessons and I finally began to hit the ball fairly straight and long. Niblet told the President of the improvement in my game (I had finally broken 120!) and JFK said to me on our return to Washington:

"I hear you're getting pretty good. Why don't you come out with me the next time we're at the Cape?"

We were returning to Hyannis Port in two weeks and, to prepare for the match, I spent three days at Greenbrier, Sam Snead's home course in

West Virginia. Sam went out with our foursome the first day, as my partner. He had no comment on my form through the first nine holes, except for frequent expressions of sympathy. I had an unattractive 58. But on the back nine he began to give me a little advice and I came in with a 47. On one hole, in fact, I even beat Snead (with a stroke handicap, of course), who was, by that time, a thoroughly shaken man.

The next Sunday I strode confidently to the first tee at Hyannis Port with the President, David Ormsby-Gore, and Charles Spalding. The bets were made and Spalding, who could afford it, agreed to be my partner. The President's caddy was my son, Marc.

JFK's psychological warfare began immediately.

"Why don't you hit first, Pierre? That way you'll have the honors at least once today."

I teed up my ball before the large gallery that was always around the first tee when the President was playing, took a couple of nervous practice swings and let fly. The ball flew off the toe of my club at a sharp right angle, narrowly missing the crowd—and hit the clubhouse.

JKF said nothing. I went back to my bag, got another ball and hit it down the middle 200 yards. I was now lying three. Two sand traps and three putts later I came in with 10 on the first hole.

I had a good drive on the second hole. But my fairway wood was a low, screaming hook that came within two feet of hitting the President on the head. At this point, a Secret Service agent, Roy Kellerman, came up to me and said, only half jokingly, "I wonder if you ought to play with the President? I can protect him from the crowd but who's going to protect him from you?"

That did it. At the end of nine holes, the team of Spalding and Salinger had lost every bet and the vote was unanimous that we end the match right there.

The President never asked me to play golf with him again. And my son, Marc, never volunteered after that to caddy in the same foursome with me.

I always seem to arouse strong emotions around a golf course. I was in the locker room of the El Dorado Country Club in Palm Springs, California, the weekend after losing my Senate seat to George Murphy.

One of the members, an elderly Republican, shook a finger in my face and said: "I was against you, you carpetbagger." And with that he fell to the floor in a dead faint.

Even dogs conspire to shatter my equanimity on a golf course. I was playing with Bill Lawrence of ABC and Al Silverman of the Cleveland *Plain Dealer* at Palm Beach one day. Bill was 4-up going into the fourteenth hole. If he won it, Al and I were dead. Lawrence hit a poor approach shot, short of the green, but Silverman laid his up next to the flag. Suddenly, a small dog scurried out of the rough, grabbed Silverman's ball off the green, and buried it in a sand trap. The mutt then took Lawrence's ball off the fairway and dropped it next to the hole. He had an easy putt to close out the match.

But the greatest distraction I have ever seen on the links is actor Peter Lawford, the President's brother-in-law. He is a left-handed, barefooted golfer. Just playing with a southpaw, who does everything backward, can add twenty strokes to your score. But bare feet! That's carrying distraction too far.

The older members at Palm Beach took a dim view of Lawford's unorthodox apparel, or lack of it. In fact, the board of directors held an extraordinary meeting to try to decide what to do about it. The President was keenly aware of their feelings, and when Peter played in a foursome with him, he always insisted that Peter wear shoes when he teed off on the first hole, which was right in front of the clubhouse. But once out of sight of the clubhouse, off came the shoes, and Peter felt at home again.

My own sometimes flamboyant dress once caused a modest furor at the Newport, Rhode Island, Casino. A friend invited me to play tennis with him there and I showed up in a blue sports shirt, canary yellow Bermuda shorts, and red socks. I did notice during the match that most of the other players were wearing all white, but attributed it to their lack of imagination. Nothing was said to me at the time, but I read in the newspapers the next day that I had been asked not to come back in the same decor.

There were many excellent golfers in the Washington press corps, among them Lawrence, Silverman and Carleton Kent. When the President was at Cape Cod or in Florida the press always took their clubs along. The Palm Beach Country Club and the Hyannis Port Club were most generous in extending guest privileges to the press—a courtesy that was appreciated not only by them but by the President.

I only saw Glen Ora, the winter retreat which the President used at Middleburg, Virginia, from the outside. We agreed before he started going there that we should do everything possible to discourage the press from following him. The house was only thirty-five miles from Washington, so I felt that by announcing that all news would emanate in Washington while the President was in Middleburg, it would cut down on the number of press men following him there. The tactic worked rather effectively and there were never more than a dozen reporters in the little Virginia town. They confined themselves to covering the President's Sunday attendance at Mass and satisfying themselves that he arrived and left his home safely in the helicopter. The photographers, however, as I have previously noted, were more busy, attempting to get pictures of the Kennedys from the road which ran by the house. I made only one trip to Middleburg, to examine the press facilities for those members of the press who felt they had to follow the President there. The newsmen generally headquartered at the Red Fox Inn, a combination restaurant and small hotel, which was situated in the heart of Middleburg.

The same policy later applied to the house which the Kennedys built at Rattlesnake Mountain, about seven miles from Middleburg, after their lease ran out on Glen Ora. This was another house I never saw because I had no need to go there to confer with the President. I could do all my business with him by telephone.

While the Rattlesnake Mountain home was being built, the President and Mrs. Kennedy had no place of their own to stay outside the Capital. They started visiting Camp David during this period and liked it more and more. They finally ended up occupying the home for only four weekends.

When in New York, the President would stay in a penthouse suite at the Carlyle at Seventy-sixth and Madison. The suite had a sweeping view of Manhattan and was located in the tower of the hotel.

The apartment was two stories high, with two bedrooms and two baths on the upper floor and a living room, dining room, library, foyer, and kitchen on the lower floor.

Colors in the apartment were mostly ivory with accents of pale blue, green, and orange. The furniture was provincial, having Louis Quinze pieces with azure-white painted and gilded frames and silk upholstery.

In Mrs. Kennedy's bedroom the furniture was white and gold, with pink the predominating color. In the President's bedroom, it was beige and brown. A green velvet chair, and one of green leather, provided contrast. White telephones on his desk had direct lines to the White House. On the walls were many nautical prints and two done in petit point. Over the bed was a print of Commodore Perry signing a peace treaty with the Indians.

The study on the first floor had blue walls and a white woodwork trim. Early American prints were hung on the walls.

On these weekends and in the evenings at the White House, the President had a group of friends he liked to invite and with whom he felt most at home.

To identify these friends, you have to divide them into several groups. First, there were the President's friends of old standing, either from school, Navy days, or Massachusetts politics. This list would include K. LeMoyne Billings, a New York advertising man who had gone to Choate with JFK. Billings, a bachelor, was often included on away-from-Washington weekends, and he would be the house guest of either the President or other members of the Kennedy family, all of whom were long-time friends. Billings did not consider himself an expert on national or international politics, something which the President liked, so conversation could be in a lighter vein. He had the ability to kid the President and be kidded back. Then there was Paul B. Fay, Jr., who had been a Navy friend of the President and was the owner of a San Francisco paving firm. JFK brought Fay to Washington as Under Secretary of the Navy and he was a frequent guest, with his wife, Anita, of the President on weekends. Charles Spalding had also been a boyhood friend of the President. A tall, good-looking man, he is a good athlete and a man with a great many ideas, which he tried out on the President. Jim Reed also fell into this category. JFK had known him in Massachusetts, and they had been friends for many years. Despite the fact he was a Republican, the President brought him to Washington as Assistant Secretary of the Treasury, in charge of the Customs Service, the Coast Guard, and several other Treasury departments.

In the ambassadorial field, the Kennedys saw a great deal of Hervé and Nicole Alphand in the early days of the administration. The French ambassador is a man of great charm and wit, with an ability to mimic people that is unsurpassed. He can give speeches in which he imitates prominent men in public office with such conviction that if you close your eyes you think the public figure is there. Nicole Alphand is an authentic French beauty, as intelligent and charming as she is pretty. Before the Alphands returned to France, she was one of the best dressed women in Washington, something which the leading French couturiers made sure was a fact by providing her with the latest models. The fact that Mrs. Kennedy spoke fluent French helped a great deal in this friendship.

The Alphands, however, while they continued to have the friendship of the Kennedys, were largely replaced toward the end of 1961 as constant companions of the Kennedys by the British ambassador and Mrs. David Ormsby-Gore. Ormsby-Gore had known JFK when he was attending school in England and had become a great friend there. The decision of the British government to send him to Washington was a master stroke. The Ormsby-Gores were frequent dinner guests at the White House and were often invited on weekend trips with the President and Mrs. Kennedy. There is one story illustrating the relative importance of the French and British ambassadors, which I cannot personally vouch for, but which certainly illustrates what can happen. It seems that, in 1962, Ambassador Alphand received a personal message for President Kennedy from President de Gaulle, with instructions that he was to hand-deliver it to the President. After checking around, he discovered that the President was in Palm Beach and, by telephone, made an appointment to deliver the message. The ambassador was ushered into the President's bedroom where he was resting, and delivered the message. Assured by the President that there would be no immediate response, he took his leave. As he carefully shut the President's bedroom door, the door of the opposite bedroom opened and out popped the British ambassador, who was the President's house guest.

Another long-time friend of the President was Massachusetts Congressman Torbert H. Macdonald, who had gone to Harvard with him. Macdonald is a good-looking and able politician, and if JFK had any reservations about him, it was with Macdonald's seeming lack of desire to take a chance to advance to higher political office.

And, of course, wherever the President was, Dave Powers was not far away. Dave had become a friend of the President during his 1946 race for Congress. Never had two men been so dissimilar. Powers came from a poor family and had only had a limited education. But he was a man of immense charm and wit and the President simply enjoyed having him around. The Kennedys were often accompanied on their trips by two Filipino Navy stewards attached to the White House staff. Almost from the first day, Powers nicknamed them Quemoy and Matsu, after the two islands offshore from China which had been much in the news during the famous Kennedy-Nixon debates. The names stuck and very few people ever found out the real names of these two efficient gentlemen.

There were also newspaper friends. The two principals in this group were Ben Bradlee, then bureau chief of *Newsweek* magazine (now managing editor of the Washington *Post*) and Charles Bartlett, then a columnist for the Chattanooga *Times*. Ben and Toni Bradlee and Charlie and Martha Bartlett were frequent dinner guests at the White House, as well as frequent weekend visitors at Hyannis Port, Palm Beach, or Glen Ora. Also falling into this group were columnist Joseph Alsop and his wife, Susan Mary, and columnist Rowland Evans and his wife, Kay. While conversation at these dinners and weekends often turned on matters of great national and international importance, not once did these newsmen violate the confidence of the President. There were a couple of instances where items appeared which the Kennedys considered to be a violation of their privacy, but after remonstration with the person responsible, the friendships continued.

Other frequent guests and friends of the President included Under Secretary of Commerce Franklin D. Roosevelt, Jr., and his wife, Sue, the Arthur Schlesingers, Jr., and artist Bill Walton, who had had a very successful career in the newspaper and magazine writing field. In Florida, Mrs. Kennedy saw a great deal of Jane Wrightsman, wife of Texas oilman Charles B. Wrightsman, who had an oceanfront house not far from the Paul residence. Mrs. Wrightsman was a member of Mrs. Kennedy's committee for the renovation of the White House. The Kennedys would traditionally pass New Year's Eve with the Wrightsmans at an elegant dinner and dance. Another occasional White House guest was Nan McEvoy, an heir to the fortune accumulated by the founders of the San Francisco *Chronicle*, who was then working for the Peace Corps in Washington.

There were several foreign newspapermen who were occasionally invited to the White House for dinner. These included Adalbert de Segonzac, the flying hero of the French resistance movement and the Washington correspondent of the Parisian newspaper *France Soir*, and Henry Brandon, the Washington correspondent of the London *Sunday Times*.

Mrs. Kennedy went out of the way to make the White House and the various summer and winter retreats of the President places where his friends could congregate. Her friends became, for the most part, wives of the friends of the President, like Toni Bradlee, Sue Roosevelt, and Martha Bartlett. Her principal and closest companion was her sister, Lee, the wife of Prince Stanislas Radziwill. It was to Lee that Jacqueline turned whenever she had major problems and it was Lee who would always comfort Jacqueline in such moments as the death of her son and the assassination of the President.

The relationship between Jacqueline and Lee was helped a great deal by the fact that the President liked Prince Radziwill enormously. The prince, descendant of an old and noble Polish family, is a very successful London businessman. The prince did not speak a great deal, but when he did he was very droll. He was the very opposite of what has become the stereotyped version of the Kennedy friend. A miserable athlete, Stash, as he was known, still put a great deal of effort into everything he did. The President admired him greatly when at the height of the fifty-mile hike craze, the prince volunteered to make the walk (and made it) although unable to walk for several days thereafter. Although Lee was deathly afraid of airplanes, she made frequent trips to the United States to be with her sister, and Mrs. Kennedy seemed happiest when she was around.

As for the President, his closest friend and confidant was his brother, Robert. Much has been written on the relationship between JFK and Bob, but the bond between the two men cannot be overemphasized. It was complete and mutual. Bob had the greatest admiration and love for his brother. There was nothing he would not do for him. His advice to JFK was sound and his judgment good. And the President knew that when he turned to Bob for advice, he was going to get it straight, whether he liked the advice or not. It was to Bob that JFK turned also in moments of crisis. It is not insignificant that in the greatest disaster of the Kennedy administration, the Bay of Pigs, it was to Bob that the President turned to head up the inquiry to find out what had gone wrong.

There were two particularly sad moments during the administration of President Kennedy, and on both occasions the presence of Bob gave the President the added strength he needed.

The first was the stroke of Joseph P. Kennedy in December 1961. Ambassador Kennedy was stricken while playing golf at the Palm Beach Country Club, and rushed to St. Mary's Hospital in West Palm Beach. The very day of his father's attack, the President had stopped in Palm Beach after a trip to Venezuela, Colombia, and Puerto Rico. He had found him well and in good spirits and had returned to Washington only to learn, an hour after his arrival at the White House, of the elder Kennedy's stroke.

At the hospital, Ambassador Kennedy hovered between life and death. About the third morning I remember going to the hospital with the President at about four o'clock, without notifying the press. The end of Ambassador Kennedy seemed to be sure, and he was administered the last rites of the Catholic Church. Then, when all hope seemed gone, he rallied. The illness of his father was a severe blow to the President. He loved and respected him, even though they might have critical differences from time to time on political issues. To see a man who had been so active, so vibrant, unable to communicate was wrenching to the heart.

The second crisis was even worse. One afternoon in August 1963, I was in my office when the President called and told me to be ready to leave the White House in five minutes—Mrs. Kennedy had been rushed to the hospital at Otis Air Force Base and the birth of her child was imminent. We flew to Cape Cod and found that not only had the baby been born, but that he was critically ill with hyaline membrane disease. This illness, which occurs in infant children, makes it very difficult for them to breathe and get oxygen. The child, named Patrick Bouvier, was taken by ambulance to a hospital in Boston where a massive effort to save his life began. The President, worried about his wife and worried about his child, shuttled between Hyannis and Boston. As hard as the doctors worked, the condition of the baby worsened. Finally, in a desperate, last-ditch effort to save his life, he was put in a large steel compression tank. It was in that tank that Patrick Bouvier Kennedy stopped breathing. Bob Kennedy, Dave Powers, and I were with the President when he got the news. He walked away from us and through a door into the hospital's boiler room. There, he wept for ten minutes, finally coming back to the three of us where Bob put his arm around his brother's shoulders. We then helicoptered back to Cape Cod so the President could be with Mrs. Kennedy when she learned of the death of her son.

The death of the infant was one of the hardest moments in the lives of both President and Mrs. Kennedy. The White House had brought about a closeness in their relationship, a wider understanding of one another. The death of their baby brought them even closer.

There were also moments of high humor at the White House. Such an occasion was the last birthday party of President Kennedy on May 29, 1963. The staff decided to give him a party in the staff mess and both the President and Mrs. Kennedy turned up. All of the presents were in a humorous vein, like small boxing gloves (to arm the President for his continuing struggle with Alabama's Governor George Wallace).

Another even more amusing incident was provided by the mass invasion in early 1962 of the White House grounds by a determined group of starlings. This bird, which shares with the sea gull and pigeon a disrespect for historical edifices and personages, was drastically altering both the exterior appearance of the Executive Mansion and the dressing habits of its occupants. We all bought hats.

A genius in the National Park Service came to our rescue. He found (where, I will never know) a recording of a distressed starling and it was played, night and day, from loudspeakers hung in trees around the grounds.

Excerpts from one of my press briefings tell the rest of the story.

Q. Is it true that the White House has been playing a recording of a distressed starling on the lawn and has it been successful in its purpose?

A. The White House has had a problem for some time with starlings who have created nuisances in front of the White House. For the last two days they have been playing a record of a distressed starling to discourage other starlings from appearing on the premises.

Q. Has it worked?

A. It has so far.

Q. What does a starling in distress sound like, Pierre?

A. I have the record here and I am going to play it for you. But first I have to tell you that they had to get the call of a distressed Washington, D.C., starling, because any other starling would be ineffective in this plan.

Q. How do you tell a D.C. starling from an out-of-town starling? Are they square? Do they hang out in the wrong places?

A. You can always tell people from out-of-town. I will play for you now the call of a distressed starling.

(The piercing wail of an anxious starling was the background for the rest of this colloquy.)

Q. Is this problem a legacy from any other administration?

A. It is a problem that has hung over from Republican and Democratic administrations. I wouldn't want to make it a partisan one.

Q. What is this starling in distress over?

A. I don't know.

Q. You are chasing them away to other buildings—

Q. —where other records of other distressed starlings are playing?

A. May I turn off the starling, please? It is beginning to distress me.

A President, with all his responsibilities, is often called upon to do strange things. Robert Donovan, the Washington Bureau Chief of the Los Angeles *Times* (then of the New York *Herald Tribune*) wrote a book called *PT 109*. Donovan's book was an action-packed and accurate account of the exploits of Lieutenant John F. Kennedy in the Pacific, including the sinking of JFK's boat, the *PT 109*, by the Japanese destroyer, *Amigiri*. The book was made to order for the movies and Donovan had hopes of making a sale. The President had enjoyed the book. He particularly had been appreciative of the great amount of research done by Donovan, including a three months' trip to the South Pacific where he had found the natives who had rescued Kennedy and his crew, as well as the Australian coast-watcher who had played a key role in the affair. To help out Donovan, Ambassador Joseph P. Kennedy, who had had a career himself in the motion-picture production field, called Jack Warner, the president of Warner Brothers, to tell him about Donovan's book. Warner bought the book for a movie over the telephone. The price included a fat fee for Donovan, as well as payments to all the survivors of the crew of *PT 109*, something which President Kennedy insisted on personally. Also in the contract were two other provisions—which in retrospect were disastrous. One of these provisions gave the White House final approval rights on the script and the other final approval on the actor to play Lieutenant Kennedy.

The White House, unfortunately, is not set up by experience or temperament to be a part of motion picture production. President Kennedy gave the assignment to me and to George Stevens, Jr., head of the motion picture section of the USIA, to act as liaison with Warner Brothers on the production.

The President had some definite ideas on the actor to portray him in the movie. His choice was Warren Beatty, a young actor who had made only one movie, *Splendor in the Grass*, which had won great critical acclaim. But this was to develop into a problem.

Jack Warner assigned Bryan Foy as executive producer on the picture. Warner himself was going to act as the over-all producer. Warner and Foy came to Washington to see the President, but before going to the White House they lunched with Stevens and me. It was apparent early in the lunch that Foy did not get on with Stevens. Stevens, son of the great Hollywood producer George Stevens (*Giant, The Greatest Story Ever Told*), had lived in the motion picture business. His work with the USIA was superlative. (In fact, under his leadership a USIA-produced movie won an Oscar as best documentary of 1963.) Yet Foy considered him a young upstart who shouldn't give his views on how to produce a movie. We were batting around ideas on possible directors for the picture when Stevens brought up the name of Fred Zinnemann, a many-time Oscar winner.

"Look, kid," Foy growled. "Don't tell me how to make an exploitation picture."

And the weakness in Foy's whole approach was that he merely looked upon *PT 109* as an "exploitation" film. As for me, Foy had no problem. He knew that I knew nothing about movies, so he didn't have anything to resent. The lunch also revealed that Foy had a rather broad-brushed view of Hollywood. Everybody, to him, was either a Communist (or sympathizer) or an anti-Communist, a homosexual or a red-blooded American.

Foy said at the lunch that Beatty should not play the part of Lieutenant

Kennedy. He described Beatty as a mixed-up actor and said if he played Kennedy, the President would also emerge as "mixed-up."

Foy had with him the first draft of the script, which I understood had been written by Los Angeles newsman Vincent X. Flaherty and script writer Richard Breen. It left a great deal to be desired.

Even after I reported back to the President on the conversation, he suggested I might go to Los Angeles and see if Beatty would play the role. I had another assignment on the West Coast, anyway, so I flew to Los Angeles and met Beatty at the home of Peter Lawford. Beatty turned out to be an intelligent, sensitive young man. He told me there was nothing in the world he would rather do than play President Kennedy, whom he admired, but he saw no future for the picture in the hands of Bryan Foy.

Foy responded to Beatty's refusal to play the role of Lieutenant Kennedy with a blistering attack in the Hollywood *Reporter*, a motion picture trade daily. "Maybe you'd like it better if we made the President a conscientious objector—or maybe have you fight your way *out* of the Navy. You're lucky this isn't Soviet Russia," Foy quoted himself as telling the actor.

With Beatty's decision, we were faced with the problem of what to do about the picture. Jack Warner had put a lot of money into the effort and Donovan had worked hard to produce his book. The President felt that to call a halt to the project would be unfair to both of them. I told him of my misgivings about Foy, but the President said that if Jack Warner was able to find a good director, even the Foy problem could be overcome.

In the director field, Warner started with Raoul Walsh. The President suggested Stevens and I take a look at a picture which Walsh had directed. I called the motion picture exchange to get the latest Walsh picture and was rewarded with a little under two hours of *Marines, Let's Go!* The President slid into the movie theater during the showing and came to the conclusion that it was not his kind of picture. I had several conversations with Warner on the subject, and he finally agreed to assign Lewis Milestone, a director of great ability, to do the job.

We still had the problem of the actor, however. Warner and Foy decided that the solution was to test a number of actors, known and unknown, and send the tests quietly to the White House for screening. For several hours, one afternoon, I looked at tests and finally made a choice. I asked the President to come and look at the tests, also. He agreed with my choice, Cliff Robertson, and Robertson got the role.

There was one final eruption before the picture was finished. Shooting went on location in the Florida Keys, and one morning around two o'clock, I received an urgent telephone call at my home from Cliff Robertson. Milestone, he said, who was making great progress with the film, had been fired that day by Foy and was replaced by Les Martinson, who had a number of good TV credits to his name up to then, but had never directed a full-length motion picture.

I called Warner in the morning, but he told me the decision had been made and could not be reversed. Milestone, he said, was directing the picture at too slow a pace. This was an action picture, he added, and needed an action director.

Several months later, at Warner's invitation, I flew to Hollywood to see the first cut of the movie. At that time it was almost four hours in length and went very slowly. The film, however, was finally cut down to a little over two hours. I must say frankly that I liked it. But the critics didn't, the public didn't, and it turned out to be one of the greatest bombs ever produced by Warner Brothers. With all the changes that had taken place, the price of the picture had ballooned up to $5,000,000 and Warners took a healthy loss on the picture which was finally removed from circulation.

The whole thing was a valuable lesson—and when, a year later, the rights to JFK's book, *Profiles in Courage,* were sold, he wanted nothing to do with the production, only the right to pass on historical stories which were added to the ones included in his book.

Whether it was movies or cooks or starlings, life in the White House had its high and low moments. You felt that it was always a living thing. Some Presidents have considered the White House a prison. In the Kennedy administration, it became a home.

# VII

## THE ESTABLISHMENT

It is said, quite accurately, that no amount of preparation or indoctrination can really prepare a man for the presidency. He finds out what the job is all about from the minute he becomes President.

In a lesser way, the same is true for anyone who works at the White House.

My contacts with the press over fifteen months of campaigning, my studies into the methods of Jim Hagerty and previous Press Secretaries, my reading of the historical relationships between the Presidents and the press—none of these prepared me for the task I undertook on January 20, 1961.

I sat down at my desk for the first time about two hours after John F. Kennedy was sworn in as President. After the speech there had been the parade down Pennsylvania Avenue. I had rushed from my position in the rows of seats behind the President for the car in which I was to ride in the parade, only to find it fully occupied. As the parade moved off, I jumped into the open, 1956 Cadillac convertible which serves as a vantage point for Secret Service agents driving right behind the presidential car. It was intensely cold that afternoon, and by the time I reached the front of the White House, my face was pink from the arctic wind. I jumped out of the car and walked by the northwest gate guard and into the West Wing of the White House.

As I walked into my office for the first time, warmth began to steal slowly back into my cold bones.

This time, on my arrival at the White House, there was no Jim Hagerty to greet me—and not much else either. Tradition permits outgoing Presidents and their staffs to strip the executive offices not only of their personal possessions but of all documents and files, private and public. My little office off the West Lobby was bare except for the furniture, two ancient copies of the budget, an exposé, *The Truman Scandals*, and a shillelagh with a note from Hagerty advising me to wrap it around the skulls of combative reporters.

I sat behind the desk for the first time, feeling a little ridiculous in my rented morning coat, striped pants, and top hat. The dusty silence was broken only by the keening of bagpipes from the parade and the chattering of the wire service teletypes in an adjoining john. I was in awe of my new surroundings. I had driven by the White House or seen it from the air a thousand times. I had been in this very office at Hagerty's invitation. Our energies for more than a year had been devoted to bringing us to this place. But nothing can prepare you for that first awareness that you are not only *in* the White House but that you *belong* there.

That was the only quiet moment I was ever to have behind that desk.

Eight inches of snow fell on Washington Inaugural Eve, turning the Capital into one giant traffic jam. I had spent most of the day closing my offices at the Democratic National Committee, national headquarters for Kennedy for President, and was to meet my wife at a cocktail party at the home of Philip Graham, publisher of the Washington *Post*. We were to go from there to Frank Sinatra's and Peter Lawford's Inaugural gala at the National Guard Armory. But because of the blizzard, I never got to Graham's and my wife never got to the gala. We finally met at 2 A.M. at the Mayflower Hotel, where I had been living that final, hectic week to save the driving time from my home in Falls Church, Virginia. I didn't see the President-elect until 2 A.M. at a dinner his father was hosting in his honor at a downtown restaurant. None of us got to bed until 4 A.M.

I met JFK four hours later at his colonial residence in Georgetown. Narrow N Street was a jumble of TV cameras and cables. Crowds of reporters and photographers, many wearing fur parkas or earmuffs against the thirteen-degree temperature, were waiting below the front steps. The junior senator from Massachusetts was at the table, putting away his normal breakfast—a large glass of orange juice, two poached eggs, three strips of crisp bacon and coffee with both sugar and cream. He was in a jubilant mood. This was the day he had been waiting, planning, and working for since his first plunge into politics in 1946. He had the Inaugural address at the table, reading and re-reading it for possible refinements even at this late moment.

The late Marguerite Higgins, the Pulitzer Prize-winning correspondent, asked the President-elect at the gala if he had a good Inaugural speech.

"It's a smash," he said with a big smile.

He asked me if I had read it. I told him I had and thought it was great. The Inaugural was *his*. He had sought the advice and criticism of others but the writing was his own. Although he had spent weeks working on it, the final draft was not written until three days before its delivery on a flight from Palm Beach to Washington. One of the persistent regrets of this Pulitzer Prize-winning historian was that he had too little time to draft his own major addresses. He was determined, however, that the words that "would go forth from this time and place, to friend and foe alike," would be his and his alone.

Shortly before 9 A.M., JFK drove to the Holy Trinity Roman Catholic Church in Georgetown, the oldest parish in the Capital. A cavalcade of limousines was waiting for him on his return and we left for the White House. I rode two cars behind him and Mrs. Kennedy in the press pool car with the senior correspondents of the wire services and networks. My wife and three children were already in the Inaugural stands at the East Front of the Capitol.

Dwight D. Eisenhower, the oldest living President in American history, was waiting on the steps of the White House to greet the man who, ninety minutes later, would become the youngest. They went inside with their wives and had a cup of coffee. A half hour later, the motorcade left for the Capitol, President Eisenhower and Senator Kennedy riding together in the bubbletop. A correspondent for the New York *Times* was to observe a humorous footnote to history. Both the President and the President-elect were extremely self-conscious in their top hats. Eisenhower had worn a Homburg at his own Inauguration and JFK wore a hat only on state occasions or in a driving rain. On the brief drive to the Capitol, he nervously took his topper off, then put it back on, every half block.

At 12:51 P.M., before a frost-bitten crowd of thousands milling in front of the Capitol—and eighty million more in front of their TV sets—the exchange of presidential power took place. John F. Kennedy took the oath that would pass the torch to "a new generation of Americans."

No two institutions in the country have a more important relationship than the government of the United States and the press. Each is powerful and each has almost inexhaustible resources.

Despite periodic phases of relative calm, the government and the press in the last analysis cannot expect to live happily together. No President in our history has emerged from his term or terms of office without having some major disagreement with the press. And no President in our history has escaped the periodic attacks of an outraged press.

Thomas Jefferson gives us a word's-eye picture of George Washington at a Cabinet meeting after being attacked by a journalist named Philip Freneau: "The President was much inflamed, got into one of those passions when he cannot command himself, ran on much on the personal abuse which had been bestowed on him, defied any man on earth to produce one single act of his since he had been in the government which was not done on the purest motives . . . and that by God he had rather be in his grave than in his present situation."

Jefferson, himself, on achieving the presidency, started out on a very friendly basis with the press. This changed later in his term to contempt and disgust, manifested in a letter he wrote a friend who had inquired as to Jefferson's view on whether he should become a journalist:

> To your request of my opinion of the manner in which a newspaper should be conducted, so as to be most useful, I should answer, "by restraining it to true facts & sound principles only." Yet I fear such a paper would find few subscribers. It is a melancholy truth, that a suppression of the press could not more compleatly deprive the nation of it's benefits, than is done by it's abandoned prostitution to falsehood. Nothing can now be believed which is seen in a newspaper . . . I really look with commiseration over the great body of my fellow citizens, who, reading newspapers, live & die in the belief, that they have known something of what has been passing in the world in their time . . . General facts may indeed be collected from them, such as that Europe is now at war, that Bonaparte has been a successful warrior . . . but no details can be relied on. I will add, that the man who never looks into a newspaper is better informed than he who reads them; inasmuch as he who knows nothing is nearer to truth than he whose mind is filled with falsehoods & errors . . .
>
> Perhaps an editor might begin a reformation in some such way as this. Divide his paper into 4 chapters, heading the 1st, Truths. 2d, Probabilities. 3d. Possibilities. 4th, Lies. The first chapter would be very short, as it would contain little more than authentic papers, and information from such sources, as the editor would be willing to risk his own reputation for their truth. The 2d would contain what, from a mature consideration of all circumstances, his judgment should conclude to be probably true. The 3d & 4th should be profesedly for those readers who would rather have lies for their money than the blank paper they would occupy.
>
> Such an editor too, would have to set his face against the demoralising practice of feeding the public mind habitually on slander & the depravity of taste which this nauseous ailment induces. Defamation is becoming a necessary of life; insomuch, that a dish of tea in the morning or evening cannot be digested without this stimulant. Even those who do not believe these abominations, still read them with complaisance to their auditors, and instead of the abhorrence & indignation which should fill a virtuous mind, betray a secret pleasure in the possibility that some may believe them, tho they do not themselves. It seems to escape them, that it is not he who prints, but he who pays for printing a slander, who is its real author.

The basic reason for the controversy between press and President is the fact that the objectives of the two institutions collide. The press, rooted in American history and a tradition of freedom, attempts to find and report every single piece of information. The government naturally wishes to present its programs and positions in the best possible light. It therefore resists—sometimes rightly and sometimes wrongly—the pressures brought on it by the press. The struggle between government and press becomes more difficult in the areas of national security. Two outstanding examples of these problems—the Cuban missile crisis of 1962 and the Vietnam war—are studied in some detail later in this book.

The White House, as a focal point of the government of the United States, mirrors this struggle at its most intense level.

Before one can understand the struggle, however, one must understand the opposing forces.

That first week in the White House, I became aware of a subtle change in my relationship with the press. I was no longer the publicity man for a candidate but the spokesman for a President. My on-the-record statements at a press briefing could hit the front pages of hundreds of newspapers two hours later. Even a "no comment" could be of tremendous significance. But the necessity for greater discretion and accuracy on my part was only one aspect of this new relationship with the White House correspondents, some of whom had been with us on the campaign trail.

JFK's campaign was far better run than Richard Nixon's. But despite the vast efforts that went into planning, it was often a capricious exercise. Luggage was lost. Impromptu briefings were held at all hours of the day and night. Broken schedules would cause reporters to miss their deadlines. And the weather or the candidate's sudden decision to climb out of his car and shake a thousand hands could throw an entire day out of whack. The traveling press was generally willing to accept such foul-ups in good humor. There could be little respect for protocol—or for deadlines—when not even the candidate was immune from the unpredictable.

But now it was different. I was on *their* ground and they had their own way of covering a President—a system of rules and prerogatives built up through a quarter of a century or more. They also had a code of tribal mores that would confuse a Nobel laureate in social anthropology. Although more than 1200 reporters had White House credentials, the ruling establishment had no more than fifty or sixty members at most. To complicate the structure even further, this establishment had many inner factions—all intensely distrustful of each other and all maneuvering to improve their position in the press hierarchy.

The sachems of the tribe were the senior correspondents for the wire services—Associated Press and United Press International. Each service has thousands of client newspapers and radio and TV stations, and can transmit the news minutes after it breaks. This is a power no President or Press

Secretary can ignore. A single reporter can rough you up in the one city where his newspaper circulates but an unfavorable AP or UPI story can hurt you around the world. Because of their great influence, the wires demand and receive privileges that are denied to other news media at the White House. For instance, the AP and UPI are always in the pool—the four or five reporters chosen by the Press Secretary to be the eyes and ears of their colleagues when it is impossible, because of space limitations, for the entire press corps to cover an event. The representatives of AP and UPI fly with the President, ride behind him when he travels by car, and are always present in his office when he holds informal press conferences with heads of state or important foreign diplomats.

The wires had still other prerogatives. Like my predecessors, I would invite their senior correspondents into my office on the morning of a press conference and tell them whether the President would have a major announcement. They, in turn, would advise me of the probable line of questioning he could expect. There was no great benefit either to the President or to the wire services from this ritual, but I stuck with it out of respect for the custom. At the press conference itself, it is traditional for the President to turn to AP and UPI for the first two questions. And the senior wire service correspondent had the authority to end the press conference just by saying, "Thank you, Mr. President."

But it is the strength of the personalities they send to the White House, not merely the extent of their circulation, that enables the wire services to protect and expand their privileges. Merriman Smith of United Press International is both amiable and tough. He has an immense sense of humor, an encyclopedic knowledge of the White House after more than twenty years on the beat, and a gentle disdain for a succession of Press Secretaries he believes have been put there to complicate his work.

Marvin Arrowsmith, senior correspondent for AP when I first became Press Secretary, was much more patient and tolerant than Smith. But, like his successors with AP—Whitney Shoemaker and Frank Cormier—he was fiercely defensive of his prerogatives.

The television and radio networks are the second most powerful faction in the establishment. They came into their own during the Eisenhower administration when they began to allot much more prime time to news and to hire on-camera personalities who were highly competent newsmen in their own right, not just actors reading a script. JFK's decision to go for live TV and radio at his press conferences brought them to a still higher zenith of influence. Because of their tremendous audience, the networks demand, but do not yet have, complete equality with the wire services.

It was my practice to place one network reporter in the pool, rotating the privilege among Sander Vanocur of NBC, George Herman of CBS, Bill Costello of Mutual, and John Edwards (later replaced by Bill Lawrence) of ABC.

The networks have a committee of Washington bureau chiefs which has the responsibility of maintaining liaison with the White House. When a President of the United States wants to make an address to the nation on a subject of importance (the Berlin crisis of 1961; the Oxford, Mississippi, crisis of 1962, etc.) it is this network committee which has the first knowledge. Under the arrangement, I would call the chairman of the committee, a job which rotated every three months, and tell him the President had an address of importance to make and wanted time on a certain evening. The chairman would then poll the networks and come back to me with various offers of time. From these offers, I would make a choice and then announce the President's speech.

I had a commitment from members of the committee that they would not reveal, even to their own correspondents, that an address of urgent national interest was imminent. But this pledge was broken on several occasions, giving certain reporters a definite time advantage to ferret out the story.

The combination of wire services and networks enabled the President to communicate with unbelievable speed both to the nation and the world. Ten minutes after I gave a presidential statement of major significance, it would be on the air and on the teletype machines of newspapers here and abroad. There were desperate moments during the Cuban missile crisis when communications between JFK and Khrushchev were running hours behind because of the total inadequacy of diplomatic channels. We decided to release JFK's statements directly to the networks and wire services, knowing that Moscow was monitoring our radio frequencies and news wires and would have the word hours faster. Khrushchev did the same with Radio Moscow and Tass, and the speed-up in communications may very well have been a factor in preventing escalation of the crisis. This necessity for instantaneous communication was the reason for prompt agreement, after the Cuban crisis, on installation of the hot line (teletype system) between Washington and Moscow.

JFK gave television some other very important advantages in addition to the televised press conference.

On at least two occasions, television cameras were permitted to follow him around in his daily work, giving the American people an unprecedented view of the President at work. One of these occasions resulted in the ABC television program *Crisis*, which showed the President and Attorney General Robert F. Kennedy actually in discussion in their offices making the important decisions on what to do to integrate the University of Alabama. The fact that Alabama's Governor George C. Wallace also allowed the cameras for the same show access to his decision making meetings resulted in as important a view of the American presidency in action as television has ever been able to present.

The President also granted exclusive interviews to television. The sole criterion for such an interview was that the request contain an idea of some merit. An outstanding example was the President's interview with David Schoenbrun of CBS, a difficult but erudite reporter. Schoenbrun was the greatest expert in the press on the subject of the European Common Market. The President had started the year 1962 by sending to the Congress an extremely complicated piece of legislation to facilitate United States trade relations with its allies—particularly the Common Market. At the time the bill was sent to Congress, a very small percentage of the American people even knew of the existence of the Market, and fewer still of its importance to American export and import trade. The President used this interview with Schoenbrun to give a clear and incisive analysis of the United States trade pattern and to explain the importance of doing business with the Common Market. This was just one phase of a vast educational campaign conducted by the government on this important point.

Walter Cronkite of CBS also had an exclusive interview with JFK to kick off the network's change-over from a fifteen- to a thirty-minute evening news show. But this one had an unfortunate aftermath. CBS shot half an hour of questions and answers, mostly on Vietnam, but cut the footage to twelve minutes for actual broadcast. The result was a partial distortion of JFK's opinion of President Ngo Dinh Diem.

In the actual interview, which was filmed, President Kennedy spoke of his respect and sympathy for the problems of President Diem. When the film was shown to the public, only the unfavorable presidential remarks remained, and JFK's praise of Diem had been deleted.

The impression was left that JFK had no confidence at all in Diem, and when he and his brother, Ngo Dinh Nhu, were later shot to death in a military coup, there were persistent charges from Madame Nhu and others that the President's statements had given aid and comfort to Diem's enemies. JFK was deeply hurt by the accusations.

The President also gave an exclusive to NBC's Huntley-Brinkley show when it went to thirty minutes. It also had to be cut to fit their time format, but this time JFK was insistent that the White House have final approval of what was shown on the air, and NBC agreed.

The most dramatic of JFK's appearances, A Conversation with the President, was seen and heard on all TV and radio networks on the evening of December 17, 1962. His own office was the setting for the informal, hour-long conversation with Lawrence of ABC, Herman of CBS, and Vanocur of NBC. An audience of tens of millions heard his candid appraisal of the triumphs and disappointments of his first two years in office. Never before had the American public had such an intimate glimpse of a President: his personality, his mind at work, his sense of history—and his sense of humor.

The most penetrating answer on the President's attitudes and feelings about his job was elicited by a question from Bill Lawrence in which he asked:

"As you look back upon your first two years in office, sir, has your experience in the office matched your expectations? You had studied a good deal the power of the presidency, the methods of its operations. How has this worked out as you saw it in advance?"

The President's answer was very revealing. "Well, I think in the first place the problems are more difficult than I had imagined they were. Secondly, there is a limitation upon the ability of the United States to solve these problems. We are involved now in the Congo in a very difficult situation. We have been unable to secure an implementation of the policy which we have supported. We are involved in a good many other areas. We are trying to see if a solution can be found to the struggle between Pakistan and India, with whom we want to maintain friendly relations. Yet they are unable to come to an agreement. There is a limitation, in other words, upon the power of the United States to bring about solutions.

"I think our people get awfully impatient and maybe fatigued and tired, and saying 'We have been carrying this burden for seventeen years; can we lay it down?' We can't lay it down, and I don't see how we are going to lay it down in this century.

"So that I would say that the problems are more difficult than I had imagined them to be. The responsibilities placed on the United States are greater than I imagined them to be, and there are greater limitations upon our ability to bring about a favorable result than I had imagined them to be. And I think that is probably true of anyone who becomes President, because there is such a difference between those who advise or speak or legislate, and between the man who must select from the various alternatives proposed and say that this shall be the policy of the United States. It is much easier to make the speeches than it is to finally make the judgments, because unfortunately your advisers are frequently divided. If you take the wrong course, and on occasion I have, the President bears the burden of the responsibility quite rightly. The advisers may move on to new advice."

I tried, early the following year, to set up a similar interview with correspondents from France, Great Britain, and West Germany for simultaneous telecast in their countries. The President was particularly anxious to reach the French audience because of his increasing difficulties with General de Gaulle over the Common Market and France's determination to build its own nuclear force.

London and Bonn quickly agreed to the proposal but the French would have no part of it. One of the stipulations I had put on the interview was that it be carried in full, with no deletions. This the French refused to do. They insisted on the right to edit the President's remarks for their state-controlled television network. The American representative of the French TV network told me the decision had been made "at the highest levels" (I assumed he was talking about General de Gaulle himself) not to permit President Kennedy a free hour of time on French TV without any choice of editing. Because France was the primary target, the President told me to call off the entire exercise.

One of the most memorable television events of the Thousand Days took place on February 14, 1962, when Mrs. Kennedy took millions of TV viewers on an hour-long tour of the Executive Mansion. There had been much publicity on her restoration of the White House, and when CBS came to her with a proposal that she show and describe the new decor to the nation, she was happy to do it. But when NBC and ABC heard of the CBS project, they blew their tops. We had no right, they said, to give a story of such great national interest to only one network. They were insistent that I require CBS to furnish them with tapes of the tour for simultaneous telecast on all three networks.

I thought their demand was ridiculous. It was my position that a TV network had as much right to an exclusive as a newspaper or a magazine. This story belongs to CBS, I told the rival networks, and you have no right to hitch a ride on their enterprise. Develop an exclusive of your own. If it's good, we'll do it. But I got nowhere with this argument. NBC and ABC were adamant and the pressure on me kept mounting. I finally had to go directly to the President for a decision. He overruled me—not because of the pressure but because he felt the President's home was in the public domain—and CBS had to share one of the most fascinating TV documentaries of all time with competitors who had absolutely nothing to do with its creation. It must have been galling to NBC and ABC, however, to have to give CBS full credit on the air.

The third ranking power bloc in the press establishment are the "specials"—the big city dailies that staff the White House. Most of their reporters deeply resent the special privileges held by the wire services and networks and are constantly fighting for greater recognition. The fact that a number of these newspapers now service other newspapers throughout the country—a specialized type of wire service—adds great weight to their arguments. The articles of reporters for such important papers as the New York *Times*, Washington *Post*, Los Angeles *Times*, New York *Herald Tribune*, Chicago *Tribune*, New York *Daily News*, and Chicago *Daily News* are widely syndicated in the United States.

The two most influential newspapers in the Capital are the New York *Times* and the Washington *Post*.

The New York *Times* has long been recognized as America's greatest daily newspaper. Its Washington bureau is the largest of any daily newspaper and staffed with dozens of experts on every variety of government work. No top policy maker in Washington starts his day without reading the *Times* and as a result the newspaper has a much greater impact on Washington thinking than other New York newspapers. It has achieved this position through excellence. The fact that a reporter works for the *Times* gives him far greater access to policy makers than the reporters of other newspapers—no matter how unfair that situation may appear to be. Other newspapers which cover the government carefully are aware of the *Times'* edge in this respect, and it does not make them happy.

The deference of the government to the *Times*, however, was sometimes the subject of sharp debate within the administration. Although it has a large New York circulation, and a modest readership outside New York, certain political specialists on our staff charged the President and me with paying too much attention to the *Times*.

"Nobody in Iowa or California reads the *Times* or even cares what it thinks editorially," Ken O'Donnell said to me one day after a *Times'* editorial had gotten JFK's day off to a gloomy start. "You and the President exaggerate its importance." I plead guilty. But I'm still willing to bet that from now into infinity, it will continue to be the first newspaper our Presidents glance at every morning and its reporters will continue to receive the red carpet treatment at the White House.

The Washington *Post* also derives its importance from being read every morning by Washington officialdom from the President on down.

The *Post* generally presents a liberal political view in a forceful and erudite way. The daily cartoons of Herbert Block (Herblock) can cause as much pain or joy in Washington as the rest of the Washington *Post* put together.

JFK was a compulsive reader—and pilferer—of newspapers and magazines. When he came into my office and saw one he hadn't read on my desk, he would invariably walk out with it. No one on the staff was safe from his shoplifting. He scanned, regularly, the New York *Times*, *Herald Tribune*, *Post*, and *Daily News*; the Washington *Post*, *Star*, and *Daily News*; the Baltimore *Sun*; the Atlanta *Constitution*; the Chicago *Tribune* and *Sun-Times*; the St. Louis *Post Dispatch*; and the *Wall Street Journal*. (I once put out a list of White House newspaper subscriptions and, inadvertently, left out the Washington *Daily News*. I got an angry letter from the circulation manager. "You, of all people, should know that President Kennedy has been a long-time subscriber to the *Daily News*. For six months before his inauguration it was delivered to his home at 3307 N Street, Georgetown, by a carrier named Marc Salinger." (Marc is my son and JFK had, indeed, been one of his customers.)

The President also read *Time*, *Newsweek*, *U.S. News & World Report*, *Look*, *Life*, *Harpers*, *The Reporter*, *New Republic*, *The Economist*, the *Saturday Review*, the *Manchester Guardian Weekly*, and the London *Sunday Times*.

The President read no West Coast newspapers, a fact that reflects not on their merit but on the provincialism of most Presidents born in the East. He simply felt more comfortable with newspapers he had read since boyhood and had a higher regard for their publishers and pundits because they were Easterners, too. He read the Atlanta *Constitution* and the St. Louis *Post Dispatch* as the liberal voices of two distinct and formidable geopolitical areas. The other exceptions—the Chicago newspapers—were read because of the city's economic importance and JFK's fascination with Cook County politics.

In recent years, the Los Angeles *Times* has begun to command the attention it deserves at the White House. It is not only the biggest newspaper in the most populous state, but has built a much stronger Washington bureau, led by Robert Donovan, formerly of the New York *Herald Tribune*. I can't understand many of its political endorsements (George Murphy for Senate!) but I will grant that is is approaching the New York *Times* in quality and extent of national coverage.

One of the biggest newspaper flaps of the administration had to do with a "special"—the New York *Herald Tribune*. The President had become increasingly unhappy with the coverage of the *Herald Tribune*—particularly during the time of the Billie Sol Estes case. His unhappiness stemmed from what he considered to be the unfairness of the *Herald Tribune* toward Agriculture Secretary Orville Freeman. Concurrently, an important Washington story was also breaking—the so-called stockpile scandal. This case centered on special treatment allegedly tendered some powerful Republicans, including George M. Humphrey, Secretary of the Treasury during the Eisenhower administration, in the purchases of goods from the government stockpile. The *Herald Tribune*—in the President's view—was playing down the stockpile scandal because it involved a Republican administration, and giving wide attention to the Billie Sol Estes case because it affected some Democrats. The fact that the publisher of the New York *Herald Tribune*, John Hay Whitney, was an owner of one of the companies mentioned in the stockpile case, did nothing to diminish JFK's suspicions as to the motives of the *Herald Tribune*. Several times, the President told me to cancel the subscription of the White House to the *Herald Tribune*. I ignored his requests because I felt his anger would abate. But one day, he happened to run into Jack McNally, the man responsible for White House newspaper subscriptions, in the hallway and ordered him to cancel the *Herald Tribune*. McNally carried out the order immediately, although it was my feeling that the President was merely letting off steam at that particular moment. In any event, the President was aghast when the story of the cancellation hit the newspapers. For several months, until it could be arranged to bring the paper back into the White House, we had to bootleg copies of the *Herald Tribune* to him daily.

The news magazines—*Time, Newsweek,* and to a lesser degree, *U.S.*

*News & World Report*—have somewhat equal rank with the dailies. All three have extensive readership in the middle and upper income brackets —the thought leaders and political activists in their communities. Because of their once-a-week deadline, they also are given certain privileges. For example, if the President was going to deliver a major speech on Monday—the day the news magazines hit the stands—I would let them have a peek at it on Friday or Saturday. I would also advise them in advance on important legislation that was going to the Hill on Monday, or the announcement of a high appointment or resignation. Never once did a reporter for a news magazine violate this trust by leaking such information to a friend on one of the dailies, who would have been able to score a clean beat on his competitors.

Because of the huge readership of magazines such as *Life, Look, Mc-Call's, The Saturday Evening Post, Ladies' Home Journal, Good Housekeeping, Redbook,* and others, their writers had special access to the Kennedys. The most memorable magazine spread of the Kennedy years was *Look's* "The President and His Son," the marvelous pictures of JFK playing with John in his office. When writer Laura Bergquist and photographer Stanley Tretick first came to me with the idea, Mrs. Kennedy was dead set against it. She felt it was too much an invasion of the family's privacy. The President smiled when I told him of her objections.

"Let's hold off on it for a while, then," he said. "We'll take another look at it the next time she leaves town."

A week or two later, Mrs. Kennedy went to Italy and Miss Bergquist and Tretick spent two hours in the President's office shooting the pictures that were to break a nation's heart when they ran in *Look* the very week of the assassination.

When Mrs. Kennedy came back from Italy and I told her what we had done, she was very upset with me.

"Wait and see, you'll love the pictures," I told her.

"You always say that," was her crisp reply.

We come, then, to the ladies—the distaff reporters whose assignment was Mrs. Kennedy and the social and family life of the White House. Mrs. Kennedy had her own very able Press Secretary, Pamela Turnure, but it was agreed that I would release all news from both the President and Mrs. Kennedy at my press briefings. It didn't work at all. I found it impossible to jump from an announcement on nuclear testing to a precise description of Mrs. Kennedy's latest hat, or from a denial that a Cabinet member was on the skids to the love life of one of Caroline's hamsters. I finally gave up and threw all questions involving society, zoology, and millinery back to Pamela in the East Wing, the headquarters of Mrs. Kennedy's staff.

The lady reporters at the White House were a formidable force, however. Except for the first news section, the society pages of the Washington

*Post* and *Star* have the largest readership in the Capital. For reasons I will never understand, both papers have a policy of printing news off the women's beat only in the women's section, regardless of its importance. I am convinced that if the wife of a senator were to announce at a society tea that she was divorcing her husband because he was selling military secrets to the Soviet Union to finance a secret liaison with a world-famous actress, you would find the story next to a recipe for fudgecake on the society pages.

Superimposed on the White House establishment was another very important segment of the Washington press—the influential columnists whose words are read daily throughout the United States.

The ranking members of this fraternity were James (Scotty) Reston of the New York *Times*, Walter Lippmann, Joseph and Stewart Alsop, Marquis Childs, Doris Fleeson, William S. White, Rowland Evans and Robert Novak, Joseph Kraft and Drew Pearson.

Because of their influence throughout the country, most of these columnists got special treatment. A request from one of them to see the President personally was usually honored, and White House staff members at the policy level like Ted Sorensen and McGeorge Bundy made sure that they had the administration's views on prevailing problems.

In any crisis situation, it was standard operating procedure to be in touch with these columnists to give them background on the government's actions. The President, himself, frequently took part in these background sessions. He would, for example, call Lippmann or invite him to the White House.

I made it a point to lunch with these correspondents from time to time to find out what their problems were and to keep them abreast of the administration's thinking.

In talking about the White House press establishment, it should also be noted that other press establishments exist in Washington. Most prominent of these are the newspaper reporters who cover the State and Defense Departments—specialists in foreign policy and defense policy who have also established their prerogatives and inner structure.

The government is not without its own press establishment.

It is an interesting commentary that the White House, the center of the government information apparatus, has a smaller information staff than any of the Cabinet departments. The budget of my office at the White House ran about $150,000 a year. This should be compared with the State Department's press budget of over $1,000,000 and the Defense Department's information budget of close to $30,000,000. The size of the White House press office has not grown, in effect, since the advent of the first so-called "modern" Press Secretary, Steve Early, who acted in that post for Franklin D. Roosevelt.

My White House press office consisted of one Press Secretary, one associate, one assistant, and five secretaries. The only change from Early's time was my addition of the assistant.

This has not taken into account the staggering growth of work for the White House press office during these thirty years. For example, when Early was Press Secretary, radio was in its infancy and television was not even a factor. He had to deal with a complement of about seventy-five accredited correspondents, compared with the 1200 who were accredited during my tenure. Airplane travel has also seriously complicated the problems of the press office. In Early's day, when President Roosevelt traveled by train (except in campaign years) he was usually accompanied by a dozen reporters compared to the fifty or sixty who accompanied President Kennedy in domestic travel and the more than a hundred who accompanied him when he went overseas.

Because of the growth of reportorial specialization in Washington, each Cabinet department has its own press organization. This extends down to such specialized agencies as the Civil Aeronautics Board and the Federal Communications Commission.

I spent an average of six days a week at the White House—and the hours were long. An Army sergeant from the transportation pool would pick me up at my home in Falls Church at eight-thirty. He would bring with him the morning editions of six major Eastern newspapers for me to scan on the twenty minute drive into Washington. My first chores at the office were to return the most urgent of my telephone calls and read the thick sheaves of wire service copy that had come in overnight on the four teletypes.

Around nine-thirty I would go into the President's office to discuss with him the late news developments around the world and the policy line I should follow in presenting his reactions to the press at my eleven o'clock briefing. He, too, had already seen the important Eastern newspapers and was often in a black mood if he thought a columnist had been unfair to him.

"I want you to call that ———," JFK might instruct me, "and tell him exactly what I think." And then, a second later, "Never mind, I'll do it myself." But he rarely did.

After leaving JFK, I would prepare myself further for the briefing by contacting his policy advisers in the White House and in the executive departments for their analysis of overnight events. After the briefing, I would dig into my mail, which often ran as high as a thousand letters a week. I would refer many of them, of course, to more appropriate departments and could answer two-thirds of the rest with form letters. But I still had to squeeze in two to three hours a day of dictation between office appointments.

I could count on at least a letter a day from women demanding to know why the President was always two or three paces ahead of his wife in pictures showing them walking together. When I told JFK about it, he said: "The answer's simple. Jackie ought to walk a little faster."

I would usually eat lunch, always a hasty affair, with one of the correspondents or a national columnist or commentator, and would call on the President again in the early afternoon to prepare for my four o'clock briefing of the press. Then there would be another batch of mail and telephone calls and more office appointments. Neither I nor the regular correspondents left the White House until the President left his office, usually after seven o'clock. If I didn't have a speaking engagement, an official function to attend, or a poker game, the Army sergeant would return me to my home between eight-thirty and nine. Very often the children were already in bed, and I would have a late dinner alone with my wife.

But it was a rare evening at home that I didn't spend half my time on the telephone. More than two hundred reporters had permission to call me at any hour through the White House switchboard. Four of the eight extensions in my home were connected directly to the White House, and I even had a jack on the shore of Lake Barcroft, fifty yards down the hill from my house.

I also had a hot line, junior grade, between my office and sixty of the correspondents. If I had to summon them to the White House after hours for an important press conference or announcement by the President, the secretary in the office had only to press a button, and a magnetic tape system in her telephone would automatically dial the reporters' home numbers. On February 10, 1962, it was possible for me, through this system, to assemble all the White House regulars within forty minutes for the 3:16 A.M. press conference at which I announced the exchange of master Soviet spy Rudolf Abel for U-2 pilot Francis Gary Powers. It was, I should explain, 8:16 A.M. in Berlin, where the dramatic exchange had taken place on the Glienicker Bridge, connecting the Western and Communist zones.

It was difficult to get some of the reporters out of bed that night. The reporter for the Voice of America (a government employee) had to be assured that the President had not declared war. At one home, Chris Camp got the reporter's wife on the phone and identified herself as my secretary.

"May I speak to Mr. ———," she asked.

"You cannot!" the wife replied heatedly. "He's sound asleep. Now just who did you say you are?"

Chris repeated her credentials again and told the wife I was calling an important news conference.

"Well I don't care who you are and you've got your nerve calling my husband at this hour and I will deliver no message to him." She hung up. The reporter did not show up and his 840,000 Midwestern readers (four major dailies employed him) were deprived of his byline coverage of the Powers-Abel story the next day.

When an important item of business broke after regular business hours, I used the telephone to put out the first bulletin. What I would usually do would be put in a conference call first to the AP, UPI, Reuters, and Agence France Presse. I would follow this with a conference call to NBC, CBS, ABC, and the Mutual Broadcasting System. Thus, inside ten minutes the item of news could already be winging around the world.

My routine was broken, of course, during times of crisis, when I might live in a hotel close to the White House for as long as eight or ten days. I would also accompany the President when he left Washington (the visit to Dallas was a rare exception) and an unbelievable backlog of paperwork would accumulate in my absence.

Not all the matters I got involved in had to do with the press. There were dozens of people a week who came to see me because they had problems with the administration and they thought I could either help them solve them or point them in the direction of someone who could. Certainly the most novel of these approaches came in 1961 from Juan Lechin, the leftist Vice-President (now deposed) of Bolivia.

One day my secretary announced Lechin had called asking for an appointment. I was puzzled by the request but set up a date for that afternoon.

Lechin arrived in my office armed with a letter of introduction from a San Francisco artist, Antonio Sotomayor, a Bolivian, whom I had known quite well as a boy. The Vice-President came right to the point.

"Mr. Salinger, if my government does not have $1,000,000 by the close of business tomorrow night, it will not be able to meet its payroll."

I was flabbergasted by the statement and inquired why Lechin had not seen persons in the government directly concerned with Latin American affairs. He assured me he had seen everyone he could in the State Department and the Agency for International Development. "I cannot get them to take any action. I am coming to see you as a last resort," he said.

I told him to call me in the morning and took the problem to President Kennedy. The President had not heard of the visit of the Bolivian Vice-President but he was extremely concerned about that country which gave all indications of going in the direction of a Cuban-type Communist regime. In a matter of hours, he had top officials in both State and AID meeting at the White House and arranged for a special mission to go to Bolivia. The work of that mission resulted in Bolivia getting a special loan from the United States, West Germany, and France in the amount of $20,000,000 which eased its pressing monetary crisis.

A year later, when members of the Bolivian tin mine workers union, which Lechin headed in addition to his government post, kidnaped and held hostage three AID officials in that country, I sent a message to

Lechin reminding him how I had helped him when he had come to me in dire trouble. I don't know whether the letter did the trick, but the AID officials were released several days later.

But, from the first day to the last, there was never a dull moment and in spite of occasional flareups the press and I managed to maintain our good humor and respect for each other. This was not always easy—particularly because of a number of changes which we instituted at the White House —not all of which were particularly welcome.

My first day and my last day at the White House—not to speak of all the days in between—had their elements of controversy.

Frantic is the only word to describe my White House debut on Saturday, January 21, 1961. At my first briefing for the press and in my first announcement of a major presidential action, I was to be party to a $27,000,000 error.

In his campaign visits to West Virginia and other distressed areas, JFK had been appalled at the sub-standard diet of hundreds of thousands of families and had promised to increase the allotment of federal surplus food. His first act as President was to issue an executive order doubling the ration and extending it to new areas of high unemployment. I had a specialist from the Department of Agriculture with me at the first briefing to answer the more technical questions.

"Exactly how much is all this going to cost?" was one of the first queries.

The specialist, who shall remain nameless, multiplied the four million beneficiaries by an approximate unit cost of $9 a month and came up with $36,000,000 a month—and that's what went out over the wires. But two hours after the briefing, he came running into my office. He had been guilty of a slight miscalculation. It wasn't $9 a month per person but $9 for a family of four. The correct cost was $9,000,000, not $36,000,000. I hastily summoned the reporters and gave them the correct figure.

"Don't lose any sleep over it, Pierre," said one. "It's just a trifling detail."

I had two more flaps that first week. Most of the news pictures and television footage shot at the Inaugural did not show JFK's hand on the Bible when he took the oath. The switchboards of newspaper offices and TV stations across the country lit up with calls suggesting a religious significance, and I was beset with questions at one of my press briefings. I had seen him touch the Bible but they wouldn't take my word for it. But they did take his. He had put his hand on the Bible only briefly through the first words of the oath and then let it fall down to his side.

My old nemesis from Palm Beach, Bill Lawrence of the New York *Times*, was the first to give me a bad time as Press Secretary. Traditionally, VIPs who call on the President and who are willing to face the press, leave the White House through the press lounge in the West Lobby. That first week, JFK met with Democratic congressional leaders who left, on their own volition, through another exit. Lawrence was convinced that gagging of presidential visitors was a new White House policy, and would not believe my flat statement that neither the President nor I had told the legislators to avoid the press.

I lost my temper. "I resent the implication that I am trying to keep you from covering the news. I am here for exactly the opposite purpose, Mr. Lawrence." (I would address a correspondent as "Mr." only when I was seething. Otherwise, we were always on a first-name basis.) But after the hassle with Lawrence, I made it a point to ask, specifically, that visitors leave by the West Lobby, if the purpose of their call was not highly confidential.

There was one humorous exchange that first week. The President still had a number of top ambassadorships to fill and the press corps kept badgering me for the names of probable appointees. Obviously, I could announce nothing until JFK was ready to send his nominations to the Senate.

"You never give us hard news, just tidbits," said one reporter. I told him he was wrong, that I had a story of major importance that day. I paused for dramatic effect.

"The cat is here."

"What cat?"

"Caroline's cat."

In mock seriousness, the press shoved closer to my desk, their pencils at the ready.

"What's the cat's name?"

"Tom Kitten."

The impatient reporter who had accused me of handing out only tidbits was now almost on top of me.

"What color is this cat? I came here for news. I've got to leave with something."

I didn't know Tom Kitten's color but I did send them racing to their telephones with the announcement that he would sleep in a box on the linoleum floor of the nursery, and that the decision as to whether he would roam at night was still pending at Cabinet level. Unfortunately, Tom Kitten caught a cold that first night and I had to issue almost daily medical bulletins on his recovery.

On my last day, March 19, 1964, Merriman Smith led a delegation into my office at 4 P.M. to protest what he and others considered to be a violation of some of the rights of the White House press corps.

"Give me just two hours and I'll take care of the problem for you," I promised.

I resigned at 6 P.M. to return to California to run for the United States

Senate. But I am certain that the delegation was waiting for my successor, George Reedy, the next morning, and that similar protests from the establishment still are an important order of business with his successors, Bill Moyers and Bob Fleming.

# VIII

## FIRST SKIRMISH

Establishment or no establishment, I was determined, my first months in the White House, to effect a number of radical changes in the press operation. All except one were to prove acceptable to the senior correspondents but the exception was to explode into a front-page controversy over censorship and news management.

I was convinced that both the President and his staff should be much more accessible to the reporters. Under Jim Hagerty, and others before him, a presidential adviser could not grant an interview without first clearing it with the Press Secretary. Even when Hagerty gave such permission, he often sat in on the interview to be certain it didn't stray off the policy track.

I felt this was an unnecessary obstruction to the flow of news from the White House. All of JFK's staff had his full confidence. And, certainly, they had an expertise in their specialties that I could not hope to match when the questions flew thick and fast at my press briefings. I let it be known that hereafter the White House would be an open beat. Any reporter could interview any staffer on any subject and without clearing with me.

Over the next three years the new system was to prove generally successful, if not entirely popular. A small number of reporters had been content to sit on their duffs all day in the lobby, waiting for me to spoon-feed them the news at my briefings. Under the new, competitive system, they either had to go to work or be shown up by their more energetic colleagues.

For the enterprising reporter, however, the open beat offered avenues of communication in the White House which had been closed for years.

James Reston of the New York *Times* later stated that "access to policy makers" had been greater during the Kennedy administration than at any other time "during the twenty years I have been a reporter in Washington."

In all the discussion about management of the news which ebbed and flowed during my term of office, I considered—and still consider—*access* to information and policy makers the central point of a successful press policy for the government and the White House. There can be no legitimate complaint about the government's press practices if those who are involved in the policy-making process in Washington are accessible and candid with the press.

I can think of no key member of the White House staff who did not speak to the press with frankness—in fact, from the President's point of view, with too much frankness from time to time.

This points to the danger of the open beat. Not only were the members of the White House staff policy makers and planners with the President, but they were also, in most instances, articulate men who had firm personal views about the needs of the world and the nation. Sometimes these views did not coincide with those of the President, but the mere fact that a person was a key aide to the President was sufficient for the reporter interviewing him (or just lunching with him socially) to attribute the staff member's views to the President.

One staff member, for example, could not wait for the Labor party to come back to power in England, and whenever discussing European politics would make this point. Some reporters attributed this view to President Kennedy, even though at that particular time he had what he considered a superb working relationship with Prime Minister Harold Macmillan, a Conservative.

On another occasion, I recall a story in a leading European daily that had a series of highly unorthodox views from JFK on the very ticklish points of West German policy and Berlin. The President called me into his office.

"Have you seen this story?"

"I have."

"Does it even come close to expressing my views on Berlin?"

"No."

"Then find out what it's doing on the front page."

After a little digging, I came up with the name of the apparent miscreant—Fred Holborn. Fred was a highly intelligent young man, and a keen student of the German question, who had been on JFK's Senate staff. He had spoken informally to a foreign reporter on the diplomatic alternatives in Berlin, without once suggesting that the President was considering a shift in policy. The reporter chose to interpret the alternatives as probabilities and put them in the mouth of the President,

1. The President and the Press Secretary. *(Henry Grossman © 1960)*

2. Senator John McClellan swears in Pierre Salinger during a session of the Senate Select Committee on Improper Activities in the Labor Field. Mr. Robert Kennedy is seated to the left of his brother John, then the junior senator from Massachusetts. (*Paul Schutzer, Life magazine © 1958 Time, Inc.*)


3. OPPOSITE PAGE JFK and Pierre Salinger walk through the falling snows of Wisconsin during the 1960 Democratic primary campaign. When only a few people showed up for the senator's speeches, Mr. Kennedy quite lucidly suggested to the Press Secretary that this not happen again. It didn't. (*Ollie Atkins, Saturday Evening Post*)

4. OPPOSITE PAGE President and Press Secretary on the lawn of Ambassador Joseph P. Kennedy's Massachusetts home, on Election Day, 1960. (*Photograph © copyright Jacques Lowe*)

5. President and Mrs. Kennedy seem delighted by cryptic message engraved on birthday gift for the President. (*White House*)

6. A classic study of the President and his Press Secretary in the oval office of the White House. (*Cornell Capa/Magnum*)

7. Mrs. Jacqueline Kennedy and Pierre Salinger chatting at a Washington cocktail party. (*Photograph © copyright Jacques Lowe*)

8. Pierre Salinger leans into drive as President Kennedy carefully follows
flight of ball. Hyannis Port, July 28, 1963. (*White House*)

even though Holborn's principal duty at the White House was to draft greetings in the name of the President to trade conventions.

Another hazard of the open beat was that staff members frequently disagreed on policy. An alert reporter, by interviewing two or more, could come up with a story whose lead might read: "There was sharp division among President Kennedy's top advisers today over recognition of the new Asian state of Outlandia." JFK didn't like this public debate among staffers on pending policy decisions but thought it was preferable to muzzling the staff as a source of information. He would not tolerate the airing of family quarrels *after* the policy was in effect.

I also felt very strongly that the President himself should be more accessible to the press. He was, without question, the most articulate and persuasive Chief Executive since FDR. He had bold and controversial concepts for moving the nation ahead that had to be sold both to the Congress and to the public, and no one could sell them more effectively than he. I found him totally receptive to my suggestion that he remove many of the traditional obstacles that have stood between the President and the press. The rule against live television at his press conferences was but the first barrier to go. His greater availability for exclusive interviews on TV and in all other media was another advance. He was also to sur-pass all other Presidents in the number of briefings, or backgrounders, he held in his office with large numbers of reporters—both foreign and Ameri-can. Many of his comments were off-the-record, but they gave the press a clear reading of his attitudes and objectives. Because of such briefings, he was able to reduce substantially the publication or broadcast of false or misleading speculation that could react to his disadvantage both at home and abroad.

The President came up with the idea of inviting the country's leading publishers to lunch on a state-by-state basis. My office made up the lists of invitees for the twenty-five such lunches he held. Usually we would take the twenty or so largest papers in the state. (With the small size of the states these got down to papers with a circulation of barely 10,000 people.) Then to fill out the lunch, we would invite the officers of that particular state's weekly press association. This gave the President a good cross section of the state's press.

The lunch would be preceded by a short cocktail session. The President would come in as lunchtime approached and go around and shake hands with each of the publishers personally. At the lunches in the State Dining Room, the President would converse with his neighbors at the table until dessert was served. Then he would give a short review of his views on current domestic and international affairs. At the close of his talks, he would open up the luncheon for discussion.

These discussions were wide in nature, but there was virtually no dis-cussion on the role of the press and the White House. During 1961, the principal subjects were Cuba and Berlin. In 1962, the subjects of the greatest interest were taxes and foreign trade.

It was interesting how a publisher could attack the President on the spending policies of his administration and then return to the discussion several minutes later with a question for the President as to why he was not building this or that dam or public building in his state. The President was quick to point out these inconsistencies.

"On the one hand," he told one publisher, "you ask me to cut back the domestic spending of the government and on the other hand you ask me for special treatment for your state. You cannot have both. And the fact that you hold that position shows some of the problems of the presidency. Everybody is for less government spending and less taxes. And everybody has some pet project they would like to see made an exception. That's what makes life so interesting around here."

Another subject of conversation was foreign aid. Most of the publishers who attended these lunches were against the President's foreign aid program, but quite a few changed their minds after he explained that some eighty per cent of the goods purchased for foreign aid came from American manufacturing firms and the entire military aid program consisted of the United States government buying arms from its own defense plants.

The publishers were generally pleased with the President's frankness —and with the honor of being invited to the White House for lunch. My files are full of letters from publishers who, on arriving home, wrote to say they had a far better understanding of the President and his problems than they had had before. One wrote me: "I will never be able to write another glib editorial attacking the President without thinking of that lunch and the great burdens of an American President."

The lunches were not without their humorous and non-humorous aspects.

One publisher (I suspect he had imbibed of cocktails too freely) insisted on taking one of the gold spoons of the White House service as a "souvenir for my daughter." The publisher was sitting next to me and I fruitlessly attempted to persuade him that this would be a bad idea. The President, sitting opposite me, finally heard the conversation and it took a personal request from him to the publisher to avert the loss of the spoon.

All but one of the affairs was cordial. The exception was the Texas lunch when E. M. Dealey, publisher of the Dallas Morning News, scornfully told the President: "We need a man on horseback to lead this nation, and many people in Texas and the Southwest think that you are riding Caroline's bicycle." The other news executives listened in embarrassed silence and one of them, the publisher of the afternoon Dallas Times Herald, later sent JFK a note assuring him that Dealey spoke only for himself. "I'm sure the people of Dallas must be glad when afternoon comes," the President replied. In a later speech, he struck out at those who "look suspiciously at our neighbors and our leaders. They call for a 'man on horseback' because they do not trust the people." The same day the President was assassinated, the Dallas *Morning News* ran a full-page ad, paid for by "American-thinking Citizens of Dallas," accusing him of pro-Communist sympathies. The day before, a *News* columnist advised the President to confine his remarks in Dallas to yachting: "If the speech is about boating you will be among the warmest of admirers. If it is about Cuber, civil rights, taxes or Vietnam, there will sure as shootin' be some who heave to and let go with a broadside of grapeshot in the presidential rigging."

A further change I was to effect at the White House was equal treatment of the foreign press. The five hundred reporters representing overseas newspapers, magazines, and networks had never been members of the establishment. The President was keenly aware of the importance of his foreign image. The old argument that a favorable story in Paris or Bonn isn't worth a single vote in Omaha no longer holds water. The impression a President creates overseas invariably bounces back to the citizens of his own country.

Not only that, what people in foreign lands think of a President of the United States is formed in great part from what they read by the correspondents of their newspapers in the United States. If the foreign reporter in the United States is frustrated—by procedures he does not understand or by a language barrier—in getting a true picture of U.S. policy and intentions, what he writes is likely to create the same frustration in his readers.

We were faced with two problems in the foreign correspondent field— those in Washington and those in New York. The latter represent better than half of all the foreign correspondents in the United States.

To attack the former problem, I recruited Jay Gildner, a young career foreign service officer who was the United States Information Agency's press officer in Toronto, Canada. I added him to my staff as a specialist to work directly with the foreign press.

Many of the overseas reporters are either new to Washington or one-man bureaus. The very vastness of the United States government bewilders many of them. There are, of course, old pros in the foreign press corps like Adalbert de Segonzac of *France Soir*, Henry Brandon of the London *Sunday Times*, Werner Imhoof of Switzerland's *Neue Zuercher Zeitung*, and Nicolas Chatelain of *Le Figaro* who could find their way around government and the White House without special assistance.

To get the program under way, I held a country-by-country series of luncheons with the correspondents to advise them of Gildner's availability and my determination that they should have equal treatment at the White House. The largest of these luncheons was with the Japanese press, which has the largest single contingent of any nation in Washington. I also lunched with the British, French, Dutch, Swedish, Canadian, and German correspondents. Unfortunately, there is no significant press representation from either Africa or South America in Washington.

I particularly recall one luncheon with the seven Soviet correspondents at Le Bistro, one of Washington's most decorous restaurants. To the horror of the *maître d'hôtel*, they trooped in with their own bottles of vodka under their arms and shook the walls with booming toasts to freedom and peace. I sent for a cigar and the waiter brought me one of slightly inferior quality.

"It has become very difficult to find a decent Cuban cigar," I said to Mike Sagateylan, the Washington bureau chief of the Soviet news agency, Tass.

"The more difficult it is for you, the simpler it is for us," he cracked back.

Gildner also organized special briefing sessions with foreign press for such top administration figures as Walter Heller of the Council of Economic Advisers; McGeorge Bundy, the President's Special Assistant for National Security Affairs; and White House Special Counsel Ted Sorensen. Special briefings were arranged at the State and the Defense Departments. In addition, with the assistance of Arthur Sylvester of Defense and Roger Tubby and Bob Manning of State, we organized tours of the United States for some of these correspondents so that their view of the United States would not be limited to Washington and New York, as interesting as those two cities may be.

Gildner's role at the White House led to a well-deserved promotion to a policy-making role in the USIA (liaison with the White House and State Department) and he was replaced by Malcolm Kilduff, an enterprising public information officer I stole from the State Department. Kilduff had helped me advance the President's trip to Europe in 1961 and I was impressed with the job he did. When it became time for Gildner to move on, I reached out for Kilduff to replace him. Both he and Gildner were most effective, not only in increasing the amount of White House coverage overseas but in achieving more accurate and objective reporting. There was also an important feed-back to us. Very often, the first hint we had of important developments in foreign capitals came from their correspondents. Even Communist reporters, especially those from Poland and Yugoslavia, were quite frank in discussing their government's intentions with White House personnel. In almost all cases, their tips were to prove correct.

It was Kilduff who drew the assignment to go to Dallas with President Kennedy the day he was assassinated. He did a remarkable job under fire on this most difficult day.

In our efforts with the foreign press, we organized occasional special projects. The most successful of these was the interview which the President and Mrs. Kennedy gave to RTF (French National Television) shortly before their visit to Paris in 1961. By strange coincidence, the President called me into his office one day to suggest that we might arrange such an interview and when I got back to my office, I found a call from Pierre Crenesse, the RTF representative in New York, asking if I could arrange such an interview. The alacrity with which I accepted Crenesse's proposal bowled him over. The interview was an entirely warm and appealing glimpse into the lives and personalities of the President and Mrs. Kennedy. Mrs. Kennedy, whose French is excellent, spoke with the interviewer in his own language for fifteen minutes. The interview was shown all over France the night before the Kennedys' arrival and was a factor in the tremendous reception they received in that country. That acclaim was also the top story in the United States—showing the important domestic considerations of good coverage and acceptance overseas.

The President also granted an exclusive interview to ATV, the commercial television channel in Great Britain, in which he discussed such important subjects as European unity and the need for Great Britain to be admitted to the Common Market.

The foreign correspondents in New York posed an even greater problem than those in Washington. Here, the correspondents tried to cover government events in Washington and the United Nations at the same time. Because of the limits on their time, and their inability to have direct access to government information directly, they frequently carried out their tasks by rewriting the morning editions of the New York *Times*. As much as I admire the *Times*, I did not feel this was a satisfactory way to cover Washington news.

After a series of meetings with Edward R. Murrow and Don Wilson of the USIA and Bob Manning of State, the USIA in 1962 established the New York Foreign Correspondents Center in a building close to the United Nations. This center had several purposes. The first was to bring the New York foreign correspondent closer to what was going on in Washington. This we did by installing a Washington wire service which communicated important actions by the government on any particular day. We also arranged to pipe in the daily press briefings of the State Department. In addition, we equipped the Center with an excellent reference library for the use of the correspondents.

With all of these assets, the Center would not have been a success unless it had been manned by the right person. I called Wilson one day and told him I had a candidate in mind for director of the Center. He told me he had one also. It turned out we had the same candidate, Ernest Wiener, the press officer of the U. S. Embassy in Vienna. Wiener had helped me set up the press arrangements for the meeting between President Kennedy and Chairman Khrushchev in Vienna, and he turned out to be a man of many qualities. He was excellent in his presentation of American foreign policy objectives and he spoke some five languages including Russian, German, and French. The Center got off to a slow start, but once the foreign correspondents understood we had a man in the Center who knew their problems and was ready to help them with an authentic and factual background on the United States, they began to come into the Center in numbers. I consider the establishment of the Center one of the most important single acts of the Kennedy administration in the field of press relations.

I felt that there should be some kind of rapport between those in government responsible for information. When I came to the White House I found there was also an occasional meeting between the United States and the West Germans, and the United States and the British on common information problems. But I resolved to expand these contacts to other nations. As a regular course of business, I scheduled meetings with the Press Secretaries of foreign heads of state paying a visit to President Kennedy. Thus, in a period of time, I got to be well acquainted with twenty-five to thirty top information specialists around the world. I found some of these contacts helpful from time-to-time in periods of crisis. For example, the personal relationship between myself and Fabian Velarde, the Press Secretary to the President of Panama, proved to be of immense value during the Panama Canal riots of 1964 which I describe later in this book. On another occasion, in 1962, the then Prime Minister of Italy, Amintore Fanfani, had a long and important meeting with Chairman Khrushchev. This meeting came at one of the difficult points in U.S.-Soviet relations after this country's resumption of nuclear testing. Dr. Humberto Bianchi, the Press Secretary of the Italian Prime Minister, flew to London, where I was at the time, to give me a personal account of the meeting for relay to President Kennedy, rather than committing this valuable message to diplomatic correspondence.

One of my objectives, however, was only partly realized. Because of the real problems of the Western Hemisphere, and particularly the relationships between the United States and Latin America, I wanted to organize a hemisphere meeting of information specialists to probe ways of improving understanding. It is an unfortunate fact that with the exception of key newspapers in the United States, Latin American news is really not adequately covered in this country. By the same token, there is an almost total absence of Latin American journalists in the United States. The result is misunderstanding.

I explored the plan first with Ali Caccavalle, the Press Secretary of the then President of Venezuela, Rómulo Betancourt. Caccavalle was enthusiastic and offered all of his help.

The first opportunity to put the plan into motion came with the announced plans of President Kennedy to meet with the Presidents of the Central American republics in the spring of 1963.

I went to San José, Costa Rica, in early March of that year to start making preparations for the President's trip. At the same time, Caccavalle flew there from Caracas and we met with the Press Secretaries of the other Central American Presidents. At these preliminary meetings, it was agreed to hold a formal meeting of the Central American Press Secretaries at the time of President Kennedy's visit late in March.

The result of this meeting was a resolution which pointed out the problems of "public understanding and support for the Alliance for Progress" as well as the "propaganda and subversive activities of international Communism emanating from Cuba." The resolution called for a larger meeting to include information specialists from Colombia, the Dominican Republic, and Mexico. This meeting was set for Oaxaca, Mexico, for the summer of 1963. Two dates for the meeting had to be postponed due to the inability of one Press Secretary or another to attend and I finally left the White House without seeing this step toward a real attack on the hemispheric problems of distrust and misunderstanding come to fruition.

Our efforts at public understanding also were extended in other areas. The State Department, first during the tenure of Roger Tubby and then under Bob Manning, organized briefing sessions for radio, TV, and newspaper reporters and editors from around the country, where these journalists were given briefings on current foreign policy problems by government officials up to and including the President of the United States.

Tubby and Manning also organized task forces of State Department officials that went out into the country and held foreign policy briefings for press and public. Some of these seminars were sponsored by leading newspapers in their home towns, such as the Kansas City *Star* and the Denver *Post*. These conferences proved to be of great value in improving general comprehension—and acceptance—of American foreign policy.

My final—and most controversial—change in press policy was the coordination of all important news from the executive branch of government. A majority of the press had another definition for it—news management.

In studying the press relations of earlier administrations, I was struck by what I thought was one of the great information catastrophes in our history—our initial responses to the U-2 incident of 1960. Within hours of the time Francis Gary Powers was shot down over Communist Armenia, four different Washington press officers put out four different stories. We were, to put it bluntly, caught lying in our teeth. The international reaction couldn't have been worse. I meant to take every precaution that JFK's administration would not repeat that error, and there was only one way to prevent it. The public information officers in the many departments of the executive branch must clear with the White House all statements and speeches bearing on important national and international questions. And why not? JFK certainly had a right to expect that his administration would speak with one tongue *and* in support of his policies. Actually, this co-ordination, or clearance, of top-level information was nothing new. Hagerty and all other Press Secretaries held a firm, if invisible, rein on the press officers in the executive department. My crime was to formalize the ar-rangement, to announce publicly the formation of a coordinating com-mittee that would gather weekly in my office.

I had JFK's full backing in this enterprise. His first instruction to me as Press Secretary was that I was to take full responsibility for all executive information. I was, of course, the target of sharp, if not always accurate, fire from the press, which saw the coordinating committee as a front for White House censorship. The first accusation of censorship or news man-agement came just three days after the Inaugural. An aide of Admiral Arleigh A. Burke came to me with a speech the chief of Naval Operations was planning to deliver that same week. It was extremely hostile to the Soviet Union. What the admiral did not know, was that Khrushchev was planning to free the RB-47 fliers who had been shot down on July 1, 1960, by a Soviet MIG over international waters near Murmansk. Burke's broadside against the Kremlin was an obvious threat to their freedom. I took the draft to Sorensen and Bundy, who agreed with me that the admiral should be told to tone down his remarks. The matter was never brought to JFK's attention.

Burke did soften his language but there was the inevitable leak to the press from his staff that the White House was muzzling the military—a charge that was to erupt into a full investigation. The fact of the matter, however, was that we had done nothing in this instance that was not done by the staffs of former Presidents. Burke's aide came to me with the speech—I didn't ask to see it—a clear indication that he was in the habit of doing this before JFK took office. (Earlier testimony before a congressional committee investigating freedom of information within the government showed that the Eisenhower administration also had its dif-ficulties with Admiral Burke. He was told to revise fourteen speeches or articles in 1956 alone.)

I met with the coordinating committee on Tuesday afternoons. We actually had two purposes. The first was to survey the latest executive policies and news developments within the many departments; to agree on the form and procedure for their release, and to range generally over questions of prime interest to the reporters covering the major departments.

These meetings served to inform all the top press officers of the govern-ment what was going on in the other departments. It also served as an excellent briefing session for me, and lessened the chances of my making a serious mistake in answering the questions of the press at my 11 A.M. and 4 P.M. daily press briefings.

Another end result was the passing on of information between the meetings. In this manner, the President and I often learned of plans by a government department that had not come to the attention of the White House, many of them contrary to the desires and interest of the President.

Of all the press officers who cooperated in this manner, one of the most outstanding was Arthur Sylvester. The Defense Department is a real labyrinth, and for any President or Secretary of Defense to keep on top of everything that is going on there is almost impossible. Sylvester's information to me about proposed activities of the Defense Department proved on occasion to be invaluable. For instance, he once reported to me that a plan was proceeding in the Defense Department to construct some nuclear testing sites for the United States in Alaska. When he gave me this information, the immediate thought came to my mind about the possible reaction of the Soviet Union to U.S. nuclear testing that close to their borders. I reported the matter to the President, who had never heard of the plan. A call from the President to Secretary of Defense McNamara (who had also not heard of the plan) brought the whole idea to a shuddering stop.

Another purpose of our weekly meetings was to prepare a briefing for the President for his press conferences.

Among the regular members on the committee were Bob Manning of State; Arthur Sylvester of Defense; Don Wilson of USIA; Dixon Donnelley of Treasury (now of State); Bill Lloyd of NASA; the late Duncan Clark of the Atomic Energy Commission; Stanley Grogan of CIA; and George Reedy representing Vice-President Johnson. I would enlarge the committee if another aspect of government was particularly hot at the moment. For instance, Ed Guthman of Justice would attend if civil rights were in the news and Rodney Leonard of Agriculture if farm legislation was in controversy.

Our briefing procedure—very similar to Hagerty's—was to agree among ourselves on the twenty or thirty questions the correspondents were most likely to ask the next day. The public information officers had a sharp instinct for what the press was thinking, and I can't recall a single major area of questioning they didn't anticipate. For questions in sensitive areas, we would prepare the text of an answer and an up-to-the-minute background briefing.

I would give the material to the President early in the evening and he would study it before going to bed. The next morning, with his top advisers present, we would go through a dry run at breakfast. The regulars were Vice-President Johnson, Secretaries Rusk and McNamara, Dr. Walter Heller, chairman of the Council of Economic Advisers, and Sorensen, O'Brien, Bundy, and Deputy Special Counsel Myer Feldman from the staff. I would sit directly across the table from JFK and fire the questions at him (between forkfuls of ham and eggs) in the language I thought the press would use. He might reply, "I can handle that one—let's move on." But, more often, he would give his answer and then invite comment from the appropriate Cabinet officer or staff member.

There were usually six or eight questions for which he required more facts, and I would start digging them up immediately after breakfast. The President almost always took a nap after lunch to increase his alertness for the press conference, which most often took place at 4 P.M. Bundy, Sorensen, and I would wake him around three, and run over the new information with him while he was dressing. The President and I would arrive at the State Department ten minutes before four. Rusk, State Under Secretary George Ball, and State press officer Manning would be waiting for us in a small room off the auditorium with the latest information off the State Department teletype. There was also a direct telephone line to the White House in case of a major, last-minute news break there.

Exactly at four, the President would stride onto the stage. I would follow, take a chair behind him and to his left, and keep a close watch on the wings in the event a story came over the teletype or telephone that he should announce immediately. I would also take notes on strictly provincial questions for which the President didn't have an answer—the award of a small defense contract or area redevelopment grant, for instance—and dig up the answer for the reporter when I got back to the office.

John F. Kennedy's first press conference—and the first in history to be heard and seen on live television—was held on January 25, 1961, in the auditorium of the new State Department Building. It was not at all the fiasco my tormentors at Palm Beach had prophesied.

This press conference, and the sixty-one to follow, were notable for their dignity and for the insight they gave the American people into the intelligence and wit of one of the most dramatic political personalities in our history. They were also to be the source of many of the most significant news breaks of our time. The top story at the first press conference was the Soviet Union's release of the RB-47 fliers. Captains Freeman B. Olmstead and John R. McKone, the only survivors of the reconnaissance plane's six-man crew. The Soviet action was an obvious gesture of friendship toward the new President, and was to signal, if only briefly, a hopeful new atmosphere in our relations with the Kremlin.

"I thought that went very well," were the President's first words to me as we drove back to the White House. "How many people do you think saw it?"

I said I didn't know. We would have to wait for the ratings. But it had to run over 50 million. (The actual count was 60 million.)

For a man who had given most of his adult life to politics and campaigning, in which the size of the crowds you attract is all important, the figure was staggering. He kept shaking his head. I knew he was eager to hear his wife's reaction. She had been watching at the White House. I never knew what she told him, but he was walking on air the next morning.

Preparations for the first press conference had begun late in December. I knew we had to find a new location because the Indian Treaty Room of the Executive Office Building, where Truman and Eisenhower had met the press, would be far too small.

The growth of the presidential press conference over the years has been phenomenal—and has changed drastically in character since Woodrow Wilson took the first step. Wilson was a great believer in the public having a role in public business and he instituted the practice of holding press conferences in his office twice a week. His press conferences were usually placid in nature, but on occasion he blew up at his questioners when they grew too persistent. "Damn it, man, can't you take me as you find me?" he once exclaimed at his press conference, but only a few moments later added: "Pardon me for blowing up." As his term of office wore on, Wilson abandoned the press conference. His successor, Warren G. Harding, reinstated them but instituted a rule that was to stay in effect for a long time thereafter—that nothing said at a presidential press conference could be quoted directly. Midway in his term he also established a rule that the questions at the press conference had to be submitted in advance. This rule was followed by Calvin Coolidge, who would open press conferences standing behind his desk with a stack of questions in his hand. Some he would throw on the floor. These were questions he would not answer. The others he answered, but frequently in a very laconic manner. It is interesting, in light of some of the disputes of today, that the Institute of Public Affairs, holding a meeting in Charlottesville, Virginia, in 1928, strongly condemned Coolidge for using the press for "propaganda purposes." President Hoover's press conferences, also in his office, and also under the Harding-Coolidge ground rules, diminished in number the longer he stayed in the White House. The first year he held a press conference almost every other week. His last year, the number dropped to a press conference a month.

Franklin Roosevelt started the presidency on the modern approach to press conferences. First, he held them with unfailing regularity twice a week in his office. Second, he began to avail himself of the new media of radio, with his "fireside chats." There were only thirty or forty reporters present at his press conferences—the number grew to 150 under Truman. For a time, Truman also held the press conferences in his office. But he finally switched them to the Executive Office Building. His announced reason was that the crowd was becoming too large. But old hands in the press corps insist that wasn't really why he did it. As Merriman Smith recalls it, "reporters who used fountain pens would shake them on his nice green rug when they clogged. So help me, that disturbed him very much."

Eisenhower stuck with the Indian Treaty Room because the attendance grew to 250 or more in his administration, far too many to handle in his office. JFK never had less than 400 reporters and photographers at the sixty-two press conferences he held in Washington. This, obviously, reflects the increasing importance of the President's office as a news source over the years. There were only a hundred correspondents accredited to the White House under Steve Early, FDR's first Press Secretary. I had to deal with more than 1200.

The auditorium at the new State building was ideal for our purposes. It was big enough to accommodate the maximum attendance we could expect. But we could reduce its size with partitions at the rear if attendance fell off. In this way, we would always have a "full house"—the only concession to TV showmanship to which I will plead guilty.

The President was always "up" for this half-hour challenge to his knowledgeability and poise and was always eager, afterward, for an appraisal of his performance. One local TV channel in Washington would tape the press conference and run it later in the evening. The President watched it whenever he could and was frequently critical both of himself and of the staging.

"I could have done better with that one" . . . "That's lousy lighting" . . . or "That camera angle murders me," were typical of his comments.

There was much criticism after the first press conference that we had deliberately suppressed the story on the release of the two fliers by the Russians in order that the President would have a blockbuster to announce.

The night before, David Wise of the New York *Herald Tribune* called me and said he had definite information the Soviets were going to free Captains Olmstead and McKone. Wise, one of the most enterprising reporters in Washington, had an exclusive story of momentous importance. The White House had learned just that day of the actual time Olmstead and McKone would be released. But we were also told by our embassy in Moscow that the Russians were insistent on simultaneous announcement of the story.

I leveled with Wise. I told him his story was correct but that its premature publication could very well blow the whole deal sky-high. "Let me call New York," he said. "I'll get back to you."

A nervous hour later, he was back on the line. He had spoken to Jock Whitney, the publisher of the *Herald Tribune*. The story would not run in their editions the next morning. Olmstead and McKone might still be in Lubiynka Prison if it hadn't been for the *Herald Tribune*'s willingness to kill the story in the national interest. We were to learn the next morning that the fliers *might* have been out of the Soviet Union before the

*Herald Tribune* broke the story. But they were held up twelve hours in Moscow because of a mechanical failure on the commercial airliner that was to fly them out.

When the President announced their release, they had been free only five hours.

I won't deny that the announcement was our biggest story at the first press conference, but we didn't suppress it earlier for that reason, as certain newsmen—Wise not among them—were to charge later.

Nor was it later true that we deliberately "saved" the most important news for the President to announce in the dramatic atmosphere of the press conference. The transcripts show that his opening statements—if they were the top story of the day—were almost always on developments of that same day. In fact, more often than not, it was the give-and-take of the questions and answers, not the President's opening announcements, that gave the correspondents their biggest story. I will admit to planting infrequent questions myself that might result in banner headlines and radio and TV news bulletins. I would simply call a reporter into my office and tell him that if he were to ask a certain question that day "you will receive a most interesting answer." And he always did. I had two reasons for doing this. First, a presidential pronouncement often appears more newsworthy if the press draws it out of him than if he volunteers it himself. Second, the reporters don't do as much homework for the press conference as the President. He would often come prepared to answer a question of major significance, but no one would ask it. It was important to us not only that he have the chance to express himself on such questions, but that the form of the question would elicit the exact answer he had ready.

Ed Folliard often came into my office on his own. "Here's a question I'm going to ask your man today," he would say. "You had better have him ready for it."

Folliard was one of the old-timers who recognized the press conference for what it was—an opportunity to give his readers the most direct possible access to the President's thinking. He wasn't there to catch the President off-guard, or to engage in a public debate with him. He was there to get an accurate response to his questions. The best way to do that was to let the President know in advance what was coming and give him a chance to develop the fullest possible answer.

In contrast, certain other reporters came only with questions their Republican publishers had given them—most of them hostile.

Such questions were always of the "Do you still beat your wife?" genre, and were easy to spot. Here are two examples:

On January 15, 1962: "It's been more than four months since the Soviets began their series of nuclear tests in the atmosphere, and I think you would agree it would only be imprudent to assume that they are not preparing further tests. Can you discuss what the overriding considerations are to cause us to give this potential enemy a gift of that length of time, and can you also tell us when we may expect a decision on your part in this matter?"

The President answered the question fully: "Well, as you know, we have tested underground, so that in talking about the gift of time, that matter should be taken into consideration. Secondly, of course, we were negotiating at the table of Geneva when the Soviet Union, after many months of preparation, began its tests.

"I have announced that we are making our preparations to conduct atmospheric testing if it's considered to be in the public interest when those preparations are completed. So that it's wholly impossible for a free country like the United States, with a free press, to prepare in secret the extensive—make extensive preparations which would be necessary, at the same time we are conducting a very important and vital negotiation. So that the Soviet Union has that advantage. They have advantages as a dictatorship in this cold war struggle. But they have very serious disadvantages, and I think that we have to balance them one against the other."

On April 11, 1962: "Sir, what are you going to do about the American soldiers getting killed in Vietnam?"

To this question the President gave really the only answer he could: "Well, I'm extremely concerned about American soldiers who are in a great many areas in hazard. We are attempting to help Vietnam maintain its independence and not fall under the domination of the Communists. The government has stated that it needs our assistance in doing it. It's very—and it presents a very hazardous operation, in the same sense that World War II, World War I, Korea—a good many thousands and hundreds of thousands of Americans died. But we cannot desist in Vietnam."

Still other reporters, eager to appear on the news panel shows out of Washington, would be deliberately argumentative to attract attention to themselves.

Looking back on it now, the decision to open the press conference to live TV was a proper one. President Johnson, to be certain, doesn't use the format as often as President Kennedy did, but for reasons that have nothing to do with its effectiveness. He simply feels more comfortable—and more communicative—in a less hectic atmosphere.

Most of the pencil and paper reporters now concede that they were wrong—that live TV brought about none of the dire consequences they thought it would. Ironically, many of the reporters who were most opposed to the format in 1960 are now the most adamant in insisting that LBJ should use it more often.

There can be no question that it was *right* for JFK. The ideas and philosophy of the man were best displayed during those moments of truth when he stood alone before millions of his countrymen to answer the questions of greatest moment to their lives and their very survival. Lacking the memoirs JFK would surely have written, the transcripts of his press conferences become his most revelatory legacy. They reveal as much about the man as they do about his ideas. His grasp of the infinite detail of government; his studied refusal to look at problems in over-simple terms; his quickness of mind; his capacity for righteous anger; and his quick humor are all clearly evident.

There will always be doubt, of course, whether live television accomplished one of the principal advantages I saw in it—a powerful propaganda tool the President could use to sell his domestic policies in the face of formidable opposition in both the press and in Congress. Certainly, he lost as many major skirmishes as he won on the domestic front. But I'm convinced, in my own mind, that his batting average would have been much lower without the new format.

I believe, too, that President Johnson was able to push through Congress as much of the New Frontier legislation as he did because of the educational groundwork laid by JFK.

One particular televised press conference of the President opened up another—and highly exciting—vista. It was the only press conference of the President carried live to Europe by the communication satellite, Telstar.

If anyone has any doubts that the installation of a full communications satellite system is going to revolutionize the world from an information standpoint, they have only to see what happened on this particular occasion.

During the first months of the administration, the President had been asked a number of times whether he was going to devalue the American dollar or raise the price of gold. He had emphatically denied both of these rumors, with absolutely no effect on foreign gold markets.

On the occasion of this particular press conference, the President was again asked the same question. He gave the same answer: no devaluation, no rise in the gold price. The results on the London gold market were staggering. They caused an immediate break in London gold prices as investors and speculators saw the President in person, live on television, making the statement.

Thousands of words written in newspapers had not had this effect, but the sight of the President making the statement did.

President Kennedy was amazed by the reaction his words had in England. But it also proved to him that a President of the United States could bring about massive support for his policies, if only he could be seen and heard directly. It made him a full supporter of the communications satellite concept—which is now rapidly progressing toward reality.

It is ironic that the President was scheduled to speak live to the people of Japan via the Syncom satellite on November 23, 1963—the day after he was assassinated.

I can't resist ending this chapter with Bill Lawrence, who gave me the roughest time of it at my disastrous press conference in Palm Beach when I first announced we were going live. For weeks afterward, as a Washington correspondent for the New York *Times*, he continued to insist that it was a mistake of historic proportions.

But one day in late May 1961, Bill came into my White House office breathing fire. JFK was leaving in a day or two for his first presidential visit to Europe.

"I'm not going with you," Bill said. "The paper's decided to let our correspondents over there handle the story." He was hot. "If I had a good job offer today, I'd quit."

After he left the office, I remembered that Hagerty, now in charge of ABC's TV and radio news operation, was very high on Lawrence and had told me he was going to try to hire him away from the *Times*. I called Hagerty in New York. "If you want Lawrence," I said, "I think today's the day."

Hagerty spoke to Lawrence that same afternoon and before the day was over he had signed a contract as ABC's White House correspondent and political editor. I took fiendish delight in the situation. How could Lawrence, now a TV reporter, justify his former position that TV cameras didn't belong at a presidential press conference?

Obviously he couldn't and didn't try to, and it wasn't long before he was willing to joke with me about it.

# IX

## DISASTER IN CUBA

My awareness of the first major crisis of the Kennedy administration began quietly enough with a telephone call from the President.

JFK's voice was grave. "I want you to stick close to home tonight, Pierre. You may have some inquiries from the press about a military affair in the Caribbean. If you do, just say that you know only what you've read in the newspapers."

My telephone rang again at three-thirty in the morning. This time it was the Army duty officer in the Situation Room at the White House. At that very hour, the first units of an exile brigade were invading Castro's Cuba. To avoid the appearance of extraordinary activity at the White House, I was not to come in until my usual hour.

The President's cryptic call was my first *official* knowledge of the Bay of Pigs. I was never present at the top-level conferences that led to his decision to unleash the rebel forces; nor did he, or other administration participants, ever take me into their confidence. Apart from the obvious fact that I was not one of his military advisers, there were good reasons for excluding me from the discussions. I was in daily contact with hundreds of the shrewdest reporters in the world. If I was not aware of the covert operation, I could not be drawn into a dialogue at my press briefings that might confirm the correspondents' suspicions. Also, I would never be in a position where I would have to lie to the press to protect the secrecy of the operation. I found out later that no information officer in government, not even those in State, the CIA, or the Pentagon, was aware that the invasion was shaping up. Security, in Washington at least, was airtight.

Because I was not a party to the Bay of Pigs decision, I will not attempt a post-mortem on the motives and competence of those who did advise the President. Short of conceding the obvious, that the operation was a fiasco of the first order from start to finish, I will leave it to those who did participate to write the sorry history of their proceedings. I will deal only with those events in which I did play a part—events that were to have a damaging effect on JFK's future relations with the American press.

To declare in mid-April of 1961 that I knew nothing of an impending military action against Cuba except what I read in the newspapers or heard on the air was to claim an enormous amount of knowledge.

Reports had begun appearing that the United States was training a brigade for military action against Castro as early as October 1960—three months before President Kennedy took office. The first article had appeared in a Guatemalan newspaper, *La Hora*, and had swiftly been followed by stories in *The Nation*, *Time*, the New York *Times*, and other U.S. newspapers.

In the weeks before the invasion, hardly a day passed without a story appearing in some newspaper, or broadcast over some radio or television station. It is fair to say that some of the press went after the story as if it were a scandal at city hall, or a kidnaping—not a military operation whose entire success might depend on the elements of surprise and secrecy. Newsmen sought out Cuban refugees in cafes and hotel lobbies in Miami to pump them for the latest news from relatives serving with the brigade. Through such "enterprise," they were able to publish much information of tactical importance, including exact estimates of the brigade's strength.

The volatile leaders of the Cuban Revolutionary Council in exile—the political arm of the brigade—were just as heedless of security. Only nine days before the landing, the council's president, Dr. José Miró Cardona, told the press in Miami that an uprising against Castro was "imminent." And the very next day, he appealed to Cubans still in their homeland to take up arms against the dictator. The only information Castro didn't have by then was the exact time and place of the invasion.

JFK was livid. He said to me in his office a week before the invasion: "I can't believe what I'm reading! Castro doesn't need agents over here. All he has to do is read our papers. It's all laid out for him." I left him, still not knowing that D-Day already was set.

My first involvement was on Saturday, April 15. That morning, eight B-26s flew a series of ineffectual bombing raids against air bases in Cuba, from Puerto Cabezas, Nicaragua. The pilots, of course, were rebels but the planes wore the insignia of Castro's air force. There was much consternation when two of them made emergency landings at Key West Naval Air Station and Miami International Airport. One pilot said he was a defector from the Cuban air force and had bombed his own base as he fled to freedom. The raid, of course, was the first and only pre-invasion air strike against Cuba and was undertaken with the full knowledge and consent of the President. But I didn't know that and told reporters at my press briefing that "our only information comes from the wire service stories we have read. We have no direct relations with Cuba and therefore have no firsthand information. We are trying to determine what the situation is."

Adlai Stevenson was as much in the dark as I was. Our chief delegate told the United Nations in New York that "these pilots and certain other crew members have apparently defected from Castro's tyranny." Castro promptly defied President Kennedy to bring the pilots before the UN. And Miró told the world that "spectacular things have begun to happen."

Governor Stevenson later told me that this had been the most "humiliating experience" of his years in government service. He was only partially mollified by President Kennedy's explanation that the failure to inform him of the true nature of U.S. involvement in the Bay of Pigs invasion was "a communications failure." Stevenson felt that he had been made a fool of, and that his integrity had been seriously damaged. One of the ironies of the matter was that Stevenson's very able public relations adviser, Clayton Fritchey, had been watching the articles in the New York *Times* about an impending attack on Cuba. He had become convinced that these accounts were authentic, and one evening over cocktails asked Stevenson if "you have been holding out on me?" Stevenson replied that he knew nothing and asked Fritchey if he had any facts. Fritchey replied that all he knew was what he read in the New York *Times*. Stevenson and Fritchey then contacted Arthur Schlesinger, Jr., who had the assignment at the White House for liaison with the United Nations. On the Saturday a week before the invasion, Schlesinger and a top operative of the CIA went to New York and gave Stevenson a partial briefing. Stevenson later told me, however, that "I was never told the full extent of the plan."

The stage was set for the least covert military operation in history.

The three days it took Castro to crush the rebels were the grimmest I can remember at the White House. Certainly, the Cuban missile crisis of the following year brought us much closer to war but the atmosphere then was of initiative and decision. Now, however, we could not influence the course of events, short of actual military intervention. We could only watch and wait—and the smell of disaster was in the air.

I saw the President five minutes after arriving at the White House on Monday morning, April 17. "We'll have no comment on what's happening down there," he said. "We're watching developments. That's *all*."

Over the next seventy-two hours I was in and out of his office at least a hundred times with the latest flashes off the wire service tickers. He was eager for news the first day. But as the reports from the beachhead became progressively worse, he would merely glance at the lead paragraphs, shake his head, and hand the copy back to me. JFK, who had been willing to risk his own life to save a single shipmate when *PT 109* was cut in half by a Japanese destroyer off the Solomons, felt a personal responsibility for every one of the fourteen hundred Cuban exiles who were facing Castro's jet planes and Russian-built tanks. He felt as much concern, then and later, for the lives and freedom of the invaders as he did for the shattering consequences of their defeat. This compassion was shown in his successful behind-the-scenes efforts the following spring to secure the freedom of most of the rebels in exchange for shipments of food and medicines to Castro.

The President sent for me on the afternoon of the third day. The rebels were short of food and ammunition and the end was in sight. A triumphant Castro was already claiming victory. The President had planned to spend the coming weekend on the aircraft carrier *Independence*, observing naval exercises off the coast of Florida. I had made arrangements for forty White House correspondents to accompany him.

"You had better let the press know we're canceling," he said. "I can't imagine a worse weekend to go cruising in the Caribbean." His face was drawn and ashen. "We really blew this one. How could that crowd at CIA and the Pentagon be this wrong?"

(While the President did make this statement privately to close associates, he was firm that as far as the public was concerned, failure of the operation was his responsibility and his alone. When Interior Secretary Stewart Udall later attempted to shift the blame to others, he reprimanded him seriously.)

He tried a wan smile. "I suppose the press has been giving you a bad time."

I told him no. In the past three days, I had had only a handful of questions on Cuba. The correspondents readily understood that whatever pronouncements the White House might have on the invasion would come in an official form, not in impromptu exchanges at my briefings.

"That was this week," he replied. "You wait. They're going to give us a hell of a pounding."

That night JFK had to go through the ordeal of the annual white tie congressional reception at the White House. He left his guests at midnight for a conference in the Cabinet Room with Secretaries Rusk and Mc-Namara, CIA Director Allen W. Dulles and his deputy, Richard M. Bissell, Jr., and General Lyman L. Lemnitzer, chairman of the Joint Chiefs of Staff. The CIA and Pentagon representatives said the rebel cause was hopeless unless JFK would commit our own forces. This had never been a part of the plan he had agreed to and he wouldn't buy it. The conference didn't end until 4 A.M. and Ken O'Donnell and I found ourselves alone with JFK in his office. He suddenly broke off the conversation and went outside. It was dark and there was a spring nip in the air. Ken and I stood at a window for the next forty-five minutes, watching him walk slowly around the south grounds of the White House.

The rebel brigade began surrendering the next morning.

The Bay of Pigs was JFK's first major defeat as President and the greatest disaster of his entire administration. He was to suffer the scorn not only of the Communist world but of the exiles themselves. Our own allies began to question the wisdom of his leadership. Neutral nations were now more receptive to overtures from the Kremlin. Castro was stronger than ever and would find Khrushchev more willing to listen to his plans for nuclear missiles to "defend" Cuba. But the crisis *that* would provoke was still eighteen months away. Another confrontation that arose from the Bay of Pigs had a much shorter fuse.

The adversaries were the President and the press and the issue was freedom of information. It was not a new fight at all—merely a resumption of the hostilities between Presidents and the press dating back to George Washington. There had been one hundred days of comparative calm—the cease-fire the press traditionally observes to allow a new President to study the battle terrain and deploy his forces. It came to an explosive end only ten days after the Bay of Pigs.

In the three years and two months I was Press Secretary to two Presidents, no single issue took more of my time and energies than freedom of information. My White House files on it were at least double those of the next largest classification. I wrote hundreds of letters responding to editors' and publishers' charges of censorship and news management; flew tens of thousands of miles to hear their grievances at press clubs and conventions; and met with their delegations in Washington—often with the President in attendance. But it all came to nothing. The struggle between the President and the press is irreconcilable and always will be as long as ours is a free and open society.

The press insists on its right to know and print what is happening in government. The President insists on his right to conceal or withhold information whose publication might threaten the national security. Generally, each respects the other's right. No responsible editor wants to reveal military secrets to the enemy. No responsible President wants to suppress non-secret information the people must have to participate intelligently in the decisions of government.

But the question is: *Who shall draw the line?* Is the press or the President the better judge of what is, or is not, inimical to the national interest? Only in wartime does the press defer, without too much argument, to the President. And that raises still another question: *Must there be an actual declaration of war or of national emergency before the President may invoke extraordinary controls on the flow of information?*

The press answers "yes"—there can be no justification for government secrecy in time of peace. The President answers "no"—a democratic society, if it is to survive in today's world, must be able to launch covert actions against its enemies.

JFK took the entirely realistic position that the cold war was never more than a moment away from flaring into a hot war. This being true —and what editor or publisher could dispute it?—our very survival could depend on our ability to maneuver secretly.

The Bay of Pigs demonstrated, as no other single event during the Kennedy administration, how difficult—if not impossible—it is for a free, open, and democratic society to mount a covert operation against an enemy that generally operates in secrecy.

It is possible to draw the conclusion from the events of the Bay of Pigs that a society such as that of the United States is not constituted to operate covertly. To accept this premise, however, is to admit that this country must always fight its battles with its enemies with one hand tied behind its back.

In the heat of the press-government battle which followed the Bay of Pigs, it was easy to draw the conclusion, as some newspapers did, that the President was trying to put the blame on the press for the failure of the operation. This was not his intent—and I know from many discussions with him that he did not lay the blame on the press. He was concerned, as any President involved in such an operation would have to be, with the amount of information which was printed in advance of the invasion. He thought some of the stories were irresponsible and aided the enemy.

The debate which ensued at the time of the Bay of Pigs, however, revolved around a basic disagreement about the self-discipline which should be maintained by the press in a democratic society in the interests of national security.

A host of constitutional and political factors loom behind the basic disagreement. While the First Amendment clearly guarantees the freedom of the press, it just as clearly does not require full disclosure by government. The President has powers of executive privilege that permit him to withhold information not only from the press but from the Congress.

Thus, the question finally gets down to what, for lack of a better phrase, has become the "right to know" of the American people.

This is, at best, a tricky doctrine. There are those who hold that the people have the "right to know" everything that their government does. It is obvious, however, that carried to its logical extreme, this philosophy would effectively deprive the government of one of its key weapons in the battle to protect itself—the "right of the enemy *not to know*." I do not think, in many instances, that the American people want to know facts, the publication of which would be inimical to the national interest. The Cuban missile crisis of 1962 demonstrated dramatically (and is discussed in detail later in this book) how the ability of the government to shroud its activities in secrecy for a limited amount of time can have a devastating effect on the enemy and result in a major victory for this country.

I do not mean to indicate a struggle between press and government is necessarily bad for our country because I think in the long run that the interplay has the effect of providing a check and balance system between two powerful institutions.

Of the two institutions, I find the press less introspective than the government. National governments, whether Democratic or Republican, are always participating in a kind of continuing self-analysis. The press as an institution does little of this. There are only two continuing studies of newspaper practices—the *Journalism Review* of Columbia University and the reports of the Nieman Foundation at Harvard University, neither of which has much circulation outside of the profession.

When it comes to the scrutiny of one of these institutions by the other —the press is far in front. The government, restrained by the First Amendment to the Constitution, has never attempted an effective study of the nation's press. In fact, it has shied away from even the implication that it might be considering such a study, like a mouse running away from an elephant. The press, on the other hand, has set up a formidable number of watchdog committees and associations to ride herd on the information policies of the government. There is the American Society of Newspaper Editors, the American Newspaper Publishers Association, the AP Editors Association, the UPI Editors Association, and Sigma Delta Chi, the national journalistic fraternity. In addition, the ASNE, the ANPA, Sigma Delta Chi, and the National Association of Broadcasters all have freedom of information committees that flood the White House with angry complaints of censorship. Such complaints, incidentally, are given a front-page play in many of the same newspapers that find nothing newsworthy in the Columbia and Harvard reports critical of journalistic ethics.

The most persistent and unreasonable critic of New Frontier information policies was V. M. (Red) Newton, Jr., managing editor of the Tampa (Florida) *Tribune* and chairman of Sigma Delta Chi's freedom of information committee. Newton saw a censor behind every tree in Washington and wrote literally dozens of protesting letters to me, to other information officers, and to the House Subcommittee on Freedom of Information. Most of his complaints were, from our point of view, baseless, but he was unwilling to accept even the most convincing evidence that he was wrong. I answered every one of his letters for exactly two years, then finally brought the frustrating exchange to an end.

"I do believe," I wrote him, "that under the pressures of today's world we should husband our energies for those activities which have some small hope of producing results. A review of our correspondence for the past two years leads me to the inescapable conclusion that any continuing correspondence would be fruitless. I do not see any sign in any of your correspondence of any willingness to see anybody's viewpoint but your own. This is indeed strange for a man who is supposedly concerned with freedom of information."

I never questioned Newton's sincerity, however. He honestly believed, as he wrote in his last letter, that "freedom of the press is no more" if American editors accept, without challenge, government's "management of the news."

In addition to the foregoing array of critics, the executive branch of government must also defend itself against a watchdog committee of the legislative branch. One of the most influential committees in Congress is the Special Government Information Subcommittee of the House Committee on Government Operations. Its chairman, Democrat John E. Moss of California, is a more redoubtable champion of freedom of information than most of the industry crusaders. Moss, however, generally withheld his fire until he had a substantive complaint against our policies and then was willing to listen to our side of it.

It is interesting to note that one of the organizations that does *not* have a freedom of information committee is the White House Correspondents Association—the reporters who must contend most directly with the information policies of the President. They rarely took part in the donnybrook. The most violent attacks on our press policies came, in most cases, from editors and publishers who never once set foot in the White House during the thirty-eight months I was there.

This was the background for the impending battle between JFK and many of the nation's most influential newspapers, magazines, and TV and radio commentators. Actually, there were warnings my first week at the White House that the "cease-fire" couldn't last very long. The decision that Admiral Burke should soften his verbal attack on the Soviet Union and our request that the New York *Herald Tribune* kill its advance story on the release of the RB-47 fliers were met with immediate complaints of censorship and news management. In both cases, we obviously were acting to protect the fliers but this fact didn't impress the editorial writers. I was very quickly in receipt of a letter from E. S. Pulliam, Jr., publisher of the Indianapolis *News* and chairman of the freedom of information committee of the American Society of Newspaper Editors. He had nine specific complaints, including the Admiral Burke affair ("Is this a change of policy?"); our request to the *Herald Tribune* ("Was this purely in the national interest or did it insure a better played story?"); and my weekly session with the ranking information specialists in government ("If it is for 'coordination,' doesn't that indicate censorship of their activities?").

"I hope you will believe me," he wrote, "when I say that I do not intend these questions to be carping or unfair. The committee of which I am now chairman has been attempting for years to make available more information to the American public. It has carried on its fight with Democratic and Republican administrations alike. We honestly feel that much information is being withheld, not for security reasons, but to protect individual mistakes and in a mistaken belief that 'What the people don't know won't hurt them.'"

My maiden speech as Press Secretary triggered the first exchange between the President and the press on the freedom of information issue. I told the National Press Club in Washington on January 25—just five days after JFK took office—that "we intend to have an open information policy *within the confines of national security.*" The sentence was exactly six words too long. Many of the correspondents read into it a forewarning of greater censorship, although I had intended just the opposite. But I had a valid reason for the qualifier—"within the confines of national security." That same week I had been shown a report by the Central Intelligence Agency, written during the Eisenhower administration, that was a shocker, to say the least. The CIA had assigned two college professors to the task of appraising America's entire defensive and retaliatory posture. These professors were to have access only to public documents, i.e., any documents which were generally available to the public. Their report was such an exact picture of our military capability that it was immediately classified "top secret"!

Five hours after my speech, the following question was thrown at JFK at his first press conference: "Press Secretary Salinger said today there might be a need for a tightening of information on national security. Doesn't the policy of deterrence require that the enemy have knowledge of our strength . . . and wouldn't there be a risk of possible miscalculation by tightening up information?"

The President replied that the enemy already had "very ample information" on which to base a determination of our strength. "I am anxious that we have a maximum flow of information but there quite obviously are some matters which involve the security of the United States, and it's a matter on which the press and the executive should attempt to reach a responsible decision."

From that point on, JFK was always willing to enter into negotiations with the press to reconcile their responsibilities with his own.

JFK was upset by the early sniping at our information policies. He felt, as I did, that reporters now had much freer access to the news than under his predecessors. Both he and his staff were now much more available for interviews and backgrounders. JFK's willingness to stand up before an audience of millions at his press conferences and answer the most sensitive questions involving foreign and domestic policy was another advance. The new status of the foreign press corps at the White House was improving both the quality and quantity of Washington news in other world capitals.

Anticipating a suspicious reaction to my weekly coordinating sessions with other administration press officers, I issued an open invitation to Congressman Moss to attend. He was at the first meeting and agreed that a close working relationship among top-level government information officers would enhance, not inhibit, the flow of information. It is worth noting, too, that early that first year Congressman Moss sent me a list of sixteen categories of executive information which had been withheld from the press under former administrations. Among them were suppression of polls taken among business leaders on the impact of pending tax legislation; the refusal of certain agencies to reveal the salaries of employees or to discuss contracts which had not gone to the lowest bidder; the insistence of certain advisory commissions on secret proceedings; and, generally, an overclassification of many files that would conceal them from the public for many years after the incumbent President had left office.

It was Congressman Moss' recommendation that we take a new look at the restrictions. We did and the wraps were promptly taken off all but four of the categories. Congressman Moss considered this a significant accomplishment by the Kennedy administration, and went out of his way to praise us in a report by his subcommittee.

But all of this was merely preliminary skirmishing. The major battle came the week after the Bay of Pigs. I must again preface what follows with the statement that JFK never tried to pass the buck for the disaster. The blame was his and he was willing to accept it ("Victory has one hundred fathers but defeat is an orphan").

The press' actions immediately following the disaster did nothing to improve the President's temper. He held a press conference on April 21—two days after the rebel surrender. There was still high-level concern in Washington over possible Soviet retaliation and the abrupt worsening of our relations with important allies, and JFK did not intend to be drawn into speculation that might prolong the crisis. "I know that many of you have further questions about Cuba," was his opening remark. "But I do not think that any useful national purpose would be served by my going into the Cuban question this morning . . ." Most of the reporters went along but one was insistent on knowing whether Secretary Rusk and Under Secretary of State Chester Bowles had been against the decision. JFK replied only that "the facts will come out in due time."

But back in his office later, the President had a more pungent comment.

"What the hell do they want me to do—give them the roll call vote? I can't go into that without compromising everybody involved and they ought to know that. If I'm going to knock some heads together, now isn't the time to do it with everybody looking down the barrel at us."

The A.M. newspapers were critical of his refusal to go into the Cuban question at his press conference, and he was still burning when I saw him in mid-morning.

"What could I have said that would have helped the situation at all? That we took the beating of our lives? That the CIA and the Pentagon are stupid? What purpose do they think it would serve to put that on the record?"

He shook his head. "We're going to have to straighten all this out, and soon. The publishers have to understand that we're never more than a miscalculation away from war and that there are things we're doing that we just can't talk about."

I then made a suggestion to the President that I would later regret. He was to speak six days later, on April 27, to the Bureau of Advertising of the American Newspaper Publishers Association at the Waldorf-Astoria in New York.

"Why not lay it on the line there?" I said. "It's a major forum and the timing will punch up the importance you assign to it. It could open up the whole area to serious discussion."

He agreed to do it and told me to relay my thinking on content to Ted Sorensen, who would write the speech. I gave Ted a long memo summarizing the freedom of information conflict between past Presidents and the press and outlining the steps we had taken to open up channels of information. He drafted a brilliant argument in support of the President's position, and one that will be as valid in the year 2061 as it was in 1961. It began with an admonition to the press that it must recognize "our common responsibilities in the face of a common danger: the totality of the Communist challenge to our survival and to our security . . .

"This deadly challenge imposes upon our society two requirements of direct concern both to the press and to the President—two requirements that may seem almost contradictory in tone, but which must be fulfilled if we are to meet this national peril. I refer, first, to the need for far greater public information; and, second, to the need for far greater official secrecy.

"The very word 'secrecy' is repugnant in a free and open society; and we are as a people inherently and historically opposed to secret societies, to secret oaths, and to secret proceedings . . . No official of my administration, whether his rank is high or low, civilian or military, should interpret my words here tonight as an excuse to censor the news, to stifle dissent, to cover up our mistakes, or to withhold from the press and the public the facts they deserve to know.

"But I do ask every publisher, every editor, and every newsman in the nation to re-examine his own standards, and to recognize the nature of our country's peril. In time of war, the government and the press have customarily joined in an effort, based largely on self-discipline, to prevent unauthorized disclosures to the enemy. In time of 'clear and present danger,' the courts have held that even the privileged rights of the First Amendment must yield to the public's need for national security.

"If the press is awaiting a declaration of war before it imposes the self-discipline of combat conditions, then I can only say that no war ever posed a greater threat to our security. If you are awaiting a finding of 'clear and present danger,' then I can only say that the danger has never been more clear and its presence has never been more imminent.

"It requires a change in outlook, a change in tactics, a change in missions—by the government, by the people, by every businessman or labor leader, and by every newspaper. For we are opposed around the world by a monolithic and ruthless conspiracy that relies primarily on covert means for expanding its sphere of influence—on infiltration instead of invasion, on subversion instead of elections, on intimidation instead of free choice, on guerrillas by night instead of armies by day. It is a system which has conscripted vast human and material resources into the building of a tightly knit, highly efficient machine that combines military, diplomatic, intelligence, economic, scientific, and political operations.

"Its preparations are concealed, not published. Its mistakes are buried, not headlined. Its dissenters are silenced, not praised. No expenditure is questioned, no rumor is printed, no secret is revealed. It conducts the cold war, in short, with a wartime discipline no democracy would ever hope or wish to match.

"Nevertheless, every democracy recognizes the necessary restraints of national security—and the question remains whether those restraints need to be more strictly observed if we are to oppose this kind of attack as well as outright invasion. For the facts of the matter are that this nation's foes have openly boasted of acquiring through our newspapers information they would otherwise hire agents to acquire through theft, bribery, or espionage; that details of this nation's covert preparations to counter the enemy's covert operations have been available to every newspaper reader, friend and foe alike; that the size, the strength, the location, and the nature of our forces and weapons, and our plans and strategy for their use, have all been pin-pointed in the press and other news media to a degree sufficient to satisfy any foreign power; and that, in at least one case, the publication of details concerning a secret mechanism whereby satellites were followed required its alteration at the expense of considerable time and money.

"The newspapers which printed these stories were loyal, patriotic, responsible, and well-meaning. Had we been engaged in open warfare, they undoubtedly would not have published such items. But in the absence of open warfare, they recognized only the tests of journalism and not the tests of national security. And my question tonight is whether additional tests should not now be adopted.

"Every newspaper now asks itself, with respect to every story: 'Is it news?' All I suggest is that you add the question: 'Is it in the interests of national security?' . . . And should the press of America consider and recommend the voluntary assumption of specific new steps or machinery, I can assure you that we will cooperate whole-heartedly with those recommendations . . ."

The reaction was violent. The press chose to ignore the content of the speech and to regard its timing—eleven days after the Bay of Pigs—as a presidential scolding for its pre-invasion reports on the training of the rebel brigade and the imminence of the landings. JFK was accused, in effect, of blaming the press for the outcome of the operation. Angry editorials across the country read into his speech a forewarning of official censorship or, at the very least, a demand for self-censorship. Still others took him to task for not revealing to the nation the full picture of our relations with Cuba. If he had, their argument went, he could have built public support for active American intervention at the Bay of Pigs, thus assuring the success of the invasion.

One of the most thoughtful, and least strident, of the editorials criticizing JFK ran in the Raleigh (North Carolina) News and Observer. Editor Jonathan Daniels wrote me: "I don't think any editor in America has been more enthusiastic in his support of President Kennedy and his program than I have been. I am eager to help in the things I believe he can do for America and the world. But, quite frankly, I was deeply disturbed by his remarks to the publishers in New York . . ."

His editorial led off with the comment: ". . . President Kennedy could not have chosen a worse time to lecture the press for a lack of 'self-restraint' in printing the news. His remarks to American publishers came hot on the heels of disclosures that, unknown to the press and the public, this country has been involved in a military adventure which not only cost the lives of many of our friends but also made this nation look both hypocritical and ineffectual in the eyes of the world.

"Undoubtedly, where a free press exists in a free country, facts may be published which will carry information to an enemy in whose country a strictly censored press keeps much hidden from the people and the world. Freedom does involve dangers which totalitarianism can avoid. And even in a free country dangers may sometimes justify the suppression or censorship of news. When and where that is necessary, the American press has shown that it will cooperate. No owners or operators of the news media, however, have any right—let alone any 'duty'—to decide what the people should know . . . President Kennedy should be thinking more about how the free, informed American people can contribute to the struggle, not how 'greater official secrecy' can be imposed upon them with the connivance of reporters and officials together . . ."

Daniels is one of America's great editors but even he was unwilling to enter into a dialogue with the President on how a free society can protect itself from its enemies and, at the same time, protect the people's right to know what their government is doing.

I had given JFK bad advice. The timing of his remarks, as Daniels wrote, could not have been worse. But he was still determined that the issue was critical to the national security and that another attempt should be made to open the dialogue. At his invitation, seven of the country's top newspaper executives met with him on May 9, ten days after his New York address. They were Mark Ferree, president of the American Newspaper Publishers Association and assistant general manager of the Scripps-Howard chain; Felix McKnight, president of the American Society of Newspaper Editors and executive editor of the Dallas *Times-Herald*; Lee Hills, president-elect of the ASNE and the Pulitzer Prize-winning executive editor of the Knight chain; Turner Catledge, managing editor of the New York *Times*; Ben McKelway, president of AP and editor of the Washington *Star*; Irwin Maier, publishing director of the Milwaukee *Journal*; and D. Tennant Bryan, publisher of the Richmond (Virginia) *Times Dispatch* and Richmond *News Leader*.

The conference in the President's office was a total failure. Although JFK produced a number of recent news dispatches that clearly violated national security, the news executives told him bluntly that they would accept no new security restrictions—voluntary or official—in the absence of a declaration of national emergency. The President replied that the cold war was a continuing emergency and that the requirement for greater restraint should be obvious.

One of the examples President Kennedy showed to the assembled editors was particularly revealing. An article published in a leading American newspaper completely informed its readers (and presumably the enemy) how the United States was getting intelligence on Soviet space operations, intelligence which permitted the United States government to know in advance when the Soviets were going to make a launch.

Looking back on the meeting, I am sure that a communications breakdown was involved. Either the President failed to make his point strongly enough, or the press misunderstood his objective. In any event, he elicited no favorable reaction from the newsmen present.

The President then made a specific proposal. He was willing to let the publishers appoint their own representative to come to Washington as their adviser on information affecting the national security. If newspapers were uncertain whether a story would betray our defense secrets to the enemy, they would submit it to their own representative. He, in turn, would be given a full briefing on the subject by appropriate officials in the White House, the CIA, the State Department, or the Pentagon. He would then tell the publisher whether he thought the story should or should not run. But the publisher would be under no compulsion to accept his advice.

Again, the delegation saw no merit in the President's approach. In fact, one or two of the executives later denied he even made a specific suggestion. "As I recall it," McKelway told reporters, "the President made some casual reference to the idea of establishing an authority of some sort empowered to answer queries from newspapers as to whether information they planned to print would violate security. He did not propose, however, to establish any such machinery and the newspapermen offered no comment on the idea. Had the President advanced such a proposal, it is my impression that some member of the newspaper committee would have suggested that experience in World War II demonstrated that no form of voluntary censorship would be effective without censorship of outgoing mail and news dispatches from the United States."

In other words, even if JFK had pursued the question further, the executives were in no mood to listen. He had no right, apparently, even to suggest that the press was not entirely responsible—and omniscient—in its handling of highly sensitive information. (I could cite many cases in which the press was entirely irresponsible in such matters. One was the advance disclosure of the exact position we would take at the Geneva conferences on a nuclear test ban treaty earlier that same year. This gave the Soviet negotiators a distinct advantage even before we sat down at the table.)

If the press had accepted President Kennedy's suggestion, we would still have been presented with some very serious problems. On one occasion during the Kennedy administration we had cooperated with a reporter who was writing a story on a very sensitive subject. His story came back to my office and to the Defense Department for clearance. The memorandum I received from the Defense Department indicated that the article was highly inaccurate. "In order to correct the mistakes, however, we will be forced to divulge some of the nation's innermost secrets," the Defense Department wrote me. We finally had to make the choice in favor of letting the story go out inaccurately, rather than compromising national security.

As a former reporter and editor myself, I respect and understand the press' resistance to all forms of censorship—voluntary or official. To deprive the American newspaper of its right to inquire freely into the activities of government is to deny to its readers the information they must have to form the consensus without which no government can successfully move toward its goals. But I cannot agree with JFK's critics that self-restraint is the equivalent of censorship. The effect of our early information policies was to increase the amount of information available to the press. The President's only caveat was that the greater accessibility of information should call for greater restraint in its use—particularly in a time of national peril.

The question he put to the publishers, in effect, was this: Can we not sit down together and discuss ways in which an open society can de-

fend itself against the covert operations of a secret society without re-
stricting unnecessarily the people's right to know?

Their answer was no. The President saw the futility of further overtures
to the publishers after the May 9 conference in his office and the question was left up in the air—to explode with far greater violence during
the Cuban missile crisis the following year.

# X

## THE WHITE HOUSE GOES OVERSEAS

When the average American goes on a trip, he stops delivery of the milk and the newspaper, bundles his family and luggage in the car, and takes off. But when the President of the United States travels, the White House travels with him. He must be able to do everything in Paris, Caracas or Vienna that he can do at 1600 Pennsylvania Avenue. This requires him to take along more than two hundred traveling companions, including Cabinet officers, staff members, translators, Secret Service agents, secretaries, military advisers, mail handlers, and the throng of reporters and photographers who regularly cover the White House.

A presidential visit overseas has many of the elements of a military operation: aerial and ground reconnaissance, secret intelligence reports, logistics, consultations with our allies, communications, and security. But even a brief trip to San Francisco calls for thousands of hours of planning by hundreds of government employees.

Preparations for a presidential trip are known as "advancing"—a lively art that demands a sturdy constitution, a flair for diplomacy, and a love for traveling under the most chaotic of circumstances. In the campaign of 1960 (a training ground for later presidential trips) JFK's junkets around the country were advanced by a crew of young lawyers and other professionals. A majority of them were volunteers who left high-paying positions to work for nothing. The work was that exciting and challenging. The best of the lot was Jerry Bruno, a compact little dynamo who had grown up in the maelstrom of Wisconsin politics. We first met him in the Wisconsin primary and, after the convention in Los Angeles, he came with us as a full-time advancer. Immediately following JFK's victory over Richard Nixon, he went to the Democratic National Committee in Washington to organize the President's key domestic trips. It is ironic that Bruno, who was responsible for many of JFK's most successful tours, was also the chief advancer for Dallas.

In a campaign, members of the advance party move into a city three or four days before the arrival of the candidate. Their first chore is to see to it that the host committee is doing all it can to turn out massive crowds. But they must also weigh the candidate's personal exposure against the local political realities and his responsibility to the rest of the ticket. Should he, for instance, cut short a mass rally on a university campus to drive to a small event in the suburbs to put his arm around a sagging congressional candidate? In many cities, there are rival Democratic factions who insist on running the show. Each may threaten a walk-out unless it has its way in such matters as who shall head the reception line at the airport or ride in the same car with the candidate in the motorcade. One clique might insist on hosting a $1000 per person reception for the candidate at the exact hour he is due to huddle with leaders of the opposing faction. The advance party must decide which event to attend. (The fund-raiser almost always wins out.) Bruno was a genius at finding his way through the mine fields of local politics. But crowds and events were only a small part of his work. He had to survey the parade routes himself to arrive at the closest possible estimate of driving time—and to be certain the candidate had a strong billboard showing along the way. Nothing distresses a candidate more than to find his opponent's confident face smiling at him from lofty elevations all over town. (When Lyndon B. Johnson came to Los Angeles shortly before the election in 1964, his California advertising director, James P. Keene, shrewdly bought twelve full-color Johnson-Humphrey boards on the motorcade route into the city. There wasn't a single Goldwater-Miller board to compete. LBJ was ecstatic but what he didn't know is that Keene had bought only a one-day showing. The posters were taken down the same afternoon.) JFK frequently flew from one point in a city to another by helicopter. The landing or take-off points might be a park, a campus, or even the grounds of an estate. Bruno had to arrange for the lowering of utility lines in the area and a suspension of all other low-level air traffic. Much of his time was spent with law-enforcement officials agreeing on crowd control, around-the-clock police protection, and the assignment of motorcycle officers to serve as couriers. He was also responsible for hotel reservations, luggage, transportation, and even laundry service for the candidate, his staff, and more than one hundred traveling press. To top it off, he had to supervise the installation of special telephone systems in the headquarters hotel, along the parade routes, and in stadiums and auditoriums where the candidate would appear. He also was responsible for setting up press headquarters, complete with typewriters, stationery, and local fact sheets for the traveling press— and for issuing press credentials to the horde of local newsmen and photographers. And, always, there was an army of minor candidates demanding to have their pictures taken with JFK and just as many contributors demanding "a moment alone" with the candidate to shake his hand.

At least one writer would accompany the advance party to draft "local inserts" for the candidate's speeches. He would prepare specific data on how the regional economy was suffering under the Republican administration—tariff policies that were damaging to exports of a local crop or procurement policies that had cost a local defense industry an important contract. The writer would also scan the hometown newspapers for stories on which the Senator might comment, and develop a humorous introduction that would have particular meaning to local voters and politicians.

I was one of the advance writers for Adlai Stevenson in California in 1952, working under John Bartlow Martin (whose decision to work for Adlai Stevenson the second time around in 1956, instead of writing the Teamster exposé for *Collier's*, was directly responsible for my joining the Kennedys). Martin was also the chief advance writer for JFK, and his local speech inserts were often given a bigger play in the press of that city than the central theme of the address.

Twenty-four hours before JFK flew into town, Bruno would prepare a minute-by-minute memorandum of activities, almost as intricate as the table of organization for a large-scale invasion. On arrival, the candidate and his traveling staff would assume command. Larry O'Brien, for instance, would ride herd on all the political functions, and I would take over the press operation. By that time, Bruno was hedge-hopping to another state to perform his miracles all over again.

But there were always foul-ups it was impossible to anticipate. The advance man for JFK's last trip to Los Angeles in 1960 was Vincent Gaughan, a brilliant young Buffalo lawyer—and a confetti addict. To Vince, a parade just wasn't a parade unless there was a constant snowfall of confetti from the beginning of the procession to the end. But he overdid it in Los Angeles. Literally tons of confetti were distributed to office workers in the downtown district the morning of the motorcade, and visibility was cut to almost zero as it came pouring out of windows onto the lead cars of the parade. JFK was hip-deep in ground-up telephone books.

Suddenly, disaster struck! A spark from one of the motorcycles in the police escort ignited the thick layer of paper in the street and the conflagration spread to the press bus. The reporters fled through emergency doors while the police escort, with sirens wailing, cut JFK's limousine out of the procession and sped down a side street. The police, unaware of the cause of the fire, had taken the precaution out of fear that the incident might have been a diversion for an attempt on the candidate's life. But this didn't soothe the tempers of the reporters, who weren't able to catch up with the official party until more than an hour later. The crowds lining the parade route that day were the largest in Los Angeles' history. But that important fact was buried under the more spectacular news that JFK's parade had caught fire.

Bruno and Gaughan took all such disasters in stride, however, and always left for their next assignment supremely confident that *this* timetable would work out to the split second. It never did.

JFK never forgot the disasters along the campaign trail—or the advance men who were responsible. In 1959, even before he was an announced candidate for President, he went to Oakland, California, for a speech in Jack London Square. Don L. Bradley, one of the shrewdest political brains in America and one of my closest friends, was in charge of the event. We had hoped for a crowd of five hundred but only thirty-five were waiting to hear the junior senator from Massachusetts. Late the following year, when Bradley was turning out massive and enthusiastic crowds the whole length of California, JFK would always turn to him and say: "This is a little better than Oakland, Don."

President Kennedy was the first to recognize the contribution that Bruno, Gaughan, and other advancers had made to his victory, but he took a perverse pleasure in pointing out to them that he campaigned in Alaska and lost it, but didn't go to Hawaii and carried it.

"Just think what my margin might have been if I had never left home!"

Advancing obviously became even more complex after JFK became President. The Secret Service now took an active hand in planning his visits, both at home and abroad. The presidential plane could not land at an airport until the sky was clear of all other traffic for many miles around. The limousine waiting on the ramp to carry him into town was given a last-minute security check down to the last nut and bolt. His route into the city was now chosen not only for its crowd potential but for its safety. At banquets, there was constant surveillance in the kitchen of the food he would eat and an advance security check on the waiters who would serve it. There was always an inspection of the amplifiers for the public address system under the rostrum to be certain they didn't contain a bomb.

But security and all other elements of advancing were much more difficult and extensive when the President was planning a visit abroad. Ken O'Donnell, JFK's Appointments Secretary, was in charge of all advancing. He had the final word, subject to the President's approval, on events, time schedules, and routes. I was responsible for press arrangements. Communications planning was under the direction of Army Colonel George McNally of the White House Communications Agency, and Secret Service Chief James Rowley was the security specialist. The advance party, never smaller than twenty-five, would also include State Department experts on the country we were visiting, translators, and protocol authorities.

We always flew in the President's Boeing 707, known as *Air Force One*. There was a requirement that the pilot, Colonel James Swindal, had to land the huge jet at least once at every foreign and domestic airport on the route. His radio crew also had to practice their multi-lingual communications with the control towers. While they were rehearsing landings and take-offs, the rest of us would head for the U. S. Embassy to assault the mountain of work awaiting us. *Air Force One* had the exterior appearance of a commercial 707, but it was actually an airborne executive suite and communications center. It had the most modern communications receiving and transmitting equipment available, including radio telephones with which the President could communicate almost instantly not only with the White House but with our embassies around the world or a battlefield commander in Vietnam. The amazing capability of this equipment was first brought to my attention on our first advance trip to Europe in May 1961 to prepare for the President's visits to Charles de Gaulle, Nikita Khrushchev, and Harold Macmillan. *Air Force One* was circling Orly Field in Paris when my telephone rang. Ted Sorensen was on the line from the White House.

"Pierre, I have a problem you can help me with. Could you step into my office for a minute?"

"Do you have any idea where I am, Ted?"

"No," he replied, "I just told my secretary to get you on the line."

"Well, she got me all right. I'm in *Air Force One*, looking down on Paris."

The communications section of the plane was just behind the pilot's cabin. The next compartment to the rear was the President's suite, including a small bedroom and private lavatory. Aft of that was a larger cabin with two big conference tables at which JFK held staff meetings. This section also had hi-fi and television sets. The TV reception was excellent, even at 30,000 feet, but we had to switch channels frequently. We were in and out of range of the short TV signal very quickly at 600 miles an hour. The next compartment to the rear was an office for the staff. In the tail section were accommodations for the Secret Service and a fully equipped kitchen. Our meals were actually cooked aloft by a crew of Air Force stewards.

Extraordinary precautions were taken to protect the President's life on trans-oceanic flights. A Navy ship was positioned every two hundred and fifty miles along *Air Force One*'s route in the event of a ditching; scores of planes stood by at coastal bases to join the search, if necessary; and Coast Guard weather ships in mid-ocean were constantly communicating the latest meteorological information to Colonel Swindal.

The French advance was a model of those to follow. We spent only two days in Paris but were kept hopping from meeting to meeting eighteen hours a day. There were literally thousands of decisions we had to agree on with our French hosts. Who would be in the welcoming party with General de Gaulle at the airport and in what order would they stand in the receiving line? This was a matter for U. S. Chief of Protocol Angier Biddle Duke and his French counterpart to work out. Where and in what numbers would the overseas and American press have direct access to the two chiefs of state, and who would prepare and issue their joint communiqué? Pierre Baraduc, press officer for the French Foreign Ministry, and I would hassle this out, each trying to negotiate a deal favoring the newsmen from our own country. What affairs of state would be held? This was an assignment for O'Donnell and de Gaulle's top advisers. When and where would the two principals confer on international questions and what would the agenda be? This was in the province of policy experts from our State Department and the French Foreign Ministry. Where would the President and Mrs. Kennedy stay? The French were refurbishing the palatial living quarters in the Quai D'Orsay, headquarters of the Foreign Ministry, but our Secret Service had to approve. Ken and I went with Rowley to check out the accommodations. (My one enduring recollection is of a solid gold tub in the President's bathroom.) We also had to inspect arrangements at the Elysée Palace and Versailles, where state dinners would be held, and at the Arc de Triomphe, where the President and General de Gaulle would rekindle the flame at the tomb of France's Unknown Soldier.

Mrs. Kennedy also had an elaborate schedule of her own. Her social secretary, Letitia (Tish) Baldrige, and Press Secretary, Pam Turnure, were with the advance party to handle her arrangements, down to the choice of a hairdresser and manicurist.

Press headquarters were to be in the Crillon Hotel, next to the American Embassy. In addition to reserving space for more than one hundred White House correspondents and photographers who would accompany us, I had to set up a press room off the main lobby and arrange for the installation of a battery of teletypes and long-distance telephones to speed the news of the conference back to the states. In Paris, as in all other capitals, the press coverage of official parades was my biggest headache. It is, of course, customary for the President and the receiving head of state to ride in the first car with a security car directly behind it. But after that, there are no firm rules. At home, it was my practice to have the press pool car third in line. But in Europe, foreign ministers and the nobility deeply resented mere reporters riding ahead of them in the parade. Baraduc and I finally won our point and pool reporters from AP and UPI, the leading American news services, and Agence France Presse, the major French news agency, rode with us in the third car. The press buses, containing hundreds of other reporters and photographers, were an even thornier issue. Most of the overseas arrangements committees would try to place them at the tail end of the procession, where the newsmen could see nothing and would be caught in the dispersing crowds and miss the next event. We were able to position the buses near the front in Paris but in other capitals I frequently lost the argument. This invariably led to angry charges from the American correspondents that I had been too soft in standing up for their rights.

But their rage was beyond belief when the reporters chosen to ride in the pool car didn't honor their obligation to report fully to their colleagues in the buses. There was a firm understanding that correspondents chosen for the pool would write a summation as quickly as possible and post it on the bulletin board in the press room. When such reports were late, the deadline-frantic newsmen would go off looking for their errant "representatives"—and often found them in their hotel rooms calmly reporting the story to their own newspapers. I must add that the pool reporters from AP and UPI were never guilty of this. But those who were seldom got another pool assignment from me. Similarly, a pool photographer had an obligation to share his pictures with the other lensmen. When he didn't, there were bitter recriminations against me and outright violence against the offender. During the Vienna visit, *Life* photographer Paul Schutzer felled Jacques Lowe of *Newsweek* with one punch for allegedly failing to respect this agreement.

While Ken and I were negotiating arrangements for the President and the press, Rowley was conferring with the police and military on security for the two heads of state. I can recall only one time when there was too much security, if that's possible. On the President's visit to Caracas in 1961, Venezuelan security chief Dr. Carlos Andres Perez was determined not to have a repeat of the stone-throwing violence against Richard Nixon there in 1958. Fixing his cold gray eyes on Ken and me at one of the advancing conferences, Perez said: "I can assure you, Señor O'Donnell, that your President will be safe in Venezuela. I have taken the necessary steps." He certainly had. More than four thousand politically suspect Venezuelans were thrown into jail for the duration of JFK's visit, and twenty thousand troops, with bayonets at the ready, stood facing the crowds along the parade route from the airport. Perez was not alone in his concern, however. O'Donnell and Dave Powers of the White House staff both carried revolvers and were constantly at the President's side in Venezuela. Rowley's security requirements in Paris weren't that formidable but he did have to approve arrangements for the deployment of thousands of French police and troops at the airport, along the parade routes, at the Quai D'Orsay, and at the public buildings where JFK would appear.

Simultaneously, Colonel McNally of the Communications Agency was preparing for a complex telephone system to serve the President and his staff. Each of us had a special telephone in our room that was connected not only with all other extensions of the visiting party in Paris but directly with the White House switchboard in Washington. We also had our own switchboards at the Crillon and the Quai D'Orsay with their own outside number. When it rang, the operator—a member of the Communications Agency—would answer: "Paris White House."

When the President is overseas, the local communications system must be able to absorb an increase in long-distance telephone and telegraph traffic running up to tens of thousands of messages a day. Paris could handle this easily but the situation was far different on our later visit to Caracas. The Venezuelan capital simply didn't have enough telephone and telegraph lines to keep up with the demands of the press and the presidential party. But this didn't stump the White House Communications Agency. An SOS was sent to the Navy and a communications ship took up a position six miles off the coast. Official government telephone calls were relayed to Washington through a naval communications center in Maryland, outside of the District of Columbia, with practically no loss of time. Reams of copy from the reporters were flown to the ship by helicopter, then radioed to the States.

But the sternest challenge the Communications Agency ever had to face was on President Eisenhower's trip to Brasilia in 1960. The new capital of Brazil had virtually no telephone system at all. The Communications Agency had to put up poles, string wire, and fly switchboards to the city. The system is still operating in Brasilia and serves as the core of its communications network. The officer in charge, Major Jack Rubley, won Brazil's highest civilian decoration for his efforts.

The work of the advance team, however, is only the tip of the iceberg. Even while we were in the foreign capital, hundreds of specialists at home were also working long hours in preparation for the trip. In the case of Paris, our ambassador, James M. Gavin, was working with French specialists in the State Department on extensive briefings for the President, his staff, and the traveling press. Thousands of pages of material on the social, economic, political, and military characteristics of the host country—and an appraisal of its leaders—would start flowing across JFK's desk weeks before his departure. When he did leave, he would know how the wine grape crop was coming along in the Rhone Valley; the status of French nuclear development; the exact state of de Gaulle's health; the pro- or anti-American sentiments of his principal advisers; and even the names of the valet and chef who would serve JFK at the Quai D'Orsay. The traveling staff had access to almost all of this material, except for highly secret intelligence reports on the French military capability or de Gaulle's developing détente with Communist China.

It was also of great importance that the traveling press have the fullest possible information on the host country and the diplomatic results JFK could hope to achieve from his visit. Such knowledge would preclude unduly optimistic or pessimistic reports on the outcome of the conferences.

The President, for instance, had little hope of substantive agreement with Khrushchev. Our correspondents were told this before they left at a State Department briefing and, as a result, did not interpret the grim outcome of the Vienna confrontation as either a rebuff or a surprise to the President. We issued to the traveling correspondents a massive press kit on the upcoming visit. It was full of such facts as the telephone numbers of embassy physicians in the event of sudden illness; the rates of currency exchange; maps of the foreign capitals and diagrams of the public buildings the President would visit; the power voltages for the guidance of newsmen using newsreel cameras and tape recorders; a brief history of the country; the leading restaurants and scenic attractions; and even advice to photographers on what labs were safe for film processing.

On take-off day, the newsmen would find still another kit waiting for them on the plane. It would contain copies of the public statements the President would deliver and an exact schedule for the tour, even listing the time at which their luggage had to be in the lobby for the flight home.

Simultaneously, kits containing not only the President's statements but biographies of him and the principals in his party were sent ahead for the convenience of the foreign press awaiting our arrival.

One such biography of me, written in the U. S. Information Agency, caused me more than a little embarrassment after our visit to Ottawa, Canada, in 1961. It described me as "a dynamo who resembles tireless competence in motion—a jaunty hunk of a man whose affable manner covers a steel-trap mind. Precocious since childhood, Salinger is accustomed to outdistancing his contemporaries."

*Battle Line*, the propaganda organ of the Republican National Committee, promptly accused me of writing the biography myself. And the New York *Herald Tribune* kept the uproar going with a highly critical editorial. But the newspaper had to eat its own words a day or two later when we discovered that the overeager USIA writer had lifted the description verbatim from an article in the *Herald Tribune*.

The pace in the press section of the White House was frantic just before a foreign visit. Every one of the President's statements was sent to the State Department for translation into a minimum of twenty languages for distribution in the foreign capital to reporters from all over the world. There were hundreds of requests for interviews with the President or Mrs. Kennedy, most of which we had to turn down because of the tight schedule. There was a last-minute cable I could always expect to receive from my press officer counterpart in the foreign capital—an urgent request that the President leave his plane by the rear door because the wing would hide him from the photographers if he left by the front. JFK always left *Air Force One* by the rear door and for exactly that reason. But it still amazes me that this apparently insignificant point would always occur to every foreign press officer and always at the eleventh hour.

Advancing the President was always a back-breaking exercise. Ken and I rarely had more than three or four hours' sleep a night and ate most of our meals on the run—cruel and inhuman punishment in cities like Paris and Vienna with their world-famous cuisine. But despite the inconveniences and our difficulties with the host committees, the trips were always diverting—possibly because O'Donnell was such an off-beat traveling companion.

On our trip to Vienna in 1961, Ken and I found ourselves with that rarest of advancing luxuries—a free evening on the town. The Vienna State Opera was performing Mozart's *Magic Flute* and I made arrangements through our embassy for O'Donnell and myself to attend. We were to receive the full treatment: the presidential box, Ambassador H. Freeman Matthews' limousine and chauffeur, and the chief protocol officer of the Austrian government as an escort.

But an hour before we were to leave, we were informed that our presence was required later that evening at a confidential meeting in a downtown hotel. Reluctant to offend our Austrian hosts by not showing up at the opera at all, we decided to catch part of the first act.

Word had spread through the auditorium that two of President Kennedy's aides were in the presidential box, and we were the object of much attention before the curtain went up. At the end of the first scene, we stood up to leave and the Austrian protocol officer paled: "Where are you going?"

We tried to explain that we must keep our appointment at the hotel.

"But you can't leave," our escort pleaded. "The opera has just begun. It would be an insult to the performers."

We said it would have been a greater insult if we had not made even a token appearance.

With that, the protocol officer, who couldn't have been much taller than five feet, put his back to the door and flung his arms out to stop an end run: "I am sorry but you must stay."

Ken eyed him for a long moment with something of the same malevolence he must have directed against opposing linemen when he played football for Harvard. The Austrian saw there was no stopping Ken and finally crumpled, trembling and perspiring, into a chair and let us pass.

When our meeting was over, we went to the Three Hussars, one of Vienna's leading restaurants, for dinner. We were having a drink at the bar, waiting for our table, when the owner dashed across the room shouting, "Welcome, Herr Salinger," in a voice that rattled the chandeliers. We were promptly given the best table and a dinner I would rank as historic. On our way back to the embassy, we stopped at a fashionable bar for a nightcap. Again the owner rushed toward us yelling, "Welcome, Herr Salinger." I felt like an international celebrity until I found out later that our chauffeur, after dropping us off, had telephoned the owners of both the restaurant and bar and told them President Kennedy's Press Secretary was their guest.

My rather extensive personal publicity on the advance trips was the source of much frustration for O'Donnell and much humor at the White House. I was frequently quoted and photographed while abroad for the very obvious reason that I was dealing directly with the press while Ken was huddling behind closed doors with government officials. But President Kennedy always ribbed O'Donnell about his poor showing in the press. When we were reporting to JFK after our return from such trips, he would always ask Ken: "How many times did Pierre get his picture in the paper this time?"

In 1963, when we were flying to Dublin to advance the President's visit to Ireland, I told Ken: "A joke's a joke. But Ireland is your country —the home of your ancestors—and you should be the spokesman for the President when we arrive. Just to be sure I don't get in your way, I won't even leave the plane until the press has left."

Ken's big moment had come. The President's impending visit was the biggest story in Ireland since the advent of St. Patrick and scores of reporters and photographers were waiting when Ken walked down the ramp alone. But the first question from the first reporter was "Where's Salinger?"

"Still inside the plane," said O'Donnell, and then had to run for his life as the newsmen surged toward the ramp. What I hadn't told Ken was that in all our prior correspondence with the Irish government, my name was given as the press contact. He never had a chance.

The most unforgettable character I ever met on an advance trip was, of course, an Irishman—Andrew Minihan, chairman of the New Ross Urban Council in Wexford County. JFK was to visit the little seaport town because his great-grandfather, Patrick Kennedy, had sailed from there to the New World more than a century earlier.

Minihan, a tall, white-bearded gentleman, was determined that New Ross would take the presidential visit in stride.

"We'll put on no frills or fancies for your young man," he told me. "He'll see us exactly as we are."

I had no argument with this. President Kennedy would not want his Irish hosts to alter the ancient characteristics of the town with paint or banners. But I did think Minihan ought to do something about a huge dung heap only twenty-five feet from the dockside, from which JFK was to thank New Ross for its hospitality.

But Minihan wouldn't bend. "It's good Irish dung and it stays where it is." And stay it did.

The grimmest moments I can remember on an advance trip were when I was taken to the Brandenburg Gate and Checkpoint Charlie to look across the Berlin Wall from the same points JFK would be gazing into East Berlin on June 26, 1963. I was frankly afraid for him when I saw the heavily armed Communist guards glaring at me from close range. When the President went to the same points on the Wall, the East Germans cut off his view at the Brandenburg Gate with huge banners. But he did have a good look from Checkpoint Charlie.

The foreign press officer who always gave me a bad time of it was Pierre Baraduc. My first run-in with him came during the President's Paris conference with General de Gaulle on the way to Vienna. I had been told in advance by the American correspondents that Baraduc was notoriously chauvinistic and would do his best to give Agence France Presse an early scoop on major developments. Obviously, the most important news to come out of the conference would be the joint communiqué by the two heads of state, summarizing the results of their discussions. I had what I thought was the only copy and was to release it just before we left Paris. But, to thwart Baraduc, I had a number of extra copies run off and gave them to the AP and UPI correspondents.

"Hold onto them until I give you the word," I said. "I'll guarantee you at least five minutes' lead time on Agence France Presse."

Exactly five minutes before I was to read the communiqué at a huge press briefing, I gave the signal to AP and UPI. They came back from the press room a moment later, shaking their heads in disgust. Agence France Presse had moved the story minutes earlier. I still don't know where Baraduc got *his* advance copy of the communiqué.

I was also the victim of another incident in Paris that had far graver implications. On the night of de Gaulle's dinner for President and Mrs. Kennedy at the Elysée Palace, I was struggling into my white tie and tails in my suite at the Crillon when I had a call from O'Donnell, who was with the President at the Quai D'Orsay.

"For your information," he said, "Secretary Rusk won't be arriving tomorrow because of the situation in the Dominican Republic."

"What situation?"

"General Trujillo has been assassinated."

Ken said it to me in such a matter-of-fact way that I assumed the news had already broken. Actually, the State Department in Washington had only a report of the assassination, but no confirmation at all. On my way to the dinner, I stopped by the press room on the main floor of the Crillon.

"Is Rusk still due here tomorrow?" one of the correspondents asked me.

"The Secretary won't be here tomorrow," I replied.

"Why?"

"Because of the situation in the Dominican Republic."

"What situation?"

That was my warning but I didn't recognize it. "The assassination of General Rafael Trujillo," I said. In a split second, more than a hundred reporters were dashing for their phones. Within the hour, headlines around the world read: SALINGER ANNOUNCES ASSASSINATION OF

TRUJILLO. Radio Havana broadcast bulletins that the murder of the Dominican dictator must have been plotted in Washington. How else could I have advance knowledge of it?

The President couldn't believe his ears when I met him at the Quai D'Orsay and told him what I had done. He was never angrier with me than at that moment.

"We now have later intelligence," he said, "that Trujillo may not be dead."

"Mr. President," I replied, "if he's not, I am."

Midway through the dinner, a waiter summoned me to the telephone. It was Rusk in Washington, but I didn't need the telephone to hear him.

"Are you out of your mind?" he shouted. "We haven't the slightest confirmation of this from the Dominican government or any other responsible source. This can be most serious. You have to straighten this out—and right now!"

I went back to my place at the table, where another waiter had another message for me—this one from the press room at the Crillon. Minutes before, the Dominican government had officially announced the assassination of General Trujillo.

I will not recount my activities for the rest of that night except to say that I did not go to bed until six o'clock in the morning.

# XI

## THE RUSSIANS IN VIENNA

John F. Kennedy and Nikita S. Khrushchev met in Vienna June 3 and 4, 1961—the only face-to-face confrontation they were ever to have as heads of state. It was an ominous two days. The Bay of Pigs six weeks earlier had brought American prestige to its lowest point since the Francis Gary Powers U-2 incident in May 1960. Khrushchev, sensing the time was right to force important American concessions on the German question, came to Vienna not to negotiate but to dictate to the young American President. It was not one of his wiser moves. Within two months it was he, not JFK, who was backing down on Berlin, the hottest issue at Vienna.

President Kennedy went to the Austrian capital knowing that the atmosphere would be unfavorable to the give-and-take that might produce important agreements. He was there largely to size up Khrushchev and to establish a personal relationship that might prove useful later.

"I would rather meet him the first time at the summit, not the brink," he said.

The President found Khrushchev a fascinating study. To prepare himself for Vienna, he read scores of intelligence reports on the Russian leader and every available word he had ever spoken or written for the public record. JFK, then and later, was never misled by the Premier's foot-stamping tantrums. He saw him as a tough and vigorous exponent of his own system who was confident that it would prevail in a peaceful competition with capitalism, and who would be willing to take the first step back from the brink. But he was also convinced that Khrushchev would not shrink from pulling the nuclear trigger if his back was to the wall. The entire U.S. strategy in the Cuban missile crisis a year later was based on this analysis, which proved to be correct. Because Khrushchev was given leeway to maneuver, he did not reply in kind to our show of force against Soviet ships and his Communist ally, Castro.

The President's greatest concern over Vienna was that it might create another false "Spirit of Camp David." U.S.-Soviet relations had taken an abrupt turn for the worse after the apparently successful Khrushchev-Eisenhower conference at the Maryland retreat in 1959. JFK was not going to be party to another such disappointment. His instructions to me long before we left for Vienna were specific:

"Let's not build this up into something it isn't. We're not likely to accomplish very much over there, and it would be dangerous to stir up false hopes at home."

His judgment was correct. Although the Soviets had sent out the first feelers for the conference, Khrushchev and his chief adviser, Foreign Minister Andrey Gromyko, had nothing new to propose. JFK and Secretary of State Dean Rusk were given a choice of alternatives that had always been unacceptable to the West. There was an agreement to press harder for a cease-fire in Laos. But the two leaders left farther apart than ever on the most explosive issue—Germany.

But when *Air Force One*, carrying the presidential party, came in for a landing at Vienna's rain-swept Schwechat Airport, I was thinking only of the massive press contingent that would be waiting to cover the event. For the next two days, I would be the official spokesman for the President. I also had a second, and less public, chore—to sidetrack possible Soviet efforts to distort the significance of the conference.

Before I left Vienna, however, I found myself caught up in a series of improbable events that would later have a dramatic effect on U.S.-Soviet communications. In rapid sequence, I would meet Khrushchev's son-in-law in a television debate; become a secret courier between the President and the Soviet premier; set up the first interview of an American President by a Russian journalist; and spend fourteen hours with Khrushchev himself.

It all began because of a woman who doesn't know what the word impossible means. Mrs. Lucy Jarvis, then co-producer of NBC's television series, *The Nation's Future*, came to me in Washington a month before Vienna with a most interesting proposition. Would I be willing to go on her show with another American and debate two top-ranking Russian journalists on the subject of a free press? If I agreed, she would go after Aleksey Adzhubei, Khrushchev's son-in-law and chief editor of *Izvestia*, and Mikhail Kharlamov, press chief for the Soviet Foreign Ministry in Moscow. Mrs. Jarvis was thinking of Clifton Daniel of the New York *Times* as my partner. Daniel is the son-in-law of former President Truman, and having him on with Khrushchev's son-in-law was a twist Lucy found hard to resist.

I readily agreed to her tentative plans for the debate. But, privately, I didn't think she could carry it off. The Russians, I felt, would never accept a debate on American television, under American ground rules, with all the implications it would have for reciprocity on Soviet TV. In fact, on the damp morning of our arrival in Vienna, I had all but forgotten it.

But Lucy, who speaks fluent Russian, was plowing full speed ahead. She was already in Vienna to nail down the two Russians and had spoken to Kharlamov, who was there as Khrushchev's official spokesman. I met with him the morning of my arrival and we agreed, through interpreters, on procedures for handling the joint American-Soviet communiqués on the conference.

"I've met your Mrs. Jarvis," he said. "What do you think of her idea for a debate on American television?"

"I'm all for it," I replied. "But it's not just for American television. We would expect you to show it in the Soviet Union. How do you and Adzhubei feel?"

"I'll speak to him when I return to Moscow," he said. "I think it can be arranged." I still had my doubts.

President Kennedy and Premier Khrushchev met that first morning in the music room of the American Embassy. They had met only once before, when the Soviet leader was visiting the U.S. in 1959 and held a brief discussion with the Senate Foreign Relations Committee. Khrushchev now recalled that JFK had been late for the meeting in Washington, and President Kennedy remembered that the Premier's only comment to him was on his youthful appearance.

Their first conversation was alternately bristling and friendly. Khrushchev's principal theme was that the U.S. must acknowledge the right of Communism to exist, not only in the Soviet Union but in other nations where the people voluntarily chose Marxism over capitalism. There was no point, he said, in arguing the relative merit of the two systems, or in blaming the Soviet Union for the importation of Communism to other areas of the world. The U.S. was myopic, he said, if it saw a Russian behind every tree in these countries that were turning to Communism. Historical inevitability, not Soviet subversion, was the impetus for pro-Communist "wars of liberation," and we should desist from active intervention against them. He had no intention, he said, of forcing Communism on other nations at the point of a gun. He was willing to let history take its course, but we were not.

President Kennedy reminded him of Mao Tse-tung's statement that power came out of the end of a gun, and Khrushchev angrily replied that Mao could not have said this. The Red Chinese leader was a Marxist and all Marxists knew they would prevail without recourse to war.

The President could not accept the Premier's contention that Marxists were willing to submit to the test of historical inevitability. He cited instances where Communist minorities, through both internal subversion and outside military intervention, were attempting to overthrow democratic regimes that had the popular support of the people. Capitalism, he said, was not on the offensive against Communism. It was the other way around. We had no argument with Communist regimes that had come to power with popular consent, and were not interfering in their national affairs. But the Marxists were attempting to sabotage democratic regimes, and this is what had brought U.S.-Soviet relations to an often dangerous point.

There was agreement between the two heads of state, however, that ways must be found to resolve the issue short of a direct confrontation between the major exponents of the competing systems. Khrushchev said the Soviets' willingness to negotiate general disarmament was evidence of their confidence that a non-military solution could be found. President Kennedy replied that his "one ambition is to secure peace"—and he was hopeful that their conversations would be a positive step in that direction.

Although their hour-long conversation had not been entirely cordial, they were both smiling when they came into the embassy dining room for lunch. The Premier was wearing a decoration on his coat that JFK didn't recognize.

"What is that?"

Khrushchev proudly told him it was the Lenin Peace Medal.

"I hope you do nothing to make them take it away from you," the President replied. Khrushchev laughed.

The conversation then went to space exploration and JFK proposed that we pool our research and "go to the moon together." Khrushchev again chuckled but after a thoughtful pause said, "All right, why not?" (But he told the President the next day that it would not be "practical" because both countries were using the same missiles for both scientific and military purposes.)

The Premier had an obsession with agriculture—probably because of the Russian's persistent failure to raise their productivity to American levels. He listened with great interest at the luncheon as Secretary Rusk told him of a new fast-growing American corn that would produce two or more crops a year in the same field.

"Remarkable," said Khrushchev, "but do you know that we have found a way to make vodka from natural gas?" He turned to the President. "What do you think of that?"

"It sounds like another of Rusk's corn stories," said JFK.

But if the conversation was light, the luncheon menu was not: Coquilles de foie gras en gelée; coeur de filet de boeuf Wellington; légumes divers; salade mimosa; biscuit glacé à la crème de menthe, and fruits. The wines were Gumpoldskirchner (Spätlese Rotgipfler) 1957; Château Mouton (Rothschild) 1953, and Perrière (Jouët Brut) 1953.

The two leaders met for three hours that afternoon, and Khrushchev went back to his earlier theme that U.S. attempts to topple Communist governments, as in Cuba, were the most volatile friction points between East and West. But he also introduced the new element that America, not the Soviet Union, was largely responsible for the proliferation of Communism. Fidel Castro, he said, was being forced into the Marxist camp because our economic sanctions had left him nowhere else to go. In Korea and Iran, our support of reactionary regimes had left the people no choice but to turn to Communism. He himself was not born a Communist. A study of capitalism and its methods had forced him to become one.

President Kennedy disagreed. We had taken economic action against Castro not because he had thrown out American business interests but because he was converting the island into a Communist base that was a direct threat to democratic governments in Latin America. Would Khrushchev stand idly by if a pro-American government were to come to power in Poland and begin subverting its Communist bloc neighbors to capitalism? Of course not. And we could not tolerate Castro's overt attempts to import Communist revolution into Latin countries against the popular will of their people.

The important thing, JFK continued, was that our two countries avoid miscalculations that might lead to nuclear war. We would, of course, continue to have conflicts of national interest. We would have to accept the inevitability of political change around the world. But we must be able to recognize the point at which such change would dangerously upset the balance of power and pose a clear danger to the very security of either the U.S. or the Soviet Union. Only if we were determined to stop short of such an eventuality could we be certain of the peaceful competition that would decide which system was the more durable.

Khrushchev again said that such an understanding was not very likely if the U.S. continued to view indigenous Communist movements as part of a world conspiracy directed by Moscow.

JFK became impatient with Khrushchev's doctrinaire responses and brought the conversation around to Laos—a subject on which a specific exchange of views was possible. To his surprise, the Premier promptly agreed that both nations should use their good offices to secure the uneasy cease-fire in Laos between neutralist and Communist forces.

The session finally broke up at 6:45 P.M. Kharlamov and I were waiting for the two heads of state in the embassy lobby to prepare a joint communiqué for the press. The principals agreed that we would omit all specifics and describe the first day's conversations merely as "frank, courteous, and wide-ranging." Kharlamov and I went into a side office and I reduced the communiqué to two typewritten paragraphs. We then left for a joint press briefing at the historic Hofburg Palace.

I can only describe the scene as bedlam. More than 1200 reporters and photographers, representing at least thirty nations, were jammed into the auditorium. Hundreds of television cables were strewn around the floor. Correspondents were struggling to adjust headsets to hear the instantaneous translation in six languages. TV and still photographers were scrambling for positions in front of the stage on which Kharlamov and I would appear. To preserve at least a semblance of order, we had agreed on White House rules for the briefing. No one could enter or leave the auditorium until it was over.

I read the joint communiqué, emphasizing the key phrase, "frank, courteous, and wide-ranging." But Kharlamov, always the propagandist, had his own game to play. When he took over the mike, he said he had "nothing to add" to my statement. "This was all that was decided to communicate today so that the meeting tomorrow could be as *fruitful* as today."

"Fruitful" went much further than the statement on which we had agreed, and Chalmers Roberts of the Washington *Post* was the first to pick it up.

"Mr. Salinger, could you accept Mr. Kharlamov's characterization of the meeting with Khrushchev as fruitful?"

"I will stand with the statement I made at the outset," I answered—an obvious tip-off to Western reporters, at least, that all was not as rosy as Kharlamov would have them believe. I was to spend much time the next two days spiking a series of Russian "leaks" that Khrushchev was bringing JFK around to his point of view.

Apart from Kharlamov's little word game, the most memorable feature of the briefing was a heroic outburst of Churchillian combativeness. Sir Winston's son, Randolph, was covering for the London *Evening Standard* and other Beaverbrook newspapers. At a critical point in the questions and answers, and in total violation of the rules, he decided to leave. When the guards told him he couldn't, he lowered a beefy shoulder and crashed through them and the doors. He said to me later in London: "Sorry, old boy, but I was just plain bored by the stupid questions."

Although it was one of the most hectic days in my life and, I am certain, Kharlamov's, the redoubtable Mrs. Lucy Jarvis was able to persuade us to meet with her the following morning in the Soviet Embassy—scene of the second day's conference. While the leaders of the two most powerful nations in the history of the world were upstairs arguing momentous issues of war and peace, Lucy, Kharlamov, and I sat down in an anteroom to discuss a television show.

The Russian agreed in principle to the debate and was certain Adzhubei would go along. We tentatively agreed on June 24 in New York City. Mrs. Jarvis was no longer considering Clifton Daniel at his own request. Daniel felt my partner should be a correspondent who had spent time in the Soviet Union. What did I think of another New York *Times* man,

Harrison Salisbury, a veteran of more than five years in Moscow? I told her it would be great to have him on my side.

If the debate came off, I told Kharlamov that morning, the President would like him and Adzhubei to come to Washington for a chat with him and general discussions with me on the whole subject of freer communications.

A major proposal I had been considering was a series of direct television exchanges between JFK and Khrushchev on significant U.S.-Soviet disagreements. They would not be debates, as such, because the principals would never be face to face. Each would film his comments on a pre-agreed subject, such as Berlin, nuclear testing, or Laos.

We would then exchange film segments and they would be shown together, not only on American and Soviet networks, but in all other nations with television. The series would certainly command the greatest TV audience in history, and could be of immeasurable benefit in clarifying long persisting issues. Kharlamov was intrigued by the idea and said he would discuss it with Khrushchev and let me know. I was not too hopeful, however.

Although I didn't discuss it with Kharlamov in Vienna, I was also considering another proposal. We would encourage one of our journalists to go to Russia to write a daily column on American life that would appear in either *Pravda* or *Izvestia*. The Soviets, in turn, would assign one of their reporters to a major American newspaper for the same purpose. They would have absolute freedom to write as they chose. We could expand the project even further by exchanging Russian and American radio news analysts for a five-minute daily commentary. I felt then, and still do, that this would have been an important breakthrough in communications with the Russian people. But impending events were to rule it out.

Except for firming up their agreement of the day before to work for an effective cease-fire in Laos and to support the neutralist government of Prince Souvanna Phouma, the second round of conversations between President Kennedy and Premier Khrushchev not only was barren of results but had ominous portents for the future.

At the morning session in the Soviet Embassy, the Russian leader was unyielding in his approach to a nuclear test ban treaty. He would consider it only within the context of general disarmament. JFK's counter-argument that general disarmament was far in the future, but a halt to nuclear testing was not only an early possibility but a positive step toward relieving world tensions had no effect on Khrushchev.

Despite his dour manner over the conference table, Khrushchev was an amiable luncheon host. There was a series of toasts in which both leaders spoke with respect for each other and with optimism that happier relations were possible. The Russian chef, I must add, outdid his American counterpart. We had caviar, fish cartilage pie, stuffed soodak fish, salad of wild fowl, asparagus, cucumbers, cauliflower, tomatoes, consommé Borshchok, crab meat in sauce, Tabaca chicken, ice cream, almonds, and fruit. Plus vodka, four wines, and cordials.

This sumptuous spread did nothing to improve Khrushchev's mood when he met with the President for their final, brief discussion that afternoon. He could no longer postpone a settlement of the Berlin question, and would sign a separate peace treaty with East Germany in December. Once that was done, he would recognize no continuing American rights in West Berlin. If the U.S. chose to go to war over this, "that is your problem." The President replied that "It is you, and not I, who wants to force a change." Khrushchev shrugged. His decision was final.

"It's going to be a cold winter," were JFK's last words to him.

Despite their failure to reach accord on major East-West conflicts, both heads of state left Vienna with greater personal respect for each other. Khrushchev later told me: "I like your young President. He knows what he's talking about." JFK found the Russian leader "tough but not unreasonable. He talks hard but his actions are cautious." Their mutual regard was to pay off later in a remarkable exchange of personal correspondence in which I was to serve as one of the couriers.

I drove back to the American Embassy with the President. It was still his opinion that the press reports were deceptively optimistic. Khrushchev's unyielding position on East Germany could only aggravate an already deepening crisis. He had me invite James Reston of the New York *Times* to the embassy and gave him an extremely candid statement of his views. Although the presidential party was leaving immediately for a working visit the next day with British Prime Minister Harold Macmillan, JFK instructed me to stay behind briefly to counteract the euphoria that was developing among some American reporters.

I backgrounded as many of the important by-liners as I could while they were filing their stories, and we all left for the airport together in the early hours of June 5 to catch up with the President in London. But one of the wheels of our Pan American charter plane sank through the concrete as we were taxiing down the runway. Although it took five hours to fix, Pan American's bountiful store of spirits took much of the edge off our irritation.

Six days after my return to Washington, I had a call from Lucy Jarvis. Adzhubei had agreed. The impossible debate was set. Almost simultaneously, I heard from the Russian Embassy that both Adzhubei and Kharlamov would be happy to accept the President's invitation to come to Washington after the debate.

My work was all cut out for me. With the help of an interpreter, I read everything I could find on Soviet press policies. I dug through a stack of the most current issues of *Pravda* and *Izvestia*. I had a series of briefings from the State Department and the USIA on the points I should press and the tack the Russians were most likely to take with me. It was also important that I understand the personalities and backgrounds of my opponents.

Adzhubei and Kharlamov had one qualification in common. They were both tough, competent newsmen. Kharlamov, who was then forty-eight, was very short but had commanding presence. He had been press chief of the Soviet Foreign Ministry for three years after serving, successively, as a sub-editor of Communist Party publications, a political officer in the Red Army in World War II, a *Pravda* correspondent in China, and a foreign intelligence director of the secret police. Khrushchev had great confidence in Kharlamov. He was at the Premier's side on most of his foreign junkets, and had written a two-volume work for Khrushchev on Soviet relations with India.

From my first meeting with him in Vienna, I found Kharlamov a thoroughly likable man. He limped from a war wound. He had sharp gray eyes under a shock of brown hair—and a fey sense of humor. Many Western correspondents in Moscow remember their first encounter with Kharlamov a little sheepishly. One evening, shortly after his appointment as press chief in the Foreign Ministry, a number of reporters were complaining bitterly at a Moscow cocktail party over the censorship policies of his predecessor, Leonid F. Ilichev.

"What we have to do," said one, "is grab hold of this new boy and lay what we want right on the line."

He was overheard by a stranger, whom most of the reporters thought was a new Polish correspondent in Moscow. Suddenly the stranger spoke up:

"I would like to meet you all, and often, to discuss this matter. I am Mikhail Averkiyevich Kharlamov—the new boy."

Adzhubei had none of Kharlamov's subtlety. He was arrogant most of the time and a braggart when the vodka was flowing. He was not popular, either with his staff at *Izvestia* or with the public. His marriage to Khrushchev's daughter, Rada, was the inspiration for two lines of doggerel frequently heard in Moscow:

> *Why have a hundred friends, they say.*
> *You just have to marry like Adzhubei.*

There's no doubt that Adzhubei's family connections had much to do with his success. But even without it, I believe he would have cut out an important career on his own. Tall, blond, and hard-driving, he was one of the most energetic men I've ever met. He took over as chief editor of *Izvestia* at the age of thirty-five in 1959—the year after his father-in-law became Premier. *Izvestia* was at that time one of the dullest newspapers in the world. Adzhubei quickly brought it to life with a brighter format, punchier headlines, and more pictures and human interest stories. Within two years, its circulation shot up from slightly more than two million to almost five million.

Adzhubei met and married Khrushchev's daughter in the early 1950s while both were students at Moscow University. He, like Kharlamov, was a war veteran, and had held minor positions in the Communist Party structure.

After his marriage, he became editor of *Komsomol'skaya Pravda*, the official newspaper of the Soviet youth movement. But his father-in-law had much bigger plans for him. In 1958 he became a deputy of the Supreme Soviet and an officer of the Bureau of the All-Union Komsomol Central Committee, the governing agency for all Soviet youth activities. He left there in 1959 to become chief editor of *Izvestia*.

Unlike Kharlamov, who was entirely affable, Adzhubei had a fierce temper. At the Austrian Youth Festival in 1959 he got into a violent argument with an American.

"You Americans are finished and don't know it," he shouted. "We are so strong we could crush you like this." And he broke the neck off a wine bottle. At the same conference, he was overheard bragging that the Soviets could capture West Berlin in twenty minutes and France in two hours.

Salisbury and I would be facing a pair of formidable adversaries. I flew to New York the day before the debate to huddle with him on strategy. I didn't have the heart to tell him that my win-loss record in high school debates was substantially under .500. I met Adzhubei for the first time the next day at a luncheon Mrs. Jarvis put together for the principals in the Hotel Carlyle. It was here that I also met the amazing Georgi N. Bolshakov for the first time. He was editor of the magazine *USSR*, the leading Soviet propaganda organ in America. But that, I was to learn later, was the least dramatic of his many assignments from the Kremlin.

The luncheon before the debate went off smoothly. The Russians said we could count on a rebroadcast of the debate in the Soviet Union—a commitment I had no reason to suspect at the time. They were looking forward, they said, to their visit to Washington. Although we were to go on camera that afternoon, *The Nation's Future* would not be broadcast until late in the evening. The first social affair on the Russians' calendar would be a barbecue at my home in Falls Church, Virginia, after which we would sit down together and watch our performance.

The debate, which had an extremely high audience rating, brought the essential differences between the American and Soviet press into sharp focus. Salisbury struck home the point that Russian reporters had no freedom to criticize the government, or to develop stories that might embarrass the Kremlin. In contrast, it was always open season on the administration for the American press—a fact with which I, at least, could ruefully agree.

Adzhubei argued that reporters had no more freedom here than in Russia "because your American publishers tell them what to write." I pointed out to him that I had worked thirteen years for a Republican-owned newspaper (the San Francisco *Chronicle*) and almost every two years would take a leave of absence to work for Democratic candidates the paper was opposing. "They had no objection to it. They let me come back to work. They never told me once what to write for their paper."

Adzhubei and Kharlamov spent most of their time blaming America for the unhappy state of the world and criticizing the American press for its sensationalism. "If Kharlamov and I were hired by the New York *Times* for two weeks," said Adzhubei, "it would be the best newspaper in the world. They would increase their circulation by a factor of, well, five, without any sensational stories, and all America from the youngest to the oldest would read only the New York *Times*."

It was Adzhubei's most spectacular flight of ego, but *Times* man Salisbury quickly brought him back to earth. Under questioning, he had to admit that even *Izvestia* had a fling at sensationalism now and then.

"Yes, we reported about the great disaster that Marilyn Monroe had divorced Arthur Miller," said Adzhubei. "Now I like Arthur Miller and I said, 'Let's print that,' and I got a letter from the readers saying, 'Stop printing nonsense and stop spoiling our relations with the American people.'"

"Having had a look at that story in Mr. Adzhubei's newspaper, I think his readers were right," said Salisbury.

"I won't do it again," Adzhubei promised.

My principal point of conflict with our opponents was the secrecy that surrounds most major events in the Soviet Union. An example was the historic flight of Yuri Gagarin, the first human space traveler, who was shot into orbit earlier that year.

"No Soviet reporter saw him take off or land," I said. "On the other hand, the flight of Commander [Alan] Shepard was done in full view of five hundred reporters and millions of people watching television all over the world. Many of the reporters who were present at Cape Canaveral came from foreign lands. If Soviet reporters had requested permission to come to Cape Canaveral and watch Commander Shepard's flight, that permission would have been granted."

Adzhubei had a lame reply. "We are modest people. First we fly, then we write about it. Otherwise, if one writes first it may not turn out."

Adzhubei had been critical earlier of "untruthful and inaccurate stories" on Russia in American newspapers. His answer on Gagarin gave me an opportunity to rebut his charge. If not even the Soviet press was told of important events there, how could he expect foreign newspapermen to report them objectively?

Despite many points of disagreement, the tone of the sixty-minute debate was generally positive. Kharlamov had the best on-camera summation.

"I think we have had a good discussion here. Regardless of our differences on particulars, partly due to mutual ignorance or misunderstanding, it is better to seek mutual understanding than to seek war. It is better to seek cooperation in order to prevent war than to emphasize the differences that exist among us."

We were all agreed that an improvement in press relations between our two nations could relax at least those tensions that grew out of honest misconceptions, and all of us were willing to explore the question in greater depth in Washington.

We had quite a party that night at my home in Falls Church. Waiting for us to arrive from New York were Edward R. Murrow, director of the USIA; Merriman Smith, senior White House correspondent for UPI; Mikhail Sagatelyan, Washington correspondent for the Soviet news agency Tass; and Roger Tubby, Assistant Secretary of State for Public Affairs. It was a humid evening and Kharlamov, Bolshakov, and Sagatelyan were eager for a swim in Lake Barcroft, a hop, skip, and jump down the hill from my home. The baggy trunks I lent them and their bellowing in stentorian Russian were a sight and sound my neighbors in Falls Church may never forget. It was no weather for coats and neckties and I gave each of the Russians a sports shirt from my collection. The one Kharlamov chose was a "his and hers" model and I told him to take the extra one back to Moscow for his wife.

It was a happy scene, straight out of suburbia—the hi-fi blaring, the guests pouring their own drinks from the patio bar and their aproned host presiding masterfully over the barbecue. Through a slight miscalculation on my part, however, the chicken came to the table somewhere between blood and medium rare. But by that time the Russians, enlivened with vodka, were ravenously hungry and ate every last drumstick.

The time finally came to watch *our* show on television. It was dark now and I brought a portable set out to the patio. Adzhubei never took his eyes from the screen for the entire hour. He would shake his head impatiently when Salisbury or I got in a good lick, but would smile broadly when he or Kharlamov were on the offensive.

Five minutes after the show was over, I had a call from President Kennedy, who had been watching it at the White House.

"You and Salisbury were great," he said. "I thought you won hands down. Tell him that for me."

The next day, a Sunday, I took the Russian visitors for a cruise down the Potomac on the presidential yacht *Patrick J*. Kharlamov, who never took a day off from politics, told me there was "grave concern" in the Soviet Union over the laggard pace of disarmament negotiations.

"We are both spending too much on missiles," he said. "It is time we spent more on goods the people can use. But your new President is even harder to bring to the bargaining table than Eisenhower. Our patience is great but not inexhaustible."

I told him he was wrong. President Kennedy was most eager to break the disarmament stalemate, and his negotiator, John J. McCloy, had instructions to explore the widest possible area of agreement.

Kharlamov shook his head. "I don't know. Sometimes I think all you want to do is make sure your grandchildren have jobs in the office dealing with disarmament."

Bolshakov, who had been waving happily at every passing boat, finally became arm-weary and sat down with us. We fell into a discussion of our allies, and Bolshakov said, "You Americans have too many and they're always fighting among themselves. You ought to decide which ones are important and get rid of the rest of them. But you won't. You're like the man who got engaged to fifteen girls in his younger days and now, at the age of thirty-five, can't decide which one to marry."

The *Patrick J.* is a Navy vessel and naval tradition requires that all hands stand at attention briefly as it comes abreast of Mount Vernon, George Washington's home on the Virginia shore of the Potomac. But on this Sunday afternoon my son Stephen, then ten years old, decided to enliven the ceremony. He ran to the stern and wheezed out his own interpretation of "The Star-Spangled Banner" on his quarter-size violin.

For the Russians—patriots and music lovers all—this was the high point of the cruise.

The next morning, the last day of their visit to Washington, Adzhubei and Kharlamov spent more than an hour with President Kennedy at the White House. Bolshakov and I sat in on the conversation. Just the day before, Premier Khrushchev had made a speech describing the United States as "a worn-out runner" and predicting that the Soviet Union would pass us in gross national product in 1978.

"I don't think you can do that at your present rate of growth," the President said to Adzhubei. "You're like the high-jumper. He can raise the bar a foot at a time until he reaches a certain height, say six feet. But for the next foot he must raise it by inches, and after that by fractions of inches."

"Well, you use one set of figures to measure our growth and we use another," said Adzhubei.

"I'm not minimizing your effort," the President replied. "You've made remarkable economic advances. This is the kind of peaceful competition I would like to see us have. But you must do more than you are to see that the peace is kept. Do that and we'll all be around in 1978 to find out whether Mr. Khrushchev's estimates are correct."

Adzhubei also took issue with the President over American troops in

West Berlin. "Their presence makes it difficult for us to believe you want a peaceful solution."

"Our force of 10,000 is token in nature," said JFK. "It is a symbol of our commitment to West Berlin—a commitment we fully intend to maintain."

"I think you ought to let us have a token force in West Berlin," said Adzhubei. "We would start with seventeen pretty nurses."

The President laughed. "We might just be able to work that out."

When it was time for his Russian guests to leave, JFK took them into the Fish Room to show them an ivory ship model Khrushchev had sent him.

"Now that's the kind of ships we ought to exchange," Adzhubei commented. "Little toy ships like that."

I saw the Russians to a car that was waiting for them outside. There was much hand-shaking and back-slapping as they said their goodbyes to me. Once home, however, they welshed on their absolute commitment to run the debate on Soviet TV. But their American visit was the prelude to a bizarre chain of events that would leave a permanent imprint on U.S.-Soviet communications.

# XII

## SECRET COURIER

My next encounter with Mikhail Kharlamov was on the night of September 23, 1961. In the three months since our television debate and his visit to Washington, the world had come perilously close to the brink. John F. Kennedy's last words to Nikita S. Khrushchev at Vienna, "It's going to be a cold winter," were proving out.

The Russian leader was still threatening to recognize East Germany before the end of the year—a decision that would almost certainly provoke military action between East and West over our access rights to Berlin.

In a grim television address to the nation on July 25, President Kennedy said the U.S. would go to war, if necessary, to defend free Berlin. He was tripling the draft call and summoning 250,000 reservists to active duty. Our long-range nuclear bomber force was on fifteen minutes' alert.

His warning to Khrushchev could not have been clearer. ". . . If war begins, it will have begun in Moscow and not Berlin. For the choice of peace or war is largely theirs, not ours. It is the Soviets who have stirred up this crisis . . . It is they who have rejected an all-German peace treaty and the rulings of international law. And as Americans know from our history on our own old frontier, gun battles are caused by outlaws, and not by officers of the peace."

The President was hopeful that his mobilization of military manpower would dissuade the Kremlin from reckless action in Germany. "We seek peace but we shall not surrender . . . West Berlin has now become the great testing place of Western courage and will . . . We cannot and will not permit the Communists to drive us out of Berlin, either gradually or by force . . . Three times in my lifetime our country and Europe have been involved in major wars. In each case serious misjudgments were made on both sides of the intentions of others, which brought about great devastation. Now, in the thermonuclear age, misjudgment on either side about the intentions of the other could rain more devastation in several hours than has been wrought in all the wars of human history . . ."

Khrushchev was conferring with our disarmament negotiator, John Mc-Cloy, at a vacation retreat in the Crimea when word of the speech reached him. Their conversations had been proceeding smoothly until then, but McCloy later reported that the Premier flew into a foot-stamping, bellowing range that made further negotiations pointless.

What could have been the first miscalculation came on August 17 when the East Germans, after occupying all crossing-points in Berlin, began to build their infamous Wall. Was it to serve as a dam to the flood of East Germans fleeing to the West? Or as a shield from behind which the Communists would strike militarily at Allied forces in the free sector of the city? No one could be certain. Shrill demands that the U.S. bulldoze the Wall were rejected by President Kennedy on the grounds that the Ulbricht regime probably had the legal right to close off its borders, and no one imagines, said the President, "that we should go to war on this point." But to reassure the West Germans of our intention to stand by them in the event the Wall had a more sinister purpose, JFK sent Vice-President Johnson to Berlin to pledge "our lives, our fortunes, our sacred honor" to the defense of the city. He also reinforced our Berlin garrison with 1500 additional infantrymen. It was a nervous weekend as the troops, riding in armored cars, moved down the Autobahn, through Communist checkpoints, to be greeted in Berlin by the Vice-President. But there was no incident. It was JFK's private assessment that the odds were one in five that the Wall and our reaction to it might have ignited World War III.

Against this already ominous background, the Soviet Union broke the three-year moratorium on nuclear testing on September 1 with a high-megaton blast in the atmosphere—a clear violation of Khrushchev's pledge to President Kennedy at Vienna:

"We will never be the first to break the moratorium. You will break it and that will force us to resume testing."

The Russian decision came as a bitter shock to JFK. Even at that early time, a nuclear test ban treaty with the Kremlin was one of his prime objectives. Now it was even further in the future. Khrushchev's offer to cancel the rest of the test series if the West would accept his position on Germany drew an appropriate reply from the President: "Nuclear blackmail." We resumed testing, but underground, on September 12.

I went to New York with the President on September 22 for a historic session of the UN General Assembly. The world organization was still in shock over the death of Secretary-General Dag Hammarskjold four days earlier in an air crash in northern Rhodesia. Although JFK did not have a close relationship with Hammarskjold, he saw him as a martyr to the central purpose of the UN. (The Secretary-General was on a peace mission to the Congo when his plane went down.) The President was also aware that the death of Hammarskjold would deprive the UN of a stabilizing force at a time when its peace-keeping mission was of critical importance and when its own future was in doubt. His prediction that the Soviets would try to impose a leadership subservient to their own interest was borne out with their prompt demand for a three-nation directorate, or troika, to replace Hammarskjold.

It was in this atmosphere of crisis that JFK would speak to the UN for the first time. The world was anxious. His statement of American policy could signal either a step toward or a step away from nuclear disaster.

The night of our arrival in Manhattan, I had a call from Georgi Bolshakov, a one-man troika himself. The Russian interpreter, editor, and spy said it was most important that I have dinner with Kharlamov, who was in town as press spokesman for Andrey Gromyko, chief Soviet delegate to the UN. This was hardly the time for a White House staffer to be seen hobnobbing publicly with a Soviet official of Kharlamov's importance. I replied merely that I was tied up for dinner but could see Kharlamov at seven-fifteen the next night—a Saturday—in my room at the Carlyle. Because a crowd of reporters was almost always standing watch in the lobby of the hotel when the President was there, I told Bolshakov to bring Kharlamov to a side entrance. A Secret Service agent would be waiting to bring them upstairs in a back elevator.

In contrast to the general air of apprehension in New York, the two Russians were all smiles when I met them at the door.

"The storm in Berlin is over," was Kharlamov's opening shot.

*Over?* I told him I didn't think the situation there could be much worse.

"Just wait, my friend," was his mysterious reply. He then came straight to the point of his visit. Earlier that month in Moscow, Khrushchev had given an exclusive interview to Cyrus L. Sulzberger, Paris correspondent of the New York *Times*. But he had also given him a most urgent message for JFK. Had Sulzberger delivered it yet? I said I didn't know.

"Then I will repeat the message to you," said Kharlamov, "and you will deliver it to the President."

His words were tumbling out almost faster than Bolshakov could translate. I told him to sit down and take his time. The President had gone to a Broadway play, was having a late supper with friends, and wouldn't return to the hotel until after midnight.

The message was urgent. Khrushchev saw the increase in our military forces in Germany as an imminent danger to peace. He was now willing, for the first time, to consider American proposals for a *rapprochement* on Berlin. He was eager for an early summit but would leave the timing up to JFK because of the President's "obvious political difficulties."

The latter reference was to be a recurring note in Khrushchev's informal communications with JFK. What he meant, in effect, was that I, Khrushchev, have total freedom of action in negotiating with you, Mr. President. I don't have to concern myself with political opposition or public opinion. But you do. You must prepare your country for the compromises a settlement of the Berlin question will require, and I am willing to give you time to do that.

But not too much time, said Kharlamov. There was intense pressure on Khrushchev from within the Communist bloc to recognize East Germany. But, apart from that, the danger of a major military incident in Berlin was too great to delay a settlement very much longer.

The Russian had one final word from Khrushchev. "He hopes your President's speech to the UN won't be another warlike ultimatum like the one on July 25. He didn't like that at all."

It was now apparent why the Russians were double-planting the Khrushchev message with both Sulzberger and me. It was crucial that JFK know of the summit bid and of the Premier's more conciliatory attitude on Germany *before* he spoke to the UN. It might prompt him to desist from another "ultimatum."

It would be at least three hours before the President would return to the penthouse, and Kharlamov and Bolshakov were in no hurry to leave. I sent down for drinks. My guests, like most Russians I knew, dutifully drank straight vodka in public but scotch and soda in private.

I was still upset with Kharlamov for breaking his promise to rebroadcast our television debate on freedom of the press. "You and Adzhubei must have figured you lost it," I said. "What other reason could you have for being afraid to show it over there?"

Kharlamov said it wasn't his fault—that NBC had not sent him a tape compatible with Soviet TV equipment. I knew better. NBC had sent him two 16-mm transcriptions that were entirely compatible. Moreover, Kharlamov had since been designated chairman of the State Committee on Radio and Television and was in a personal position to honor his commitment.

"Let's not argue over what is past," he said. "When you come to the Soviet Union with your family to visit Adzhubei next summer, I will put you on live television and you can say whatever you want."

I had almost forgotten Adzhubei's casual invitation to me three months earlier at my home in Falls Church. In fact, I had written it off as party conversation.

"No, he was most serious," said Kharlamov. "He likes your children very much. He wants them to know his children."

I told the Russian I would have to clear it with my superiors and would let Adzhubei know.

Kharlamov still had no word for me on my proposal at Vienna that

President Kennedy and Premier Khrushchev engage in a series of "remote" television debates. But he said there was great interest in it in Moscow and he would have an answer for me soon.

Cy Sulzberger's interview with Khrushchev earlier that week gave me an opportunity to brace Kharlamov on another point. All the Russian Premier had to do to command a direct audience of millions in this country was to invite an American correspondent to his office. In addition to Sulzberger, Walter Lippmann and Drew Pearson had been given recent interviews and all received tremendous circulation in the American press.

But until now the Kremlin had never permitted a Soviet journalist to interview President Kennedy. I told Kharlamov the time had come for a little reciprocity. JFK was entirely willing to receive a prominent Russian reporter. When could he expect one?

Kharlamov shook his head. "It would be most difficult. You have chosen a very bad time to ask." He was referring to the case of fifteen Soviet correspondents, due in New York for the UN session, who had been denied visas by the State Department on a technicality.

"I will try to clear that up," I said, "if you will try to arrange the interview." When he agreed, I said Adzhubei would be an ideal choice. Kharlamov threw another name into the pot—Pavel Sutukov, the extremely able editor of *Pravda*. Adzhubei was then in Rome for an audience with Pope John XXIII—the first ever given to a ranking Communist. Kharlamov said he would speak to him on his return.

After two hours, the Russians stood up to leave. They would return to my room at eleven-thirty the next morning if the President's reply to Khrushchev was ready. Although Kharlamov understood my reason for having a Secret Service agent bring him and Bolshakov upstairs in a back elevator, he had to have his little joke with me at the door.

"No bodyguard? You trust us to find the back way out?"

I had left a call for the President and he sent for me at 1 A.M. I found him sitting up in bed, reading and chewing on an unlit cigar. He hadn't heard from Sulzberger. This was his first knowledge of Khrushchev's message and he had me repeat the key points a number of times. He got out of bed and stood for a long time at the window in his white pajamas, looking at the spectacular view of the Manhattan skyline.

"There's only one way you can read it," he finally said. "If Khrushchev is ready to listen to our views on Germany, he's not going to recognize the Ulbricht regime—not this year, at least—and that's good news."

Shortly before 1:30 A.M., he called Secretary Rusk for guidance on his response. They spoke for more than half an hour. Because Khrushchev had put nothing on paper, it was agreed that JFK should reply in the same informal way.

I sat on the edge of the bed, a sheaf of hotel stationery on my knee, while the President dictated a memorandum that I was to read to Kharlamov the next morning. State Department career officers wouldn't have slept a wink if they had known of the strange exercise in diplomatic communications that was taking place that night.

The President was cautiously receptive to Khrushchev's proposal for an early summit on Berlin. But first, he said, there should be a demonstration of Soviet good faith in Laos. (The Communist Pathet Lao was then threatening the shaky neutralist government of Souvanna Phouma, and there was danger that the cease-fire between rebel and royalist forces couldn't survive Pathet Lao pressure much longer. Laotian neutrality was to be a continuing friction point between the two heads of state. JFK repeatedly charged Khrushchev with failure to honor his commitment at Vienna in 1961 and the Geneva agreement of the following year. When First Deputy Premier Anastas Mikoyan came to Washington in November 1962—a month after the Cuban missile crisis—the President told him to advise Khrushchev that the abrogation of his agreement to halt North Vietnamese infiltration of Laos on the Ho Chi Minh trail could have "the most serious consequences"—a warning to the Kremlin that is as relevant today as it was then.)

In the memo he was now dictating to me, President Kennedy told Khrushchev that if the Kremlin was now willing to honor its commitments in Laos, a summit on the much more difficult question of Germany would be more likely to produce significant agreement. We would be watching and waiting.

The spirit of the memorandum was cordial, however. The President found Khrushchev's willingness to re-examine his position on Germany most encouraging. He was hopeful it would lead to a general relaxation of tensions.

Just before I left him at 3 A.M., JFK took a long look at his UN speech. He didn't change a word. It was already moderate in tone—not at all the "ultimatum" Khrushchev was afraid it might be. The U.S., of course, could not accept the Russian proposal for a troika to replace Hammarskjold. A three-nation directorate representing the Soviet bloc, the West and a neutral "would entrench the Cold War in the headquarters of peace . . . Even the three horses of the troika did not have three drivers, all going in different directions."

He then went to his central theme—disarmament. "Today, every inhabitant of this planet must contemplate the day when this planet may no longer be habitable. Every man, woman, and child lives under a nuclear sword of Damocles, hanging by the slenderest of threads, capable of being cut at any moment by accident or miscalculation or by madness. The weapons of war must be abolished before they abolish us." The U.S. now proposed "that disarmament negotiations resume promptly, and continue without interruption until an entire program for general and complete disarmament . . . has been actually achieved. The logical place to begin is a treaty assuring the end of nuclear tests of all kinds . . ." He was willing to continue test ban discussions, even though "others were secretly preparing new experiments in destruction" while we had been negotiating in good faith at Geneva.

It was his duty, the President said, "to report to this Assembly on two threats to peace . . . South Vietnam is already under attack—sometimes by a single assassin, sometimes by a band of guerrillas, recently by full battalions. The peaceful borders of Burma, Cambodia, and India have been repeatedly violated. And the peaceful people of Laos are in danger of losing the independence they gained not so long ago. No one can call these 'wars of liberation.' For these are free countries living under their own governments." He warned that if measures were not taken "to protect the small and the weak from such tactics," the freedom of all nations in both hemispheres was in danger.

The second threat to peace was "the crisis over Berlin and Germany . . . It is absurd to allege that we are threatening a war merely to prevent the Soviet Union and East Germany from signing a so-called 'treaty' of peace. The Western Allies are not concerned with any paper arrangement the Soviets may wish to make with a regime of their own creation, on territory occupied by their own troops and governed by their own agents . . . If there is a dangerous crisis in Berlin—and there is—it is because of threats against the vital interests and the deep commitments of the Western Powers, and the freedom of West Berlin. We cannot fail these commitments . . . but we believe a peaceful settlement is possible . . . The possibilities of negotiation are now being explored [and] if those who created this crisis desire peace, there will be peace and freedom in Berlin."

The President was convinced that all East-West differences could be resolved over the negotiating table, and we were ready to sit down. "Together we shall save our planet or together we shall perish in its flames . . . Mankind must put an end to war, or war will put an end to mankind."

Although firmly restating our position on the most explosive points of difference between Washington and Moscow, the speech was far more conciliatory in tone than his July 25 TV address, and there was nothing in it that was likely to send Khrushchev off on another tantrum.

Minutes before he left for the UN, the President gave his approval to the typescript of his memorandum to the Russian leader. A half hour later, I read it to Kharlamov and Bolshakov in my room. Although they were eager to leave to transmit JFK's message to Moscow, I held them for a moment at the door.

I had spoken earlier to Roger Tubby, Assistant Secretary of State for Public Affairs, concerning the visas for the fifteen Soviet correspondents. Were they being held up for legitimate reasons of national security or merely as a retaliation against recent Soviet treatment of American newsmen? Tubby said he didn't know but would find out. He called me back within the hour and said there were no security reasons for withholding the visas and they would be issued immediately. I informed Kharlamov of this fact and said I would now expect him to follow through with Adzhubei on the interview with President Kennedy. He said he would but couldn't resist a final swipe at State for its "stupidity" in not admitting the correspondents in the first place.

# XIII

## THE KENNEDY-KHRUSHCHEV
## CORRESPONDENCE

Friday, September 29, 1961, was a lazy fall day in Newport, Rhode Island. The President and his family were there for a brief vacation at the Narragansett Bay-front home of Mrs. Kennedy's mother and stepfather, Mr. and Mrs. Hugh D. Auchincloss.

I held a press briefing that morning at the Newport Naval Station. The big story of the day was Richard Nixon's decision to run for governor of California against incumbent Pat Brown—a miscalculation that was to wipe him out in 1964 as a presidential contender. The correspondents were looking for a White House angle.

"Does the President have any reaction to Mr. Nixon's announcement?"

"He does not," I replied.

"As a Californian, do you have a reaction?"

"No."

"Not even as a patriotic American?"

"No."

(The question was later put to the President directly at a press conference in Washington. What advice would he have given Nixon? "I would have been happy to tell him my opinion," JFK answered, "but he never asked me for it." Nixon, of course, wasn't a man to accept advice, much less solicit it. If he had, the President would have told him he was out of his mind. "He's only running to stay alive politically," he said to me after first learning of Nixon's decision. "He hasn't a chance of winning, but even if he did the risks are too great for the advantages he might win.")

After the briefing, I took off for an afternoon round of golf. When I got back to my quarters at the naval station, I had a call waiting from

Georgi Bolshakov in New York City. He said it was urgent that he see me immediately and he was willing to charter a plane and fly up that evening.

I told him to hold off. I would call him back within an hour. We had twenty or thirty correspondents with us at Newport and I knew that a sudden appearance by the Russian editor might cause a minor sensation on a slow news day. I put in calls to the President and to Dean Rusk, who was conferring with Soviet Foreign Minister Andrey Gromyko on Laos and Berlin that afternoon in New York. Their best guess was that Bolshakov had a Soviet response to JFK's memorandum on the Laotian crisis that I had read to him and Kharlamov just four days earlier. But they agreed with me that he should not be seen in Newport. I got back to him in New York. He was most unhappy when I told him the earliest we could meet would be at three-thirty the following afternoon at the Carlyle Hotel in Manhattan.

"If you knew the importance of what I have," he said, "you wouldn't keep me waiting that long."

Bolshakov had a flair for the conspiratorial—and why not? Editing the magazine USSR and serving as an interpreter for visiting Russian officials were but two of his chores in Washington. He was also, according to the CIA, a top agent for the KGB, the Soviet international spy network.

I flew to New York the next day and met Secretary Rusk who was winding up his conference with Gromyko. We met at Rusk's suite at the Waldorf-Astoria. He was most eager to find out what Bolshakov had up his sleeve. If it was the Kremlin's answer on Laos, why all the mystery? Gromyko could have given that to him at their meeting that day. I left for the Carlyle after promising to call Rusk immediately after my session with the Russian spy. Bolshakov was at my door at exactly three-thirty. He had two newspapers under his arm. Hidden in the fold of one of them was a thick manila envelope. He took his time opening it.

"Here," he said. "You may read this. Then it is for the eyes of the President only."

It was a twenty-six-page personal letter from Nikita S. Khrushchev to John F. Kennedy—the beginning of a secret correspondence that has no known parallel in the history of modern diplomacy. (The letters are now in the archives of the Kennedy Library. Their publication at a future time would depend on many factors—the state of U.S.-Soviet relations, possible injury to statesmen who may still be alive, and the risk that their publication might foreclose such personal and confidential exchanges between heads of state in the future.)

Khrushchev's first letter was a direct response on Laos but sections of it also dealt with the highly volatile situation in Berlin. Khrushchev was now ready to back off from the unconciliatory positions he had taken at Vienna. He saw no reason why negotiations in good faith could not produce settlements in both Southeast Asia and Germany. He was willing, if JFK was, to take another look at positions that had been frozen hard through fifteen years of cold war.

It was the most hopeful overture from Khrushchev since the release of the RB-47 pilots eight months earlier. I read the letter twice while Bolshakov sat smugly on the edge of the bed savoring my surprise. This first of many personal letters the Russian Premier was to write the American President was remarkable not only for its contents but for its candor. In contrast to the sterile gobbledegook that passes for high-level diplomatic correspondence, Khrushchev wrote with almost peasant simplicity and directness. He said, in effect, that you and I, Mr. President, are the leaders of two nations that are on a collision course. But because we are reasonable men, we agree that war between us is unthinkable. We have no choice but to put our heads together and find ways to live in peace.

Bolshakov had spent an entire night translating the letter from the Russian. But he also gave me the original in Russian to permit a comparison by our own translators. I was to deliver the letter to the President personally and to regard it as highly confidential. The only Russians in the United States who knew of it, Bolshakov said, were himself and Gromyko. Not even the Soviet ambassador to the United States, Mikhail Menshikov, had been told. The only Americans who knew were the President, the Secretary of State, and myself.

But Bolshakov had still another surprise for me. My recommendation to Mikhail Kharlamov that an important Soviet editor interview President Kennedy had been brought to the attention of Premier Khrushchev. He was all for it. Either Aleksey Adzhubei or Pavel Sutukov of *Pravda* would fly over for that purpose within the next two months.

This was great news. But I told Bolshakov we would expect the interview to run in full in the Soviet Union, and after agreement on our part that the Russian translation was accurate. He saw no difficulties.

Two minutes after Bolshakov was out the door, I had the President on the line at Newport. "Get that letter over to Dean Rusk as quickly as possible," he said, "then bring it up here to me."

The Secretary of State was not at the Waldorf-Astoria but would be back at seven-thirty. I was waiting for him. He also read the letter twice but did not want to give JFK a snap reaction. It was agreed that he would take the letter to Washington that night and have a State Department messenger return it to me at seven-thirty the next morning at the Northeast Airlines terminal at La Guardia, where I would be waiting for a plane to Providence. I gave it to the President two hours later on his return to the Auchincloss' from church. Immediately after reading it, JFK spoke to Rusk in Washington. They agreed that I should contact Bolshakov and inform him that the President would respond promptly, probably within the week. This settled the fact that Bolshakov and I would again serve as couriers—a role we were to play many times in the future.

I held another press briefing at the naval station that afternoon. I didn't know the Secretary of State and I had been seen together in New York by a newspaperman and one of the first questions came as a surprise.

"Is there anything you can tell us about your meeting with Secretary Rusk yesterday?" I came up with the fastest "no" of my career, and they didn't press me.

On this autumn weekend, there came into being a system of personal and direct correspondence between the two heads of state that was to continue until the President's murder more than two years later. It was to prove most useful in preserving the peace. But it also forced upon JFK the most fateful decision of his life during the Cuban missile crisis a year later.

Khrushchev would always initiate the exchange of letters. If I was in Washington, I would have a call from Bolshakov, who would tell me simply that "there is a matter of urgency." We would agree on a rendezvous, either on a Washington street corner or in a bar. If I wasn't available, the Russian would contact the President's brother, Bob, Ted Sorensen, or another White House staffer. When I was the courier and JFK's answer was ready, I would call Bolshakov and arrange to deliver it to him. He almost broke me up one night on a rainy street corner. After furtively slipping an envelope out of his pocket and into mine, he clapped a fraternal hand on my shoulder.

"Every man has his Russian," he said, "and I'm yours."

Early in November, Bolshakov told me Adzhubei had been chosen to interview the President, and he and I were to work out the arrangements. We quickly agreed on the date—November 25, and the place—Hyannis Port.

The chief editor of *Izvestia* arrived in Washington November 20 and I had a dinner party for him at my home. He brought gifts from his father-in-law—a Ukrainian blouse for my wife and a hamper of vodka and Armenian brandy for me. With Adzhubei were Yuri Barsukov, an *Izvestia* correspondent in Washington, and the omnipresent Bolshakov. Among the American guests were John C. Guthrie, director of the Soviet desk at the State Department, and his wife.

After a round of toasts to Soviet-American friendship and to all heroes —living and dead—of both countries, we sat down to dinner. My wife had spent all afternoon preparing stroganoff, one of her specialties. But Adzhubei, still distrustful of the Salinger cuisine after my blood rare chicken on his last visit, said he wasn't hungry. I broke open a bottle of his father-in-law's brandy for him and he held forth conversationally while the rest of us ate.

Adzhubei was a unique Communist. His antagonism toward the West was always tempered by a respect, which he never tried to conceal, for

Western technology and culture. He bought his trim-fitting suits in London and was a fair authority on French wines and American motor cars.

"I'm a New Frontier Russian," he often told me, implying a contempt for the doctrinaire old guard in Russia that saw nothing redeeming in the non-Communist world.

Adzhubei was much taken with my son, Stephen, on his first visit to Falls Church—probably because of that impromptu violin recital on the Potomac—and we had pursued the idea of exchanging sons for a summer. Stephen would spend his vacation with the Adzhubeis in Moscow and his oldest, Nikita, would live with us in Virginia.

But nothing had come of our discussion. Adzhubei hadn't been able to sell it to his superiors and the FBI and Secret Service had told me the cost of maintaining a summer-long, twenty-four-hour-a-day vigil over Khrushchev's grandson would be staggering.

After his second or third brandy that evening, Adzhubei became more than a little critical of his father-in-law. He said Khrushchev had not given the Adzhubeis a wedding present or any other gift in all the fifteen years of their marriage.

"I went hunting with him once in the woods outside Moscow," Adzhubei said. "I had a severe pain on my right side but said nothing until it became unbearable. When it was apparent that I had acute appendicitis and would have to be rushed to a hospital, he said he hoped I would be all right. That was the only personal interest he has ever shown in me."

Adzhubei's general political theme that night was that the Soviet Union and the United States were the only important world powers and should resolve their differences without paying too much attention to their allies. Neither the French, the British, nor the West Germans were reliable friends, he continued, and we should not permit them to complicate our relations with the Kremlin. But he quickly dropped the subject when Guthrie asked him if the Soviets would be equally willing to discard allies that had been particularly troublesome to us—East Germany and China, for example.

There was a reference to the interest of the Kennedy family in the arts and Adzhubei cut in with the comment that America had no corner on culture. He spoke glowingly of Rachmaninoff, Chaliapin, and Tolstoi. When it was pointed out to him that all three were pre-revolutionary figures, he came back with Shostakovich—although admitting that he didn't care for his music personally.

We had a musicale of our own after dinner. Barsukov was an excellent pianist and accompanied Bolshakov, who sang magnificently. I performed a little Bach—but not without interruption.

My daughter Suzanne, then ten years old, had taken quite a liking to Adzhubei. Whenever he caught her peeking at him over the top of the piano or around a corner, he would leap from his chair and chase her wildly through the downstairs rooms. It was on that note of hilarity that we all said goodnight.

Adzhubei and I flew to Hyannis two days before the interview and took rooms at the Yachtsman Hotel. With us were Bolshakov, who would translate for Adzhubei; Alexander Akalovsky of the State Department, who would translate for the President; and Jack Romagna, the official White House stenotype reporter, who would prepare the English transcript. Akalovsky had been the translator of the Eisenhower-Khrushchev conversations at Camp David, the Nixon visit to the Soviet Union, and the Kennedy-Khrushchev "summit" at Vienna. He was our best.

Adzhubei and I were now agreed on all the ground rules. We would both have to approve the transcript and he was to run the interview in full—a promise he kept with one unimportant exception. I was disappointed when he told me the interview would appear only in the Moscow edition of *Izvestia*, but I was in no position to haggle.

I can best describe Adzhubei's mood as cocky. He was looking forward to the exchange with JFK and even offered to give me his questions in advance so the President would know what to expect. When I declined, he said he was even willing to ask questions I might suggest, to be certain JFK had an opportunity to develop particular points for the Russian audience. I declined that offer, too, and he shrugged, as if to say:

"Well, don't blame me if it doesn't go your way."

The night before the interview we had dinner together at the Captain's Table in Hyannis. I recall it only because of an incident involving Al Spivak, a White House correspondent for UPI. Spivak was sitting at a table across the dining room and came over to see me. He didn't catch my eye immediately, but Adzhubei was aware of his presence. Suddenly, he twisted around in his chair and shouted: "You agent!" This was Adzhubei's idea of a joke, but to this day, Spivak is known to some of his colleagues in the White House press corps as "The Agent."

The next morning the President and Mrs. Kennedy met us at the door of their home in Hyannis Port. She introduced Adzhubei and Bolshakov to Caroline and John, and then left us. The interview began at 10:20 A.M. in the sun-bright living room. The President sat in a rocking chair and the two Russians on a sofa facing him. Akalovsky and I sat to one side. There was a preliminary exchange of hopes that the interview would create a new atmosphere of understanding between their two countries. Then Adzhubei swung into his questions, which he had written on large white cards. He would ask them in Russian, wait for the translation, then steal a peek at the next question as the President spoke.

The next two hours were notable on many counts. First, the interview was totally unlike any that JFK had ever given to an American newsman. Adzhubei, a man of spectacular ego, would introduce almost every question with a propagandistic defense of the Soviet position before inviting JFK's view on the same issue. He would then comment rather incisively on the President's answer.

We knew this was likely to happen but were confident that the President would more than hold his own. Adzhubei was there not only as a reporter but as an important Communist official. That, and his relationship with Khrushchev, gave him little choice. He must try to come home with an interview in which the American President came off second best to the chief editor of *Izvestia*.

JFK, impatient with Adzhubei's propagandistic prelude to every question, accused him early in the interview of being both "a newspaperman *and* a politician." The editor was only briefly dismayed. "In our country every citizen is a politician, because we like our country very much. The young and the old like the socialist system of our country and we are ready to fight for it until its victorious end."

The President took the line that there would be much less to fight about if the Russians would demonstrate a sincere desire to negotiate a nuclear test ban and a realistic settlement of the Berlin question. Adzhubei said "coals from the last war" were still burning in "the heart of every Soviet citizen . . . Thus, a solution of the question of a [German] peace treaty is the hope and tranquillity in the heart of every Soviet man. After all, we are still singing songs about those who did not come home from the war. I know that you participated in the war, that you are a hero of the war, and this is why I am talking to you in such lofty words."

JFK agreed that "the Soviet Union suffered more from World War II than any country . . . [but] I will say that the United States also suffered." In his own family, "my brother was killed in Europe—my sister's husband was killed in Europe. The point is that that war is now over. We want to prevent another war arising out of Germany. I think the important thing between the United States and the U.S.S.R. is not to create the kind of tension and pressure which, in the name of settling World War II, increases the chances of a conflict between the Soviet Union and its allies on one hand and the United States and its allies on the other."

Adzhubei could find no fault with that answer. "I will communicate your words to our readers with a feeling of satisfaction. We have always thought and still think of the Americans as realists." But we were not being realistic, he felt, in thinking that "the social changes which are happening in the world today are the result of actions in which Moscow has its hands."

The President was not at all certain that every country that had embraced Communism since World War II had done so voluntarily. "We have been under the impression that the Yalta Agreement and the Potsdam Agreement provided for a free choice for the peoples of Eastern Europe. They do not, in our opinion, have a free choice. You may argue that they may want to live under Communism, but if they do not they are not given the opportunity to change. We believe that if the Soviet Union . . . will permit the people of the world to live as they wish to live, relations between the Soviet Union and the United States will then be very satisfactory . . ."

Late in the interview, Adzhubei foolishly set a trap for himself with one of his own questions. If the President were a Soviet Navy veteran of World War II, wouldn't he be gravely disturbed by the rearmament of West Germany?

JFK's answer was devastating. "If I were a Soviet veteran, I would see that West Germany now has only nine divisions, which is a fraction of the Soviet forces. Nine divisions. It has no nuclear weapons of its own. It has a very small Air Force—almost no Navy, I think perhaps two or three submarines. Its nine divisions are under the international control of NATO . . . I don't believe West Germany is a military threat [to the Soviet Union] . . . Then I would look at the power of the United States and I would look at the power of the Soviet Union, and I would say that the important thing is for the Soviet Union and the United States not to get into a war which would destroy both of our systems."

The President added that "Chairman Khrushchev did not, nor did I, make the arrangements in 1945 in regard to Berlin," which he had described earlier as the issue most threatening to peace. "Our responsibility, given the situation, which is a difficult one, is to bring about peace, and I believe it can be done. In short, if I were a Soviet naval officer, I would feel . . . that the important thing now is to reach an accord with the United States, our ally during that second war."

Adzhubei replied weakly that "you answered this question not as a veteran of the Soviet armed forces but as President of the United States, and that is quite natural."

On my own visit to the Soviet Union the next year, most of the comment on the interview centered on this one answer. It was the most hopeful statement yet from the new President that peace was possible and that he was willing to work for it. But, beyond that, the manner in which Adzhubei chose to preface his question gave tremendously more impact to the answer. The average Russian citizen knew that JFK was not only a Navy veteran but a hero of World War II, and his answer was that much more moving and convincing.

Although the interview was always cordial on the surface, it was apparent the two principals did not hit it off personally. There was no warmth or humor at all—merely cold politeness. When it was over, the President was convinced he had done badly. He gestured for me to stay behind when Adzhubei said his perfunctory goodbyes and left with the translators for the hotel.

"That might have been a mistake," he said. "Your arrogant Russian friend got in as many shots as I did."

I suggested that he reserve judgment until he saw the transcript. When he did, he agreed with me that Adzhubei's clumsy polemics had made his own comments that much stronger.

I put Adzhubei, Bolshakov, and Akalovsky on an Air Force courier plane to New York with Romagna's transcript about five hours after the interview. There, Bolshakov translated the transcript into Russian and Akalovsky re-translated the Russian version into English to check its accuracy. The agreed translation was in Adzhubei's hands thirty-six hours later.

On November 28—three days after the interview—I got a two-word cable from Adzhubei:

INTERVJU OPUBLICKOVANO (INTERVIEW PUBLISHED).

It had been printed that day in the Moscow edition of *Izvestia*. I immediately released the transcript to AP, UPI, and all the foreign wire services and it ran the next day in every major country in the world. It was a sensation everywhere. Within hours, all copies of *Izvestia* were sold out in Moscow. Worn, much-read copies were still being passed hand-to-hand in Russia months later. The major point it had struck home to Soviet citizens was that John F. Kennedy was a reasonable and mature man. He had personal knowledge of the horrors of war. He was determined to avoid another. And he was certain it could be done. To the Russians, who had suffered the most casualty losses in World War II, this was the message, above all, they had been eager to hear from the young American leader.

The London *Daily Mail* called the interview "the most remarkable event of its kind for many years." A Norwegian paper described it as "sensational." The *Manchester Guardian* said it was "a remarkable attempt by the leaders of the western world to put the western case to the Soviet people." "The beginning of a new thaw in East-West relations," was the response of an editorialist in Sweden. In France it was hailed as a first step toward "an effective summit conference."

There was dissent, of course. The press in both East and West Germany found the interview lacking in concrete proposals. *Izvestia* itself did not comment but Tass, the Soviet news agency, also criticized the President for failing to suggest new alternatives in Berlin. It did praise, however, his "inclination toward serious talks." Red China damned it by ignoring it, a policy consistent with Peking's total opposition to the Khrushchev line. Radio Havana called JFK a hypocrite for picturing "warmongering Yankees as little Angels." An important newspaper in India said that America's recognition of anti-Communist regimes, "however undemocratic," belied the President's commitment to self-determination in the interview.

But world reaction was at least 10 to 1 in favor. Here was a positive and hopeful indication that the world's two nuclear giants were now a little more willing to talk to each other.

JFK, as always, was a realist. "It was important for me to speak directly to the Russian people, if only to try to convince them that we're not all that bloodthirsty. But it was a propaganda stroke for Khrushchev, too. Just by letting the interview run, he took the steam out of the argument that the Kremlin is afraid to let the Russian people hear the truth.

"When you add it all up, maybe the biggest plus is that Khrushchev held still for it. Do you think he might be softening up a little?"

Adzhubei kept his promise to run the interview verbatim, with one exception that wasn't worth quibbling over. The English transcript quotes him as saying that Khrushchev's visit to America in 1959 was not "completely satisfactory." It came out in *Izvestia:* "The positive results of that trip were wrecked and brought to nothing by the well-known actions of the then American administration." His motive for changing it was obvious. His original statement left it in doubt whether Khrushchev or his host was responsible for the failure of his mission. I never chided Adzhubei for tampering with the transcript. I probably would have done the same if the quick-tempered Khrushchev had been my father-in-law.

Finally, there had been much low-level grumbling in the State Department that the interview should have been arranged through diplomatic channels, not by me. But a couple of days after the interview ran in *Izvestia,* I got a letter from Llewellyn E. Thompson, the United States ambassador to the U.S.S.R. I didn't know him at the time. But we became friends on my trip to the Soviet Union and even closer friends later around a series of poker tables.

His letter read: "Just a line to tell you how delighted I am with the President's interview with Adzhubei. I must confess I was very dubious about the exercise as I did not think they would publish such a forceful statement of our position, and anything less than that would have misled the Soviet people. While the interview has only been published in the Moscow *Izvestia,* this in itself covers a good many people. What particularly pleased me was the tone of the President's remarks, which has made a great impression on the Russians I know, while at the same time getting across our point of view on specific issues."

"Getting across our point of view"—that had been JFK's only purpose in granting the interview and he had succeeded. The next phase almost brought us to a television confrontation between President Kennedy and Premier Khrushchev.

# XIV

## TV BOMBS OUT

January 18, 1962, was a day of uncommon excitement at the White House. That evening President and Mrs. Kennedy were to be hosts to Igor Stravinsky at a formal dinner in honor of the composer-pianist's eightieth birthday. Many of the most famous names in American music were on the guest list, and I had been looking forward to the event with great eagerness.

Stravinsky had been an idol of mine since the age of five, when I undertook the study of piano at the Toronto Conservatory of Music. But this was my first opportunity to meet him and to express my admiration for him and his music.

From the time I was four until I was eleven, it was my parents' intention that I should pursue a career in classical music. My instructor at the Toronto Conservatory was the brilliant Clement Hambourg, and it was as much a tribute to his iron discipline as to my own skill that I was able to perform my first concert at the age of six at the Canadian National Exposition in 1931.

My father's work as a mining engineer had taken us to Toronto in 1929, but we came back to San Francisco in 1932, where I continued my piano instruction under virtuoso Lev Shorr and studies in composition and conducting under Ray Green.

The atmosphere of my home was entirely musical. My father was an impresario for a time in Salt Lake City, staging concerts with Madame Schumann-Heink and pianist Harold Bauer. Many of the most important names in music—Pierre Monteux, Ernest Bloch, Isaac Stern, Yehudi Menuhin, and Edgard Varèse—were guests in our home.

But at the age of eleven I began to rebel. I was then studying not only piano, composition, and conducting, but also the violin. I had no friends of my own age—and had rarely swung a baseball bat or thrown a football.

My parents made the wise decision that I should de-emphasize music for a time and enroll in public schools. But once free of its rigorous disciplines, I never went back to music, except for the entertainment of my friends and family musicales with my children—Suzanne on the guitar, Stephen on the violin, and Marc joining me at the piano. My own abandonment of a concert career did not detract, however, from my love for music or the anticipation with which I was looking forward to the appearance of Stravinsky.

On the day of the event, I had lunch with Scotty Reston at the Metropolitan Club. The New York *Times* correspondent felt very strongly that the White House staff was defaulting on an important historical trust.

"Eisenhower left an excellent record behind for his own use or for that of future historians," he said. "But Kennedy's way of doing business is much too informal."

Reston said I should keep a White House diary containing the names of JFK's visitors, his off-the-record conversations, and events and disputes leading up to major decisions. I had always kept a record of my own conversations with important visitors in order to advise the President of them later. But I told Reston my position at the White House would be untenable if JFK and my colleagues thought I was jotting down their every chance remark. I did promise, however, to keep a general record of comings and goings at the White House. (Considering the avalanche of books on John F. Kennedy, during his administration and since his death, it would appear that Reston's worries were unfounded).

When I got back to the office I had a call from *my* Russian—Georgi Bolshakov. As always, it was most urgent that I see him. We got together that evening in the bar of the Hay Adams Hotel, just across Lafayette Square from the White House.

Bolshakov had three messages for me and the first was clearly the most important. Premier Khrushchev had agreed to my proposal for a series of television exchanges between himself and President Kennedy. He was ready to enter into specific negotiations at a time and place to be decided upon jointly.

This was great news. Although the Aleksey Adzhubei interview almost two months earlier had given JFK his first chance to speak directly to the Russian people, it was strictly a one-shot deal. The TV exchanges with Khrushchev would afford him not only a continuing opportunity to crack the Iron Curtain, but through the medium in which he was most effective in projecting his strong personality and convictions.

Bolshakov's next message was a personal one. Adzhubei's invitation to me and my family to visit him in Moscow was now official. He would like us to come over in April. In addition, the Soviet Union also would be most receptive to a visit from the President's brother, Attorney General Robert Kennedy, who was planning a tour of Europe that summer. The Kremlin would appreciate the earliest possible answer to both invitations.

As we were leaving the bar, the Russian editor told me that Adzhubei and his wife, Rada, were then in Havana on the final stop of a South American tour, and would be passing through Washington on their way home. I didn't mention it to Bolshakov but it struck me that the time was right for another chat between the President and Adzhubei, who had been a most useful line of communication to his father-in-law.

I went directly back to the White House for the Stravinsky dinner. Many of the world's most prominent musicians were on hand to honor the great Russian-born composer and pianist. After most of the guests had left, JFK summoned me to join him and Stravinsky.

"Mr. Salinger is also a pianist," the President said.

"Then I must hear him play," Stravinsky replied.

I was only halfway through one of my own compositions—a lively Gershwinesque suite—when Stravinsky walked out. I could only conclude that he had another engagement of great importance. Conductor Leonard Bernstein stuck it out until the last note, however.

"Interesting, very interesting," he said. But he never did invite me to appear as guest soloist with his New York Philharmonic.

I met with the President in his office shortly before midnight and told him of my conversation with Bolshakov. He said I was to proceed immediately with negotiations for the joint TV appearances with Khrushchev. He was also in favor of my visiting the Soviet Union, but told me to delay my answer for a time. He took a dim view, however, of the invitation to his brother Bob.

"I don't think he should be in this picture at all. The press would blow it up into something it wasn't, and it would certainly ruffle a lot of feathers over in State. I think we'll decline that one, but let's do it quietly and before the Russians announce it."

As for Adzhubei, the President said he would be happy to have him and Khrushchev's daughter to the White House for lunch.

JFK spoke to Bob the next morning and his brother concurred that he should not go to Russia. But on January 21, the day before I was to advise Bolshakov of the decision, the New York *Times* ran a page-one story by Max Frankel announcing the Soviet invitation to the Attorney General.

Bob quickly announced that long-standing commitments in other European capitals would not permit him to visit Moscow. But the damage was done. The New York *Daily News* carried a statement from Bolshakov that the turn-down was "a direct affront to the Soviet Union." There were angry mumblings from Moscow.

All of this couldn't have come at a worse time. Although the pressure was off in Berlin because of Khrushchev's retreat from recognition of East

Germany, the nuclear disarmament conference in Geneva was nearing collapse over Russia's unwillingness to accept inspection, and the situation in Southeast Asia was worsening.

Who was responsible for the leak? The only persons in the administration who knew of my conversation with Bolshakov—apart from the President and the Attorney General—were Secretary Rusk, the State Department's Soviet expert, Charles E. (Chip) Bohlen, and the then Assistant Secretary of State for European Affairs, Foy D. Kohler. We had only one clue. Scotty Reston had alerted Bob the night before that the story was going to break and said the informant was a Russian. But JFK was dubious. He felt Scotty had laid it on the Russians to protect a State Department source, perhaps an old-line career officer who didn't want the President's brother meddling in diplomatic affairs.

Whether it was true in this case or not, JFK's frequent use of non-diplomats, including myself, to communicate with the Russians was always met with grumbling in the middle echelons of the State Department. In fairness, it should be said that Rusk, Bohlen, and Kohler did not share this attitude.

I met with Bolshakov again on the night of January 23 to arrange the negotiations for the TV exchange. He was still unhappy over the Bob Kennedy incident and denied that a Russian source could have been responsible. But he did listen attentively to my explanation of the President's position and said he would relay it to Moscow. He again became impatient, however, when I said there was still no decision on whether I would visit Russia. Privately, I felt the President had no choice but to send me or risk another "affront" to the Kremlin. I took a little of the edge off Bolshakov's ill humor by telling him the President would like to have the Adzhubeis to lunch on January 30.

We then got down to business on the TV exchange. Bolshakov said that Mikhail Kharlamov would be the negotiator for Khrushchev. I told him that Edward R. Murrow, director of the USIA, and I would speak for JFK. We quickly agreed to meet in Paris on January 28 and 29—just five days away.

Because there was no certainty of reaching agreement with Kharlamov, it was decided at the White House that we should not announce the impending TV exchange until it was a *fait accompli*. I should have a cover story for my visit to Paris. (Interestingly, Kharlamov felt the same way. He left for the French capital as a "tourist" en route to Denmark.)

Ed Murrow, who was then touring Africa, already had plans to be in Paris on January 29, and it was agreed that the public explanation for my trip was to confer with him and top American information officers from London, Paris, Bonn, and Rome. I was able to reach Ed in Lagos, Nigeria, and he said he could be in Paris a day early. I then called our ambassador to France, James M. Gavin, and told him I was coming.

The cover story quickly came a cropper. I got a wire from Gavin that the French Foreign Office had tipped the press that both Kharlamov and I would be in Paris at the same time, and hinted at an important connection between the two visits. This quickly led to speculation, here and abroad, that a summit conference was in the offing, which I had to deny vigorously. I stuck to my story that I was going to Paris merely to talk to Murrow and his information specialists.

There was never a doubt in my mind who the villain was: Pierre Baraduc, the press spokesman for the French Foreign Office. I had found him most difficult to work with during President Kennedy's visit in 1961 with General de Gaulle. And now, apparently angry because Kharlamov and I had not taken him into our confidence, he was doing his best to stir up controversy over our visit.

A throng of reporters was waiting for me when the plane set down at Orly Airport. Why was I in Paris? I gave them the cover story. Did I know Kharlamov was also there? I did. Did I plan to meet with him? Yes, if we could work it out.

Kharlamov flew in an hour later and ran through the same charade.

Our first public encounter came that night at a cocktail party in the home of Cecil Lyon, minister of the U. S. Embassy. Baraduc was also there and spent most of the time eavesdropping on Kharlamov and me. But our past relations with him had been of such an unsatisfactory nature that the Russian and I had agreed by telephone before the party that nothing would be said of the television exchange.

There had been flurries in the press about a possible shakeup in the Kremlin and the status of former Soviet Foreign Minister V. M. Molotov. Kharlamov laughed. Would Khrushchev be vacationing on the Black Sea and Deputy Chairman Anastas Mikoyan be touring Africa if there was a crisis in Moscow? As for Molotov, Kharlamov shrugged him off as "a political cadaver. No one pays any attention to him any more." (When I went to the Soviet Union on a business trip in 1965, Kharlamov himself was described as "a political cadaver." Both he and Adzhubei were demoted to minor positions after the fall of Khrushchev in 1964. Adzhubei had become assistant editor of the magazine, *Soviet Union*, and Kharlamov was running the government printing plant.) Late in the evening, an argument broke out between Baraduc and Kharlamov. The Frenchman lit into the Russian for the Kremlin's expulsion of Sacha Simon, a correspondent for *Le Figaro*. When Kharlamov reminded him that the French government had recently expelled John Rich, an American reporter for NBC, Baraduc snorted and walked away.

The actual negotiations began the next morning in the Soviet Embassy. Other than Murrow, Kharlamov, and myself, the only persons present were the Russian and English translators. I was glad to have Murrow with me. He was a man of great warmth and incisive intelligence. He had given up a $125,000 a year berth as a TV commentator for a salary of $21,000 as director of the USIA. There were, of course, many New Frontiersmen who had left private enterprise to earn a fraction of their former salaries in government, but most of them were younger men who could afford to interrupt their careers briefly. Murrow, however, made his sacrifice in middle life, and at a time when he was not in the best of health. But despite this, he was ready on a moment's notice to fly wherever the President sent him and to undertake assignments that would have exhausted a far younger man. His death in April 1965 was a tremendous loss not only to the nation he had served as a courageous reporter, but to all of us who had the privilege of knowing him and working with him.

Kharlamov had come to Paris with an absolutely free hand to negotiate a deal—a refreshing change from the usual Russian line that "I must ask my government for further instructions." My original proposal was for a series of fifteen-minute programs, with the principals dividing the time evenly. But Murrow and I quickly agreed to Kharlamov's suggestion that we double the length to thirty minutes. The order in which JFK and Khrushchev would appear on the screen would be left to the discretion of their advisers. If the Soviets felt Khrushchev should have the last word in his own country, that was all right with us. We would have the same option of running the President either first or last for American viewers.

Murrow thought the first show should have a general theme, such as "What Kind of World I Would Like to Live In." After that, the exchanges would be on specific subjects—Berlin, Southeast Asia, nuclear testing, or military alliances. Kharlamov agreed but with the stipulation that the principals could stray a little from the subject, if they chose. The whole purpose of the series, however, was to advance relations between the two countries. In no event were they to resort to diatribe or polemics.

We then agreed on March 18, 1962, as the date of the first exchange. It would be telecast simultaneously at twelve noon Washington time and 7 P.M. Moscow time. Each of us would film our principal on March 9 or 10 in 35 mm, and immediately exchange negatives so the full show could be put together. It was agreed, further, that each of us would try to promote the widest possible distribution of additional negatives among other countries in the free and Communist worlds.

Kharlamov was jubilant when the four-hour negotiations came to an end. "Who says the Russians and the Americans can't sit down and work things out?"

I felt this was an opportune time to approach the Russians directly on the subject of a "hot line" between Moscow and Washington. Our countries now had the capacity to wage intercontinental nuclear war with the touch of a button. It was obvious that we should also have an instantaneous channel of communication to minimize the possibility of a misunderstanding or miscalculation that might prompt someone to press that button by mistake. There had been much comment in the press and elsewhere on the necessity of a direct link between the two capitals, but nothing had been done about it.

I had heard from a Soviet source that Khrushchev was generally in favor of the idea. Would the Soviet Union now be willing to enter into direct negotiations? Kharlamov said he would check it out on his return to Moscow and let me know. It is a chilling, but historic, fact that the Russians did not agree to "hot line" negotiations until *after* the Cuban missile crisis of October 1962. The delay could have been fatal.

The Paris negotiations ended with a luncheon at the Soviet Embassy. Over vodka and caviar, Kharlamov began needling Murrow as a "master propagandist," and took particular issue with the content of the Voice of America broadcasts.

But Murrow had the last word. "I want you to come over and testify before the congressional committees that pass on appropriations from the USIA," he said to Kharlamov. "With your testimonial to our effectiveness, I think they might give me twice as much money."

I had to rush to catch a plane back to Washington for the President's luncheon the next day for the Adzhubeis. Kharlamov told me at the door that our agreement was final and that all he would have to clear with Khrushchev was the date of the first telecast. He would have the word on that within ten days.

The lunch with the Adzhubeis was most cordial. Mrs. Kennedy and Khrushchev's daughter hit it off from the start. Rada was a bit on the chubby side, but not by Russian standards. She had a buoyant sense of humor and spoke English and French fluently. On this trip she was wearing a new mink coat she had bought in Paris. As always on his American visits, Adzhubei brought Bolshakov along to translate. Adzhubei denied that he understood English. But, judging from his off-guard reactions, I still think he had a fair understanding of what was being said around him.

The high point of the luncheon—for me, at least—was when the President told Adzhubei that I would accept his invitation to visit the Soviet Union in April. It had already been decided at the White House that I would go and for the official purpose of conferring with leaders of the Soviet communications industry. The Adzhubeis were sorry my family wouldn't be with me.

"Aleksey always comes home with wonderful stories of your children," said Rada. I was having a reception for the Adzhubeis that evening at my home in Falls Church, and told her that after she met my wild brood, she might be glad they weren't going to be her house guests.

After the lunch, JFK took Adzhubei and Bolshakov to the Oval Room on the second floor. He had a number of comments on American policy that he knew Adzhubei would communicate directly to his father-in-law.

First, the Kremlin must not misjudge American intentions in Berlin. We were there to stay, despite the more hopeful atmosphere resulting from Khrushchev's decision to postpone indefinitely Soviet recognition of the East German regime. Khrushchev should also know that we would take stronger action in Southeast Asia if Communist Pathet Lao forces in Laos continued to harbor forces attacking the government of South Vietnam. (Two months later, while I was meeting with Khrushchev in a dacha outside Moscow, JFK sent additional United States troops into Thailand to serve notice on the Pathet Lao that we would fight to defend the free governments of both Laos and South Vietnam.)

The President had a final word for Khrushchev. We were studying the military advantages to the Soviets of their violation of the moratorium on nuclear tests. We were still testing only under ground, although most of the forty Russian tests had been in the atmosphere, including a monstrous fifty-eight-megatonner. There must be no great surprise in the Kremlin if our appraisal of the Soviet testing effort should result in further American tests in the atmosphere.

I held a press briefing after the Adzhubeis left the White House, and described the conversation merely as "informal and wide-ranging. But the President, in talking to Mr. Adzhubei, is always conscious of the fact that he is in a position to communicate our views directly to his father-in-law."

I then broke the story that I would be going to the Soviet Union in two months to try to achieve a freer exchange of information between Moscow and Washington. My friends in the press corps had never thought of me as a foreign emissary. Wouldn't I be butting heads with official organizations already negotiating cultural agreements? I didn't think so. Did I have clearance with the State Department? I did. Would I call on Khrushchev? I had no such plans. (In fact, Adzhubei had never brought up that possibility in any of our discussions about the visit.)

The reception for Adzhubei in my home that night was a reprise of his two former visits to Falls Church. There was an endless series of toasts— a songfest around the piano, led by Bolshakov with his booming basso— and a children's hour in which both of the Adzhubeis frolicked with Marc, Suzanne, and Stephen. The Adzhubeis had lunch the next day with Bob Kennedy and then flew home.

Two weeks later, on February 13, Bolshakov notified me that Khrushchev had agreed to all the arrangements but one for his joint appearances with the President. He would prefer that the first go on the air May 25 instead of March 18. I readily agreed to the five-week delay.

I met privately on February 28 with the top executives of the three major American television networks in New York. Among those attending the conference in the Carlyle Hotel were Robert Kintner, president of NBC (now a special assistant to President Johnson); Julian Goodman, chief of the news department of the same network; Dr. Frank Stanton, president of CBS; and former White House Press Secretary Jim Hagerty, representing ABC. There was much initial grumbling that the networks hadn't been brought into the picture earlier. But they finally bought my argument that I had nothing to discuss with them until I was certain we had a show. Obviously, the nets could have made a substantial creative contribution to the negotiations in Paris, but it was highly questionable that Kharlamov would have agreed to their participation. All three networks, however, agreed to run the first of the series on May 25. As we were leaving the suite, I had a call from McGeorge Bundy at the White House.

The President had come to a most difficult and reluctant decision. The Soviet nuclear tests in the atmosphere had given them a new capability that might encourage aggressive designs. We had no choice but to return to atmospheric testing ourselves. The President would announce his decision on March 2 on nationwide television if the network executives with whom I was then conferring would allocate the time. All agreed.

I didn't know it then but at the very instant I thought the TV exchange was a certainty, the whole deal was already falling apart.

Three days later the President told the nation it was his intention to resume atmospheric testing over the Pacific in late April. But he was willing to cancel the series if the Soviets would sign, before that time, a treaty "to halt permanently the testing of all nuclear weapons, in every environment: in the air, in outer space, under ground and under water." If the Kremlin would not agree to such a treaty, "then we shall be left with no choice but to keep our own defensive arsenal adequate for the security of all free men."

His decision met with solid editorial support across the country, but there was sharp criticism—mostly from Republican publishers—of JFK's intention to debate Khrushchev on television. The New York *Daily News* said it was a bad trade because the Soviet Union had only five million TV sets and we had fifty million. Actually, there were ten million sets in Russia, but the *News'* argument was still off-point. Khrushchev could, and did, appear on American TV whenever he chose, just by calling in one of the network correspondents. But the exchange would give President Kennedy an Iron Curtain audience he had no other way of reaching.

I met with the President and McGeorge Bundy in the President's office on April 5 to discuss the script for the first debate. They felt the first show would have greater appeal if Mrs. Kennedy and Mrs. Khrushchev made brief appearances. I called Bolshakov at home, where he was sick in bed, and he said he would relay the suggestion to Kharlamov in Moscow. Not more than a half hour later, he was back on the line.

"I have bad news for you. I must see you immediately." We made an appointment for the Hay Adams bar for 6:30.

It was no jolly Russian who found me waiting at a back table. For the first time since I had known him, Bolshakov was ill at ease with me. His hands were trembling but I wrote it off to the fact that he had just gotten out of a sick bed.

Then he blurted it out.

"My government wants to call off the entire Kennedy-Khrushchev exchange."

I demanded to know why.

"The fault is your own President's for deciding to resume the nuclear tests. The Soviet people would not understand it if their Premier would consent to a joint appearance with him at a time like this."

The bar was crowded with newsmen and I tried to keep my voice down. It was not JFK but Khrushchev who had broken the moratorium. How naive could the Russians be if they thought that would not force us to a decision?

Bolshakov tried to calm me down.

"None of this affects your visit to the Soviet Union. We still want you to come."

I slammed my fist on the table.

"It sure as hell does affect my visit. What's the use of trying to open up lines of communication if your people are going to behave this stupidly?" Bolshakov knew the Soviet position was wrong and didn't try to argue with me.

I got out of there while I still had a little control over my temper, and went directly to the President's office. He became almost as angry as I was, and sent for Sorensen, who already was working on the draft of his statement for the opening exchange.

JFK's first thought was for me to contact Bolshakov and cancel my own visit to Russia in retaliation.

"You might add that this is just another example of why it's so difficult for us to come to any agreement at all with the Russians."

But then he cooled off and called Chip Bohlen, the State Department expert on Soviet affairs. Bohlen said it would be unwise to react too strongly. His thought was that I should insist to Bolshakov that our two governments announce the cancellation as a joint decision, without going into the reasons. The President concurred.

"But tell him also that we are greatly displeased. Point out the criticism we've had from our own press and the great lengths we went to in good faith to bring this agreement to fruition. And you might stress *good faith*."

Bolshakov, glad to be off the hook, quickly agreed to the joint announcement. But that wasn't my last word to a Russian on the subject. I tried to revive the project with Khrushchev personally when I saw him in Moscow two months later.

# XV

## WITH KHRUSHCHEV

The announcement that President Kennedy was sending me to the Soviet Union to negotiate a freer exchange of information drew a barrage of criticism. Newspapers across the country gave a banner line play to Republican charges of "secret diplomacy." I was the target of angry comment on the floor of Congress. State Department career officers maneuvering behind the scenes also took their best shots. And criticism within the White House was just as intense, although it never hit the headlines.

The most rabid critic of my mission to Moscow was Bruce Alger, the arch-conservative Republican congressman from Texas. He said I was "a young and inexperienced White House publicity man," and that JFK shouldn't let me out of his sight, much less out of the country. A television audience of millions heard the President come to my defense at a press conference:

"I know there are always some people who feel that Americans are always young and inexperienced, and foreigners are always able and tough and great negotiators. But I don't think the United States would have acquired its present position of leadership in the free world if that view were correct. Now he (Congressman Alger) also said that Mr. Salinger's main job was to increase my standing in the Gallup Poll. Having done that, he is now moving on to improve our communications."

There was a roar of laughter from the press.

When I got back to the White House after the press conference, I found a wire from a friend in California, Don L. Bradley:

DON'T LET THEM SELL YOU THE KREMLIN.

Presidential Assistant Ken O'Donnell said, "It isn't important whether you can carry the mission off successfully or not, although I think you'll do all right. Just the announcement that you're going has already been a political minus for the President."

The opposition from the middle echelons in the State Department was much more subtle—and always anonymous. There were the inevitable leaks to the press that high-ranking diplomats were "viewing with alarm" and that the President was "privately regretting his decision." This came as no surprise. Old hands in State were still growling over my television debate with Aleksey Adzhubei and Mikhail Kharlamov and my role in arranging Adzhubei's interview with JFK for *Izvestia*. Their view was that White House personnel—and frequently the President himself—had no right to meddle in international affairs. I recall vividly a conversation with a top State Department official a month after JFK took office. The President had told me to relay a not very significant order to him.

"I don't know whether I should follow through on this or not," he said.

"But it's the President's policy," I replied.

"It may be the President's policy," he bristled, "but is it the State Department's?"

JFK finally began to have his own misgivings but he felt my plans were too far along to call off without offending the Russians. He did tell me, however, to leave my family behind.

"That way, at least, they won't be able to call it a social jaunt at government expense."

My itinerary was now firm. I would leave for Europe on May 5 and visit Bonn and Amsterdam before arriving in Moscow on May 11 for a five-day visit. My traveling companions would be Tom Sorensen, director of Policy and Planning for the USIA (and brother of White House Special Counsel Ted Sorensen), and Alexander Akalovsky, the State Department's top Russian translator. To prepare myself, I took a cram course in Russian and was given extensive briefings by Soviet experts in both State and the USIA.

Four days before my departure, I had lunch at the Soviet Embassy with Anatoly Dobrynin, the new U.S.S.R. ambassador, to settle on final arrangements. In contrast to most Soviet diplomats, who always had their guard up in the presence of Americans, the tall, elegant Dobrynin had a casual air.

"Call me Anatoly," were his first words to me.

Dobrynin, unlike his predecessor, Mikhail Menshikov, was an intimate of Khrushchev's and had his absolute confidence. The new ambassador was aware of the secret letters from Khrushchev to President Kennedy and the role Georgi Bolshakov and I had been playing as couriers.

"All that will stop now," he told me. "All further communications from the Chairman to the President will go directly through me."

Dobrynin, a proponent of informal diplomacy, was all in favor of my Russian tour. "We diplomats have been talking to each other for years," he said, "and not very much happens. The only way Americans can understand Russia is to go there and talk to the people to find out what they are thinking. That's what I want to do here. I want to have the widest possible relationship with Americans both in and out of government. I don't want to exchange angry notes. I want to exchange honest opinions."

Shortly before leaving Moscow, Dobrynin and his wife had seen Mrs. Kennedy's television tour of the White House. "A most charming woman," said the ambassador. "She and my wife will like each other."

He also told me that Khrushchev was "much taken with Mrs. Kennedy at Vienna, and you are aware, of course, of the Chairman's role in electing her husband President."

I said that I was not.

Dobrynin explained that during the presidential campaign a U. S. Embassy official in Moscow had been critical of the Soviet press for attacking Richard Nixon but not John F. Kennedy. The American diplomat felt this left the impression that the Kremlin was for JFK.

"When this statement was brought to Khrushchev's attention," Dobrynin said, "the Chairman promptly gave a speech calling the rival candidates 'two boots on the same foot,' thus creating the impression he didn't like either one."

Dobrynin smiled. "If it would be helpful to you, Mr. Salinger, I could arrange for *Pravda* and *Izvestia* to print bad things about you after you come home from your visit."

I reminded him that *Izvestia* already had given my associate, Andy Hatcher, an editorial pounding. In August 1961, on a day when I was away from Washington, Andy had announced the official U.S. reaction to the Soviet Union's resumption of nuclear testing. He said it was a cause for "uneasiness and indignation." He was immediately characterized in *Izvestia* as a "hypocritical weeper" and the modern incarnation of Job Trotter, the sly coachman in Dickens' *Pickwick Papers*, "who feigns anger and astonishment to conceal his own employer's wrongdoing."

I told Dobrynin that I already had all the criticism I could handle, and would be willing to settle for the blast at Andy.

Sorensen and I flew first to Bonn for a conference with American and West German information specialists. Akalovsky would catch up with us in Amsterdam. There had been recent friction between Washington and the West German capital over conflicting policy statements on Berlin. Our purpose was to agree on more direct lines of communication to prevent future misunderstandings.

But even while we were in Bonn, two press conferences by Chancellor Konrad Adenauer set off a new furor. The brunt of his remarks, as interpreted by the press, was that the United States should hold no further exploratory discussions with the Soviet Union on the subject of a thirteen-nation commission to arbitrate access rights to Berlin. This left the alarming implication that West Germany would now deal with the East German Communists in its own way. Washington was more than a little upset.

I had a summons to call on Foreign Minister Gerhard Schroeder at the chancellory. He was greatly disturbed. Would I please advise the President that Dr. Adenauer had been misunderstood? He had not said that he was against further American-Soviet discussions, merely that the intransigent Russian position held forth little hope of agreement. I felt the press was correct in its original interpretation but cabled Schroeder's explanation to JFK.

The next stop was Amsterdam for an address at The Hague to the Netherlands Society for Public Relations. Sorensen, Akalovsky, and I then caught a commercial Soviet airliner for Moscow. The Aeroflot TU-104 took only two and a half hours for the 1600-mile flight and the service was excellent. But the jet's most striking feature was a huge marble lavatory that would have been more appropriate to a transatlantic liner.

A large crowd was waiting at Sheremetyevo Airport. I saw Ambassador Llewellyn (Tommy) Thompson gesturing to me urgently as I ran the gauntlet of American and Soviet correspondents. Then came Adzhubei and Kharlamov with a welcoming party of Russian officials. Tommy finally got me off to one side. He said it was an entirely new ball game and my hosts were calling the signals.

"Adzhubei insists on taking you from here to the government dacha outside the city. You will spend most of tomorrow there with Khrushchev."

Not once in all the weeks of negotiation over my visit had the Russians given me the slightest hint that I would even see Khrushchev, much less spend a day with him. In fact, our most telling rebuttal to Republican howls of secret diplomacy had been that I would not be engaging in discussions with top-level Soviet leaders. I would consult only with my own counterparts in the communications field. There could be no doubt that Khrushchev himself was responsible for this sudden switch in plans and, just as obviously, I could not offend him by refusing the invitation.

Much of my briefing for the trip had been on past and present relations with the Soviet Union, but I was understandably reluctant to sit down with Khrushchev himself without last-minute guidance from Thompson. Although my hosts were clearly impatient with the delay, they agreed to drive me first to Spaso House, the American Embassy, where Tommy brought me up-to-date on the latest developments. I also cabled the President and his return instructions were specific. I was not to be drawn into a substantive discussion of questions other than communications by Khrushchev. If he went into foreign policy issues, I was merely to listen and assure him that I would transmit his views to Washington. (To counter a possible new wave of criticism at home, the White House prepared a statement to the effect that I was seeing Khrushchev at his invitation, our conversation would be entirely informal, and there was absolutely no change in my original assignment. But, strangely, there was no important revival of the earlier attack, and the statement was not issued.)

The Ogoryevo dacha, a summer guest residence for high Soviet officials, was twenty-two miles outside the capital in a forest of birch and pine. The grounds were encircled by a high brick wall and the gates were heavily guarded by security police. The turreted two-story wood and brick residence had a sweeping view of the Moscow River. Strangely, the dacha had only two bedrooms, but five dining rooms. Richard Nixon was a guest there in 1959—and later described his adventures in *Six Crises*.

Shortly after our arrival we were joined by Leonid Zamyatin, deputy chief of the American Countries Division of the Soviet Foreign Office; Viktor Sukhodrev, interpreter for Khrushchev; and Mrs. Sukhodrev, a spectacularly attractive blonde and a leading Soviet actress before her marriage.

We then sat down to the first of a series of three-hour Soviet meals. As a starter, there were huge platters of smoked salmon, caviar, cucumber salad, cold cuts, and black bread. Through this course, there was one vodka toast after another—and it was bad manners to sip. The whole jigger had to go down in one swallow. But because of the heavy infusion of food between toasts, I never felt the effects of the vodka. After the appetizers came hot entrees of fish and beef with the appropriate Georgian wines. For dessert, there were at least five varieties of cheese and huge baskets of fruit. And, finally, steaming pots of coffee and decanters of Armenian cognac. (I credit my natural temperance with the fact that I put on only six pounds during the five days I spent in Russia.)

After dinner, we all went down to a small theater in the basement to see a Russian science-fiction picture *The Amphibious Man*. The hero was half fish and could breathe only under water—an environmental disadvantage that had no effect at all on his love life.

It had been a long day for us Americans and our hosts let us go to bed early. I was entirely alone in the dacha. Sorensen, Akalovsky, and the Russians slept in cottages down the road.

When the housekeeper came into the bedroom the next morning, she took one look at the giant four-poster, glanced at me strangely, and walked out, mumbling to herself. I found out later that she thought Mrs. Sukhodrev was my wife, and couldn't understand why I had slept alone.

I was still recovering from dinner the night before and told Adzhubei

I would have a light breakfast. I got twelve pancakes and a large side order of sausage. It *was* light by Russian standards. The others at the table had eggs, pancakes, ham, sausage, toast, coffee—and brandy.

We were joined after breakfast by Rada Adzhubei and her two youngsters, Nikita and Aleksey, Jr., and Yuri Zhukov, former chairman of the State Committee for Cultural Relations with Foreign Countries. He had resigned recently to return to his first love, journalism, and wrote the "Observer" column in *Pravda*—the daily "bible" of official Kremlin policy.

Mrs. Adzhubei was briefly unhappy with me for coming to Moscow alone. "It's terrible how you Americans treat your wives," she said.

Khrushchev was not due at the dacha until shortly before noon. To pass the time, Adzhubei and Kharlamov took me for a walk in the woods— the first of three long safaris that weekend. The weather was cold and overcast and we all wore topcoats. Not far from the dacha, we came across a shooting gallery, much like those at American amusement parks. Adzhubei challenged me to a test of marksmanship and we fired away at the moving targets for half an hour, with a modicum of success, before agreeing to call it a draw.

The sharpest memory I have of Khrushchev's arrival is that the security arrangements were almost identical to those our own Secret Service uses to protect the President. A security agent bounded from the limousine even before it came to a stop and quickly scanned the small crowd waiting on the lawn. But he did not open the door for Khrushchev until five more agents, riding in a second car, had also taken up their positions.

Khrushchev was all smiles. He tipped his hat to the women and then rammed it back on his head. It stayed there the rest of the day—even through lunch. He walked toward me, his hand outstretched.

"I thank your President for having my daughter to lunch at the White House," were his first words. "No other American President has had the courage to do that."

JFK's invitation to the Adzhubeis was a central reason for the Premier's many courtesies to me over the next two days. He spoke of it frequently and always with a reference to the President's "courage."

Khrushchev did not speak English and my cram course in Russian was hardly adequate for conversations with a head of state. During all my discussions with him, either his translator, Sukhodrev, or mine, Akalovsky, was always with us.

We spent the next hour cruising up and down the bleak Moscow River in a small armada of power launches. Occasionally, a peasant on the bank would recognize his Premier and wave. Khrushchev would jump to his feet, shout, and wave back—frequently with both arms. For a politician whose tenure did not depend on the popular vote, he was as much aware of his image as a small-town alderman. The same launch had run aground on a sandspit when Richard Nixon was Khrushchev's guest three years earlier, but our cruise was uneventful except for the Premier's political exertions.

Once ashore, Khrushchev struck off into the forest. With my heavy ballast of breakfast, I had a rough time keeping up with his loping stride. Although he was sixty-eight years old, he still had the hard, vigorous physique of the miner and laborer he had been in his youth. The women didn't even try to keep pace as we plunged deeper and deeper into the misty woods.

We finally came to our destination—a skeet-shooting range. There were twin traps at each side that shot a crisscross pattern of clay pigeons. To shatter both, you had to aim and fire two blasts from the shotgun in a split second. Khrushchev was an expert. He hit the targets eight out of ten times and at least half of his volleys were doubles. Then it was my turn. I hadn't had a skeet gun in my hands for fifteen years and hit only one clay pigeon in six tries.

"Don't feel badly," Khrushchev said. "I've got generals who can't hit anything either." Then, with all the flourish of a carnival pitchman, he gave me a porcelain doll as a prize.

I had been looking forward to a warm fireplace, but my host had other plans. Pulling his hat farther over his ears to protect them from the cold, he led us down a trail that wound *away* from the dacha. We walked at least five miles during the next two hours. Khrushchev's running conversation with me was entirely non-political, except for one biting reference to Dr. Adenauer. Referring to the confusion over the Chancellor's press conference remarks at Bonn that same week, the Premier spoke of him as "a dangerous and senile old man. The only way Adenauer could reunite Germany is through war, and he hasn't got the courage to do that."

Khrushchev said President Kennedy "is much more reasonable. That was a very good statement he made on the importance of honest negotiations on Berlin." (JFK had told his press conference that we would continue to negotiate on access to Berlin, and quoted Winston Churchill: "It is better to jaw, jaw than to war, war. We will continue to jaw, jaw.")

The Premier had two fixations—Berlin and Soviet agriculture. After a long monologue on recent Russian successes with chemical fertilizers, he suddenly stopped walking, glanced at me impatiently, and said:

"I don't know why I waste my time explaining all this to you. You don't know anything about agriculture."

I had to admit that I didn't. He smiled. "That's all right. Stalin didn't either."

Of the Russians hiking along with us (the women had long since given up and gone back to the dacha) Khrushchev had the greatest affection for Zhukov, the *Pravda* columnist. Adzhubei, normally an extremely garrulous companion, was silent and almost sullen in his father-in-law's presence.

Khrushchev chided Zhukov for giving up his ministerial rank to return to journalism. "I thought it was time to step down and let a younger man take over," said Zhukov, who was then in his fifties.

Khrushchev winked at me. "Zhukov dares to talk of younger men. He wants me to step down, too. That's what he wants." Then he smiled wanly. "He's right, of course. I am much too old." Over the next two days, the Premier spoke often of his age and of transferring his power to a younger man of his own choice. He had no suspicion that two years later he would leave office involuntarily and would have no voice in the selection of his successor.

When we finally got back to the dacha around 3 P.M.—all of us breathless except Khrushchev—we found the women waiting at a huge table set up on the patio overlooking the river. The sun was out now and it was warmer.

Khrushchev beamed proudly at the massive spread of food and clapped a hand on my shoulder.

"Sit down, Gospodin Salinger. You have worked for your lunch and now you shall have it." (Gospodin is the Russian word for Mister in contradistinction to Tovarich, which means Comrade and is reserved for Communist Party members.)

The Premier tilted his hat lower over his eyes to shield them from the sun and reached for the vodka. "I've escaped my doctors today," he said, "and I'm going to have a good time."

Khrushchev, Kharlamov, Adzhubei, and Zhukov took turns proposing toasts, and the Premier drank along with us, glass for glass. But, despite his age, the alcohol had no visible effect on him. He was a great story-teller and, more often than not, the Soviet system was the butt of his jokes.

He told of a timid college professor who lived in the same apartment building with a ruthless agent of the secret police. They met one evening in the hallway.

"It's terrible what's happening in this country," said the professor. "I teach a class in Russian literature. I have a very bright student and today I asked him who wrote Eugen Onegin. And he answered back, 'I didn't.' Isn't that terrible?"

The next night the secret agent knocked on the professor's door.

"I have good news for you, old friend. You know that student of yours—the one who says he didn't write Eugen Onegin?"

"Yes."

"Well, I have had a little talk with him and now he says he did."

Khrushchev applauded his own joke, then told another. It seems that Stalin's body was taken from its crypt in the Kremlin and buried in an obscure graveyard next to the corpse of a former President of the U.S.S.R., Mikhail Kalinin.

"How are you, Joe, old comrade?" Kalinin asked his new neighbor.

"Not very good," Stalin replied. "I don't like being moved around like this."

"How long will you stay with us?"

"I don't know."

"Where will you go from here?"

Stalin shrugged. "Wherever the party sends me."

Three courses later (fish, fowl, and pork), Khrushchev told me I was staying at the dacha of "Gospodin Averell Harriman."

"I like that man very much," he said, "and I tried to hire him. I said that if he would come to the Kremlin and be my adviser, I would give him this dacha. But he refused."

"He had to refuse," I replied. "He's already an adviser to the President."

Khrushchev saw no conflict. "Why can't he advise us both? He could bring about world peace. You tell him I still want him."

After three hours at the table, I didn't think I could eat another bite. But out came the waiters again, this time with a shashlik, the lamb and rice dish more commonly known in this country as shish kabob. The Premier grabbed a plate and put it between us.

"Gospodin Salinger and I will eat this together," he said. I declined but he handed me a fork. "We will think you don't like our cooking." Taking alternate bites, we finally put it away. But Khrushchev was still going strong. He dug into a rich dessert and had at least five cognacs.

Suddenly there was an ominous change in his manner.

"Your President," he said, glaring at me under the brim of his hat, "has made a very bad mistake for which he will have to pay!" The laughter and light conversation around the table came to an abrupt stop. "He has said that you will be the first to use the bomb."

He was referring to a recent article in *The Saturday Evening Post*, written by Stewart Alsop, in which JFK had specified the conditions under which we might be forced to use nuclear weapons in Europe.

The President, McGeorge Bundy, and I had all seen the article before publication, but none of us read into it, as Khrushchev had, a warning of pre-emptive war. JFK did say that "Khrushchev must not be certain that, where its vital interests are threatened, the United States will never strike first" [with nuclear weapons]. But it was said with specific reference to our options in the event of a major conventional attack on Western Europe.

Khrushchev glowered at me. "This warmonger Alsop—is he now your Secretary of State? Not even Eisenhower or Dulles would have made the statement your President made. He now forces us to reappraise our own position." (The Kremlin did order a special military alert immediately following publication of the article.)

I told the Premier that the President had issued a statement clarifying his remarks. Its effect was that U.S. policy was unchanged. We would not use nuclear weapons first unless we or our allies were the target of mass Communist aggression.

"I have seen that statement," said Khrushchev, "but I take the President's words literally in the article. This is clearly a new doctrine."

He then said he would apply exactly the same policy to the defense of East Germany. If Western troops were to cross its borders, he would respond immediately with a nuclear attack. He shook a finger at me. "And I am talking facts, my friend, not theory."

His anger vanished as quickly as it had come. He clapped his hands and smiled. "I am now going to tell you an official state secret."

He spoke of the crisis at the Berlin Wall in 1961, when American and Soviet tanks faced each other at point-blank range at the Brandenburg Gate. He blamed the incident on General Lucius B. Clay, President Kennedy's personal representative in Berlin. "Clay is as much a general as I am a shoemaker."

Khrushchev said he held an emergency consultation with Marshal Rodion Malinovsky, the Soviet Minister of Defense. "Now even a schoolboy knows that tanks can go either forward or backward. They do not like to stay in one place. If the tanks went forward, it was war. If they went backward, it was peace.

"West Berlin means nothing to us, so I told Malinovsky to back up our tanks a little bit and hide them behind buildings where the Americans couldn't see them. If we do this, I said to Malinovsky, the American tanks will also move back within twenty minutes and we will have no more crisis."

Khrushchev grinned triumphantly over his cognac. "It was just as I said it would be. We pulled back. You pulled back. Now that's generalship!"

He had a postscript on Berlin. "I personally ordered the construction of the Wall. A state is a state and must control its own borders."

It was now nearing six o'clock. The sun was low and there was again a biting chill in the air. Khrushchev stood up, no longer smiling.

"Come, Gospodin Salinger. It is time that we speak to each other—privately."

# XVI

## A TALK BY THE MOSCOW RIVER

I spent the next ninety minutes with Nikita S. Khrushchev in a small arbor overlooking the Moscow River. We were alone except for his interpreter, Viktor Sukhodrev, and a detachment of security agents who took up positions in the surrounding woods.

I told the Premier at the outset that I was not a diplomat and had no authority to enter into substantive discussions with him. I could, however, relay his views to President Kennedy, and I would appreciate a full transcript of our conversation to avoid all possibility of error or misinterpretation. He readily agreed. (The transcript, which was given to me two days later, was generally accurate, except for the insertion of two comments from Khrushchev that he could not delay recognition of East Germany much longer. No such statements were made to me, and were obvious afterthoughts to punch up the then-prevailing Soviet line.)

Khrushchev began with the comment that since President Kennedy had taken office, the atmosphere in America—and even in West Germany—was generally more favorable for a settlement of the Berlin question. (To Khrushchev and all other Soviet officials I had met, Berlin was always the major issue—the key to peaceful co-existence. If a *rapprochement* could be found there, they were absolutely confident that agreements on nuclear disarmament and other differences would follow very quickly.) The Premier repeated that he was greatly disturbed by recent statements of JFK on nuclear policy. But, on balance, "Your President has accomplished much and shown himself to be a big statesman," said the Premier. "Please convey to the President that I want to be his friend . . . of course, Kennedy is no kith nor kin of mine. He is a big capitalist and I, as a Communist, have a very definite attitude toward capitalists."

His attitude toward Richard Nixon, however, was much harsher. "He is an intellectually limited man who not only does not inspire respect toward himself but, most of all, produces the impression of a slightly fraudulent, petty storekeeper, capable of selling tainted herring or representing kerosene-soaked sugar as good merchandise, things that an honest merchant, of course, would never allow himself. Nixon is not a serious politician and, I repeat, is a most limited person."

I was surprised by his reaction to Nixon, who had proven himself a formidable adversary in their "kitchen debate" and other encounters in 1959. But the Chairman was just warming up on the subject of Nixon. He said the former Vice-President, through a high-ranking Republican, had made overtures to the Soviet Union in an effort to influence the outcome of the presidential elections in 1960.

"It is true," said Khrushchev, "that before the elections this intermediary with whom I had established not bad relations at the time of my trip to the U.S.A., had informed us through our representatives in the U.S.A. that in the event of Nixon's occupying the White House, the former policy of Eisenhower would be reviewed. Before the very elections, he approached us with the request to release the crew members of the American RB-47, shot down in the air space of the Soviet Union. We, of course, understood that Nixon wished to make political capital out of this for himself in advance of the elections."

I responded that the release of the RB-47 fliers before the election might very well have won it for Nixon.

"Of course," said Khrushchev. "For this reason, when we in the government considered this question, I said that it would not be proper to do this. For, you see, Nixon wanted to make it appear as if he had already arranged certain contacts with the Soviet government. And this, of course, could have played a decisive role in the elections. That is why we decided to wait a while until Kennedy came to power and only after that to release the American flyers of the RB-47. Now it is obvious that we acted correctly."

Khrushchev then came back to the subject of Germany, which obviously was causing him great anxiety.

"If we succeeded in agreeing with the President of the U.S.A. concerning normalizing the situation in West Berlin, it would be a very great thing . . . If we do not succeed, then we will find ourselves on the verge of a very great test . . . We have not infringed and do not tend to infringe upon the freedom of West Berlin. To us, just as to you, West Berlin is not necessary. It is fitting to say that if we had wanted to occupy West Berlin, then we would need only an hour for this . . ."

He was concerned over the reinforcement of the American garrison in free Berlin. "It is unwise to threaten us with war, unwise to attempt to keep us from signing a peace treaty (with East Germany) with threats of war . . . I repeat we do not recognize and cannot recognize the right of the Western powers to keep their troops in West Berlin. And so you will begin a war over West Berlin with its two and a half million people. Adenauer himself says that not a single fool wants to fight over West Berlin. But if the Germans themselves say this, certainly the U.S.A. even more so will not fight over West Berlin, which it needs like a dog needs five legs."

He conceded that recognition of East Germany and the signing of a separate peace treaty with the Ulbricht regime "will entail a serious sharpening of our relations. Whether it will lead to war or not, I do not know, because this depends upon your position. But, in any event, with the signature of a peace treaty the Soviet government will not recognize any right of the Western powers to maintain their troops in West Berlin.

"We cannot foresee what steps will be undertaken by the American government but are prepared for anything. We wish to be correctly understood in the U.S.A. It would be silly on our part to attempt to frighten you, exactly as it would be foolish on your part to frighten us.

"We already have fought more than once and well know what war is and therefore do not want it. Although both we and you possess completely adequate means of destruction, at present it is indispensable to measure our forces not by the quantity of weapons but by the quantity and quality of reason on both sides. That is the main thing."

Khrushchev, however, had only one new proposal affecting free Berlin for me to communicate to the President—the replacement of American, British, and French forces with symbolic troop contingents from both NATO and Warsaw Pact countries. This "compromise solution," he said, would "bring an end to the occupation regime without any loss of moral prestige by either side."

Late in the conversation, I got around to his cancellation of the television exchange between himself and President Kennedy because of the American resumption of nuclear tests.

"We are ready at any time to carry out this proposal and consider that it would bring great advantages for all countries," I said.

"I also consider that it would be a useful thing," Khrushchev replied. "We suggested to postpone this exchange of opinions on television for the time being because an unsuitable situation has developed. In present circumstances we would have to resort to polemics, the result of which would be opposite of those we desire. It would lead only to the worsening of relations and this we do not want. We will carry out your proposal when more appropriate conditions are created for it."

He had no objection, however, to my suggestion that Kharlamov and I continue our discussions on the TV exchange. But he felt it would require a visit to the Soviet Union by President Kennedy "to clear away the obstructions now disturbing Soviet-American relations. This trip would enable the President to meet the Soviet people and personally to evaluate conditions in our country. But, really, how can we invite the President to visit us now if we were to be compelled at every meeting to accuse him of the fact that the U.S.A. is carrying out nuclear explosions?

"No, we want to invite Kennedy to the Soviet Union not to insult him, but so that his trip would contribute to improving relations between our countries."

Khrushchev had doubts that JFK was negotiating in the same good faith as his predecessor on another major issue—a nuclear disarmament treaty.

"I recall my talks with former President Eisenhower at Camp David. I felt then that he sincerely wanted to come to an understanding. He said that it would be good if we could put our signatures under such a historic document. In general I think that although Eisenhower, of course, executed the wishes of the American monopolies, all the same he was inclined toward good deeds. This opinion is confirmed by his behavior during the second world war."

But the Premier was not at all certain the Kennedy administration "really wants disarmament or whether it is participating (in the Geneva negotiations) merely for the sake of lulling public opinion."

I reminded him that President Kennedy had been willing to cancel our new series of nuclear tests if there had been agreement at Geneva on a general disarmament plan, but had found the Soviet Union unwilling to grant the slightest concessions.

"No more than two months ago," I continued, "the President said that the biggest disappointment during the first months of his administration was the fact that an agreement had not been achieved on the prohibition of nuclear tests. I can assure you that the President is wholly sincere in his desire to achieve an agreement."

Khrushchev then defended the Soviet position against international control of nuclear disarmament—the principal obstacle to agreement at Geneva.

"If the U.S.A. in the future will continue to insist on its position on the question of control, then our views will continue to differ. We will never accept the conditions put forth by the United States regarding control. We will not tolerate on our territory any sort of control posts before the realization of general and complete disarmament. And now, evidently, you will conduct nuclear explosions and we will have to conduct them until a more general understanding of the need of general and complete disarmament appears."

This brought him back to the Alsop article in *The Saturday Evening Post*. He could not reconcile my assurance of President Kennedy's sincerity on disarmament with "his statement that you will be the first to use the bomb."

He shrugged fatalistically.

"I do not know how our relations with the U.S.A. will develop further, under President Kennedy. That depends on him. West Berlin, too, is an important test—it is a Rubicon. If we cross it without war, all will go well. If not, it will be too bad.

"The key is in the hands of President Kennedy, because he will have to fire the first shot. You see, it was he who said that a situation could arise in which the U.S.A. would be the first to deliver an atomic strike."

He shrugged off my objection that the President had been misunderstood.

"So what, we are ready to meet this strike. But I want to warn you— we will not be slow to deliver a retaliatory strike."

The discussion came to an end with Khrushchev expressing disappointment that I had not brought him a personal message from the President. But his manner was cheerful as we began walking back up the path toward the dacha.

"I ask you to convey to the President and his wife the best wishes of Nina Petrovna and myself. And you must not forget. Tell him what a great honor it was for Nina Petrovna and me to have our daughter eat with him at the White House."

Khrushchev's limousine was waiting for him in front of the dacha. He walked toward it. Then, apparently on an impulse, he turned to Adzhubei.

"What is Gospodin Salinger doing for lunch tomorrow?"

His son-in-law replied that he was taking me to the Aragvi, a famous Georgian restaurant in downtown Moscow.

"No," said Khrushchev. "I have had such a good time today I think I will do it again tomorrow. You will bring Gospodin Salinger here for lunch." With that, he once again tipped his hat to the ladies, climbed in the back seat, and was still waving back at us as the car disappeared around a curve into the forest.

Sorensen, Akalovsky, and I left immediately for the American Embassy. Ambassador Thompson had had a hectic day reassuring Bonn, Paris, and London that JFK's thirty-six-year-old Press Secretary had not spent the afternoon negotiating the future of Europe with Khrushchev. (Every day of my visit in the Soviet Union, a cable had to be sent to Bonn to quiet Dr. Adenauer's suspicions that dark deeds were afoot.) I was met outside Spaso House by a throng of reporters and gave them only the sketchiest outline of my day. I also had to deny a totally irresponsible charge by Republican Senator Homer E. Capehart of Indiana that I had deliberately insulted Ambassador Thompson by not staying overnight at the embassy. Tommy had been in the difficult position of not being able to give the correspondents an hour-by-hour rundown on my activities at the dacha.

But it was ridiculous for Capehart to try to build this into an international incident.

The embassy itself was also a scene of frantic activity. The ambassador and his wife, Jane, were packing to leave Moscow and the corridors were jammed with packing boxes and personal files. (Tommy's next assignment was as Special Assistant to the Secretary of State for Soviet Affairs, a position in which his great personal knowledge of Khrushchev was to prove most important in the Cuban missile crisis later that year. Tommy is one of America's ablest foreign officers, and a career diplomat since 1929. He was in Moscow in October 1941 when German troops were pushing across Russia and stuck to his desk even when there was danger the capital might fall into Nazi hands. President Eisenhower made him ambassador to Moscow in 1957 and JFK kept him at his post for the simple reason that he was the best.)

I was up until long after midnight, dictating to relays of secretaries a full account of my formal and informal conversations with the Russian Premier. The many thousands of words were immediately cabled to the White House. Simultaneously, Tommy transmitted to the State Department his expert analysis of Khrushchev's statements to me on Berlin and American-Soviet relations. His work was interrupted briefly by a call from Adzhubei inviting him and his family to join us at the dacha the next day.

Early that Sunday morning, Adzhubei took us on a tour of the Kremlin, including Lenin's office and living quarters. We then drove to the dacha, arriving shortly before noon. Khrushchev, his wife, Nina Petrovna, and a son, Sergei—a rocket engineer—drove up minutes behind us.

Nina Petrovna's English was excellent. She was plump and grandmotherly and took immediate charge of Adzhubei's sons, Nikita and Aleksey, Jr. The Premier would frequently join her for a romp with the boys on the lawn. There was obviously a deep affection between Khrushchev and his wife. She rarely took her eyes from him. He would often glance toward her and shrug his shoulders as if to say, "I'm sorry but this is business." She would smile back and nod her head. As on the first day, Adzhubei kept a respectable distance from his father-in-law and had little or nothing to say.

I had been fearful all morning that Khrushchev would lead us on another forced march through the forest, and that's exactly what he did. There was a slight drizzle and the air was bitterly cold but he clapped a hand on my shoulder and said:

"We walk twice as far as yesterday, yes?"

He must have walked a mile before he finally stopped to let the women catch up. Khrushchev took advantage of the break to reprimand me for editorials in American newspapers critical of the Kremlin.

"Such comments create a bad atmosphere," he said. "You should not permit the publishers to say such things."

I told him I had no control over what the newspapers printed.

"Adzhubei does," he replied.

I said that our positions were not at all comparable. Adzhubei, as chief editor of a government newspaper, had absolute powers of censorship over its news and editorial content. I, as Press Secretary, could only present the President's policies as effectively as possible. But there was nothing I could do about it if the newspapers chose to criticize those policies.

"You are too modest about your power," he said.

It struck me as strange that Khrushchev, with his extensive knowledge of the power blocs operating in American politics and government, could be that naive regarding the relationship between the White House and the press.

"I can't believe you are serious in your belief that I could stop the American papers from criticizing you," I said.

"I am entirely serious," he grumbled. "You could stop it if the President told you to."

Khrushchev was particularly impatient with the strong editorial reaction in America to the Soviet violation of the moratorium on nuclear testing.

"Why all the bother?" he said. "Even before the tests, we could wipe out all of West Europe, Africa, and Asia with one salvo."

Their reason for resuming the tests, he said, was that the Soviet Union now had warheads in the fifty megaton range, and "it was necessary to relate them to our rockets."

Khrushchev then said that America would gain nothing by resuming its own tests in the atmosphere. "Every time you explode one, we will explode a bigger one. I will not hide the fact that our engineers and scientists are now urgently preparing to carry out further nuclear weapons tests."

The Premier was the most mercurial man I had ever met. His mood could change in an instant from blustery anger to gentle humor.

The next leg of our safari brought us to a collective farm bordering the grounds of the dacha.

"When I first came here fifteen years ago," said Khrushchev, "this farm was in terrible condition. I went to Stalin and I said I want to do something to help that farm. But Stalin wouldn't let me. Wasn't that awful?"

He winked at me. "But now I give the orders and I have done many things to help this farm. I have even planted trees myself."

"A moment ago," I replied, "you were discussing death-dealing bombs and now you speak with much greater interest of planting trees."

"Of course," he said. "You see, trees are life, but weapons are death."

He quickly came back to Stalin.

"He understood only Marxism-Leninism. But he didn't know how to apply it to agriculture and industry. He was no good at practical things. I wish he could see this farm now. Then he would know I was right—

that even an important man in government should take time to help the farmers—even with his own hands, as I did."

As we walked deeper into the woods, we came to a long, pine-studded slope. Khrushchev said that he and his predecessor as Premier, Nikolai Bulganin, had spent many afternoons skiing there.

"When we came back to the dacha," he said, "Bulganin's wife always had hot mulled wine waiting for us." He obviously was fond of Bulganin, despite his role in exiling him to the provinces as the director of a remote power station.

The drizzle mercifully became a driving rain and Khrushchev had no choice but to take his little army back to the dacha. Foreign Minister and Mrs. Andrey Gromyko were waiting for us on the porch and the smiling Premier accused them of being late to escape the walk. Gromyko didn't deny it.

We had lunch inside because of the weather. It was another eight or ten course affair with a liberal sprinkling of vodka, cognac, and Khrushchevian humor. Mrs. Thompson had brought the Premier a gift—a trick jigger that was almost solid glass and held no more than a teaspoonful of liquor. He drank all the toasts from it and made much of the point that he was the only temperate person at the table.

He also had another anti-Stalin joke concerning an argument between an American and a Russian over which country was more democratic.

"I can walk into the President's office," the American said, "criticize everything he's doing, and the President will still receive me well and shake my hand when I leave."

"It is the same in the Soviet Union," the Russian replied. "I can walk into Stalin's office, criticize everything the American President is doing, and Stalin will still receive me well and shake my hand when I leave."

Gromyko also had a Stalin story.

Roosevelt, Churchill, and Stalin were holding a summit meeting and Roosevelt said: "I had a dream last night that I was President of the world."

"That's strange," said Churchill, "I had a dream last night that I was Prime Minister of the world."

"Impossible," said Stalin. "I don't recall appointing either one of you."

Late in the luncheon, Zhukov said he had heard the reports that Ambassador Thompson was leaving Moscow for a new assignment.

Khrushchev pounded a fist on the table in mock anger. "I haven't agreed to that." Tommy laughed the loudest.

We then drew the Premier into a discussion of his office routine. He complained that he spent most of his time reading "dull reports from ambassadors."

Mrs. Khrushchev glanced nervously at Tommy. "You mean our own ambassadors?"

"Of course," her husband replied.

Khrushchev said he had a simple procedure for keeping up with his paper work at the Kremlin.

"I have my secretaries divide all the reports into two piles—one that I should read and one that I should not waste my time reading.

"Then I read the unimportant pile first," he said. "It's always more important than the important one."

After lunch, Ambassador Thompson spent fifteen minutes alone with Khrushchev to advise him of President Kennedy's great concern over new Communist military activity in Laos. (During the previous night, JFK had dispatched additional troops into neighboring Thailand to remove all doubt of our intention to fight, if necessary, to protect the neutralist government of Souvanna Phouma.)

The day finally came to an end and Khrushchev walked with me to the embassy car.

"We have had good fun, yes?"

I told him it had been a wonderful two days.

"You will come back," he said, "and we will have more fun."

I was sorry to say goodbye. I had come to like Khrushchev very much. For all his public tantrums and rocket-rattling, he was a man of great warmth, humor, and courtesy. It struck me on the ride back to the embassy that I had spent fourteen hours with him and not once in all that time had he taken a telephone call or left his guests for even a minute to consult with his staff.

I never saw him again. Two years later he was thrown out of office and with him Adzhubei and Kharlamov. Bolshakov is the only one of "my Russians" who still holds a position of authority in the Soviet Union. I saw him on a business trip to Moscow last year.

I was in Bolshakov's office at the Novosty News Agency and I asked him about Khrushchev. Bolshakov said that the former Premier was in good health living at a dacha outside of Moscow.

"Isn't it a pity that in your system you waste the talents of a man like Khrushchev after he leaves office?" I asked.

Bolshakov smiled wanly but did not answer.

By the spring of 1965, Nikita S. Khrushchev, once one of the most powerful leaders in the world, had become a "non person."

# XVII

## THE FIFTY-MILE HIKE

John F. Kennedy, a natural athlete himself, had a passion for physical fitness that was almost the undoing of his chubby Press Secretary. I still shudder when I think of the Fifty-Mile Hike That Almost Was—a crisis in my personal life that White House correspondents still refer to as Salinger's Folly.

It all began the first week in February 1963, when JFK ran across a letter President Theodore Roosevelt had written to the commandant of the Marine Corps in 1908, suggesting that Marine officers should hike fifty miles from time to time to prove their fitness. He wrote also that he would call on members of his own staff for an equivalent demonstration of vigor.

Now I have always denied accusations of news management against the Kennedy administration, but in this one instance the President was clearly guilty. He sent a copy of Teddy's letter to General David M. Shoup, the Marine Corps commandant, with this memo:

> *Why don't you send this back to me as your own discovery? You might want to add a comment that today's Marine Corps officers are just as fit as those of 1908, and are willing to prove it. I, in turn, will ask Mr. Salinger for a report on the fitness of the White House staff.*

General Shoup was not a man to defy the orders of his Commander-in-Chief, and wrote the President that a detachment of leathernecks from Camp Lejeune, North Carolina, would set out on a fifty-mile hike the following week.

JFK gave me the commandant's letter to release to the press. "You realize, of course," he told me, "that somebody from the White House will have to go down there and march with the Marines." He was looking at my waistline as he spoke.

"Why not Ken O'Donnell? He's always in great shape."

"No," the President replied. "It should be somebody who needs the exercise—somebody who would be an inspiration to millions of other out-of-shape Americans."

I tried another tack. "I wonder if you have to take Teddy Roosevelt that literally, sir? After all, he was on horseback, not on foot, when he led the Rough Riders up San Juan Hill—and that's the way we should all remember him."

JFK was still eying my belt buckle. "There is no escape, Pierre. I intend to follow Teddy's letter to the letter."

I went back to my office for an agonizing appraisal of the shape I was in. Just before World War II, I had been a cross-country runner at San Francisco State College and had taken two tenth-place ribbons. But in both races, the eleventh man in a field of eleven hadn't been able to finish because of blisters.

After the war, I went out for the boxing team at my next alma mater— the University of San Francisco. One of my first opponents was an Austrian exchange student. I was plump but he was fat. I threw an uppercut in the first round that ricocheted off his paunch and hit me squarely on the chin. I was out cold for much longer than the count of ten. When the coach finally brought me around, I quickly agreed with him that a self-inflicted one-punch knockout was the proper note of glory on which to end my pugilistic career.

My only physical exertions since then had been an infrequent round of golf (riding in an electric cart whenever possible); an even more infrequent tennis match (conceding to my opponent the entire forecourt and both sidelines); contests of strength with stubborn wine corks; an exhausting Bach arpeggio on the piano; and weekly weightlifting exercises with the ponderous Sunday edition of the New York *Times*.

I was thirty-seven years old, five-feet nine, and twenty pounds overweight at 185. I was never without a cigar, a thirst, or an appetite. I was clearly *not* a fit representative of the New Frontier. Yet I had no choice but to start training immediately in the event the President did send me to Camp Lejeune. I had a date for lunch that day at the Hay Adams Hotel, a full block and a half away from the White House, and decided to walk both ways. I was footsore on my return and immediately informed the President of that fact.

"Try it again tomorrow," he said, "and report back."

"If I may, sir," I replied, "I should like to remove myself as a volunteer."

"You are the only man on the staff," he said, "who has shown sufficient interest in the hike to open training. You are still very much in the running."

I went home that night heavy of heart and foot. But my deliverance came the next morning—or, at least, I thought it had—in the person of Brigadier General Godfrey T. McHugh, the President's Air Force aide. He had been at a cocktail party the night before and had said, in the presence of a reporter for the Washington *Post*, that it would be "loads of fun to go on a fifty-mile hike every day."

I knew that McHugh, a handsome bachelor, had to be in shape, if only to keep up with his spectacular social life. Just the year before, at age fifty-one, he had been graduated from the Fort Benning parachute school with a class of teen-age recruits.

I actually ran into the President's office with the story from the *Post*. "If there was ever a volunteer," I said, "McHugh is it!"

"All right," JFK said, "you're off the hook. You can tell the press McHugh is our man, but let him know first."

McHugh, happily, was not at his desk and I didn't waste much time trying to find him. Within three minutes of my conversation with the President, I issued the following communiqué to the press:

> *The President noted the report in the Washington* Post *with some interest this morning. General McHugh's office has been notified that the President would consider it fitting if he would go to Camp Lejeune and join in the march.*

McHugh promptly went into orbit. "I was misquoted by the *Post*," he said. "I am not a volunteer and I suspect Mr. Salinger of self-serving motives in announcing that I am. I have spoken to the President and he accepts my explanation of the matter. I will not be going to Camp Lejeune."

I was again in imminent peril and had no choice but to renew the offensive. I did it by involving McHugh in a totally fictional controversy with Army Major General Chester V. Clifton, the President's ranking military adviser, who was, conveniently, out of town that day. I told a UPI reporter, but not for attribution to me, that Clifton was outraged with McHugh, a flier, for volunteering for the hike and thus usurping the role of the foot soldier. I said, further, that Clifton was confident he could outwalk McHugh seven days a week.

I had gone too far. McHugh, the honor of the Air Force now at stake, issued a communiqué of his own. He would accept Clifton's challenge and lead a fifty-mile hike of his own for White House personnel only. The marchers, in addition to himself and Clifton, would be "the President's naval aide, Captain Tazewell T. Shepard, and Press Secretary Pierre Salinger. I will leave it to Mr. Salinger to choose the line of march—and to keep up with the rest of us, if he can."

It took me the rest of the day to recover from the sheer savagery of McHugh's counterattack, and bright and early the next morning I tried to secure a presidential stay of execution. But JFK had no sympathy for me at all.

"I could have told you," he said, "that a civilian always loses when he tries to meddle with the military. You have been outflanked by McHugh and you might as well face up to it."

"Mr. President, what if I got on a train and walked up and down the aisle until it had gone fifty miles? Couldn't I say I had walked fifty miles?"

"You could not," he said. "And, very frankly, I don't understand what's worrying you. You're in your thirties and McHugh is in his fifties. You ought to be able to keep up with him."

"But he's trim and I'm twenty pounds overweight."

"You won't be at the end of fifty miles," the President replied.

I had my marching orders and told the correspondents "the time has come for the Press Secretary to demonstrate his physical fitness." The White House fifty-mile hike would start at 7 A.M. on Friday, February 15, and would follow the towpath of the Chesapeake & Ohio Canal, which runs along the Potomac. (I chose the canal because it was readily accessible to ambulances and other emergency equipment, and Friday because it would give me a full weekend to recover.)

McHugh began his psychological warfare almost immediately. He strode manfully up and down the White House driveway outside my window, rehearsing for the TV cameras the killing pace he would set on the actual hike. I got tired just peeking at him through the curtains.

The White House reporters, most of whom I had thought to be my friends, were just as heartless. All that day they came into my office bearing gifts (and malice): a pair of crutches, a compass, corn plasters, bottles of liniment, splints, rubbing alcohol, and a pedometer.

I struck back at my afternoon press briefing. I told the correspondents that I would be guilty of supressing the news if I did not insist on full coverage of the hike. I would expect all White House reporters to accompany the march from beginning to end. "When I walk, everybody walks."

Veteran newsmen who had known war and pestilence grew pale at the prospect.

"Pierre, do you actually see any real and present danger of this hiking gag escalating into the real thing?"

"I think there is every possibility it will."

"Mr. Secretary, may I ask you a personal question? How far did you go for lunch today?"

"I went to the Jockey Club—by automobile."

"You're exhausting my physical fitness," said one of the reporters.

"Pierre, in the Civil War you could buy a volunteer to take your place."

"I cannot permit that. We are all in over our heads."

"Can you arrange to have some of those St. Bernard dogs that carry little flasks around their necks?"

"Austerity is going to be our motto."

"How long do you think the hike will last?"

"Up to three days."

The response to my last answer was unprintable.

My second victory of the day was over the Navy. Captain Shepard told the press it would not be fitting for a Navy man to walk fifty miles when a parallel waterway was available. "It is my intention," he said, "to drift fifty miles down the canal in a rowboat." I had the pleasure of informing him that there hadn't been much water in the canal for years and that he would have to leg it with the rest of us.

More than fifty reporters signed up for the hike—most of them on direct order of their editors. The only legitimate volunteers were twelve White House stenographers. I told them it was strictly a stag affair but that we might be able to use them as ambulance drivers or nurses at first-aid stations along the way.

I went home that night with a certain air of confidence. Many of the reporters who would be hiking with me were in their fifties and sixties, and their only known exercise was shuffling a gin rummy deck. I might not be able to keep up with McHugh but I shouldn't run dead last in *this* field of entries. I actually began to look forward with a certain zest to a tune-up hike I was planning that Sunday—five days before the main event.

I was up at dawn and had a huge breakfast and three cognacs to fortify me against the winter cold before leading a small army down the hill from my home to the banks of Lake Barcroft. My second in command was a neighbor, retired Marine Corps Colonel Freeman Williams, whom I took along to study his military gait. The troops were my wife and three children. The only observer was Jack Perkins of NBC television. (I still regret that Perkins found it necessary to point out on the Huntley-Brinkley show that on one leg of the march, when we had to cut across the frozen surface of the lake, I sent my wife ahead to test the thickness of the ice.)

The distance around the lake was between five and six miles and we made it in slightly under two hours. I was, understandably, more than a little cocky when we got back. But bad news was on the way.

That same Sunday, Attorney General Bob Kennedy had taken off on a fifty-mile hike from Washington to Camp David, the presidential retreat in Maryland. His co-marchers were Ed Guthman, the sturdy public information officer of the Justice Department, and David Hackett, who was executive director of the President's Committee on Juvenile Delinquency and Youth. Hackett had been a U.S. olympic ice hockey player in his youth.

I couldn't believe it when I heard on the evening news shows that only Bob had gone the distance. Guthman and Hackett, who were in far better shape than I, had given up after only seventeen miles.

I was even more shaken the next morning by Art Buchwald, the columnist for the New York *Herald Tribune,* and by a squib on the UPI wire.

Buchwald, whose waistline was even more bulbous than mine, made the flat prediction that I would not survive the hike, and would go down in history as a martyr to fat men everywhere. He was willing to share my fate. He would go the full fifty miles with me—but in a horse-drawn surrey complete with picnic hamper of cold chicken and champagne.

UPI advised me to profit from the experience of Pheidippides, "the gentleman of Athens who inaugurated the marathon race by running to enlist the aid of the Spartans against a Persian invasion of Greece in 490 B.C. Once the battle was won," the UPI continued, "Pheidippides raced 22 miles to Athens with the news. 'Rejoice, we conquer!' cried Pheidippides, and dropped dead."

I tried to put up a brave front at my first press briefing of the day. The first question was from Merriman Smith of UPI.

"With Bob Kennedy and all the other volunteers getting into the fifty-mile hike act, do you think our own participation is still necessary?"

"Are you asking that question from the point of self-interest?"

"I am."

"Have you been assigned to cover this?"

"Not yet. But if it remains necessary, shouldn't you consider an age limit, saying nobody over fifty could go?"

"How about nobody over thirty-five?" I replied.

"We're all for that."

I then told the reporters of my practice spin around Lake Barcroft.

"How far did you go?"

"Five and a half miles."

"Did you have a support unit?"

"No."

"Did you actually hike around the lake or just among the homes of friends?"

"I resent that implication."

When the reporters left my office, I came to one of the wisest decisions of my life. I would fink out. But time was drawing short. The Camp Lejeune Marines were marching the next morning. If a strategic retreat was at all possible, now was the time to start running.

I went in to see the President.

"Sir, I took a walk around Lake Barcroft yesterday. I felt all right last night, but this morning I am feverish and creaky. If you should need me today, I'll probably be in the White House dispensary."

His eyes narrowed. "What are you trying to tell me?"

"I am trying to tell you, sir, that I can't walk fifty miles. You are backing a loser."

"You're sure?"

"I'm sure."

He grinned. "All right, if you can't make it, you can't. But you're going to have to come up with a good reason for calling it off."

"I will think of something, sir."

"I'm sure you will. But it had better be convincing. If it isn't, you hike."

I tried all the rest of that day to dream up a face-saving cover story: a NATO information crisis requiring my immediate presence in Paris, threatening weather conditions, an almost forgotten invitation to address the Manila Press Club.

"Sorry," said the President, "you'll have to do better than that."

It came to me the next morning—the obvious out! It was simple, it was logical and it was almost honest.

I put in a call to Dick Snider, the administrator of the President's Council on Physical Fitness.

"We feel at the White House," I said, "that the fifty-mile hike craze is getting out of hand. Don't you agree there's a danger that people with bad hearts or other infirmities might do permanent harm to themselves by attempting hikes that are clearly beyond their capability?"

"You might have a point there," he replied.

"In that case," I continued, "wouldn't it be in the national interest for the President's Council on Physical Fitness to issue a statement advising unfit people against such hikes?"

There was a long silence at the other end of the line.

"Pierre, are you speaking for yourself or for the President?"

"I am speaking for myself, but I can assure you the President is aware of my interest in this matter."

"All right," Snider said, "we'll give some thought to issuing such a statement at the appropriate time."

"The appropriate time is right now," I said. "In fact, I just happen to have a statement in front of me that I could dictate to you over the phone."

"No," he replied, "we're quite capable of writing our own statement. When would you like us to put it out?"

"Within the hour, if possible."

"We'll do it."

The council gave its advice to the nation at eleven and I took it at twelve.

With the assistance of Ted Sorensen, I wrote a statement canceling the hike and went into my noon briefing free of panic for the first time in a week. The first question gave me my opening:

"Mr. Secretary, all the publicity about what the Baltimore *Sun* has fearlessly called Salinger's Folly brought a statement from the President's

Council on Physical Fitness this morning. It warns that while fifty-mile hikes are OK for Marines, the physical activity of ordinary citizens should be 'consistent with their physical condition.' We suspect you may have written that statement."

A. I deny it.

Q. The council advised that those who are not used to exercising regularly should begin moderately and gradually increase the pace. We all know, of course, of your eagerness to demonstrate your physical fitness. But some of us wonder if you might be unselfish about this and, instead of encouraging us to walk away what little physical fitness we have along the C & O Canal on Friday, set a good example of some more moderate and appropriate type of exercise—like jumping off the spot on which all of this has put you.

A. A long question like that deserves an answer.

Q. Did you write the question, too?

A. May I make my statement, please? The President's Council on Physical Fitness this morning issued a statement commending those in the nation who are successfully attempting the fifty-mile hikes, but warning that those who are not in good shape should not attempt such a feat. My shape is not good.

Q. Are you referring to your condition or your proportions?

A. May I please finish my statement? While the facts laid out by the President's Council have been apparent to others for some time, their full significance was pressed upon me . . .

Q. Is this a resignation?

A. . . . as a result of a six-mile hike last Sunday . . .

Q. You have gone up half a mile.

A. . . . I have done little walking since, except to go from my office to the White House dispensary. Even that trip required the use of an elevator. I believe the fitness of this administration has already been amply demonstrated by the Attorney General.

Q. When he walks, he walks for others.

A. A further demonstration on my part would be superfluous and possibly disastrous. I am therefore rescinding the hike previously announced. I may be plucky but I am not stupid.

Q. Hear! Hear!

A. I am moved not only by the generous advice volunteered by many doctors throughout the country, but by my compassion for those members of the press who might have been forced to join this undertaking. While many brave reporters have vowed to go the last mile with me, it is not clear that some of them could go the first. I hope that my decision will not discourage those who are determined to demonstrate that they are in better shape than I am. They are.

I am grateful to the many citizens who have taken the time to wire or write me their support. I am grateful to Mr. Art Buchwald of the New York *Herald Tribune* for his moving and eloquent defense of the role of the fat man in our society. The essence of the message of the President's Council to fat men was: Moderation should be the rule in all things, including exercise. I have received that message. I intend to take seriously the advice of the council and gradually increase the tempo of my walking, so that by next year—who knows? That is the end of my statement and I am out of breath.

Q. Has the President approved this statement?

A. Well, he hasn't seen this statement in this form. But I told him I was going to make a statement.

Q. Was the President pleased with your decision and is he still going to keep you as Press Secretary?

A. He hasn't commented on it.

Q. Does your statement commit the military aides, too?

A. My statement speaks only for myself.

Q. Does your statement imply that the New York *Herald Tribune* is now being read at the White House?

A. Mr. Buchwald has always been read at the White House.

Merriman Smith, speaking for a happy mob of colleagues, brought the briefing to an end.

"Thank you, Mr. Secretary—in more ways than one."

Over the next week, thousands of fat men sent me telegrams and letters applauding my decision. I also got an invitation from Jersey City to appear as a one-man marching unit in the St. Patrick's Day parade, with my own color guard and band bringing up the front and rear. I declined on grounds of national origin but said I might be available on Bastille Day.

Marine Commandant Shoup sent me a replica of the engraved calendar President Kennedy had given to staff members after the Cuban missile crisis. But this one was for the month of February 1963, and the raised dates, according to the general's inscription, were for "the red letter days of Mr. Salinger's build-up for the hike-up and the Black Tuesday of his capitulation . . . Some Cabinets may have better legs, but your footwork is superb."

The President had only one criticism of my retreat. "You also let McHugh escape, and I think he could have gone fifty."

But it was left to Carleton Kent of the Chicago *Sun-Times* to place the entire incident in its true historical perspective:

"Thank God, the Press Secretary is a coward."

9. President Kennedy braces himself against the brisk New England breezes as Press Secretary Pierre Salinger looks on. This picture was taken during the America Cup Races held in Newport, R. I., in 1963, aboard the Navy destroyer USS *Joseph P. Kennedy, Jr.* (*R. L. Knudsen*)

10. Pierre Salinger met Premier Khrushchev in the spring of 1962. They spent over seven hours talking. This picture was taken in the woods outside Moscow, near the Premier's dacha. (*Tass Sov-Photo*)

11. Premier Khrushchev and Pierre Salinger pose for the photographers. Mr. Salinger and Premier Khrushchev got along splendidly during the presidential Press Secretary's trip to Russia. (*Tass Sov-Photo*)

12. OPPOSITE PAGE Aleksey Adzhubei, Khrushchev's son-in-law and editor of *Izvestia*, Ambassador Llewellyn Thompson, Pierre Salinger, and Mr. Salinger's interpreter, Alexander Akalovsky, grouped around a coffee table in Moscow airport. (*From Look magazine. © Copyright 1962 by Cowles Communications, Inc.*)

13. James Hagerty, presidential Press Secretary under President Eisenhower, offered invaluable assistance in briefing the new Press Secretary on the ins and outs of his new and complex job. (*White House*)

14. While President Kennedy addresses the General Assembly of the United Nations, a distinguished audience listens. From l. to r. (front row) unidentified woman; Mrs. Jacqueline Kennedy; Mrs. Sargent Shriver; Mrs. Stephen Smith; and Mrs. Peter Lawford; (back row) unidentified woman; Pierre Salinger; Mrs. Robert Kennedy; and Mrs. Dean Rusk, September 25, 1961. *(UPI)*

15. OPPOSITE PAGE Pierre Salinger passes on a bit of information to the President during a 1963 fund-raising banquet in California.

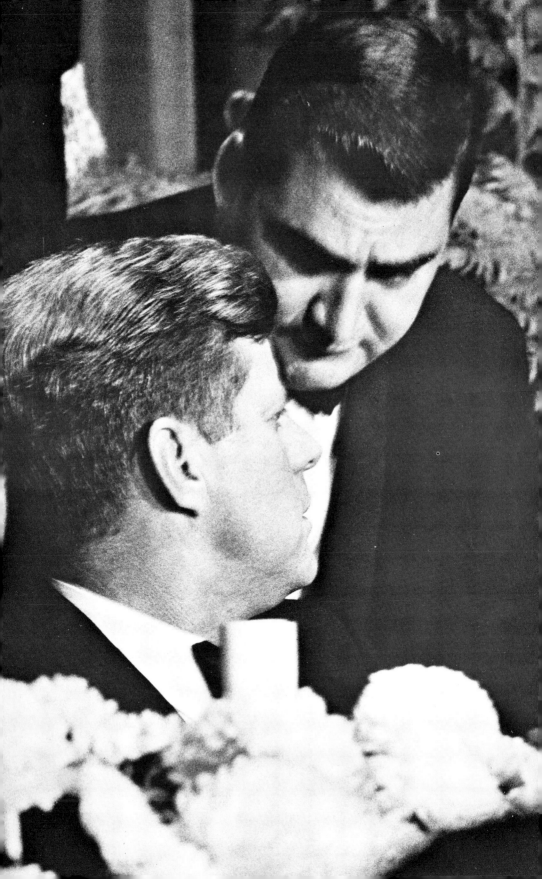

16. The President's coffin is borne up the steps of the Capitol. (*White House*)

# XVIII

## EYEBALL-TO-EYEBALL

The President was in a black mood on the morning of Tuesday, October 16, 1962.

There was no smile, not even his daily opener "What's up?" when I went into his office to clear a number of routine announcements to the press. I thought he was still angry over the actions of Prime Minister Ahmed Ben Bella of Algeria, who had been his guest at the White House the day before and had then flown directly to Havana to see Fidel Castro. JFK felt Ben Bella had no right to accept a formal invitation to visit Washington as an opportunity for calling on the dictator of a hostile state. What was even worse, the Algerian leader promptly issued a joint communiqué with Castro demanding our withdrawal from Guantánamo.

The President sat at his desk, drumming his teeth impatiently with his fingertips, as I ran through my collection of minutiae: his proclamation of National Cultural Center Week, the appointment of the North Carolina Tercentenary Commission, the guest list for a White House luncheon that day honoring Crown Prince Hassan al-Rida al-Senussi of Libya.

He cut me off abruptly.

"I haven't time to hear the rest of it. But I have one you can put on top of this list. I'm going to see Gromyko here Thursday."

Soviet Foreign Minister Andrey Gromyko was then in New York for a session of the UN Security Council, and there had been speculation that he would call on the President before returning to Moscow.

I said the reporters would want to know the purpose of his call.

"I don't know what he wants," JFK replied. "He's coming on his initiative, not mine." He stood up from his desk. "There's another thing. I expect a lot of traffic through here this week—Rusk, McNamara, Stevenson, the Chiefs of Staff. If the press tries to read something significant into it, you're to deny that anything special is going on."

I didn't pursue it. When he was ready to tell me, he would.

The next day, Wednesday, I flew with him to Connecticut where he spoke at Waterbury, Stratford, and New Haven in behalf of the Democratic ticket in the mid-term elections. Among the candidates was Abraham Ribicoff, who had resigned as Secretary of Health, Education and Welfare to run (and successfully) for the U. S. Senate. When the President spoke at the New Haven Green, he was the target of jeers and boos from the predominantly Republican Yale students. He took it in good humor.

We were back in Washington at midnight. Over the next two days, I kept a log of the high-ranking government officials who met with the President: Vice-President Johnson, State Secretary Rusk, UN Ambassador Stevenson, Defense Secretary McNamara, Attorney General Kennedy, Treasury Secretary Dillon, CIA Director McCone, former ambassador to Moscow Llewellyn Thompson, State Department Soviet specialist Chip Bohlen, and General Maxwell Taylor, the new chairman of the Joint Chiefs of Staff.

A number of Under, Assistant, and Deputy Secretaries of State and Defense also were present for the series of secret conferences, as were McGeorge Bundy, Ken O'Donnell, and Ted Sorensen of the White House staff. (This gathering of presidential advisers later became known as EXCOM—the Executive Committee of the National Security Council—and more pithily, as the "think tank" or "war council.")

Not since the Bay of Pigs, eighteen months earlier, had there been such a formidable collection of top brass at the White House. Although an international crisis obviously was building, the President did not cancel a weekend political swing into Ohio, Illinois, Missouri, New Mexico, Nevada, and California, and a non-political stop at the Seattle World's Fair.

We left on Friday morning. The helicopter that was to shuttle us to the presidential jet at Andrews Air Force Base had to wait forty-five minutes on the White House lawn while the President was winding up still another EXCOM session in his office. He was met by huge crowds in the public square in Cleveland and in Springfield, where he spoke at the fairgrounds and laid a wreath at Lincoln's tomb.

It was dark and a light rain was falling when *Air Force One* landed at O'Hare International Airport in Chicago. Despite his successes of the day—and it was vital that he increase his congressional majorities in the approaching election—JFK was gloomy as we drove from O'Hare to our hotel, the Sheraton-Blackstone. An anti-Castro picket in front of the hotel, carrying a sign, *LESS PROFILE—MORE COURAGE*, did nothing to improve his mood.

I wasn't in my suite more than a minute before I had a call from Washington. It was Richard Phillips, second in command to Bob Manning in the State Department Public Affairs Bureau. He said the President should be told that columnists Robert S. Allen and Paul Scott were about to go out with a story that we were preparing to invade Cuba. Seconds after I hung up, Carleton V. Kent of the Chicago *Sun-Times* was on the line.

"Pierre, we have it on good authority that the 18th Parachute Corps is standing by for a jump on Cuba. I want a comment from the White House."

I said I would look into it and check back with him. Two calls within a minute, from points half a continent apart, and both reporting the imminence of military action against Cuba, had to be more than coincidence.

I went upstairs to see the President. When the Secret Service let me into his suite, he was standing in his undershorts, talking to Washington. Ken O'Donnell was with him. When he hung up, his face was tense and drawn. I told him of the calls from Phillips and Kent.

"You call Kent right back," he said, "and tell him he's wrong. We are not planning to invade Cuba." Then, to O'Donnell, "You call McNamara and tell him to straighten out Allen and Scott."

Kent took the denial without comment but was obviously skeptical. I then spoke to Art Sylvester at the Pentagon to cue him on the President's official comment on the rumors.

"Maybe we're not going to invade," he said, "but something big is coming up."

I decided to take a run at O'Donnell, whom I knew had been present at the secret White House conferences all that week. JFK had already left for a $100-a-plate Democratic dinner at McCormick Place and I found Ken alone in the presidential suite.

"You're going to have to cut me in pretty quick," I said. "I'm flying blind with the press."

"All I can tell you is this," he said. "The President may have to develop a cold somewhere along the line tomorrow. If he does, we'll cancel out the rest of the trip and head back to Washington."

Ken's poker face was as grim as I had ever seen it.

"If I were you," he said, "I'd stay away from the reporters tonight, even if you have to hide out somewhere."

That I couldn't do. I had a date for dinner in the Pump Room with friends from the *Sun-Times*, whose Carleton Kent was already on my tail. O'Donnell agreed that if I didn't show up it could only arouse further suspicion.

Despite the mounting atmosphere of tension, I had a great evening with Larry Fanning, editor of the *Sun-Times*; Dick Trezevant, the Sunday editor; cartoonist Bill Mauldin; and columnist Irv Kupcinet. The steak, the wine, and the company were all first rate. But Kupcinet brought me back to reality over brandy.

"How's your supply of Cuban cigars holding out, Pierre?"

"Haven't been able to find one in months."

"The way things are looking," Irv said, "you had better get used to the domestic variety."

The next morning, a Saturday, I met with the press at nine-fifteen to outline the President's schedule for the day—a series of outdoor political speeches in Chicago and St. Louis before we caught a plane to Albuquerque. Midway through the briefing, Carroll Linkins, our traveling representative for Western Union, came up to me and whispered that I was to go to the President's suite immediately.

I found JFK, still unshaven and in his pajamas, with O'Donnell, Dave Powers, and Rear Admiral George G. Burkley, the White House physician. The President was playing it straight.

"I have a temperature and a cold," he told me. "You had better go back downstairs and tell the press I'm returning to Washington on the advice of Dr. Burkley." Then, as I was halfway to the door, "Wait a minute. Let's be sure we're all saying the same thing."

He then took out a piece of Sheraton-Blackstone stationery and wrote: "*99.2 degrees temperature. Upper respiratory infection. Doctor says he should return to Washington.*"

He gave it to me. "There, tell them that."

I had to call the reporters back from their buses in front of the hotel to read them the "medical bulletin." No one questioned it, although many of them must have had a hunch that it was a cover for a more critical reason for returning to the capital.

We were airborne at 11 A.M. At one point in the flight, I found myself alone with the President in his private compartment.

"Mr. President, you don't have that bad a cold, do you?"

"I've had worse."

"Then there's something else?"

His unprintable answer sent a chill through me.

We were back at the White House at one-thirty. As we left the helicopter, JFK took my arm.

"You'll be around?" I nodded.

After another press briefing on the President's cold, I sent my staff home for the day to create the impression of routine Saturday activity. But my date book for the rest of that day—October 20—records the frantic pace of rumors and events.

2:15 P.M.: A call from the Virginia *News Pilot*, reporting intense activity at the Norfolk naval base. Was there a connection with the President's return to Washington? I said no.

2:30 P.M.: Bob Kennedy, McNamara, McCone, General Taylor, and Edward McDermott, director of the Office of Emergency Planning, slip into the White House through a side entrance to confer with the President.

(There were others from Defense, State, and the White House staff that I was not aware of until later.)

2:35 P.M.: A call from AP, reporting a large-scale movement of Marines from California to Florida. "Must be part of the Vieques exercise," I replied. (The following week, Marine amphibious units were to practice landings on the island of Vieques, just off the east coast of Puerto Rico. It was not a covert activity. In fact, military correspondents from the Pentagon were going to cover it.)

2:45 P.M.: A call from David Wise of the New York *Herald Tribune*, reporting that Secretary Rusk was canceling his speaking engagements for the next week. What's up? I gave him an honest answer. "I don't know."

3 P.M.: Mac Kilduff, who had been standing by in the Situation Room, informs me that we have intelligence reports of a massive buildup of Soviet warplanes in Cuba, including Ilyushin-28 jet bombers, capable of delivering a nuclear strike.

3:10 P.M.: A call from the Washington *Post*, reporting that Vice-President Johnson is cutting short a political junket to Hawaii because of a cold and is returning to Washington. Epidemic or coincidence? I have no comment.

3:45 P.M.: A call from Charles von Fremd of CBS. His office is convinced that a major crisis is at hand. Should he cancel his social engagements for the evening? I tell him no.

4 P.M.: A call from Sylvester at Defense. The Pentagon is canceling the Vieques maneuvers but will delay the announcement to the press as long as possible.

5:30 P.M.: The EXCOM session ends. O'Donnell tells me the President wants me to go home but stay close to the telephone.

9:38 P.M.: The President calls me at home. I tell him of the many questions on Cuba and remind him I'm still in the dark. "You're lucky," he answers, and asks me to call him if I have further press queries to report.

10:08 P.M.: A call from Eddie Folliard of the Washington *Post*. He informs me that columnist Walter Lippmann has just told *Post* editor Al Friendly at a party that we're on the brink of war. I call the President back. He's angry. "This town is a sieve." Then, after a pause, "Pierre, how much longer do you think this thing can hold?"

"Whatever the story is," I reply, "too many good reporters are chasing it for it to hold much longer. I would say through tonight and maybe tomorrow."

"All right, Pierre. I'll have Bundy fill you in on the whole thing in the morning."

I met Bundy at 9 A.M. in the Situation Room. There were guards outside the door—huge maps of Cuba and its sea approaches on the walls—a continuous clatter of teletypes.

Mac didn't pull his punches. He told me we were, at that very moment, on the brink of nuclear war. We had absolute evidence of offensive Soviet missiles in Cuba—missiles that could destroy Washington, New York, and all other major cities on the Eastern seaboard and in the South.

"They're not yet fully operational," Bundy told me, "but they will be in a matter of days. We intend to take whatever action we must— probably a blockade—to force their removal before that time. The President should reach his final decision today and announce it on national TV tomorrow."

Bundy said the next move would be Khrushchev's and "we frankly don't know what he's likely to do."

Bundy then told me what our evidence was—aerial photographs on which the missile sites and launchers were clearly visible. He also gave me a chronology of events leading up to the President's sudden decision to return to Washington.

Early in September, on JFK's personal order, our U-2s had taken pictures of every square inch of Cuba. There was absolutely no sign of unusual activity, although Republican Senator Kenneth B. Keating of New York had been insisting for weeks that the Russians already had offensive missiles on the island. He would not, however, furnish the "evidence" to his own government. (Keating, of course, was wrong. No such weapons were on the island when he first said they were. But whatever his evidence was—probably reports from unreliable Cuban refugees— he at least thought he was right. The same cannot be said for Republican Senators Barry Goldwater, Homer Capehart, and Strom Thurmond, who had no supporting information at all but tried to turn Keating's charge into an election issue. Their line was that JFK was "soft on Castro" for refusing to invade or take other action against Cuba to remove a missile threat which was then non-existent!)

It wasn't until October 14, after a hurricane swept away the cloud cover over Cuba, that our U-2s found what they were looking for—a series of medium and intermediate missile bases in various stages of readiness. Bundy brought the pictures to the President the next morning in his bedroom. JFK told Mac to convene the first EXCOM session at eleven forty-five, then had his breakfast and went to his office to greet astronaut Walter M. Schirra, Jr., and his family.

(Over the next seven days, the White House was the scene of almost continuous EXCOM meetings, with and without the President. He kept most of his early out-of-town political commitments that week to forestall suspicion in Moscow and Havana that we were aware of this new threat to our security and were mounting the necessary counteraction. He did not cancel the West Coast phase of the tour and return to the capital until the time had come for his personal decision on what that counteraction would be.

(The choices were many: an invasion of Cuba, an aerial strike against the missile bases, a blockade, secret diplomatic approaches to Khrushchev, or no action at all except for presentation of our case to the UN. Communist retaliation to our decision could also take many forms: an invasion of West Germany, bombardment of our missile bases in Turkey and Italy, direct intervention in Southeast Asia, an attack on Guantánamo, or execution of the Bay of Pigs survivors still held in Cuban prisons.

(The final agreement on a blockade as the action most likely to effect removal of the missiles without escalating the crisis into nuclear war was not unanimous. But it can serve no useful purpose to speculate now on whether Adlai Stevenson was a "dove" or this or that Cabinet officer or general a "hawk." To the contrary, it can only discredit reputations and damage the effectiveness of many who are still in action against a Communist menace that is as ominous today as it was in the fall of 1962.

(Although I did not sit in on EXCOM until after the decision was a *fait accompli*, many of the principals, including the President, later took me into their confidence. I have no intention of violating that confidence.)

After my briefing by Bundy, the President's mood and events of the preceding week were no longer mysteries. On Tuesday morning, when I was wasting his time with the guest list for the Prince Hassan luncheon, he was weighing the momentous alternatives of war and peace. (JFK's one great fear was that he might have to be the President to start a nuclear war. He knew that events beyond his control could force that dreadful decision and he was determined that no action of his—or failure to take action—would push the world over the brink. He was insistent that we continue disarmament negotiations at Geneva even when the prospects of success were apparently hopeless. He later spoke of the Nuclear Test Ban Treaty as his most significant achievement. His prime concern, through all the crises with the Soviet Union, was that we not push Khrushchev into a corner where he might order a nuclear strike as his only way out. He felt that his choice of a blockade against Cuba, instead of direct military action, gave Khrushchev such an out—and he was right.)

In light of what Bundy had told me, I could also understand JFK's grim anticipation of Gromyko's visit on Thursday. Just a month earlier, Soviet Ambassador Dobrynin had given the President Khrushchev's personal pledge that he would do nothing to complicate U.S.-Soviet relations during the congressional elections! Dobrynin also gave his assurance that the weapons the Soviet Union was then shipping to Cuba were strictly defensive, and no threat at all to American security.

While the President was stumping Connecticut on Wednesday, a new flight of U-2s shot definite photographic evidence that the Russians not only were accelerating the construction of missile bases known to us, but were launching construction of new ones. This information was given to the President brief hours before he sat down with Gromyko.

The Foreign Minister lied in his teeth. He told JFK he would speak "frankly," but the first words out of his mouth were a denial that Castro was receiving offensive weapons. It must have been difficult for the President to restrain his anger. But if he had given Gromyko the slightest hint that we knew the truth, the Communists would have been ready for our counteraction. And, although the announcement of our response was only four days away, the President still did not know what form it would take.

EXCOM was still hassling over the alternatives on Friday when we took off for the political swing into the Midwest. The call the President was taking in his suite that night in the Sheraton-Blackstone, when I told him of the crisis queries from the press, was from his brother Bob. The Attorney General said that EXCOM was narrowing its decision to a blockade and that the Justice Department was already preparing the proclamation.

Another call from Bob the next morning that EXCOM was ready to present its recommendation, and that security was beginning to fall apart, was the impetus for our hasty return to Washington. JFK gave his tentative approval of the blockade to EXCOM on Saturday afternoon, but another meeting was set for the following morning. Bundy was preparing for it when I left the Situation Room and went upstairs to my own office.

Every man in Washington who knew what the next day or two might bring must have had the same thoughts I did that Sunday morning. Washington was certainly within range of both Soviet and Cuban missiles and was, unquestionably, a primary target.

Security precludes a full discussion of the subject, but it is obvious that the President must leave the Capital in the event of nuclear war and take with him certain personnel to maintain his continuity of command. I was among those who would evacuate with him. But none of us could take our families with us—not even the President. (JFK told his wife that weekend that she ought to consider leaving Washington with their children, as the wives of other officials did, to be closer to her assigned bomb shelter. But she chose to remain with him at the White House.)

Almost two years earlier, when Jim Hagerty was briefing me on information procedures for just such an emergency as this, he said simply and without emotion:

"If the order ever comes for you to evacuate with the President, you'll face the toughest thing you've ever had to do in your life. You're going to have to tell your family, 'Goodbye—you're on your own.'"

A messenger came into my office that Sunday morning with an envelope —the evacuation orders for my family if an attack was imminent. They were to pack their clothes and other necessities, have the car ready and stand by for further word from me. If that word came, they were to drive to a location outside the nuclear impact area of Washington and join the wives and children of other White House personnel.

I had no choice, of course. I had to place duty above family, but it was a cruel decision at the time. Thank God, I never had to place that call to my family in the frightening days ahead.

A highly secret and intricate plan exists for converting our national government from its many and cumbersome peacetime activities to a single-purpose instrument of war. My areas of responsibility were to maintain the President's communications with the people, no matter where he might be, and to halt the flow of all information that might prove useful to the enemy.

Shortly before noon that Sunday, I met in my office with Colonel Justice Chambers, deputy director of the Office of Emergency Planning. The colonel, a Congressional Medal of Honor winner in World War II, had conferred with me frequently over the past twenty-two months to update our emergency information procedures. All we had to do that morning was set the plan in motion.

The colonel's first action was to place on standby alert a nation-wide communications system, most of it underground. This system would be available if war came only to top government officials and the news services and networks. Our next concern was the pool of White House correspondents and photographers who would accompany the President if he had to evacuate Washington and who would remain with him for the duration. Colonel Chambers and I reviewed pre-evacuation instructions for the reporters we had previously worked out and that I was to relay to them at the appropriate time.

Finally, we made plans to summon to Washington some of the Censorship Advisory Board—a panel of fifteen nationally prominent news executives who would enforce government censorship in the event of war. The board had been in existence since World War II, when its policy director was Byron Price. It was, however, somewhat of an anachronism in the atomic age when the almost certain brevity of all-out war would render censorship a rather academic exercise. We went ahead, however, with plans to activate the board because even if war did not come, the President might still have to declare a state of national emergency in which official censorship would become necessary.

After the colonel left my office, I made arrangements with Art Sylvester of Defense and Bob Manning of State to meet with me at my home that afternoon—away from the watchful eyes of the press—to work out a general policy of news coordination.

My telephone rang constantly that morning. Press speculation was now at a fever pitch. In the absence of censorship, there was no way to conceal the movement of ships, planes, and troops toward the Caribbean. And the President's hasty return, the parade of VIPs through the White House, and the all-night activity at State and the Pentagon were unmistakable signs of emergency.

After Bundy's briefing, I could no longer issue a flat denial that important developments were imminent. My one answer to all questions was "no comment."

One of the most persistent queries was why the President hadn't gone to Mass. I went into his office to see him.

"You always go on Sunday," I said. "If you don't today, the press is going to draw its own conclusions."

"Don't worry," he replied. "I'm going." Then he smiled. "Aren't you glad you didn't know all this before you had to?"

He then told me he was convening another session of EXCOM, within the hour, and that I was to attend it and all future strategy conferences for the duration.

"I'll expect you to know what's going on every minute," he said. "You'll have to be on top of every word that comes out of here, State, and the Pentagon."

It was a somber gathering in the Cabinet Room as the President came in last and took his position at the center of the long walnut table, his back to the windows facing on the flower garden. In contrast to his mood of impatience and anxiety through most of that week, he was absolutely calm now that he had come to a decision. I had seen that same facet of his character two years before in Hyannis Port while we were sweating out the election returns. As Richard Nixon cut deeper and deeper into his early lead, he was still able to go to bed and sleep soundly—not knowing whether he would wake up the next President or an also-ran. Then, too, a decision had been made and events would run their own course. It may have been the fatalism of a man who had been close to death three times—twice after surgery and once in the Solomons. But whatever it was, he was the calmest person in the Cabinet Room that morning.

A number of significant actions were taken. The first was a decision, after much debate, to delete from the President's TV address to the nation the next night a proposal for an immediate Kennedy-Khrushchev summit conference on Cuba. It was felt that this might blunt the main thrust of his message: the blockade and our reasons for imposing it. Moscow might even read it as a sign of weakness, and that could prove to be a dangerous miscalculation. It was agreed to hold off on the summit bid until after our ships were in position and there could be no question of our resolution to enforce the blockade. (JFK did not have to ask for a summit the following week because of the rapidity with which Khrushchev agreed to pull back his missiles.)

There was also a discussion of whether to call our action a blockade or a quarantine. The question had both legal and semantic aspects. A blockade is an act of war, and we were not ready to characterize our initial move against Cuba as that. The word quarantine was chosen because of its less bellicose tone and because it would prove more palatable to certain of our reluctant allies. Consultations were to be held the next day with the Organization of American States. Although it was our intention to proceed with or without their concurrence, the President was insistent that we at least try to organize hemispheric unity behind our actions.

JFK told EXCOM that morning that he was sending former Secretary of State Dean Acheson to brief President de Gaulle and the North Atlantic Treaty Organization. Ambassador David Bruce would inform Prime Minister Macmillan and Ambassador Walter C. Dowling was recalled from a Georgia vacation to call on Chancellor Adenauer. Copies of the U-2 photographs and other data supporting the quarantine decision would go out the next day to all foreign embassies in Washington for immediate transmittal to their governments.

The strategy was also laid down for the presentation of our case to the UN Security Council, which Adlai Stevenson, who was present, would handle brilliantly two days later.

EXCOM approval was also given to a bold plan by Don Wilson, deputy director of the U. S. Information Agency, for carrying our message directly to the Cuban people. The Voice of America, our government's only propaganda broadcast into Cuba, was on a short wave frequency, and had a very small audience. But ten commercial radio stations on the Atlantic seaboard had medium-range signals with clear audibility in Cuba during the nighttime hours when there was little competing traffic to interfere. Wilson's plan was for the President to ask the stations to turn their transmitters over to the government from sunset until sunrise for Spanish-language broadcasts in support of our actions. I was to transmit the request to the stations in time for them to carry the President's address. In the interim, Voice of America technicians would rig special cables from Washington right up to their front doors, without the knowledge of the stations.

Immediately following the meeting, the President gave me three instructions. The first was to ask the networks for a half hour of time at 7 P.M. the next night, "but hold off as long as you can. Too much is out of the bag already." I was also to organize simultaneous briefings, immediately after his speech, for the three Washington press contingents covering the White House, the State Department, and the Pentagon. Finally, I was to work with Larry O'Brien in bringing key congressional leaders back to Washington for a briefing in the President's office at 5 P.M. the next day.

I then left for my meeting with Sylvester and Manning, waving at the reporters in the West Lobby as if I were on my way to Falls Church for a leisurely Sunday dinner. But my performance at home when I gave my wife the envelope with her evacuation instructions was not quite as convincing. Although I told her the odds were heavily against her ever having to carry them out, my own concern was all too apparent to her. And the arrival of Sylvester and Manning minutes later was hardly reassuring.

Sunlight streaming through the windows and Bach on the hi-fi set an incongruous atmosphere for our discussion. It was agreed that Sylvester would handle all press announcements on the military phase and Manning would be responsible for the diplomatic front. But nothing would come out of either the Pentagon or State without prior approval of the White House. This would require instantaneous communication among the three of us.

I put in a call to the White House Communications Agency from my home and made arrangements for our own three-way "hot line." That same afternoon, a special telephone was put on each of our desks with a direct line bypassing the switchboards. All I had to do was pick up the receiver, press a buzzer, and Sylvester and Manning, or both, would answer at their end. The system was in almost continuous use the following week.

We then left for Manning's office to go over the latest diplomatic and press cables, including those from Tass. But there was nothing on the Soviet news agency wire even suggesting a direct confrontation between Washington and Moscow. While we were in Manning's office, UPI correspondent Don May caught us together. I'm certain he didn't believe our story that nothing much was up.

I then went back to the White House, entering through a side door to avoid the press, to assist O'Brien in calling the congressional leaders back to the Capital. My assignment was to work with Brigadier General Godfrey McHugh in arranging jet transportation for the senators and representatives.

The election was less than two weeks away and many of them were reluctant to cancel political appearances without knowing the exact nature of the crisis. I must add, however, that their dramatic return to Washington had political advantages for the incumbents. A wire service photograph of Republican Senator Thomas H. Kuchel of California strapping himself into an Air Force jet had to add to his later plurality over Democrat Richard Richards. The most difficult to contact was Democratic Representative Hale Boggs of Louisiana, who was fishing that day in the Gulf of Mexico. A bottle containing the request that he return to Washington was thrown to him from an Air Force plane. He was then flown by helicopter to New Orleans, where a jet was waiting to carry him to the Capital.

I was back home at four in the afternoon. The telephone rang all evening and most of the night with urgent queries from the press. I spoke to the President four times to alert him that security was crumbling. Certain reporters had the entire story, except for the actual time the quarantine would take effect. (Although I had nothing to do with it, the President interceded that night with both the New York *Times* and the Washington *Post*, who agreed to withhold publication in the interests of national security. If they had run the story—if Khrushchev had been given a full day's advance warning—we might have lost the initiative that was to prove crucial in the days ahead.)

But it wasn't only the telephone calls that kept me awake most of that night. I knew that when I left in the morning, I would not be returning home for an indeterminate time. I would have to be available to the President around the clock, and that meant sleeping in the White House or a nearby hotel. My wife and children would have to fend for themselves if the worst came. I got up at four-thirty, without waking the family, threw extra clothes into an overnight bag, and was at my desk at six.

The White House was ready for the approaching crisis. Arrangements had been made for staff members and their secretaries to sleep in the bomb shelter in the basement. The White House mess would be open night and day to feed us. We all were given specific instructions in the event of impending attack. And, for the first time since my naval service in the Pacific, I had to set a twenty-four-hour watch schedule. Mac Kilduff, Andy Hatcher, and I would all be on duty during the day, and would rotate the watch during the night. At least one secretary would be on stand-by during the night and would sleep in the bomb shelter. I took a room in a hotel a block away but also had a cot moved into my office.

The President spoke on the telephone that morning to former Presidents Eisenhower, Truman, and Hoover to advise them of the crisis and his plans for meeting it. Cables were sent to our ambassadors in Latin America and elsewhere, forewarning them of possible anti-American demonstrations and instructing them to take all necessary precautions to protect embassy personnel. Another session of EXCOM was held to review the orders that would go out to our military commands around the world.

One of my first calls that day was to Newton Minow, chairman of the Federal Communications Commission. Don Wilson and I had agreed that Minow was the appropriate government official to run interference for me in our plan to use the facilities of the ten radio stations. Minow, who was in New York, flew back to Washington for a fill-in, then telephoned the managers of the stations, instructing them to stand by for an urgent call from the White House at 6 P.M.

Following the President's instructions, I held off as long as I could before requesting time on the TV and radio networks for that night. At exactly noon, I spoke to Bob Fleming, the Washington bureau manager for ABC and chairman of the special network advisory committee that dealt with such requests from the White House.

When I told him the President would speak on a subject of "the highest national urgency"—the first time I had ever used that description with the network committee—I knew there could be no question of the response.

"Do you have a time preference?" Fleming asked.

"We do—7 P.M. and across the board." That meant a simultaneous broadcast in all time zones.

"I'll get back to you," said Fleming.

The correspondents were then called into my office for their morning briefing, and my opening announcement was their first official confirmation that a major crisis was at hand.

"We have just submitted to the networks a request for a half hour of time at seven tonight for the President to make an address to the nation on a subject of the highest national urgency. We expect to hear from the networks in the next fifteen or twenty minutes."

The first question was from a reporter with a wry sense of humor.

"Do you think they will give it to you?"

"I have a feeling they will," I replied. I then announced a meeting of the full National Security Council for 3:15 P.M., a Cabinet meeting at four, and a conference with the congressional leadership at five.

The answer came from Fleming while the reporters were leaving my office.

"The time is yours—all networks, all live."

My afternoon was as frantic as the morning. The President gave me a long backgrounder to prepare me for the questions I would have to answer after his speech. I took down his direct quotes on the key points:

1. "We chose a quarantine over an air strike because there is no certainty of hitting all the targets. We are also uncertain how many of the sites are operational. While we were hitting one, another might launch its missiles against us. A quarantine is far less likely to provoke a nuclear response.

2. "The argument that we should do nothing at all and turn the matter over to the UN gives the Russians time we can't let them have. They could rush work on bases that are still not operational, and the danger to our security would become that much greater. All of this has been done secretly, and while the Russians were denying that it was being done. We have to read this as evidence that they might use them at any time. There are other risks in doing nothing. It would induce the Russians to make incorrect assumptions about the reliability of our commitments in other areas of the world, particularly Berlin. It would create grave problems in Latin America, where there would be a feeling that the balance

of power in this hemisphere was shifting away from us—that the Russians could throw their weight around right on our own doorstep.

3. "We didn't act earlier because we didn't have proof of the offensive nature of these weapons until last Tuesday. If we had acted without such proof, it would have been impossible to organize support for an action of any kind against Cuba. All we had before Tuesday were reports from refugees and they have frequently been inaccurate.

4. "It has to be made clear that there's a big difference between offensive Soviet nuclear weapons in Cuba and our own in Turkey and elsewhere. Ours are an attempt to redress the balance of power in Europe—much the same as NATO is meant to balance the Warsaw Pact countries. We don't deny that ours are there. Their locations and capability certainly are known to the Russians. But what is happening in Cuba is far different—a provocative change in the delicate status quo in this hemisphere. That status quo poses no threat at all to the Soviet Union. Just last month, the Russians were saying they didn't need offensive missiles in Cuba, and have since denied that they were moving them in. The very secrecy of this operation, and attempts to guard that secrecy even by Khrushchev himself, poses an obvious danger to us that we can't ignore."

JFK then told me that the "quarantine is our first move, and we hope we won't have to make others. The next move is up to the Russians. If they turn their ships around, there will be a breathing spell to talk things over. If they don't, we will take whatever actions are necessary."

I met again with the press at 4:10 P.M. and parried a host of questions with the statement that the President would answer most of them himself in his address to the nation, now less than three hours away.

I was challenged for the first time on my announcement in Chicago that the President was returning to the Capital because of a cold.

Q. Mr. Secretary, it has been suggested that the President's cold was a diplomatic illness. Or, to put it another way, a phony.

A. I read you the first time.

Q. I would like you to answer that question.

A. The President definitely had a degree of temperature in Chicago.

Q. Does he still have a cold?

A. No, he is fine.

The transcripts of my press briefings don't record incredulous glances, but they were the general reaction to my comment.

The President had a long-standing appointment to confer that afternoon with Prime Minister Milton Obote of Uganda, and could not cancel it without offending the African leader. The Cabinet was kept waiting while the President and the Prime Minister spent forty-five minutes ranging over subjects from trade to American assistance to African schools. It was a measure both of JFK's innate courtesy and coolness under fire that he did not give Obote a token five minutes and then rush him out. When their meeting was over, the President took his visitor to the White House door through a mob of reporters. JFK's only response to a barrage of questions:

"It has been a very interesting day."

At 5 P.M., the congressional leaders were taken into his office, shown the aerial photographs and told of the quarantine announcement that would come only two hours later. Senator Richard B. Russell, chairman of the Armed Services Committee, argued instead for an invasion, and had support from Senator J. William Fulbright. The President heard them out, but said he would not change his strategy.

Promptly at 6 P.M., Soviet Ambassador Dobrynin was summoned to the State Department and advised by Rusk of the quarantine decision and given the text of the President's TV address for immediate transmission to Khrushchev. Minutes later, Ambassador Foy Kohler delivered the same message to the Kremlin. (In forming the pool that would be in the President's office when he read the speech, I deliberately chose Mike Sagatelyan of Tass. "Why me?" was his surprised reaction. "I want to be sure that you read the President loud and clear," I told him.)

I also had messages of my own to deliver at 6 P.M.—to the ten radio stations. The form of the request had been gone over very carefully by Minow and attorneys for the FCC. There must be no suggestion that the government, which has regulatory control over radio stations, was demanding the use of their facilities. Their participation must be entirely voluntary. We must also emphasize that we were willing to reimburse them for lost revenue and for the additional cost of operating their transmitters through the night.

My first call was to Ralf Brent, president of WRUL in New York City. He quickly agreed to the use of his station but didn't think he had time to rig the cables for the President's address an hour later.

"The cable is already at your front door," I said. "All you have to do is hook into it."

The other nine calls went the same way. It is to the credit of all the stations that not one of them tried to pin me down on how much money we were willing to pay for this extraordinary service. That very night, the President found time to send each of the owners a thank you telegram.

The White House mimeo section produced the press copies of the President's speech to be given to the correspondents when JFK actually went on the air.

(The distribution of texts of major addresses was always a mob scene to which I was unwilling to expose the girls in the office. Deadline-frantic reporters would jam outside my office and almost knock each other down trying to grab a copy from the pile Hatcher or Kilduff would take to the door.)

When the senators and congressmen left the President's office at 5:45 P.M., the network crew took over. There was space in the office for the cameras of only one network, which would provide a direct audio-visual feed to the others. On this night, it was CBS' turn to pool its facilities.

Extensive preparations were necessary. Canvas was spread over the floor to protect the rug. The President's desk was cleared, except for a small reading lectern. Furniture was moved out to make room for the three cameras, recorders, and a battery of lights. Chairs were set up for the press pool.

But this was only for TV. Except for microphones on the lectern, all the radio equipment was in the adjoining office of Mrs. Evelyn Lincoln, the President's personal secretary. It was necessary for each network and station to have its own commentator standing by to sign on with, "Ladies and Gentlemen, the President of the United States," and to close with an ad lib analysis of the Chief Executive's remarks.

JFK entered his office at six-forty. It took ten minutes to adjust the lighting (he wore no make-up) and to focus the cameras from their stationary positions. At six-fifty, he went into the Cabinet Room for a last reading of his speech—easily the most important of his life. At six fifty-nine, he sat down behind his desk, watching the director who would cue him when he was on the air.

Tens of millions of Americans were waiting with the nervousness that always accompanies a major presidential pronouncement when JFK's face came on their screens at 7 P.M. He wasted no words.

"Good evening, my fellow citizens: This government, as promised, has maintained the closest surveillance of the Soviet military buildup on the island of Cuba. Within the past week, unmistakable evidence has established the fact that a series of offensive missile sites is now in preparation on that imprisoned island. The purpose of these bases can be none other than to provide a nuclear strike capability against the Western Hemisphere."

The new weaponry on Cuba, he said, includes "medium range ballistic missiles capable of carrying a nuclear warhead for a distance of more than 1000 miles. Each of these missiles, in short, is capable of striking Washington, D.C., the Panama Canal, Cape Canaveral, Mexico City, or any other city in the southeastern part of the United States, in Central America, or in the Caribbean area . . .

"The urgent transformation of Cuba into an important strategic base . . . constitutes an explicit threat to the peace and security of all the Americas . . . This secret, swift, and extraordinary buildup of Communist missiles . . . is a deliberately provocative and unjustified change in the status quo which cannot be accepted by this country, if our courage and our commitments are ever to be trusted again by either friend or foe."

He then announced "a strict quarantine on all offensive military equipment under shipment to Cuba" and more intense aerial surveillance of Cuba. "Should these offensive military preparations continue, thus increasing the threat to the hemisphere, further action will be justified. I have directed the Armed Forces to prepare for any eventualities . . ."

Then came the most chilling paragraph in the speech.

"It shall be the policy of this nation to regard any nuclear missile launched from Cuba against any nation in the Western Hemisphere as an attack by the Soviet Union on the United States, requiring a full retaliatory response upon the Soviet Union."

There was more: reinforcement of our base at Guantánamo and the evacuation of the dependents of military personnel; a call for immediate deliberations by the UN Security Council and the OAS to "take action against this latest Soviet threat to world peace"; and an appeal to Khrushchev to "abandon this course of world domination, and to join in an historic effort to end the perilous arms race and to transform the history of man."

And, finally, "The path we have chosen for the present is full of hazards, as all paths are, but it is the one most consistent with our character and courage as a nation and our commitments around the world. The cost of freedom is always high, but Americans have always paid it. And one path we shall never choose, and that is the path of surrender or submission.

"Our goal is not the victory of might, but the vindication of right; not peace at the expense of freedom, but both peace *and* freedom, here in this hemisphere, and, we hope, around the world. God willing, that goal will be achieved."

The waiting was over. The crisis had formally begun.

I waded through the snarl of TV cables on the floor of the President's office and went back to my own to meet the press.

The number of correspondents at the White House that night was the largest in my history as Press Secretary, and surpassed only on the weekend of President Kennedy's assassination and funeral. I must have taken a hundred questions in fifteen minutes.

Is the President getting out of Washington?

"He plans to stay here, at least for the foreseeable future."

Will he call Congress back into session?

"I have not heard that subject discussed yet."

Will the President appear personally before the UN?

"I have not heard that he will."

Did the President call Gromyko a liar to his face last Thursday?

"He did not."

Are the President and Vice-President canceling all political tours for the duration?

"They are."

Would I speculate on our next move if the blockade did not succeed?

"I am not in charge of speculation. That's your job."

When the briefing came to an end, I sent, one by one, for the White House reporters who would accompany the President if we had to evacuate Washington. I told them they were never to be more than fifteen minutes away from the White House and were to let me know where to reach them every minute of the night and day.

I then put in a call to Bill Steven, the very able editor of the Houston *Chronicle*, whom we had chosen to serve as executive officer of the Censorship Advisory Board. Could he fly to Washington immediately? He could and did.

It was after two o'clock before I finally left the White House for my hotel, after rousing Hatcher out of a sound sleep on the cot in my office and telling him to take over the watch.

The next six days were the most anxious and active of my life and, certainly, the grimmest of the Thousand Days of John F. Kennedy's presidency. But I never knew him to be more in command of himself or of events. And I can never forget his courage, his smile, and his optimism that this crisis, too, would pass.

# XIX

## KHRUSHCHEV BACKS DOWN

For five days, an anxious world waited and hoped.

But inside the White House, there was no time for waiting and the first Soviet responses to the President's decision gave us no reason for hope.

The Kremlin instructed its Warsaw Treaty forces—East Germany, Czechoslovakia, Poland, Hungary, and Rumania—to "raise the military preparedness of the troops and fleets." Through Ambassador Kohler, Chairman Khrushchev sent a bristling message to JFK, branding the quarantine an act of "piracy," and accusing him of war provocations. Our own military preparedness left no doubt that we could go much further than the quarantine if Russian-Cuban action made it necessary. The greatest manpower mobilization since World War II—more than 100,000 troops—was assembling in Florida and other southeastern states for a possible invasion of Cuba. Ninety U.S. warships, including eight carriers with their sixty-eight squadrons of aircraft, were ready to proceed to their blockade assignments. Our Strategic Air Command and Polaris submarine fleet was on instant alert. As Secretary of State Rusk put it, the two most powerful nations in the history of the world—each with the capacity to destroy the other—were "eyeball-to-eyeball."

Our activities fell into a definite cycle. We spent sixteen hours a day analyzing Soviet reactions, developing a counterstrategy, drafting messages to the Kremlin, and then sleeping for a fitful four or five hours.

While we slept, the Kremlin was studying our messages, revising its own strategy, and sending countermessages.

Two factors became immediately apparent to us.

First, every word that came out of the White House would play a fateful role in determining the course of events. Second, communications between the White House and the Kremlin were perilously obsolete in the nuclear age. A message sent from the President to Ambassador Kohler for delivery to Khrushchev took more than four hours to reach him through normal diplomatic channels. Even though the government had this diplomatic channel to Moscow, the process of coding, transmittal, decoding, and translating was nerve-rackingly slow. And Khrushchev had to suffer the same delays in communicating with JFK.

The two governments arrived almost simultaneously at the same decision: to bypass diplomatic channels and issue their proposals and responses directly to radio and press news-gathering agencies. This cut the time lapse considerably and was a key factor in the swift resolution of the crisis (and in the later decision to install a "hot line" linking the two capitals).

The Soviet bloc correspondents continued, of course, to attend my press briefings, and I was very much aware that the statements I issued on behalf of the President—and my own answers to questions—were being read in the Kremlin within an hour.

Volumes already have been written on the events of that fateful week, and I will not attempt still another precise chronology of our actions and Soviet counteractions. But my notes taken at the Executive Committee meetings at the White House define the most crucial elements of the first and, hopefully, the last direct confrontation of nuclear powers.

*Tuesday morning, October 23: President approves plans for issuance of "A Proclamation of Interdiction of the Delivery of Offensive Weapons to Cuba"* (the technical instrument authorizing the quarantine, which was given greater legal force later in the day by a 19 to 0 vote of the Organization of American States). *President consents to retaliatory air strikes against Cuba if a U.S. plane is shot down.*

*Tuesday afternoon, October 23: EXCOM approves language of interdiction proclamation and decides to issue it that night, to take effect at 10 A.M. the next morning. The proclamation limits the cargoes we will intercept to missiles and bombers. McNamara advises that at least twenty-five Russian ships are en route to Cuba.*

At this early point, the indications were that Khrushchev and Castro might react militarily to the quarantine. The evidence from our U-2s was that Soviet and Cuban technicians were now working around the clock on the missile sites, and many more IL-28 bombers were seen on Cuban airstrips. There were also reports that Russian submarines (probably with a nuclear capacity) were accompanying the freighters bound for Cuba. The President took the news impassively. "I guess this is the week I earn my salary."

*Wednesday, October 24: First reports that most of the Russian ships are either changing course or moving toward Cuba at reduced speed. But President orders immediate attention to our alternatives if Russia should move on West Berlin, and our state of preparedness in the event of an air attack on southeastern states from Cuba.*

Word that the Soviet ships were either turning away from our blockade fleet or delaying the first confrontation was met with cautious relief. It was, of course, a hopeful sign. But there was also the possibility that the Russian captains had been instructed to sortie until the Kremlin could make up its mind what to do. One vessel, the tanker *Bucharest*, was still holding course and speed and would reach the blockade line the following morning. All we could do was wait. The President speculated that the Russians might test the blockade with only those ships carrying non-military cargoes, such as the *Bucharest*, but divert vessels actually transporting missiles or bombers. Our interference with "peaceful" merchant ships would be a propaganda advantage for the Russians. At the same time, they would not risk having highly secret and sensitive military hardware fall into our hands.

*Thursday, October 25: President orders Navy to pass Bucharest through blockade line without search. Also orders night reconnaissance flights over Cuba and approves adding missile fuel to list of contraband we will intercept.*

JFK let the *Bucharest* proceed to Cuba without interference for two reasons. A tanker, lacking the huge hatches necessary to conceal an ICBM below decks, would have to carry them topside, and none were visible on the *Bucharest*. Second, this was the first Soviet vessel to reach the quarantine line and her captain may not yet have had his instructions from Moscow.

*Friday, October 26: Department of Defense announces the first boarding and search of a freighter under Soviet charter—the Marucla, of Panamanian registry. There is no resistance.*

The Navy ship that stopped the *Marucla* was the destroyer *Joseph P. Kennedy, Jr.,* named after the President's older brother. It was a complete coincidence, but JFK told me: "The press will never believe we didn't stick the *Kennedy* in the way of the *Marucla* just to give the family publicity."

At noon that same day, the Soviet Union made its first specific overtures for a peaceful settlement of the crisis—not directly to the U.S. government but through John Scali, the diplomatic reporter for ABC-TV. The offer, made to him over lunch by Aleksandr Fomin, a counselor of the Soviet Embassy in Washington, was for immediate removal of offensive missiles in Cuba and dismantling of their bases in exchange for a U.S. pledge not to invade the island.

On Friday evening, President Kennedy received a long letter from Khrushchev. It was alternately belligerent and conciliatory, but contained the same general proposal that Fomin had made to Scali earlier in the day. For the first time, there was real hope that our strategy was succeeding and that the Soviet Union was backing down. The President met with EXCOM the following morning to consider a reply to the Khrushchev letter.

*Saturday morning, October 27: Decision to accept Khrushchev proposal, contingent on UN observation of missile and launcher removal. A new letter from Khrushchev arrives imposing further conditions, among them removal of our Jupiter missiles from Turkey.*

The high hopes of the night before were shattered. The latest Soviet proposal was totally unacceptable, and two later developments that day brought the confrontation to its most critical stage. One of our U-2s was missing over Cuba and presumed to have been shot down by Castro's surface-to-air missiles. The President already had announced we would respond to such an incident by bombing Cuba, but he held back on the order until we could be certain the U-2 had been lost as a result of enemy action.

*Saturday evening, October 27: Secretary Rusk announces that a U-2, based in Alaska, has flown over the Chukotski Peninsula in Siberia because of a navigational error. Soviet fighters rose to meet it, but there was no shooting. I am told to tell press nothing concerning either U-2 incident unless Cuba or Russia releases the news. Acting on Bob Kennedy's suggestion, President decides to ignore second Khrushchev letter and respond only to the first EXCOM meeting set for 10 A.M. tomorrow (Sunday) to discuss air strike against Cuba if latest intelligence shows U-2 was shot down.*

In the President's reply to the first Khrushchev letter, released directly to the press at 8 P.M. to hasten its receipt in Moscow, he told the Premier, "the key elements of your proposals . . . seem generally acceptable . . . You would agree to remove these weapons systems from Cuba under appropriate United Nations observation and supervision; and undertake, with suitable safeguards, to halt the further introduction of such weapons systems into Cuba. We, on our part, would agree—upon the establishment of adequate arrangements through the United Nations to ensure the carrying out and the continuation of these commitments—(a) to remove promptly the quarantine measures now in effect and (b) to give assurances against an invasion of Cuba . . ."

It was my clear impression when we left the White House late on Saturday night that time was running out. There was no certainty at all that Khrushchev would seriously consider the President's reply to a peace proposal which the Russians themselves had apparently withdrawn. We were waiting for a thunderous Soviet propaganda reaction to the U-2 overflight of Siberia, and our missing U-2 over Cuba would compel a decision to retaliate the next morning.

The least U.S. response would have been air strikes against the Russian SAM sites in Cuba. The strongest response would have been an outright invasion of Cuba with a high cost in U.S. lives, although the military were confident we could take Cuba in a week to ten days. Whether an invasion would have brought a nuclear response from the Soviet Union, no one will ever know. But in my view it would have been impossible for the Soviet Union to stand by and watch its one satellite in the Western Hemisphere go under without retaliating in a forceful way—particularly when casualties would have been high among the thousands of Russian soldiers and technicians in Cuba at that time.

(I have in my files a note I slipped to Ken O'Donnell during the Saturday EXCOM meeting: *"What is amazing is how the key presidential choices, mostly made in the dark, have worked out in a crisis situation."* There was also the remark that night of Bill Foster, director of the U. S. Arms Control and Disarmament Agency: *"This is not a good night for disarmament."* And, finally, the disturbed statement of the President: *"That's the trouble with all that we're doing. Once we walk out of this room, people can start to get killed."*)

I was driving to work on Sunday morning, October 28, when I heard a flash on the radio that Khrushchev had sent a message to the President, in response to JFK's of the night before, agreeing to withdraw his missiles and tear down the launching sites if the U.S. would guarantee not to invade Cuba.

The crisis was over but I couldn't believe it. Only a handful of the President's advisers thought that Khrushchev would back away from his latest demands that quickly. But he had, and for reasons the world may never know. Instead of discussing air attacks against Cuba that morning—perhaps an actual invasion—there was nothing left for EXCOM to do but draft the President's reply to Khrushchev, hailing his "statesmanlike decision" as a "welcome and constructive contribution to peace."

Not once during this final meeting did the President join in the general spirit of triumph. His manner was entirely businesslike. This crisis had passed, but there would be others to contend with next month and next year. One of his advisers said he was now "ten feet tall" and would have more weight in settling future blow-ups around the world. "No," he said, "this will wear off in about a week, and everyone will be back thinking only of their own interests."

I had my first good sleep in a week that night. It was hard to believe that brief hours before we had been perilously close to nuclear war because of the U-2 incidents on opposite sides of the world and the feverish activity at the missile bases in Cuba. Khrushchev later wrote that the U-2 over the Chukotski Peninsula "might have been taken for a nuclear bomber . . . intruding when everything [in the Soviet Union] had been put into combat readiness." We also had definite information that Sunday morning that the missing U-2 over Cuba had, in fact, been shot down by Castro's forces. The slain pilot was Major Rudolf Anderson, Jr., who had taken the aerial photographs on October 14 definitely establishing the presence of offensive missiles in Cuba.

The role of ABC newsman John Scali in settling the missile crisis is a fascinating footnote to history. It points up both the dangerously obsolete nature of our communications with the Soviet Union before the "hot line" and the Byzantine-like character of Soviet diplomacy.

The Russians chose Scali as their intermediary with the U.S. government for a number of reasons—all of which are a tribute to his enterprise and integrity as a reporter. The Soviet Embassy knew that he was held in great respect in our own State Department and would have swift access to Secretary Rusk—a critical factor in their plan. But they also had confidence in Scali themselves. Unlike many diplomatic correspondents, who look only to our own State Department for news, Scali was in regular contact with the most important foreign embassies in Washington, including those of the Soviet Union and its satellites.

I participated in the decision to ask Scali to hold his silence on the secret negotiations in which he was a principal, but the story has since been leaking out in dribbles from other sources. Now, and with his permission, I print for the first time the significant sections of his reports to President Kennedy and Secretary Rusk.

On the morning of Friday, October 26, Scali received a telephone call from Fomin, who held the title of counselor at the Soviet Embassy but was known to be the chief Russian intelligence agent in Washington.

Following is Scali's first memo to Roger Hilsman, director of the Bureau of Intelligence and Research for the State Department.

"Aleksandr S. Fomin, Soviet Embassy Counselor, at lunch which he sought urgently, asks if State would be interested in settlement of Cuban crisis along these lines: Bases would be dismantled under United Nation's supervision and Castro would pledge not to accept offensive weapons of any kind, ever, in return for U.S. pledge not to invade Cuba.

"I said I didn't know but that perhaps this is something that could be talked about. He said if Stevenson pursued this line, Zorin [Valerian Zorin, Soviet ambassador to the UN Security Council] would be interested. Asked that I check with State and let him know. He gave me his home telephone number so I could call him tonight, if necessary.

"Fomin claimed that Cuban delegate to UN during Security Council debate asked for such no-invasion assurances in return for dismantling but that he got no reply. I told him I'd followed the UN debate very carefully but could not recall any such remarks on Cuba's part . . ."

Scali got this memo to Rusk, through Hilsman, directly after leaving the Soviet official. The Secretary of State immediately brought the newsman to the White House to secure the President's reply. I rushed up to Scali in some agitation when I saw him in the back corridor near the Cabinet Room—an area that was off-limits to the press.

"What the hell are you doing here?" I asked.

Before he could answer, Rusk came up to me from behind and said, "It's OK, Pierre, I brought him."

Fomin's proposal to Scali was an acceptable basis for settlement of the crisis, and Scali was instructed by the President to convey that message to the Russian, but without attributing it to JFK. Following is Scali's second memo:

"At 7:35 P.M. [October 26] I met Fomin in the Statler Hotel lobby as per his suggestion [and] we went to the coffee shop in the hotel to talk. I told him: 'I have reason to believe that the United States government sees real possibilities in this and supposes that the representatives of the USSR and the United States in New York can work this matter out with U Thant and with each other. It is my definite impression that time is very urgent . . .'

"He listened attentively and then asked whether my information came from high sources. I told him the information came from the highest sources in the United States government. He asked for a second time if I were absolutely sure it came from the highest sources. I reiterated this a second time. He then said that if the information did not come from the highest sources and he reported it, he could be made to look like a fool at a very critical time. I replied that I would be the most irresponsible man in the world if I lied about something as important as this at this very critical time.

"He then seemed assured that I was telling the truth. At this point he said he wanted to be sure that we both knew the arrangements we were discussing. I then told him my understanding:

"That the offensive Cuban missile sites would be dismantled under United Nations supervision, that Castro would publicly pledge never to receive offensive weapons again, that the Soviet Union would also promise not to ship them again, and that in return the United States would publicly promise not to invade Cuba.

"He agreed that this was precisely what he had mentioned. At this point, Fomin asked whether I knew if it would be possible to have the United Nations inspectors also check the American military bases in Florida to make sure that there would be no invasion of Cuba. He also asked whether it would be possible to inspect surrounding Caribbean countries. I replied I did not know because this was a completely new element which he was introducing for the first time. He agreed that he had not mentioned it before, but 'I am a layman and a small fry and I am just asking.'

"I replied I could only answer as a reporter since I did not have any official information. It was my impression, I said, that this would raise a terrible complication because there are no American offensive missiles pointed at Cuba as there are [offensive missiles] in Cuba so that the situations were different. Furthermore, I pointed out that once the missile bases in Cuba were dismantled and that Cuba pledged never to receive them again, the need for the mobilization of American forces in Florida would not exist, so presumably these forces would return to their posts and the situation in Florida would revert to normal.

"But, I said, to ask the President to agree to allow foreign inspectors in Florida at this time would put him in a difficult position at home, because many right-wingers in the United States were demanding that Cuba be invaded at all costs and that they would interpret this that the President was going 'soft.'

"Fomin then asked how the Soviets could be sure that the coast of Florida and the nearby Caribbean countries would not be used as the jumping off point for a future invasion. I said on this that he would have to rely on the word of the United States government, that it did not intend to invade Cuba itself and that it did not intend to allow Cuban refugees to use American soil for such attacks.

"I repeated again that any effort to insist that inspectors check the American mobilization in Florida or Caribbean countries would raise a terrible complication at a period when time was of the essence in settling the Cuban problem.

"He then told me that he could assure me that this information would be communicated immediately to the highest Soviet sources and simultaneously to Mr. Zorin. He reiterated this a second time. He then said he wanted to get right back to the embassy and left with me so quickly he did not wait for his change at the cashier's cage. As we said goodbye in the lobby, he said he might be in touch with me again and that he had both my office and home telephone number. I told him I would be glad to talk with him at any time.

"I got the impression that the new element that he raised was something that he was trying out for size on me. When I told him of the domestic and other repercussions which would make acceptance extremely unlikely, he raised no objection. The entire meeting took twenty minutes."

There can be no question that Fomin was acting on orders from Ambassador Dobrynin and was speaking directly for Khrushchev. The eventual settlement was on almost precisely the terms Fomin presented to Scali at their first meeting. Similarly, Scali's statement that he was relaying the tentative acceptance of "the highest sources" in our government left no doubt that he was speaking for the President. It must be understood that other contacts between Moscow and Washington, both diplomatic and informal, were taking place at the same time as the Fomin-Scali exchange. The reason both governments would resort to such clearly unofficial approaches is obvious. In the event of their failure, the Kremlin could disown Fomin as a minor functionary who had no authority to enter into such negotiations, and we could describe Scali merely as a conscientious private citizen who was relaying information he had received.

When Khrushchev's second letter, demanding the removal of our missiles from Turkey, came through the next morning, Scali felt—and with justification—that the Russians had been using him to gain time to bring the Cuban missile emplacements to a point of greater combat readiness. Actually, the mystery of the conflicting Khrushchev proposals has never been solved. Was Khrushchev overruled on his first letter? Did he even see the second message sent out over his signature? We may never know. But, whatever the case, Scali had good reason to believe that Fomin had not dealt with him in good faith.

He telephoned Fomin at four o'clock Saturday afternoon and arranged to meet him fifteen minutes later at the Statler Hotel. The Russian said he was totally mystified by the second message from the Kremlin and that he and Ambassador Dobrynin were "waiting anxiously" for further word from Moscow on the original proposal.

From Scali's memo to Rusk that same day:

"I told him I found it exceedingly difficult to believe; that, as a reporter, I had no alternative but to conclude it was a stinking double-cross. He professed to be amazed. The formula mentioned by Radio Moscow, I pointed out, had no connection whatever with what he and I discussed last night. He agreed. He reiterated again that it was his opinion that the message had not been received by Moscow in time, because of the heavy cable traffic originating from New York, London, and other points. I again found it exceedingly difficult to believe." (Scali could have held no other opinion because the *first* communication from Khrushchev the night before, stipulating terms for a settlement, was almost identical to Fomin's proposal.)

"At this point, he said: 'Well, the [second] formula mentioned by Moscow is not new. After all, Walter Lippmann mentioned it and many other prominent Americans.' I told him I didn't give a damn if Walter Lippmann or Cleopatra mentioned it—that it was completely, totally, utterly and perpetually unacceptable. It was unacceptable in the past, I told him, is unacceptable today, would be unacceptable tomorrow and into infinity—that the American government just wouldn't consider it. If the Soviets want to talk about the location and number of American bases overseas, they should do this within the framework of disarmament and not as part of any deal. He claimed that they had brought it up in disarmament talks and that it had been rejected.

"I stressed that I was speaking only as a reporter but that almost certainly some government officials would ask what happened to the idea that I talked about, particularly in view of what I had told him last night about its being something that could be discussed. He said that he and the ambassador are 'small fry'—that in a situation like this Khrushchev received suggestions from many sources. But, he insisted, he still expected a reply and would get in touch with me immediately when it came . . .

"I can't tell whether this guy is telling the truth or not. He seemed genuinely to disbelieve anything about an earlier note, repeated about half a dozen times that he and the ambassador were awaiting a reply. He seemed upset. But it could all be an act."

The reply came, of course, the next morning and brought tremendous relief to Washington, the nation, and the world. Scali met Fomin again at 12:55 P.M. and the Russian said, "I am instructed to say that the information you provided yesterday was very helpful to the Chairman in making up his mind quickly."

The nation and the world owe John Scali a great debt of gratitude. He chose to put aside his tools as a newsman in favor of the greater national interest at a crucial time in history. This meant immobilizing himself as a reporter and permitting others to end up with what was the greatest story of his life. I have known Scali for a long time and have found him to be the meanest man who ever sat down at a poker table. But his role in averting nuclear catastrophe was of enormous importance, and I have him down in my book not only as a great reporter but as a great American.

At the President's suggestion, Scali met again with Fomin on October 29 and November 3 and his memos to Rusk were extremely valuable in assessing Moscow's post-crisis positions. From Scali's report of October 29:

". . . The main points he [Fomin] made in a long, rambling conversation: Castro is a very hard person to control. The Soviets have urged him repeatedly to concentrate his energies on Cuba, not to try to stir up trouble elsewhere, but Castro doesn't listen . . . Three or four times Fomin asked if the time was right for a summit conference. I told him, as a reporter, I felt Mr. Kennedy would not be very receptive, for a time, until he knew beyond a shadow of a doubt that the Soviets were carrying out their promises . . .

"Fomin said that Secretary Rusk should talk with Ambassador Dobrynin three times a day for at least an hour a session 'so both sides can understand each other better.' I said that this didn't leave time for Rusk to do much else. He replied that there is nothing more important in this nuclear world than better Soviet-American understanding . . .

"The only point I made, insistently, was that the terrible dangers of the past few days made it imperative for both sides to get together and start some sane nuclear disarmament. I said that the President is determined to try again more urgently than ever, that the Soviets will find that the inspection to be carried out in Cuba will be a reasonable kind, not an excuse for espionage as always claimed, and perhaps from this, both sides can go on to agree on inspection which is indispensable, as he well knew, to disarmament. There was no tendency on the administration's part, I said, to humiliate or embarrass Mr. Khrushchev at this time. He replied that this consideration 'represents statesmanship of a high order' by the President and that he and the Ambassador understood this. The Soviet government, he said, despite everything, recognizes that the Kennedy administration is better and more reasonable to deal with than the last, even though there are belligerent statements from the Pentagon which are difficult to understand. It's of course also difficult to understand how Walter Lippmann, a close friend of the President, can be wrong and how I, who work for Republican James Hagerty [then ABC's top news executive] can defend the administration. 'You should be fired by Mr. Hagerty,' he said with a smile. I replied that everything Mr. Lippmann writes does not come straight from the White House, that he is frequently wrong, and that if the Soviets were going to seek to judge administration intentions by following the words of reporters, they should back-read (journalese for re-read) or listen to different reporters than the ones they have been following . . ."

From Scali's memo of November 3:

"Main points Fomin made were: The United States must be 'patient' with Soviet efforts to convince Castro to behave . . . It's like trying to convince a 'stubborn' woman to have relations with you. If you use force, you never achieve your objective, but if you use gentle persuasion you overcome her pro forma objections. He emphasized repeatedly that the Soviets need 'reciprocal concessions' from the United States at this time. You must not keep the blockade on unchanged, he said, but relax it gradually so as to create a better atmosphere . . .

"Castro is adamant, he claimed, against inspection on Cuban territory. The way to solve this, he said, is for the United States and Russia to put Castro aside and carry out the agreement between them. Castro won't even allow inspection inside his territorial waters, so why not have inspection aboard [the ships], 'let's say, thirteen miles out at sea.' Fomin emphasized that if the United States 'forces the issue' it won't do any good, because 'we have to live with Castro.' He ridiculed the idea that Russia could be persuaded to pull out the SAM sites while it is pulling out the offensive equipment. 'What, and leave a king (Castro) naked?', he asked when I urged this on him. Russia intends to leave behind some defensive technicians, he said, those training Cuba's strictly defensive equipment . . .

"Fomin seemed still quite disturbed by the narrow margin by which the United States and Russia avoided war. He blamed the 'aggressive spirit' of the administration on 'Bobby' Kennedy, saying he 'is the worst of the whole lot and we know this. He was the one who was urging rash action.' I pointed out that Rusk and McNamara were unanimous in support of the administration decisions and that it would be a mistake to believe it was the result of only Robert Kennedy's influence . . ."

Scali's information from Fomin was regularly reported to the EXCOM.

It so accurately mirrored what the Soviets were telling Ambassador Stevenson and John McCloy at the UN that President Kennedy once wryly observed: "Why don't we just invite John in to the EXCOM meetings."

My history with the Russians, from my initial contacts at Vienna through my visit to the Soviet Union, always had an eerie quality to them. It was a shadowy world of covert diplomacy but continuing contact.

It was not surprising, then, that Khrushchev sent one of his most trusted advisers—Yuri Zhukov—to Washington on October 31 to seek out those of us he knew in the administration. His purpose: To find out what the score was between Washington and Moscow in the wake of the missile crisis. I had met Zhukov on my visit to the Soviet Union earlier that year when he wrote the party line column "Observer" for *Pravda*. He was now its foreign editor.

At the EXCOM meeting of October 29, JFK turned to Ambassador Thompson and asked if Zhukov was an important person.

"He certainly is," said Thompson. "I'm going to see him Friday."

Secretary Rusk smiled. "I guess Zhukov doesn't regard me as part of the ruling circle. He hasn't asked to see me."

The President cracked back: "Pierre must outrank both of you. Zhukov is seeing him for lunch on Wednesday."

The laugh that followed the President's remark broke the tension in a room that had just heard a report that the day after Khrushchev's pledge to remove the missiles, an American plane had been fired on over a Cuban air base while photographing a new concentration of Soviet IL-28 bombers.

During the week of the missile crisis, Zhukov had been attending a Ford Foundation conference on communications at Andover, Maine, but apparently was in close communication with Moscow.

On the same Friday that Fomin was broaching the Soviet terms to Scali, Zhukov asked Norman Cousins, who was also attending the conference, if President Kennedy was likely to crow about his victory, or take more aggressive action against the Soviet Union, if the Kremlin withdrew its missiles.

The editor of the *Saturday Review*, speaking as a private citizen, responded that the President was unlikely to do anything that would humiliate Khrushchev or provoke a new crisis.

The Fomin-Scali and Zhukov-Cousins conversations are significant when placed in the same time period. Also significant was information Cousins gleaned from other Russian delegates to the Andover conference. In reporting back to Khrushchev on his October 18 conversation with the President, Foreign Minister Gromyko omitted all mention of his assurance to JFK that no offensive missiles were in Cuba. At that late day, he apparently had no authorization from the Chairman to deliberately lie to the President, and chose to forget that he had done it.

I met Zhukov at the Rive Gauche restaurant in the Georgetown section of Washington on Wednesday, October 31. One of the members of his party was Georgi Bolshakov—secret agent, editor of the *USSR* magazine, and my fellow courier in the confidential exchange of letters between JFK and Khrushchev. This form of communication, incidentally, was not used during the missile crisis, probably because of the great amount of time required for transmittal, translation, and decoding.

Zhukov's manner was deadly serious. There was none of the friendly banter and humor he had shown during my two-day visit with Khrushchev a year earlier. He began by asking for my appraisal of the long-range impact of the missile crisis on U.S.-Soviet relations—a question for which I had been intensely briefed.

I said there had been hopeful signs of *rapprochement* in the past two years: the release of our RB-47 pilots immediately after the Inauguration, the cease-fire agreement in Laos, and the Soviet decision to postpone recognition of East Germany. Although our continuing negotiations on Berlin and nuclear testing had not produced satisfactory solutions, there was at least a feeling of integrity in communication, particularly in the personal exchange of letters between the two heads of state.

But, I continued, the clandestine Soviet decision to equip Cuba with offensive missiles was a harsh blow to our confidence that the Soviet Union was genuinely seeking a peaceful answer to our many differences. I reminded Zhukov that high-ranking Soviet officials had deliberately lied to President Kennedy in denying that such missiles were in Cuba.

The situation now, I said, was very clear. Khrushchev's commitment to remove both the missiles and their launchers must be swiftly and demonstrably carried out. If it was not, still another crisis was inevitable.

Zhukov, who had been silent until this point, nodded his shaggy head vigorously. "That is right, of course. We must both keep our agreement exactly. Neither must show the slightest weakness. If your President were to back down on his position, it would place Chairman Khrushchev in a most difficult position with Castro."

Zhukov then sounded me out on the possible U.S. reaction to a Soviet bid for a summit conference "to finalize the present agreements." This, he said, "would open the way for the settlement of other wide-ranging problems." He then told me he had discussed a summit with Scotty Reston the day before, but the New York *Times* correspondent did not think the time was right. I replied that I could speak only as an individual, not as a member of the government, but a summit at that time would place both governments in an awkward position if it did not produce important agreements.

Zhukov then returned to the Cuban question. "We are greatly concerned," he said, "by reports your State Department is circulating that Castro has sent a message to Communists in Latin America instructing them to begin acts of sabotage. This is most dangerous. Castro sent no such message and, further, Castro is not the boss of Communists in Latin America. Such talk could cause Latin countries to take action against Cuba and that would be most unfortunate. The fate of the world is in question here. Let U Thant settle these problems."

Zhukov had one more complaint—this one against a movie called *We'll Bury You*, released by Columbia Pictures. He described it as a distortion of recent Soviet history and an "insult" to both Lenin and Khrushchev. "If we made such a film about President Kennedy, you would immediately recall your ambassador from Moscow."

I pointed out to Zhukov that, unlike the Soviet Union, the U.S. government does not control the motion picture studios. He said he was aware of this but "we want you to know we don't like such pictures."

The luncheon came to an end on a pleasanter note. There had been fears that Khrushchev would sign a separate peace treaty with East Germany immediately after the fall elections in the U.S. Zhukov said he had no such intention. "We do not want to solve this problem without your participation."

I was to see Zhukov only once more. It was in Tokyo in August 1964 after I had resigned from the White House to become a candidate for the Senate. He was there as a Russian delegate to the conference commemorating the anniversary of the nuclear attack on Hiroshima. He expressed great regret at the assassination of President Kennedy and said that Khrushchev hoped to be able to work with President Johnson as he had with JFK. I assured him that this was also President Johnson's hope. But Khrushchev was deposed six weeks later and with him went Yuri Zhukov. When I visited the Soviet Union in 1965, I was told that I could not see him.

Bolshakov was recalled to Moscow shortly after attending my luncheon with Zhukov. On Saturday, October 20—only two days before the President's dramatic announcement of Soviet perfidy—Bolshakov had foolishly told columnists Stewart Alsop and Charles Bartlett that there were no offensive Soviet missiles in Cuba. He was quoted by name in their column and, after such a whopping lie, the Kremlin correctly assumed that his usefulness in Washington had come to an end. In 1965, however, Bolshakov was still very much in evidence in Moscow. I went to see him in his spacious office at Novosty (a Soviet feature news agency), where he was head of the radio-TV department. American newsmen there told me he had put Novosty on a paying basis. In fact, he had just closed a deal with a major American network to sell them color films of the latest Russian space flight for $25,000.

In the week following the Cuban missile crisis, I found myself in another confrontation. It was a direct outgrowth of the missile crisis, but this time the adversaries were not Russian, but my friends in the Washington press corps.

# XX

## WAS NEWS A WEAPON?

The storm that broke over the news handling of the Cuban missile crisis cannot be put on the same plane with the events that moved the nation during those fateful days.

Nevertheless, it proved to be my most serious struggle with the press— and illustrated once again the fundamental chasm that exists between the interests of the press and the government in a crisis situation. The crisis centered on the same issue I had seen come into play during the abortive attack at the Bay of Pigs—how a government handles its news in a national security situation which cannot, for a number of reasons, be called war.

The news crisis exploded the day after Chairman Khrushchev announced he was taking the missiles out of Cuba. There had been some grumbling during the week of the crisis about our handling of the news, but in my opinion, it would have passed without any serious problem had it not been for an interview granted by Assistant Secretary of Defense Authur Sylvester to the Washington *Star*'s military correspondent, Richard Fryklund.

During that interview, Sylvester agreed that reporters had had a tougher time covering the U.S. blockade of Cuba than they had in covering World War II. Then he added: "I cannot think of a comparable situation, but in the kind of world we live in the generation of news by the government becomes one weapon in a strained situation. The results, in my opinion, justify the means."

As true as that might be on sober reflection, it was the kind of statement which was to provide the flame to explode the powder keg of press resentment.

But, to put Sylvester's words in context, it is important to review what happened during the crisis week as it related to the dissemination of news.

As I have indicated, a considerable amount of planning went into the handling of the critical week between October 22 and 28. There had also been the firm decision made by the President on October 15, when he first learned of the existence of missiles in Cuba from U-2 photographs, that there should be absolute secrecy clamped on this information so that the government would have a short breathing spell in which to make the vital decisions it would have to make to counter the Soviet move.

To implement that decision, President Kennedy directed that no more than a dozen top officers in the government be informed of the presence of the missiles to minimize the opportunity of this information leaking to the press (I was not one of those twelve officers).

It was the President's feeling that if the U.S. government could sort out the alternatives available to it in five or six days, without the knowledge of the Soviet Union, then the United States could seize the initiative in what was to be the first nuclear confrontation of the nuclear age. The President had been aware of the number of times the Soviet Union had seized the initiative against the United States merely on the basis of premature release of information we had in our possession. In the case of the Cuban missile crisis, the stakes were the highest possible, the lives of hundreds of millions of persons, and the President was resolved that no news leak was going to impede the possibility of the United States making its decision and implementing it without the knowledge of the Soviet Union and Cuba. It was this policy which made it possible for the United States to have its ships on station and the blockade in effect when President Kennedy went on nation-wide television on the night of October 22, 1962.

Yet one of the early and persistent charges about our handling of news during the Cuban missile crisis was that we had deliberately lied to the press in the days preceding the President's announcement.

The House Subcommittee on Freedom of Information headed by Congressman John Moss prepared a long memorandum based on the complaints of reporters which alleged that administration spokesmen had "deliberately" lied to the press. Cited as evidence, for example, is the following statement:

"A Pentagon spokesman denied tonight [October 19] that any alert had been ordered or that any emergency measures have been set in motion against Communist-ruled Cuba."

The fact was that on October 19, only three top officials in the Defense Department, including Secretary McNamara, knew anything about the Cuban missile crisis, and one of the officials who did not know anything of what was going on that time was Assistant Secretary Sylvester, who was in charge of drafting statements for "Pentagon spokesman." In retrospect, also, it must be said candidly that for the spokesman to have said otherwise would have shattered the news blackout ordered by President Kennedy and given our enemies information they could not otherwise have obtained at this time. The same House report charged me with "lying" to the press when I announced the President's cold in Chicago on October 20. As my previous recital has indicated, I knew nothing of the Cuban missile crisis on the morning of October 20, and again, in retrospect, if I had it would hardly have been in the national interest for me to announce that the President was rushing back to Washington because of the discovery of missiles in Cuba—before the final U.S. government decision had been made, and, more importantly, before the Russians and Cubans knew we had discovered the missiles.

If there was one key element in President Kennedy's successful policy at the time of the Cuban missile crisis, it would seem to me it was the fact that we caught the Russians and the Cubans by surprise on the night of October 22, that they had not been forewarned about the blockade, and that they therefore were faced with urgent considerations of what to do in the face of this powerful U.S. move.

Of course, the whole subject of lying to the press also came back to haunt us with another statement attributed to Sylvester at Syracuse, New York, that ". . . it is inherent in our government's right, if necessary, to lie to save itself when it is going up in nuclear war. This seems to me basic." Sylvester denied making the statement, but it was widely quoted and also contributed to the press crisis. Sylvester did subsequently testify before the House Committee on Information:

"The government does not have a right to lie to the people, but it does have a right in facing an enemy, if information is not accurate and is intended to mislead the enemy, I think that any people will support their government in not putting out information that is going to help the enemy. And, if necessary, misleading them."

Once the President had made his announcement, however, there is no question that the entire information policy of the government was rigidly and directly planned. The policy planning for news dissemination was put into the hands of the Executive Committee of the National Security Council. The coordination of EXCOM decisions was put in my hands, with the military news being handled by Sylvester and the diplomatic news by Manning. We decided that any information which could conceivably be of assistance to the enemy should be cut off at the source in the Defense Department. Because of the delicate balance we were trying to accomplish—striving to give the press all the information it was possible to give in a crisis situation and still holding back information of a vital nature to the enemy—I decided it would be helpful to brief some of the top leaders of the news industry on our plans and the philosophy behind them.

At 6 P.M. on October 23, the day after the President's speech, I met with leaders of the nation's news, radio, and TV industries. Those present at the meeting included Benjamin McKelway, editor of the Washington *Star* and president of the Associated Press; Wes Gallagher, editor of the AP; Bill Beale, head of the Washington Bureau of the AP; Whitney Shoemaker, White House correspondent of the AP; Mims Thomason, editor of the United Press International; Lyle Wilson, head of the Washington Bureau of the UPI; and Merriman Smith, White House correspondent of the UPI. Representing the networks were Jim Hagerty of ABC, Blair Clark of CBS, and William McAndrew of NBC, all news directors of their respective organizations. Finally, also present were Sylvester and Manning.

My major point to these gentlemen was that while we did not have a clear-cut war situation, we were locked in a crisis that could lead to nuclear war. I told them that we did not want to impede the orderly flow of news, nor, at the same time did we want to give out any information of help to the enemy. I was assured that the news organizations represented were as patriotic as the government, and had not in the past nor did they now want to help the enemy, either. I was asked how I was going to implement this general policy. At this time, I produced for the participants a draft of the White House's twelve points on information of value to the enemy which I asked them to read. I told them these twelve points would be issued by the White House the following day as a guide to the press on what the government felt was information helpful to the enemy. At the same time, I told them that the Defense Department was putting out a version of the twelve points to all of its commands—telling them that this was information which they were prohibited from releasing by the government. With the Defense Department directive and the twelve-point memorandum to the press, I felt that we were as close as possible to plugging any loopholes. And, to make doubly certain, I had Sylvester establish a twenty-four-hour-a-day office at the Pentagon which would be available to the press for consultation if they came across a piece of information where they were in any doubt whether the publication of such information would be in the national interest. I pointed out to the editors that the twelve-point guideline to be issued by the White House was advisory in nature, and could not be considered binding on the press since we were not at that time considering the establishment of formal censorship. I asked for their cooperation in this very difficult period.

I was not altogether pleased with the meeting. I felt a certain hostility on the part of some of the press representatives there, particularly Gallagher and McAndrew. They bridled at the idea of even a suggestion of censorship—no matter how voluntary it might be—and they pressed me on what they considered a vital point.

This point was the refusal of the administration to allow reporters to sail from Norfolk on ships destined for the blockade. It was their contention that in World War II and in the Korean War the government had allowed reporters on Navy ships engaged in action. It was inexplicable to them that we would not allow reporters on ships during this crisis.

It was a decision of the Executive Committee of the National Security Council, however, that reporters not be allowed on these ships. Their reasoning was simple. To allow reporters to tell their readers what the blockade ships were doing would be to deprive the United States of a certain amount of flexibility in passing and stopping ships. It would also inform the Russians how the blockade was operating and give them valuable information which they could pass on to their own ships. Even with the blockade in place, President Kennedy wanted to avoid a direct showdown with the Soviet Union until Chairman Khrushchev had had a chance to see the gravity of the situation he had created by placing the missiles in Cuba and, perhaps, take action which would reduce the tension and the confrontation. It was also brought up at the meeting that the administration had refused to allow reporters to go to our naval base at Guantánamo. I replied that, at the proper time, reporters would be permitted to go to Guantánamo, but that at this time the Executive Committee had also barred this possibility on the grounds that to report any buildup of U.S. troops there would be helpful to the enemy. Neither of these decisions particularly pleased those present, and in the days that followed I was bombarded with telephonic and telegraphic requests to bring about a reversal of these policies.

The upshot of the meeting was a promise from the organizations represented to disseminate our twelve-point guidelines to all their affiliates and bureaus. But, as Jim Hagerty pointed out, a television or radio network is a "loose confederation" at best and they could only speak with any precision for the radio and television stations owned outright by the networks. Of all the persons attending the meeting, the most sympathetic to our problems was Hagerty, who brought eight years of experience as Press Secretary to President Eisenhower to the meeting, who had worked on the inside of government, and who had some clear idea of the monumental problems facing us during this crisis. After the meeting, I asked Hagerty to stay for a private talk.

I filled Jim in on the censorship plans we would put into motion should a full-scale war break out. I pointed out that the major problem with any censorship program was to have someone heading it whom the press trusted. Such had been the case during World War II when the censorship program had been headed by a hard-nosed newsman, Byron Price. In my work in Washington, I had not met a single newsman who did not think that Price had administered the program fairly and impartially. It would have been easy to turn to Price again in this emergency, but Price was getting old and it was the view of those who knew him that he would not want to take on such an arduous post again. I had brought Bill Steven, the able editor of the Houston *Chronicle*, to Washington to be available to play a role in the censorship plans. Steven was willing to help out, but did not want to direct the program. He was willing to be the number two man. I told Hagerty I needed someone of unquestioned honesty and integrity to head up the program. Then—and I had discussed the matter with President Kennedy—I put the problem to him. The only man, in the President's view and mine, who fitted the necessities of the time was Hagerty himself. He told me quietly that he was flattered by the confidence the President and I had in him, and that because of his past experience he would never turn down a direct request from the President of the United States—no matter who he was or what party he represented—to serve his government. He argued, however, that he did not feel he was the man for the job. We discussed it for some time, and although Hagerty never came out and said he would not take the job, it was my feeling that he would rather not. I understood his reluctance and finally came up with a compromise proposal. We would set up a new advisory committee on our censorship program and Hagerty would head this committee. He agreed to do this on the spot and also countered with the suggestion that perhaps I was selling Price short, and he was the answer to my problem—even on a short term basis.

Following our meeting, I took Hagerty in to see President Kennedy, and he repeated his thoughts to him. The President thanked Hagerty for agreeing to head the advisory committee and we agreed that Price would be called immediately on a standby basis. He agreed to serve if full censorship became necessary.

On October 24, I handed out the twelve-point guidelines to the press. In retrospect, they seem more reasonable in content than the press thought at the time:

MEMORANDUM TO
EDITORS AND RADIO AND TELEVISION NEWS DIRECTORS:

The following information is considered vital to our national security and therefore will not be released by the Department of Defense. Despite this fact, it is possible that such information may come into the possession of news media. During the current tense international situation, the White House feels that the publication of such information is contrary to the public interest. We ask public information media of all types to exercise caution and discretion in the publication of such information.

(1) Any discussion of plans for employment of strategic or tactical forces of the United States including types of equipment and new or planned location of command or control centers or detection systems.

(2) Estimates of United States capability of destroying targets, including numbers of weapons required, size and character of forces required, ability of these forces to penetrate defenses, and accuracy or reliability of our forces or weapon systems.

(3) Intelligence estimates concerning targets or target systems, such as numbers, types and locations of aiming points in the target system, enemy missile and bombers forces, etc.

(4) Intelligence estimates of enemy plans or capabilities, or information which would reveal the level of success of United States intelligence efforts or operations with respect to Cuba or the Communist bloc.

(5) Details as to numbers or movements of United States forces, including naval units and vessels, aircraft, missile forces or ground forces, ammunition, equipment, etc. Announcement may be made of such unit movements after the movement has been completed.

(6) Degree of alert of military forces.

(7) Location of aircraft or supporting equipment. Presence of aircraft observable in the public domain may be confirmed.

(8) Emergency dispersal plans of aircraft and units including dispersal capabilities, times, schedules or logistical support.

(9) Official estimates of vulnerability to various forms of enemy action, including sabotage, of United States Armed Forces and installations.

(10) New data concerning operational missile distribution, numbers, operational readiness. Estimates of effectiveness of strike capability of missile forces.

(11) Details of command and control systems, including new or planned posts and facilities, estimates of ability to survive enemy attacks, security measures, etc., including sea or airborne command posts.

(12) Details of airlift or sealift capabilities, including size and nature of forces to be lifted, time limits for such lifts, and supply capabilities, with respect to possible specific areas of operation.

Editors having doubts about information and wanting to establish whether or not it is within the purview of this memorandum should contact the News Desk, Department of Defense, at OXford 5-3201, Washington, D.C. Such advice will be on an advisory basis and not considered finally binding on the editor(s).

In handing out the memorandum I said: "As the memorandum makes clear, this is not a binding matter on editors. In other words, they can either take our advice or reject it as they see fit, but it was felt that if the editors had in front of them a memorandum of the categories of information which we consider not to be in the national interest to print at this time, it would be helpful to them in making these judgments that we ask them to make."

I was asked if there had been breaches of security in the preceding week and I answered that I felt there had been. As an example, I cited the case of a major news network, which interviewed a woman who had just been evacuated from Guantánamo to the Norfolk, Virginia, naval base. The questions posed to her were directed solely to how many ships were in the harbor, how many troops had moved into Guantánamo in the preceding forty-eight hours, and other questions of a military significance.

Another question was how these guidelines would apply to foreign reporters. The fact of the matter was that there was no way of enforcing the guidelines with foreign reporters unless you set up censorship of all dispatches leaving the continental limits of the United States. This I was not prepared to do at this stage of the crisis. The next question dealt with how I proposed to get the cooperation of Russian reporters on this matter.

"Well, I would think in the interests of American national security that we would have some desire on the part of American newspapers to assist in this program. Obviously, Russian reporters are going to print anything they can get their hands on. But a lot of the stuff they print they read in American newspapers, and if they are not reading it in the American newspapers, it makes it a little more difficult for them to get it."

In the rough-and-tumble press conference which followed, I clung to the point that our guidelines were not even voluntary censorship, since the press had the final right to make news judgments. But I had the feeling at the end of the conference that the press had not been very convinced.

The next major press flap occurred the following day, October 25. At eight o'clock that morning, the Navy intercepted the Soviet tanker *Bucharest*. Convinced, from information the government had received that the *Bucharest* was not carrying contraband materials, it was permitted to pass.

The Executive Committee heard the report at its morning meeting and ordered the news released through the Defense Department at the end of the morning. Meanwhile, under a plan set up by Secretary Rusk and approved by the President, key members of Congress were being briefed almost daily about the developments in the missile crisis. Such a briefing took place the same morning in New York. One of the representatives being briefed was Congressman James E. Van Zandt, a Republican from Pennsylvania. On that particular morning, Congressman Van Zandt showed he was a man who knew how to get his name in the paper. He rushed out after the briefing, held a press conference, and to the consternation of everyone, announced the *Bucharest* story. The news hit the wires at 11 A.M., some forty-five minutes before the Defense Department was to make the announcement. The President was outraged—particularly that such sensitive information had been given to Van Zandt in the first place. The press was outraged (and rightfully) that they had to learn of the first major blockade incident involving a Russian ship from a Pennsylvania congressman holding a press conference in New York City.

The morning press conference at the White House was again emotionally charged. The press was disgusted that it had had to get such vital information from a congressman and wanted to know what the White House was doing to prevent such a thing. Another suspicion had arisen in their minds—if Van Zandt had not made the confrontation with the *Bucharest* public, the government would never have said anything to them about the incident in the first place. The latter charge was untrue on its face. The Executive Committee had specifically authorized me to direct Arthur Sylvester to make this information public—but not only this information. At the same morning briefing at the Defense Department, Sylvester announced the dramatic news that some dozen Soviet ships heading toward the U.S. blockade had turned back. As to the former, I was under strict instructions not to get into a public debate with Van Zandt, although at the morning State Department briefing it was made amply clear that Van Zandt had violated the ground rules under which he had been given the briefing.

A third major discussion with the press arose over the distribution of pictures of the missiles in Cuba. In this particular argument, I agreed completely with the press.

Following the President's speech of October 22, a news briefing had been held at the Defense Department, during which pictures of the missiles in Cuba had been shown to the press. Again the next day, Ambassador Stevenson showed the pictures to the United Nations while making his dramatic presentation of the United States' case. Still, with the press practically battering down the doors to my office, I could not obtain permission for the release of the pictures from EXCOM. The final straw was when the pictures were released, in London, to British television by Ambassador David Bruce and his public affairs officer, William Clark. Ambassador Bruce checked with someone at the White House before releasing them and his argument was that the pictures were badly needed to button up the U.S. case before the British public. There was great skepticism in Europe about the whole relationship between the U.S. and Cuba and it had been heightened after the Bay of Pigs. So skeptical were the British that even *after* the publication of the pictures in Great Britain, the military editor of the prestigious *Times* of London wrote a front-page story in which he called the pictures a complete fabrication and delusion by the United States. The publication of the pictures in Great Britain finally won the argument for me. I pointed out to the President it was untenable for us to have the pictures printed in the British press and shown over British television and to consider them classified in the United States and not release them to our own press. I was finally empowered to give out the pictures, which I did shortly before one o'clock in the morning of October 24. Why there was ever any argument over the release of the pictures, I shall never know. They were dramatic evidence of the Soviet Union's duplicity.

One final fact is needed to put into context the furor that arose from Sylvester's statements. In the latter part of the week of October 22–29, there were stories in a number of leading newspapers, quoting unnamed sources in the Defense and State Departments, some of which included information which the President felt were violations of the guidelines we had issued to the press.

"How can we expect the press to cooperate with us," he asked, "when people at Defense and State put out information we are asking the press not to publish?" This, indeed, has always been a central problem—not only during the Cuban missile crisis, but at other times. It involves the public official who wants to make a hero of himself with the press by giving it information. Often, the official in question knows only a piece of the policy or decision about which he is speaking, with the result that misleading and only partially true (if not in some cases wholly untrue) stories appear. In the heat of the Cuban missile crisis, the President was in no mood to take the matter lightly. He ordered me to have Sylvester immediately institute a policy in which all officials of the Defense Department reported, by memorandum, their contacts with the press, the questions they had been asked, and the responses they had given. This policy went into effect on October 27. A similar policy went into effect at the State Department four days later.

No matter how volubly we protested that both the Secretary of Defense and the Secretary of State had a right to know what their subordinates were telling the press on policy matters, the press protested vigorously and actively on the grounds that the new policy reeked of censorship. It was useless to point out to them that Defense and State Department officers were not barred from seeing or speaking to members of the press. But the press argued—with some justification—that a Defense Department or State Department aide would be much more inhibited in talking to the press if he knew he had to write a memorandum to the Secretary telling him what he had told the particular reporter. I was in accord with the President on the policy at the Defense Department. I could see great justification for this policy in the cavernous Pentagon, with its inter-service rivalries and the constant jockeying for position and credit which took place there. I thought, however, that the policy was a mistake at the State Department, and so told the President. Bob Manning, the Assistant Secretary of State for Public Affairs, felt even more strongly. The President's hand was strengthened, however, when a cabled message from Ambassador Adlai Stevenson to Secretary Rusk was put out over the wires of one of the two leading wire services before Secretary Rusk even had a chance to read the message.

The message, which included the ambassador's report of his conversations with UN Secretary-General U Thant after the latter had seen Fidel Castro, was received by the State Department's Diplomatic Telegraph Branch at 1:35 A.M. By eight o'clock in the morning, 105 copies had been distributed to key officials in the department. At 10:32 A.M. the contents of the message, including some of its wording, were in the hands of John Hightower, the able Associated Press correspondent who covers the State Department. Secretary Rusk had not yet had time to read the message.

The State Department policy, however, lasted less than a month. In announcing that the rule had been suspended, Manning wrote a thoughtful letter to top officials of the State Department.

In it he enunciated two principles which had accompanied the original order and which had largely, if not completely, been ignored by the press in their discussion of the policy:

"First, that it is essential both to the public and the government that there be the fullest possible dialogue between policy officials and newsmen, and that it is the policy of the department, as interpreted and carried out by the Bureau of Public Affairs, to encourage this dialogue, not to inhibit it.

"Second, that there were some specific steps that the suggested procedure explicitly was *not* designed to include, namely the requiring of advance permission for press interviews or contacts or the presence of a public affairs adviser or other third party at such interviews."

Manning then went on to make the key point of support for the policy:

"A point of important principle is involved. In the conduct of the public business for which he is responsible, the Secretary of course has the right to know what his policy officers are doing in this regard; whether, for example, they are paying sufficient attention to this important aspect of foreign affairs. It is equally necessary that the Assistant Secretary for Public Affairs, who is charged by the Secretary of State with responsibility for informing the public, has the right to know and to examine the flow and pattern of relations between the department and the communications media. It is obvious that any attempt to build a better, speedier, and increasingly forthcoming program of information requires at least a rudimentary sense of the pattern of the department's relations with the press."

Despite all these points, in my opinion the Cuban missile crisis would have faded into history without a major confrontation between the press and the government had it not been for Sylvester's interview of October 29 in which he talked of the "generation of news . . . becomes one weapon in a strained situation."

Sylvester's statements, coming on the heels of the problems we had had with the press during the crisis week, were just the kind calculated to raise outcries in the nation's press. It did not take twenty-four hours for these voices to be heard. In the months that followed, the administration's press policies were castigated by newspapers across the country.

Newspaper associations like the American Society of Newspaper Editors, the American Newspaper Publishers Association, and Sigma Delta Chi wrote strongly worded resolutions condemning the administration—and Sylvester's "generation of news" quickly became "management of the news." In fact, the whole issue was written in such a way that "management of the news" was pictured as something entirely new, which had been thought up by the Kennedy administration. The fact was that the phrase, "management of the news" had first been used by James Reston of the New York *Times* to describe the activities of James Hagerty in the Eisenhower administration.

The Washington *Star* editorial was typical of those written across the country. Mr. Sylvester, said the *Star*, had "let the ugly cat out of the bag." Quoting Sylvester, the *Star* went on: "Weigh those words. Their meaning is truly sinister. In an administration that is becoming quite notable in its efforts toward achieving managed control of the news, Mr. Sylvester may have overlooked one likely result of 'the methods we used.' The result is that Mr. Sylvester and his superiors, from this time on, are suspect. They have in our opinion recklessly and thoughtlessly forfeited the confidence that in this country has been the rule rather than the exception. What they say from now on, as arbitrarily established sources of information, may be the truth. But that truth will be accepted with a grain of salt. The 'kind of world we live in' seems now to be a world in which the truth given the American people of what has happened is that part of the truth selected by officialdom to piece together a desirable image. That image may be a distortion, the inevitable result of an attempt to use the press and its news as an instrument of national policy."

A contrasting editorial appeared in the Detroit *News* of November 26. ". . . The President very properly closed all channels of official information until he was quite ready to disclose to the American people what he had done and what he proposed to do in the immediate future. The right of the press to have this type of information made available to it because of the Constitutional protection of the free press does not exist, this right having been superseded by the *prior and fundamental right of a nation to protect its own existence from an enemy.* (Author's italics.) The First Amendment with its free press guarantee does not intend that a nation shall commit suicide rather than keep a secret. No prudent editor is questioning the actions of President Kennedy in the Cuban crisis insofar as news disclosures were concerned. Those who are include a noisy minority which has elevated the 'right to know' into a constitutional absolute indefensible at law."

The President's first press conference after the missile crisis, held in the State Department auditorium on November 20, was studded with questions about the administration's information policies.

One questioner noted that the President's administration "like others, is being criticized for its handling of information. The point is being made that reporters are being hampered in carrying out their role as a link between the government and the American people, that we're not keeping the American people well-informed as a result of government policies."

The President, in answering, reviewed the events of the crisis. He agreed that the fact the U.S. had discovered missiles in Cuba had been "kept in the highest levels of government. We didn't make any public statement about it." Then he added:

". . . We did not want to indicate to the Soviet Union or to Cuba, or anyone else who might be our adversaries, the extent of our information until we had determined what our policy would be and until we consulted with our allies and members of OAS and NATO. So, for these very good reasons, I believe this matter was kept by the government until Monday night.

"I have no apologies for that. I don't think that there's any doubt it would have been a great mistake and possibly a disaster if this news had dribbled out when we were unsure of the extent of the Soviet buildup in Cuba, and when we were unsure of our response and when we had not consulted with any of our allies, who might have been involved in great difficulties as a result of our action."

The President then said that during the actual week of the crisis until the Sunday "when we received Mr. Khrushchev's first message about the withdrawal, we attempted to have the government speak with one voice. There were obvious restraints on newspapermen. They were not permitted, for example, to go to Guantánamo because obviously that might be an area which might be under attack. Since that Sunday, we have tried to, or at least intend to attempt to, lift any restraints on the news. And I'm really—as a reader of a good many papers, it seems to me that the papers more or less reflected quite accurately the state of our negotiations with the Soviet Union."

In answer to another question, the President cited his central thesis. "I can assure you that our only interest has been, first, during this period of crisis and over a longer period to try—not to have coming out of the Pentagon information which is highly sensitive, particularly in the intelligence areas, which I can assure you in my own not too distant experience has been extremely inimical to the interests of the United States. Now that is our only interest."

It is useless here to get into a long discussion of the charges and countercharges which flew back and forth during the hectic days following the missile crisis. It is still held as an indisputable fact in some circles, regrettably, that the American people were somehow not told the truth during the crisis.

The press made the point over and over again, and in at least two incidents after the crisis attempted to demonstrate his view. The first revolved around a series of sensational articles which appeared in the Hearst papers, as well as elsewhere, that the Russians had somehow managed to hide the missiles in the caves of Cuba rather than take them out of that country. Their information came from unnamed Cuban refugees. Some members of Congress even repeated the charges in statements issued from their offices, but when the President sent specialists from the CIA to the Hill they refused to reveal their sources, causing the President to remark wryly at one of his press conferences that the government of the United States was not, after all, "a foreign power."

The New York *Mirror* ran a scare headline: *PINPOINT CUBA'S MISSILES* and listed "literally dozens of secret bases" where missiles were hidden in caves. They attributed this startling information to "refugees and underground sources" compiled by the "Cuban Information Service of Coral Gables, Florida." The "Truth About Cuba Committee, Inc.", told the United Press International that there were twenty-one secret caves and other subterranean sites where missiles were hidden. Each report was patiently checked out by U.S. intelligence officials. Each day, U.S. planes flew low reconnaissance flights over Cuba and turned up not one scintilla of evidence to back up these scare stories. Government officials naturally agreed that even the best intelligence is not foolproof, but it was the best judgment and information of the entire U.S. intelligence apparatus that the missiles had left Cuba and had not been planted in caves.

The second incident was triggered by the Scripps-Howard newspapers and their sensational handling of a report that high-flying Soviet reconnaissance planes had overflown Florida during the Cuban missile crisis, causing U.S. fighter planes to scramble into position to intercept them. The story was totally untrue and when questioned by Scripps-Howard (after they had published the original story without making any effort to check it at the White House, Defense, or State Departments), I made a definitive statement that the story was without foundation. The next day, the Washington *Evening News*, a Scripps-Howard paper, reprinted the story in even bigger type, quoting my denial, but saying in bold type that they didn't believe me and that they liked their sources better than mine. I hit the ceiling and took the article to the President. He had already read it and was fuming. He ordered me to call Walker Stone, the editor of the Scripps-Howard newspapers, and offer to put any official of the United States government he would believe on the telephone to talk to him about the story. When I got Stone on the phone, I told him that I had authority to tell him that any government official in whom he had trust would call him, if he would guarantee in advance to believe that official. I offered to have the President, the Secretary of Defense, the head of the Defense Intelligence Agency, or the head of the North American Air Defense Command (NORAD) call. I was astonished and stunned when Stone told me it would be of no use to have any of the men listed call. "We believe our source and nothing is going to make us change our story." I asked Stone if he realized that he was in effect calling the President of the United States and some other top officers of the government liars. Stone replied that he did not look on it that way, but that the Scripps-Howard newspapers were standing by the story. Their source turned out to be a reserve lieutenant colonel on the staff of the military reserve unit headed by Senator Strom Thurmond of South Carolina (then a Democrat, now a Republican). When NORAD, through its commanding officer, General John Gerhart, put out a statement on December 6, 1962, you needed a microscope to find the story in the Washington *News*.

"I want to say," General Gerhart's statement said, "as the commander-in-chief of the North American Air Defense Command, which is the command responsible for the aerospace defense of the North American continent, that *no* Russian aircraft of any type have overflown any part of the continental United States during or since the Cuban crisis. This headquarters has released this statement previously, but due to the continuing discussion of this in the press, I feel it necessary for me personally to reconfirm this fact."

The Cuban missile crisis, when carefully analyzed, is a symptom of a much greater problem which has never really been seriously attacked in a mutual way by the American press and the U.S. government. That question is how a democracy, constituted with the freedoms of the United States, defends itself in a cold-war situation against an enemy which can operate in secret. This is, in my opinion, one of the central issues of our time—and, in all the charges and countercharges that have flown between the press and the government over the spurious issue of management of the news, this basic issue has for the most part been overlooked.

To analyze recent history, the handling of the press in a situation like World War II or even the Korean War presents no basic problems. Battlefield censorship can be imposed and the press, while in a state of war, will tolerate restraints and restrictions which it will not accept in peacetime. But the dangers posed by this whole question loom larger as we move into the second half of the twentieth century. I believe the first major news crisis—which became a national crisis—engendered by our ambivalence and lack of desire to come to grips with this issue revolved around the shooting down of Francis Gary Powers and his U-2 plane over the Soviet Union in 1960. In our haste to satisfy what has come to be accepted as the doctrine of "need to know," our government rushed out on four fronts with press releases to explain what Powers was doing there in the first place. Unfortunately, the four stories did not gibe and the Soviet Union was faced with what to do about the bald-faced admission by the United States that it was sending spy planes over its national territory. Put into this position by the U.S. statements, the Soviets had really only one response—and that was the response they made—violent anger at the United States, a public trial of Powers, and the withdrawal of the invitation to President Eisenhower to visit the Soviet Union. I do not counsel here, in hindsight, that the government should have said nothing about the incident. But one carefully worded statement, issued by the Defense Department speaking for the entire government, might well have put a damper on the whole incident. Under these circumstances, Khrushchev might not have felt compelled to take the hostile actions he did.

Again, another example resolves around our press handling in Vietnam during the period 1958–64. During these years, with a force of up to some 20,000 Americans in Vietnam acting as "advisers" to the South Vietnamese government, we were faced with a non-war situation. Yet the United States was doing certain necessary things in Vietnam during those days which it was far better for the enemy not to know about. (I go to greater lengths on the press handling of the Vietnam war by the Kennedy administration in the next chapter of the book.)

As disastrous as was the invasion of the Bay of Pigs, it was, as I have pointed out earlier, an effort by a free and open democratic society to mount a covert military operation. It failed miserably. While the advance notice in the press that the invasion was imminent was certainly helpful to Fidel Castro, one cannot in any way blame the American press for the failure at the Bay of Pigs. Yet this incident is also symptomatic of the central problem.

It is not my contention that the American press as an institution is single-mindedly devoted to the publication of the nation's innermost secrets to the benefit of our enemies. Nor am I naive enough to advance the postulate that the U.S. government is always pure in its motives on handling of the news. There have been vital secrets published in the press and there has been information withheld by the government which should not have been.

This does not take away, however, from the thesis that there must be some dialogue on how a democracy operates in the present gray areas of world politics. Some great democracies like France and Great Britain have solved the problem in their own way. French governments, including the present regime of President Charles de Gaulle, have seized entire issues of newspapers and magazines when they felt that some of the material published was against the national interest (and even for the more flimsy reason that it offended some minister in the government of the nation's Chief Executive). In Great Britain, there are instances when so-called "Q" notices are issued to the press on sensitive security matters. The "Q" notices forbid newspapers to publish any information on the subjects included in the notice. I do not cite these examples as a possibility for the United States, but rather to reinforce the point, which is sometimes overlooked in these press-government debates over freedom of information, that the United States is the most open democratic system the world has ever seen—with the widest latitude of press freedom the world has ever seen.

What other government would have dared to conduct the space exploits this nation has attempted in full view of whirring television cameras, with all the dangers that this entails for the national prestige?

You then come down to the two Sylvester statements. Unfortunate as was their timing, there was a modicum of truth in both.

To disassociate the handling of news from an over-all crisis situation is to wish for something that never was and never will be. Certainly it was a key factor in the crisis when certain messages to Khrushchev were released to the press even before they had been received by the Soviet Chairman. In this case, it had been determined that the ordinary channels of communication were too slow for the rapidity with which the crisis was developing.

Certainly the statements I put out at the White House on three occasions during that fateful week, pointing out that the Soviets were continuing to work on their missile sites, were as important in keeping the pressure on the Soviet Union as the movement of troops into position for a possible invasion of Cuba.

And most importantly, the fact that on the night of October 27, 1962, at the meeting of the National Security Council, we were informed that the Alaska-based American U-2 plane, because of a mechanical failure in its navigational system, had wandered some 800 miles inside the limits of the Soviet Union, was critical also. To have announced that the U-2 had overflown Russia at that particularly difficult time in the crisis would, in my opinion, have taken away from Chairman Khrushchev some, if not all, of the few options he had left at that time. We might very well have confronted him with another Francis Gary Powers situation—and in this particular nuclear confrontation this would have been unthinkable. The Executive Committee of the National Security Council, to a man, decided that night that I should say nothing about this errant U-2, leaving to the Russians the decision to say something if they so desired. (The Soviet Union never said a word about the plane, but the next morning, Chairman Khrushchev announced he was taking the missiles out of Cuba.)

We need a consistent and determined policy to handle this problem. In my view we now have neither. It is easy for an Arthur Krock, from his desk at the New York *Times*, to castigate the Kennedy administration for what he considered the evils of secret diplomacy, and turn around two years later and attack the Johnson administration—as he did during the Vietnam peace offensive of 1965—for carrying on its diplomacy in public. It is also easy (although a bit painful) for a government to counter stories such as the missile-in-cave flap by having its Secretary of Defense hold a two-hour televised press conference in which he has to compromise some of the nation's most important intelligence in order to combat what has appeared in the newspapers. Neither is much of a solution, however.

# XXI

## AN INDEPENDENT LADY

The Inauguration on January 20, 1961, not only signaled the beginning of the administration of John F. Kennedy; it also brought Jacqueline Bouvier Kennedy to the White House.

It is not enough to say that Mrs. Kennedy is a unique woman. That she certainly is. She is also a study in contrasts. She is fiercely independent—but at the same time shy and dependent. She had a distinct dislike for the business of politics, and at the same time an undisguised admiration for those who practice it with excellence and style. She can give the appearance of detachment from the hurly-burly world of the twentieth century, while at the same time demonstrating a keen understanding of the problems which beset mankind. She would do anything to avoid hurting the feelings of others.

I first met Jacqueline Kennedy in the spring of 1957, about the same time I met the President, but she did not materialize as a person to me until late in 1959, when the then Senator Kennedy started working in earnest for the presidential nomination.

In the months that followed, as we plowed through the snows of New Hampshire and Wisconsin and the coal mines of West Virginia, I noticed a subtle difference in her attitude toward the campaign. It does no disservice to anyone to say that at first it appeared that the last thing in the world Mrs. Kennedy wanted to do was to be involved in a national political campaign. The hours were long, the crowds were large and sometimes oppressive. At the same time, there was not the slightest doubt that Mrs. Kennedy was a considerable political asset to her husband. Dave Powers used to kid JFK by telling him that "At least half the crowd turned out to see Jackie, not you." No one was more aware of this than Senator

Kennedy himself. But, as the months went on, Mrs. Kennedy became "involved." It became her campaign as well as the senator's, and she was genuinely sorry when the impending birth of John forced her to quit the campaign trail just before the 1960 Democratic National Convention in Los Angeles.

Even though the baby was only two months away, she turned up in New York City in October to participate in a massive ticker-tape parade up Broadway that attracted more than two million people.

But it was not to be in campaigning that Jacqueline Kennedy was to make her deepest impression on the American people. Nor was it in campaigning that she was going to leave her greatest legacy.

It is ironic, however, that just the week before the assassination of the President, Mrs. Kennedy had already turned her attentions to the campaign of 1964. Mrs. Lyndon Johnson had reported to her that the press in Texas seemed to be paying more attention to her impending arrival than to that of the President. She had used this information to bolster her long-standing argument with the President that if she was indeed a political asset—and without ego she recognized herself as such—she could be of far greater help to her husband when employed politically with some discrimination. She had, on November 11, 1963, dispatched a memorandum to her Press Secretary, Miss Pamela Turnure, in which she started to plan things that could be of the greatest value in 1964. Her usual sense of humor showed through when she wrote Pam: *I guess if Pierre ends up putting me and the children on the cover of* Look *in a bubble bath, I'll have to put up with it*. She said in the memorandum that she planned to be extremely active in the 1964 campaign, and wrote Pamela: *I will do anything to help*.

It is fair to say that Mrs. Kennedy, other than wishing for the election of her husband, had not made any preparations in 1960 for her role as the wife of the President of the United States until after the election was decided. But once the election was over, she started to plan with a vengeance.

She was, of course, very pregnant on election night. John was to be born later the same month. It was actually her first tour of the White House after the birth of John that crystallized several thoughts in her mind. Mrs. Kennedy had visited the White House as a child, and had left with one impression—it was a pity that the White House did not have anything for the millions of tourists who visited it each year to take away; some literature that would tell the story of this historic house and some of its occupants. Her tour with Mrs. Eisenhower convinced her of two other things. The first was that the White House, as then constituted, was not a place for a family with growing children.

The second was that much of the historic furniture and art of the White House had, through the years, been allowed, for one reason or another, to leave the house. Some of the furniture had been sold by the wives of Presidents in need of additional funds. Other furniture had simply been moved out by Presidents and their wives who preferred Macy's Modern to the historic treasures of America's past.

Mrs. Kennedy decided to do something about all three of these problems.

With characteristic order of priorities, it was the children who came first. As the Kennedys moved in, so did carpenters and other workmen to fix up the bedrooms of Caroline and John. The President and Mrs. Kennedy left their own bedrooms for later, and spent the first several weeks they were in the White House sleeping in the Lincoln and Queen's Rooms, respectively. One other change was initiated almost immediately. Mrs. Kennedy discovered that in order to have hot food upstairs, it was necessary to have it brought up from the kitchen, in the basement, on trays. She also found she had no small dining room in the family quarters on the second floor in which to entertain in private. Just north of the private sitting room had been the bedroom and sitting room which had been organized for Margaret Truman, the daughter of President Harry S. Truman. These rooms Mrs. Kennedy converted into a private dining room with a small kitchen adjoining, and in the evenings when the Kennedys were alone or with a group of friends, Chef René Verdon came upstairs and did his cooking there.

In the weeks that followed the birth of John, Mrs. Kennedy also turned her thoughts to the major project for which she will remain known for years to come. She ordered, from the Library of Congress, every single piece of literature she could find on the White House and its furnishings. And, laboriously, she started going through this material, determining what had to be done to bring the White House back to prominence as a place of history.

It must be said that President Kennedy was largely unenthusiastic about the project at first. Not that he had any doubt about the ability of Mrs. Kennedy to carry it out, but the memory of the public uproar that had surrounded the building of President Truman's famous south porch was still in his mind.

Not only did the President start out to be against the project, but a number of people in the government were against it as well. In reminiscing about the earlier internal furor which surrounded Mrs. Kennedy's plans to re-do the White House, she recalled in a memorandum to a friend that "I was warned, begged, and practically threatened" not to undertake the renovation. In the end, however, she prevailed and her judgment was completely vindicated by the overwhelming support she received from the American people for the project.

Public funds could not be used for what Mrs. Kennedy had in mind and therefore private solicitation was going to be needed. The President did not want any criticism leveled at this fund raising or the subsequent use of the funds.

As it became evident that Mrs. Kennedy was going to go ahead with her project, the President called in the eminent Washington lawyer Clark Clifford, and had him draw papers for the formation of Mrs. Kennedy's Committee on the Arts that would both regulate the activities of the committee and leave it at all times open to any public scrutiny.

To get the committee started, Mrs. Kennedy first recruited her Palm Beach, Florida, friend, Mrs. Jane Wrightsman, the wife of Texas oil millionaire Charles Wrightsman. Together, they went to see Henry Dupont, the owner of the Winterthur Museum, the greatest single repository of historical American furniture and art, and persuaded him to become chairman of The Fine Arts Committee for the White House. Its members were persons from all over the country, with the best credentials in this field. A similar committee, dealing specifically in paintings and sculpture, was set up under James Fosburgh, a New York painter, lecturer, and collector.

Mrs. Kennedy attached a great deal of importance to this project, and she devoted a great amount of personal time to its success. The curator's staff would cringe when they saw a packing box arrive, knowing that Mrs. Kennedy would be there five minutes later wondering why the box was not unpacked. With Mr. Fosburgh she supervised the hanging of newly acquired paintings, and with equal enthusiasm saw to the placement of antique furniture as it arrived.

Once the project was under way, the President backed Mrs. Kennedy strongly in her decisions. There was one case which involved a lot of soul-searching in the White House. That was when Mrs. Kennedy decided to change the wall hangings in the Blue Room from blue to white with blue accent. The matter finally went to the President with Mrs. Kennedy's recommendation that it be done. But she had more than a recommendation—she had marshaled the historical facts to show that this was the proper coloring for the room. The room was changed.

I might insert, parenthetically, that this particular change caused me to have one of my most humorous press briefings. It started quietly enough:

Q. Is there anything to the story that the Green Room is going to be chartreuse and the Blue Room is going to be white on white?

A. I am glad that you brought that up.

Q. What was the question?

A. The question was whether the Green Room was going to be chartreuse and the Blue Room was going to be white on white. I would like to deal with this matter within the limitations of my own knowledge, but I can state equivocally that—

Q. You mean unequivocally.

A. Unequivocally, that the Blue Room will continue to be the Blue Room.

Q. You didn't answer someone's question. What is chartreuse?

A. I couldn't tell you that. The Green Room will remain the Green Room, and the Blue Room will remain the Blue Room.

Q. Pierre, I want to ask you two questions. Are these rooms going to be done over? Is the fabric going to be removed?

A. The fabric in both rooms is old and soiled and will be replaced. That is accurate. That is the only part, and virtually the only part of the story that was accurate.

Q. The man who has been making the fabrics has been quoted quite widely.

A. I can even go one step further. As far as I know, and I think Miss Turnure will bear me out, there is no contract for him to prepare the fabrics in these two rooms.

Q. What is that?

A. I said the Green Room will remain the Green Room, and the Blue Room will remain the Blue Room, and there has been no final decision on the fabrics.

Q. The colors will remain the same?

Q. Do you know when the work will start?

A. I can't tell you that.

Q. In other words, the blue stuff is being taken off the walls and will be replaced by other blue fabrics?

A. The Blue Room will remain the Blue Room and the Green Room will remain the Green Room.

Q. The Blue Room can still be called the Blue Room even if it has a white covering?

A. The story makes the flat assertion that it is going to have a white wall. There is no present contract and no final decision has been made on the fabrics which are going to cover the wall of the Blue Room. The Blue Room will remain the Blue Room.

Q. It will be blue?

A. The Blue Room will remain the Blue Room.

Q. Do you mean in name only?

A. I will stand on that statement.

One item caused a small uproar. Mrs. Kennedy had redecorated the family dining room on the first floor. This was the room used each week for the President's Tuesday breakfast with his legislative leaders. For several weeks, the breakfasts had to be moved out of the room while the renovation was being completed. Finally the morning arrived when we were allowed to use the family dining room again. The breakfasts usually started at 8:45 A.M., but on this particular morning the President sent down word that he would be a few minutes late and for the others to go ahead. As Larry O'Brien sat down in his chair, it broke, and he sank through to the floor.

"It's a good thing that wasn't the President," remarked House Speaker John W. McCormack, as they picked an unharmed Larry off the floor.

Several minutes later the President arrived and we all stood as he entered the room. As we sat down we heard another chair crack. This time it was the President's. A quick grab by Senate Majority Leader Mike Mansfield and McCormack prevented the President from sinking all the way to the floor. It is rumored that this particular aspect of Mrs. Kennedy's renovation program was the subject of some discussion that night at their dinner table.

The press, as it did with almost everything else that went on at the White House, also played a role in Mrs. Kennedy's renovation plans. One of the things Mrs. Kennedy attempted to do was to prevent word leaking out that she was contemplating buying this or that object of furniture. When such a story got into the press the result was predictable: the price of the object being considered for purchase by the White House went up and Mrs. Kennedy's office would be deluged by offers of similar types of furniture. The leaks to the press usually came from dealers who had been contacted by the White House, or wanted to sell something to the White House. Despite the stated desire that their negotiations with the White House should be kept confidential until any purchase was announced, the lure of seeing their own name in print was often too much for the dealers involved. One series of articles on Mrs. Kennedy's plans for renovation of the White House, written by Maxine Cheshire of the Washington *Post*, was almost totally based on this type of information.

The third phase of her improvement program for the White House was the launching of the *White House Guide Book*. The book was written by the then White House curator, Mrs. Lorraine Pearce, but edited personally by Mrs. Kennedy. She also took part in the layout of the pictures in the handsomely designed book which was prepared and printed by the National Geographic Society. The plan to sell the book was met with strong opposition. Mrs. Kennedy reported to a friend that she had "scores of complaints" that "it was a sacrilege to let money change hands in the White House." In addition, the Secret Service did not want anything to happen in the White House which would prevent the huge crowds of tourists from moving through the house without stopping and loitering. Despite these protests, Mrs. Kennedy went ahead—with staggering results. From July 1962, when the first books went on sale, until November 1963, the time of the assassination of President Kennedy, more than 600,000 copies had been sold—a national best seller by any standard. The profits from the sale of the guide book were used to buy additional furniture for the White House and to maintain it. This had the effect of lifting some of the fund-raising burden from The Fine Arts Committee for the White House.

The renovation of the White House was a manifestation of Mrs. Kennedy's desire for it to be a center of excellence. This extended to her feelings about culture. Some people have written that she was interested in culture for culture's sake. What she really wanted was for the White House to be the showcase for everything that was the finest in music, poetry, and the arts. It was with this in mind that she played such an important role in the cultural life of the Kennedy administration.

The high point of Mrs. Kennedy's cultural activities was the concert of Pablo Casals at the White House at an affair honoring Governor Luis Muñoz-Marin of the Commonwealth of Puerto Rico. The famed cellist had exiled himself from the United States over what he considered the unfortunate policies of the U.S. government favoring Spanish dictator Francisco Franco.

Before getting to the Casals concert, however, it would be better to set the scene on cultural activities in the White House.

The central point, as I have noted, was Mrs. Kennedy's desire to attract the best to the White House. She was primarily interested in setting a tone for the arts which would encourage culture around the country. I became involved in these activities through my own interest in music and my former career (short-lived) as a concert pianist. At a luncheon to raise funds for the National Symphony Orchestra of Washington, I had suggested the establishment of a White House music and art prize, to be used as a device for finding up-and-coming young American artists who could be honored in their own land. I had in mind the fact that such a great American pianist as Van Cliburn had to be recognized in the Soviet Union before he got any recognition here.

As a result of the speech and the interest it created, I was contacted by Isaac Stern, the virtuoso American concert violinist, whom I had known as a boy. Stern had led the fight to save Carnegie Hall in New York and was bubbling with ideas for a cultural renaissance in the United States and some definite ideas of what role the Kennedys could play in such a movement. Mrs. Kennedy invited Isaac to come to lunch at the White House and the three of us hashed out ideas for well over two hours. Mrs. Kennedy was very receptive to Stern's suggestions—which ranged all the way from concepts to elevate the National Cultural Center (now the John F. Kennedy Center for the Performing Arts) in Washington from a mere building to a living center for creative artistic effort, to ideas of national youth orchestras made up of the nation's most talented young people. At the lunch the subject of Casals came up. Abe Fortas, then a Washington lawyer and now an associate justice of the United States Supreme Court, had broached the subject to me of Casals giving a concert at the White House. Casals, it seemed, was very impressed with what President Kennedy was doing in the area of world peace and wanted to do something to honor the President. Fortas had also talked to Stern about Casals.

At the lunch it was decided to go ahead with a White House evening featuring Casals, and Stern undertook to make the final arrangements. The evening of November 13, 1961, was decided upon for the concert.

Mrs. Kennedy asked me if I wanted to submit a suggested guest list for the evening. I agreed readily and submitted a list of the nation's top classical composers—men like Aaron Copland, Norman Dello Joio, Samuel Barber, Ray Green, Leonard Bernstein, and Roy Harris. The invitations went out and the big evening arrived. It was a joyous evening. The composers were delighted. Almost none of them had been invited to the White House before, and they considered it a high-level recognition of their work. Casals played with deep feeling and beauty, finishing with a Catalán song of his native Spain.

I received a lovely handwritten note from Mrs. Kennedy the next morning, thanking me for my role in the affair:

*Dear Pierre. Last night was an unbelievable dream—and all because of you . . .*

She gave me too much credit, because without Mrs. Kennedy the evening would never have taken place.

The President followed the cultural program with interest. It should be said, in fairness, that while not a devotee of classical music, he saw the importance of the program. The Casals concert, of course, could not by itself make a cultural program. August Heckscher, who had worked for the Twentieth Century Fund, took a leave of absence for six months to come to the White House to work with the many groups that had been stimulated in the cultural field by the leadership of the White House. When Heckscher left, President Kennedy asked Arthur Schlesinger and me to study methods by which a cultural program could be continued. One of the most effective ways was a series of concerts sponsored by the members of the Cabinet and held in the State Department auditorium. There was, of course, the continuing work of raising money for the National Cultural Center, and a number of other great cultural events at the White House. These were topped by the evening during which Isaac Stern, cellist Leonard Rose, and pianist Eugene Istomin played trios in honor of French Cultural Minister André Malraux. I had arranged another evening starring clarinetist Benny Goodman and trumpeter Louis Armstrong, in which they were going to play the best of American jazz. The thinking was that jazz is such a distinctive American musical contribution that it belonged in our program of concerts. It certainly would have been an evening to remember, but the guests for whom the evening had been organized had to cancel out at the last moment.

Another important cultural event which Mrs. Kennedy personally arranged was the first American exhibit of the famous painting, the *Mona Lisa*, which hangs in the Louvre in Paris. The visit of the *Mona Lisa* came out of a series of discussions between Mrs. Kennedy and André Malraux. Mrs. Kennedy had come to know Malraux well during the President's visit to Paris in 1961, and she had been particularly moved by the fact that Malraux had insisted on personally giving her a tour of the Louvre and Malmaison, the palace of Josephine, the wife of Napoleon Bonaparte, only a few days after Malraux's two sons had been killed in an automobile accident. At that time, she had discussed the *Mona Lisa* with Malraux and the exhibition of the great work of art was finally arranged during the visit of Minister Malraux to Washington in 1962.

There have been questions raised as to the over-all value of the White House cultural program during the Kennedy administration. Certainly it was not anywhere near the complete answer to the problem of encouraging culture in this nation. But, at least when the top artists in the classical field were performing at the White House, it was a reminder that there are other things going on in the field of music than the Beatles.

With all that I have said about the renovation of the White House and culture, it should be emphasized that Mrs. Kennedy's number one and most consuming interest was her husband and children.

One cornerstone rule of life in the White House was set down by Mrs. Kennedy. It was that the children, Caroline and John, would try to live as normal a life as possible under the difficult circumstances that the White House offered. This led to some sharp exchanges of views inside and outside the White House. One of the treasures of my life is a series of memoranda from Mrs. Kennedy, asking (usually in outrage—and with justification) why this story or that picture had appeared in the press. If she was sometimes harsh on those around her for infractions of the rules she had set down on privacy, it was because she really believed in them. After receiving a steady stream of memoranda pointing out deficiencies in my efforts to preserve the privacy of the children, I received one with a heading: *Don't worry—a nice calm memo.*

Her objective was very simple and direct: To make the White House the best possible place for her husband and children to live, to make it a refuge for the President in the midst of the maelstrom of his job, and further to make the White House, both as a physical thing and through the behavior of its inhabitants, an institution in which all Americans could be proud. In carrying out this objective, she had great gentleness and great firmness. But her true intentions (and the sincerity of them) were in my opinion never really understood by the ladies of the press, who were primarily assigned to cover her activities. They considered Mrs. Kennedy aloof and hard to deal with and the brunt of their criticism fell on Mrs. Kennedy's young and beautiful Press Secretary, Pamela Turnure.

Pam Turnure had never had any experience in dealing with the press prior to taking over the post with Mrs. Kennedy.

But, despite this, Pam was ideally suited for her job. She had the confidence of both Mrs. Kennedy and the President. And when she was often criticized by the press for not giving this tidbit or that tidbit about life in the White House, she was merely carrying out the orders of Mrs. Kennedy.

These efforts at privacy created a "crisis" in March 1961, involving a National Park Service decision to improve the landscaping of the White House grounds. Among the proposals was the planting of six-foot-high rhododendrons to shield certain private areas from public gaze.

The Park Service was eager to move ahead with the plan and President and Mrs. Kennedy gave their approval. The Washington *Star* promptly came out with a story that the whole thing was President Kennedy's idea to protect Caroline's privacy, and that the rhododendrons would cut off the entire view of the White House grounds from the south—a favorite viewing place for hundreds of thousands of tourists a year.

I knew nothing about it until I got a query from a *Star* reporter at one of my press briefings, and responded that it was "too silly" to warrant comment. In fact, I said, I wouldn't even go to the Kennedys to inquire further.

Now, nothing rouses the animals of the press corps more than to be told that a question is "silly," and the reporters came back at me hard and fast.

I decided to conduct an investigation of my own and discovered that the Park Service was merely implementing the Olmstead Plan, drawn up by a consulting firm of that name in Brookline, Massachusetts, twenty-six years before. This, obviously, was long before Caroline was born, and the *Star*'s accusation against President Kennedy was, just as obviously, untrue.

In fact, even the Olmstead Plan did not call for obscuring the entire southern view of the White House with rhododendrons, merely two areas by the East and West gates.

It was true that the Park Service had shown Mrs. Kennedy the plans, but her only contribution had been to suggest tall plantings to give her children a little privacy in their small play area.

After the facts came out, the *Star* had another story, expressing "regret that it originally planted the rhododendrons along the wrong fence and thus implied that the President wanted to obscure the view of the White House from the south. The modification of the 1935 plan will doubtless be an improvement all around."

But the paper couldn't resist a final dig at me: "Although Mr. Salinger had gained in San Francisco the reputation of being a first-class newspaperman, he is relatively new in Washington and is not yet considered by the *Star* to be an expert on the degrees of silliness that can be attained in this city."

I decided on a strategic retreat. I could, of course, have taken public note of the fact that the original *Star* story was wrong by their own admission, but that would only have precipitated another slam at me. By mutual consent, we agreed to let the rhododendron crisis fade into history.

About a month later, I was invited to a private lunch with Benjamin McKelway, the editor of the *Star*, and other top editorial directors of the newspaper. I arrived with a gift for McKelway—a rhododendron bush, with a note attached. "This bush is presented to the *Star* to be planted in front of the building to hide it from the public." My relations with the *Star* improved from that moment on.

There were moments of joy provided by the children. Caroline and John roamed the White House with curiosity and appeared in the unlikeliest places. I should have had an idea of what was to come the afternoon that the President held a press conference in Palm Beach before his Inauguration. He was well into the press conference, being held on the patio of his father's house, when onto the patio came Caroline, dressed in a nightgown and wearing her mother's shoes. After a short, futile effort to get her to leave, I took Caroline by the hand and marched her back into the house.

Or the time Caroline got loose in the West Lobby of the White House where the press sat around waiting for presidential developments. One of the reporters asked Caroline what her father was doing. "Oh, he's upstairs with his shoes and socks off, not doing anything." It was Caroline's last press conference. Caroline and John would come over to the office with their father almost every morning. Part of the fun was the joy of walking over with daddy, but there was also a side bonus—a raid on the inevitable candy box which Mrs. Evelyn Lincoln, the President's secretary, kept on her desk for that purpose. After five or ten minutes, Miss Maud Shaw, the English nurse who took care of the children, would show up and take them off to the house.

Caroline went to nursery school and was joined in the last year by John. The nursery school was organized by Mrs. Kennedy so that Caroline could have children her own age studying with her, and not have to leave the White House grounds. There was a nominal tuition charge for the children, which went to pay the two teachers. Among the students in the school was Avery Hatcher, the son of Associate White House Press Secretary Andrew Hatcher. Young Avery went off to school the first morning and when he got home his mother asked him how he had enjoyed it.

"Oh, I liked it fine," he replied. "And I got to meet the President of the United States," he added.

"How did you know it was the President?" his mother asked.

"Oh, I recognized him from his pictures in the newspapers. And, you know what? He recognized me, too," the little Negro boy said.

"How do you think he recognized you?" his mother asked.

"Daddy must have told him I was the one who was going to wear green pants," was the reply.

From his office the President could see the nursery school class taking their playground time in the sandpile behind his office. On some occasions he would get up from his desk and walk out to the children to talk to Caroline, John, and the others.

Animals were also a big thing around the White House, as the Kennedy family had a great affection for them. There were never less than fifteen pets in residence at the White House, ranging from two ponies to accident-prone hamsters.

Although JFK had an allergy to dogs, he was willing to accept the discomfort because of the joy they gave to Caroline and John. He would often step out of his office between appointments, clap his hands, and then brace himself for the inevitable charge by his children and their canine friends. Among the dogs were Charlie, a Welsh terrier; Shannon, an Irish cocker spaniel that was given to the family by Prime Minister Eamon de Valera after the President's 1963 visit to Eire; and Pushinka, the daughter of Laika, the first Russian space dog, a gift to Mrs. Kennedy from Premier Khrushchev.

The happy union of Pushinka and Charlie resulted in puppies, for whom Mrs. Kennedy had to find homes. One went to Peter and Pat Lawford and two others were given away to children in a national letter-writing contest. In response to an invitation from Mrs. Kennedy, more than 10,000 boys and girls wrote her a description of the home and care they thought a dog should have. I had to reduce the mountain of mail to the hundred best letters, from which Mrs. Kennedy made the final choice. The most eloquent letter came from a boy in Chicago, but he was never in the running because he forgot to give his name and address. He wrote: *I will raise the dog to be a Democrat and to bite all Republicans.* The White House was also home to Caroline's pony, Macaroni.

Another animal figured in the news—the beautiful horse Sardar, a gift to Mrs. Kennedy from Mohammed Ayub Khan, President of Pakistan, after her visit there in 1962. Mrs. Kennedy wisely chose to decline two other gifts—an Indian elephant and a litter of tiger cubs. There was a brief flurry of criticism because Sardar was flown to Washington aboard a Military Air Transport Service plane, apparently at taxpayers' expense. But the uproar didn't last long after I told the press that it was a regular flight and the plane, like a majority of MATS flights, was returning to this country without other cargo.

Democratic Senator Stephen M. Young of Ohio, famous for his acid letters to constituents, had the last word in the controversy. A wealthy resident of Cleveland wrote him that he had horses in Europe that he would like to have flown over at public expense. Would the Senator please arrange for free MATS transportation?

"All your letter proves," the senator wrote back, "is that a horse's —— lives at —— —— Street, Cleveland."

But the most newsworthy inhabitants of the White House zoo were Caroline's hamsters. They were always running away, catching cold, or managing their own demise in ways that would delight James Bond. The White House press corps, particularly the distaff reporters, took a lively interest in the health and welfare of the hamsters.

Helen Thomas of UPI woke me out of a sound sleep one morning at three o'clock.

"I wouldn't call you at an ungodly hour like this, Pierre, if it weren't important. But we have a report that one of Caroline's hamsters has died. Would you check it out for me?"

I exploded.

"Who would you like me to call, Helen? Caroline? Mrs. Kennedy? The President himself?"

I fell back into bed without waiting for her answer. Later that morning, I found out that Helen was correct. One of Caroline's hamsters had, indeed, crawled into the President's bathtub and drowned.

In addition to the pets in residence, the White House was the temporary home of many animals sent as gifts for John and Caroline. Most of the donors were only looking for publicity and the pets were promptly given to Washington orphanages.

The most spectacular of this brood was Zsa Zsa, the beer-swilling, trumpet-tooting rabbit. She was sent to Caroline by a Pittsburgh magician —complete with horn and beer-opener.

One of my press briefings records Zsa Zsa's brief White House tenure.

Q. Mr. Secretary, do you know that this rabbit is a lush?

A. All I know about Zsa Zsa is that she's supposed to be able to play the first five bars of "The Star-Spangled Banner" on a toy golden trumpet.

Q. Could we have the rabbit come over here and run through a couple of numbers for us?

A. I can ask her.

Q. Was the rabbit playing the trumpet as it came into the White House?

A. No, the trumpet came under separate cover and it will be sent to the orphanage with the rabbit. I don't think Zsa Zsa should be without her trumpet.

Q. You're not sending her to the orphanage?

A. Immediately.

There was an insidious invasion of the Kennedys' privacy—in the commercial field. Because the Kennedy's were of great interest to the general public, there was an effort to commercialize them which never stopped—even after the death of the President.

There were some things we could do something about—and others we could not. In the latter category was the revolting exploitation of Mrs. Kennedy, primarily by the movie fan magazines, which goes on even today. Issue after issue, these magazines ran pictures of Mrs. Kennedy on the cover with suggestive titles. When you read the articles they said nothing, but the titles said just enough to sell the magazines. The pictures that were used were usually in the public domain, and therefore nothing could be done on that score, either.

Then there were the records poking fun at the Kennedys. A number of these appeared, although the only really successful one was *The First Family*, by Vaughn Meader. The President and Mrs. Kennedy took the Meader album in very good humor, although they were less pleased with some of the imitations of Meader's imitation, which came out subsequently.

But the most serious area was in products, obviously based on the Kennedys. An example of sorts were the numerous Caroline Kennedy and Jacqueline Kennedy dolls which appeared. Some were shoddy goods. Others were extremely well built, but still a strict invasion of the Kennedys' privacy. In a way, it was a compliment to the Kennedys that so many people were interested in putting out products revolving around them. But the White House has had a policy against commercialization of the presidential families for some time and has enforced this policy over the years with the assistance of the Better Business Bureau. I must have written dozens of letters and had dozens of telephone conversations with merchants during my tenure as Press Secretary, telling them to desist in the sale of certain items. Where we were able to get to the merchants, we were usually successful, and the sale of the items ceased. But the United States is a big country, and there were just too many Kennedy products on the market for us to get to all of them.

The principal members of Mrs. Kennedy's staff were her social secretary, Letitia Baldrige (now Mrs. Robert Hollensteiner), who was succeeded by Nancy Tuckerman early in 1963; her Press Secretary, Pamela Turnure; the White House curator, Mrs. Lorraine Pearce, and the executive housekeeper, Anne Lincoln. Miss Baldrige, who came to the White House with a background in business and public relations, did the general organizing of the White House social functions, and answered Mrs. Kennedy's non-personal mail. Miss Lincoln planned the menus for official dinners and luncheons, ran the household staff, and kept an eye on the food budget. Pam handled relations with the lady reporters, in many ways an assignment more treacherous than my own. The ladies were never really satisfied with the news they got on Mrs. Kennedy and the children. When there would be a large reception at the White House, representatives of the nation's social pages would be invited to cover the event. They would go around buttonholing guests at the reception, who often did not know they were talking to a member of the press. The next morning's papers would be filled with chitchat from these parties. Mrs. Kennedy felt that some of the events at the White House should not be covered by society reporters in the first place. For example, she felt that the concert of Pablo Casals should be covered by the music critics, dramatic presentations by the drama critics, and so on. Finally the open break came, and Mrs. Kennedy sent down orders that the press was not to be admitted to the next reception. They could watch from a previously selected vantage point, but they could not interview the guests. The resultant uproar proved to be the Cuban missile crisis of the East Wing. Art Buchwald even dubbed it the Eyelash-to-Eyelash crisis, and the ladies wrote plaintive stories on how they were forced to cover great social events from behind potted plants. To be frank, the heat was such that the White House caved in, and the very next party found the reporters back in their accustomed role of interviewing the guests. Pam suffered through her term of office with great good humor and grace, which was often a tribute to her tact. Mrs. Pearce served as liaison between Mrs. Kennedy and her Arts Committee and helped to bring into existence the first real catalogue of the White House contents.

Mrs. Kennedy was an inveterate memorandum writer, all in longhand and usually on long sheets of yellow paper. No morning would pass without the White House Usher's Office arriving with ten or fifteen memoranda written for Tish, Pam, Anne, or Lorraine. When the President would start to do his evening reading, Mrs. Kennedy would turn to her memoranda. Every afternoon at 4 P.M., she would receive memoranda from her staff asking for her views or approval on a number of projects. She would also receive her correspondence to sign. Mrs. Kennedy wrote the bulk of her personal letters in longhand rather than by dictating them to a secretary. On the morning after a state dinner, even if Mrs. Kennedy had gone to bed at 2 A.M. or later, the memoranda arrived, either expressing pleasure with the way the evening had gone and praising the recipient for his role, or suggesting ways in which the next state dinner might be improved. Chef René Verdon invariably got a memorandum from Mrs. Kennedy after one of these dinners, thanking him for his efforts. The chef would put the memo on the bulletin board in the kitchen for all the help to see. Sometimes, Mrs. Kennedy would draw pictures of canapés she suggested for the next dinner, sending them down to the chef or to Anne Lincoln.

Her attention to detail was legendary, and a state dinner reflected the many facets of her interests. Bouquets of flowers—like Flemish still lifes

—were turned out for these occasions by the White House flower room, which Mrs. Kennedy had had reorganized early in 1961, under the expert guidance of Mrs. Paul Mellon. (Mrs. Mellon was later to design the President's Rose Garden, a source of never-ending pleasure for President Kennedy.) The tables would gleam with vermeil ornaments and flatware, some of which dated back to the days of James Monroe, and wines were poured in goblets made of West Virginia glass—small evidence of a promise kept by President and Mrs. Kennedy that they would always remember that state and the beginning it had provided.

On the afternoon of a dinner, Sandy Fox, of the Civil Service staff for White House entertainment, would bring over the seating charts and list of people attending the dinner. Mrs. Kennedy would get down on her hands and knees on the floor of her sitting room and personally plan the seating. Some places, of course, were prearranged by protocol needs. In a dinner of 120 guests, perhaps forty had to be placed specially for protocol reasons. But Mrs. Kennedy decided where the rest of the guests would be seated.

Mrs. Kennedy was also a person who did not like to see time wasted. During the months when she was awaiting the birth of young Patrick Bouvier in 1963 (and while JFK was in Germany, Italy, and Ireland), she selected the 1963 official and personal Christmas cards, as well as all the Christmas gifts that she and the President were going to send out that year. While the cards were never mailed, she saw to it that everyone received the gifts intended for them, even in her bereavement following the assassination of the President. Her gift for me was a leather-bound collection of the Inaugural addresses of all the American Presidents with the following inscription in her handwriting on the flyleaf: *For Pierre: The President was going to give this for Christmas. Please accept it now from me with my devotion always.*

# XXII

## UPROAR IN VIETNAM

While the Cuban missile crisis presented a dramatic example of the confrontation of the press and government in a cold war situation, the war in Vietnam—in many ways—posed far more disturbing problems for both.

The handling of the delicate information policy problems of the Vietnam war between 1961 and early 1964 consumed hours of meetings, intermittent changes of policies and personnel, and, in the end, total frustration. In fact, it became a kind of angry frustration.

What follows is not a pretty chapter in the continuing relations between the government and the press. It certainly is not an apologia for the government's action, for we were responsible for a number of mistakes as we groped for the answer to handle a "non-war" in which Americans were dying. Nor, however, do I accept the premise of certain members of the press that they were totally right and that everybody in government with whom they had dealings was somehow deluded and stupid.

To understand the information problem which confronted us in Vietnam, it is first important to know some of the political decisions which had been made in that unfortunate country which has now been racked by war for more than twenty years.

When John F. Kennedy became President of the United States, the total U.S. force in Vietnam was about six hundred. It could truly be said that the United States was acting solely as an adviser to the government of South Vietnam. The activities and numbers of our troops were well within the limits imposed by the Geneva Conference of 1954 which the signers hoped would permanently settle the Indochina problem. That conference had taken French Indochina and divided it into four sections —a Communist North Vietnam, a non-Communist South Vietnam (the

Korea pattern), and two neutral nations, Cambodia and Laos. Starting late in 1959, the situation in Vietnam began to deteriorate both militarily and politically. The North Vietnamese proclaimed the existence in South Vietnam of the National Liberation Front (NLF) of Vietnam, which became better known as the Vietcong. At this time, the Vietcong became bolder in their attacks on government troops in the countryside. They also began to exercise increasing control over the little villages in the rural areas of South Vietnam. At the same time, the government of President Ngo Dinh Diem, which had had a promising start, had begun to become increasingly dictatorial and removed from the people of Vietnam.

In late 1961, the President sent his then military adviser at the White House, General Maxwell Taylor, to Vietnam, for a personal investigation of the situation. When General Taylor returned, his report was a mixture of optimism and pessimism. The general felt that the South Vietnamese could win the war against the Vietcong; at the same time he felt that the level of U.S. support, both in personnel and supplies, needed to be escalated.

President Kennedy and the Joint Chiefs of Staff concurred with General Taylor's recommendations, and the United States started a gradual buildup of troops which was to reach over 20,000 at the time of the death of the President.

The early months of the increase convinced us in Washington that a change was necessary in our policies toward the press in Vietnam. There were several very serious and complicating factors: the United States was still acting in the role of adviser to the government of South Vietnam and the South Vietnamese felt very strongly that their government should be the controlling factor in relations with the press; neither Ambassador Frederick E. Nolting, Jr., nor the U.S. military commander in Vietnam, General Paul D. Harkins, had a particularly warm relationship with the press; with the buildup in U.S. troops and supplies, this government was now going to be engaged in activities which were in clear violation of the Geneva Conference of 1954. (The fact that the North Vietnamese had been systematically violating these agreements for some time did not dissuade those in the top echelon of U.S. policy making, who felt it would be a serious tactical error on our part to concede that the United States was similarly violating the agreements.) Finally, the administration, having gone through the Bay of Pigs, and still involved in the Berlin crisis which had caused it to call up the reserves and send extra divisions to Europe, was not anxious to admit the existence of a real war in Southeast Asia. And there was the tendency of our representatives in the field (and some visiting generals and admirals) to give press conferences which painted an altogether too rosy picture of the actual situation in Vietnam.

The press on its part was vehement in the objections to the restraints under which it was forced to operate. Homer Bigart, the Pulitzer Prize-winning correspondent of the New York *Times,* was particularly harsh in his charge that U.S. representatives in Vietnam were not telling the press the truth about what was going on there.

In early 1962, with the arrival of fresh troops and scores of American helicopters in Vietnam, the top information officers at the State Department, Bob Manning and Carl Rowan; the USIA, Edward R. Murrow and Don Wilson; the Defense Department, Arthur Sylvester, and I decided that something had to be done of a dramatic nature to improve our press relations there.

At a meeting between President Kennedy and Secretary of State Dean Rusk in early February, Rowan made a powerful presentation of the need for loosening our very stringent press information policies in Vietnam. I had previously told the President that I felt we were on a collision course with the press in Vietnam and unless we did something drastic, the administration would become embroiled in a fight it could not win.

The President gave us the go-ahead for two changes. First, a new press policy to be sent to the field expressing the administration's desire for the maximum amount of cooperation between the U.S. mission in Saigon and the press; second, a change of top personnel in the information field in Saigon. While we had no particular quarrel with John M. Anspacher, then the head of the U. S. Information Service in Saigon, we felt that a change of personnel might also signal a change of attitude on the part of the administration toward our Vietnamese policies.

The latter problem we had to solve in two phases. We did not have the man we wanted for the Saigon job ready at the time of our discussions with the President. To fill the gap for several months, I suggested we send Charlie Davis, the press officer for the USIS in Tokyo, to Saigon. I had known Davis personally for more than twenty years. We had attended high school together and, in fact, had been political opponents when I made my first fling at politics, an election for editor of the Lowell High School weekly newspaper. I still remember the election with some pain (maybe it was a harbinger of things to come). I ran on the highly popular slogan of doing away with high school fraternities and sororities. Davis received 1800 votes and I received less than 300. Davis had been in the Marines during the war, ended up in Japan, and had stayed there. He learned to speak Japanese and Korean fluently and had become one of the finest press officers of the USIS had anywhere in the world. In addition, he was personally acquainted with most of the reporters then serving in Vietnam and had their personal confidence.

A cable went to Tokyo on February 17 ordering Davis to Saigon TO WORK DIRECTLY WITH THE AMERICAN PRESS, PARTICULARLY ON MILITARY MATTERS. Before going to Saigon, Davis was sent to Honolulu for a meeting there on February 19 with Ambassador Nolting, General Harkins,

Sylvester, and Rowan. The latter two hand-carried to this meeting the draft of our new press policy statement for Vietnam which was also cabled to the embassy in Saigon.

Davis reported to me by private letter after his arrival in Vietnam. The picure was not encouraging. The U.S. government people with whom he had to work regarded him with suspicion and resentment because his orders came directly from the White House. "The acrimony between the embassy and the military is normal. The lack of confidence that the newsmen have in our position is based primarily on bad communications between the press and the public information officers. The weakness of a definitive information policy is almost unreal," Davis wrote.

On a long-term basis, we decided to seek the services of John Mecklin, a correspondent for *Time-Life* with wide experience in Vietnam. Mecklin had covered the Indochina war involving the French, was well-acquainted with the country, and was also highly thought of by his fellow correspondents. Mecklin agreed to take the assignment and arrived in Saigon early in May.

We also decided, on a military basis, to send a knowledgeable Air Force officer with wide experience in public information to Saigon. For this assignment, Sylvester and Defense Secretary Robert McNamara chose Colonel Lee Baker.

The press guidance memorandum was drafted by Rowan with the help of Sterling Cottrell, a career State Department officer who was the head of the department's Vietnam Task Force. The House Subcommittee on Information, in a 1963 report, tried to place the entire responsibility for the memorandum on Rowan, but the fact was that it was read and approved by Manning, Sylvester, Murrow, Wilson, and myself. In addition, the memorandum was shown to both President Kennedy and his national security adviser, McGeorge Bundy, before being sent to the field. Copies of the memo were also approved by Assistant Secretary of State for Far Eastern Affairs Averell Harriman, Secretary of Defense Robert Mc-Namara, and Deputy Under Secretary of State for Political Affairs U. Alexis Johnson (who was later to become Deputy Ambassador to Saigon during the ambassadorial term of General Maxwell Taylor).

I devote some space to the clearing of the memorandum only because it became a matter of such controversy later. The clear intent of the memorandum, however, was to improve the situation for the press covering the war in Vietnam. The fact that certain paragraphs in the memo were later used to repress rather than give out information does not detract from the clear intent of the drafters of the memorandum to improve the situation.

Because the memo still carries a "confidential" classification, I cannot quote it directly. But its intent was clearly set forth in the first paragraph which noted the determination of the State and Defense Departments and the USIA for more flexibility in the relationships with press covering the war in Vietnam. The memo called for the greatest possible cooperation with the press as well as an appeal to the good faith of the correspondents in handling of information which might be inimical to the national security interests of the United States.

Among other things which the memorandum pointed out were that the war was clearly a Vietnamese one, in which we were acting solely in training, advisory, and support capacities. The memo noted that it was not within our power to cut off press criticism of the Diem regime, but that it should be pointed out to the press that this type of criticism made our task in Vietnam more difficult. We urged the ambassador and General Harkins to see the press as frequently as possible and to keep them informed of what the United States was doing, compatible with the needs of national security. Finally, we pointed out that sensational stories which tended to describe certain battles as decisive in the enlarging war were inaccurate in that the war was likely to go on for a long period of time.

The memorandum, which became more popularly known as Cable 1006, had been drafted with all the best intentions. It is my recollection that we felt strongly in Washington that the combination of the memorandum and the change in personnel would certainly improve our relations with the press in Saigon. How wrong we proved to be is underscored in a book which Mecklin wrote after completing his service in Vietnam (*Mission in Torment*, Doubleday & Company, 1965). In that comprehensive study of the press problem in Vietnam, Mecklin writes:

"By early 1962 difficulties with the press had reached a point where Washington ordered a reexamination of information policy. The result was a new directive, State Department Cable No. 1006 of February 21, 1962—two months before my arrival—which was supposed to 'liberalize' the policy. It was 'liberal' in the sense that it recognized the right of American newsmen to cover the war in Vietnam, but it was otherwise little more than a codification of the errors the mission was already committing."

Notwithstanding Mecklin's comments, however, we felt in Washington that Cable 1006 was a step forward. As far as reports reaching Washington in the ensuing months were concerned, it was an improvement. State, Defense, and the USIA all reported a lessening of press complaints in Saigon.

(It is an interesting sidelight that due to a mixup Colonel Baker did not get a copy of Cable 1006 for at least three months. Therefore, later charges that Baker restricted military information to the press on the basis of Cable 1006 were untrue. He simply had not seen the cable.)

When the House Subcommittee on Information issued its report on the administration's press policies in Vietnam in late 1963, it was particularly critical of Cable 1006 and very precise in pinning the responsibility for the cable on Carl Rowan, who by that time had become the U.S. ambassador to Finland. It is relevant here to cite Rowan's recollection of the government's relations with the press after the issuance of Cable 1006.

"The Moss [Committee Chairman John Moss of California] Subcommittee report states that 'soon after the press guidance was issued, however, newsmen began reporting difficulties getting information from U.S. officials in Vietnam.' The exact opposite is true. The record will show that correspondents like Homer Bigart and Keyes Beech, and magazines like *U.S. News and World Report* had complained bitterly in weeks prior to February 17 [1962]. Every report I received subsequent to the press guidance indicated that sending Davis to Saigon with authority to assist newsmen in clearing certain barriers was greatly appreciated by correspondents and virtually silenced complaints until other unrelated problems arose months later."

Thus, it is basic to the understanding of the events which followed that two points were accepted in Washington the spring of 1962: (1) relations with the press were going better in Saigon, and (2) because of the liberalization of our press policies, the government should be prepared for stories which it would rather not see in print. The first point turned out to be a delusion. The second point became true in spades.

Stories began appearing with increasing regularity describing heavy involvement of U.S. forces in Vietnamese operations, and stories of the shooting down of U.S. helicopters. Such articles are frequent now with more than 235,000 U.S. troops in Vietnam, but taken in the context of 1962-63 operations, they presented the American people with the picture of a widening war in Southeast Asia—and it was this picture which, for the reasons previously outlined, the administration did not want to present. President Kennedy was particularly sensitive about some of these articles. It was my view at the time that we should be prepared to take the good stories with the bad in Vietnam, but the President pushed hard for us to tighten the rules there under which correspondents could observe field operations in person.

One story particularly enraged the President. It described how eight U.S. helicopters had been shot down in an operation with the Vietnamese. The story was exaggerated (it turned out there were only five helicopters downed), but again the picture of massive and growing involvement by the U.S. in Vietnam concerned the administration.

Those responsible for the information policies of the government were therefore squeezed hard—between the desire of the administration to downplay the war for a whole variety of military and political reasons and the desire of the reporters on the ground to tell all to the American people. It seems to me that the solution may have well been reached in a middle position, but the hardening of attitudes by both press and government never allowed us to reach that compromise.

To complicate matters further, the Diem government, and particularly Diem's brother Ngo Dinh Nhu and his wife, developed a fanatical hatred for a large part of the American press in Vietnam. On two occasions, on instructions from Washington, Ambassador Nolting had to make personal representation to President Diem to ward off the expulsion from the country of François Sully, the Saigon correspondent of *Newsweek* magazine. Despite these efforts, Sully was finally expelled, as was James Robinson of NBC. But the Diems reserved their special hatred for three young American correspondents, David Halberstam of the New York *Times*, Neil Sheehan of UPI, and Malcolm Browne of the AP. Their dislike was reciprocated fully by the reporters, who came to the joint or independent conclusion that there was never going to be any real progress in the war in Vietnam until the Diem government fell and was replaced by one with a real understanding of the needs of the Vietnamese people.

Because U.S. policy in late 1962 and early 1963 was based on the continuing support by this country of President Diem, the three reporters became the focal point of U.S. disapproval at the mission level in Saigon and at high government levels in Washington. It is true, as Halberstam reports in his book, *The Making of a Quagmire* (Random House, 1964), that President Kennedy suggested to Arthur Hays Sulzberger, the new publisher of the New York *Times* that he might give Halberstam a vacation and remove him from Vietnam. It would have also been predictably true, as Halberstam later reports, that such a request would have the opposite effect—that it would stiffen the back of the New York *Times* and require them to keep Halberstam in Vietnam just to prove they couldn't be pushed around by the administration.

Since Halberstam, Sheehan, and Browne became such a storm center in our Vietnamese press relations, it is well to analyze their role there. To do so fairly, one must separate the military from the political aspects of the war. As far as the military were concerned, it can be said candidly that the three reporters were faithfully carrying out their mission in reporting the battles in Vietnam, even when this reporting had the unfortunate by-product of putting the United States in an unfavorable light. One can say this while not accepting Halberstam's persistent point in his book that the press was always right and the government always wrong. It is this oversimplification which weakens Halberstam's position rather than some of his actions in Vietnam as they related to the military situation, which were entirely proper.

When we get to the political situation, however, Halberstam, Sheehan, and Browne are on far less favorable ground. The three reporters devoted their activities in 1963 to the political crisis which developed in Saigon—particularly the nasty conflict between the government and the Buddhists. Whether they intended it or not, their articles reflected the bitter hatred they had for the Diem government and their avowed purpose (stated to a number of reporters in Saigon) to bring down the Diem government. It is a deep question of reportorial ethics whether the destruction of a government is within the legitimate framework of journalistic enterprise.

Mecklin became ill in February 1963, and after an examination at Clark Air Force Base near Manila, it was determined he had a malignant tumor in his chest. He flew back to the Naval Hospital at Bethesda, Maryland, for surgery.

By late April he was sufficiently recovered to be preparing to return to Saigon. Don Wilson, the deputy director of the USIA, called me on several occasions, asking me to see Mecklin. Mecklin finally came to my office and his story of the mounting difficulties in Saigon convinced me that this was something the President should hear himself. I arranged an appointment for Mecklin with President Kennedy on April 29, 1963. I felt that Mecklin should see the President alone and urged him to pull no punches in telling his story.

After the meeting, the President told me he had been deeply impressed with Mecklin's recital—but at the same time he did not feel that any new press policy in Vietnam would, in the long run, be successful because of the highly conflicting interests of the government and the press there. But after a discussion, in which McGeorge Bundy participated, he authorized me to draft a new guideline to Saigon to supersede State Department Cable 1006.

The new press policy was contained in a secret memorandum to be hand-delivered to Ambassador Nolting and General Harkins by Arthur Sylvester at one of the periodic Vietnam review meetings in Honolulu.

The memorandum recognized the press problems in Vietnam and granted additional leeway to officers in the field in handling relations with the correspondents. It urged our representatives to take the reporters into their confidence and stated that Washington would exercise patience while the new guidelines were being put into effect. What was probably most important, from the standpoint of those who received the memorandum, it noted that the President himself had been consulted on its drafting. The memo also urged a note of caution in describing the military and political situation in Saigon.

Mecklin was enthusiastic about the memorandum and went back to Saigon, convinced that at last he had a directive in hand which would enable him to bring peace to the press-government war.

The almost immediate eruption of the Buddhist crisis dashed all these hopes, and as Mecklin later wrote, brought problems with it "that probably could not have been solved if Kennedy himself had come out to buy the newsmen a round of beers at the Caravelle [Hotel] bar."

The Buddhist crisis marked the beginning of the end of the Diem regime. In its final paroxysms of power, the fading regime again concentrated its hatred and fire power on the American press. The climax was reached on July 7, 1963, when a group of U.S. newsmen were attacked at the entrance of a Buddhist pagoda by Vietnamese government plain-clothes police while covering a religious ceremony.

In a telegram to the President, signed by Halberstam, Browne, Shee-han, and Peter Kalisher, the Far East correspondent of CBS, the news-men reported that nine representatives of U.S. news organizations had been "subjected to a swift, unprovoked, and violent attack by govern-ment plain-clothes police while covering an otherwise peaceful Buddhist religious ceremony. One correspondent was knocked down and kicked. Other newsmen were shoved, jostled, and struck by rocks thrown by the plain-clothes men—all in full sight of forty to sixty uniformed metropoli-tan policemen and a squad of riot police. In the course of the attack, one camera was smashed and several damaged.

"The inescapable conclusion is that the government of South Vietnam, a country to which the United States is heavily committed, has begun a campaign of open physical intimidation to prevent the covering of news which we feel Americans have a right to know . . . Since the United States Embassy here does not deem this incident serious enough to make a formal protest, we respectfully request that you, Mr. President, protest against this attack and obtain assurances that it will not be repeated."

The fact was that the U. S. Embassy had already made representations to the Vietnamese government by the time the telegram reached the President. Without regard to any previous problems we had with the press in Saigon, this was clearly a matter which needed more than a rou-tine response. I recommended to the President that we dispatch Bob Manning to Saigon immediately for an on-the-spot survey of the situation. The President agreed and I got a telegram off to the correspondents sev-eral hours after the President had received theirs. In the telegram, I in-formed them of the protest lodged by our embassy and told them that Manning would be in Saigon the following week.

While the Manning mission did little to solve the immediate problems in Saigon, it served an important larger purpose. On his return, he pre-pared a twenty-eight-page memorandum for Secretary of State Rusk and other top State Department officials that was remarkable for its candor and insight into our problems there.

Again, as in discussing the Cuban missile crisis, we return to the key information issue of our time in reading the Manning memorandum.

That question is how a free, democratic society governs its relations with the press in the gray area of the cold war.

Halberstam devotes but one paragraph to this problem in his 323-page book. "The split between the American press and the American mission was very much the product of our country's traditional freedoms and attitudes," he writes. "There was a conflict between these and the pres-

sure of the cold war, which often push the United States into complicated, difficult, and essentially alien situations. We reporters were the
heirs of a traditional American freedom: the right of a journalist to write
what he sees, whether the news is good or bad for his own country. We
did not have to worry about the alternatives of policy making. The ambassadors and generals, on the other hand, were the heirs to a new di-
lemma: the discord between this country's traditional instincts, and its
duties and responsibilities in the cold war."

Manning put it in a different way: "The press problem in Vietnam is
singular because of the singular nature of the United States involvement
in that country. Our involvement is so extensive as to require public, i.e.,
press, scrutiny, and yet so hemmed by limitations as to make it difficult
for the United States government to promote and assure that scrutiny.
The problem is complicated by the long-standing desire of the United
States government to see the American involvement in Vietnam mini-
mized, even represented, as something less than in reality it is. The early
history of the handling of the situation is marked by attitudes, directives,
and actions in Washington and in the field that reflect this United States
desire."

The State Department official argued for "relaxation of some—but not
all—of the strictures still imposed on American coverage of the Vietnamese situation" and also called for a more "relaxed attitude on the part
of U.S. officials to the reports and assessments of the U.S. press. This
would do much to reduce the somewhat 'Alice in Wonderland' miasma
that surrounds the Vietnamese press situation, and it would help to build
a degree of mutual confidence and mutual credibility between American
authorities and American correspondents covering Vietnam."

This latter point was particularly important because it was clearly too
true that the nervousness of U.S. officials, right up to the President of the
United States, about what appeared in newspapers on events in Vietnam
was not realistic when measured against a more generous and mature
public reaction.

One of Manning's principal recommendations was that the arrival of
the new ambassador, Henry Cabot Lodge, to replace Ambassador Nolting be used as a delineation point to commence a new and more productive relationship with the American press in Saigon. It was Manning's
argument that Lodge, unburdened by participation in the long warfare with the press which had plagued his predecessor, could create a new
climate of cooperation.

This, in fact, did take place. With Lodge as the ambassador a new era
was opened in the relations between the press and the U.S. government.
The overthrow of the Diem government several months later also brought
on a new era of cooperation between the Vietnamese and the U.S. press.

I drop this recital at the time of the assassination of President Kennedy

because I played no firsthand role in Vietnamese press relations thereafter. They have continued to be troublesome but the infusion of 240,000
American servicemen in Vietnam has taken the conflict out of the so-
called "non-war" status. As such, the struggle is more amenable to the
traditional relationships between government and press that we saw during World War II and the Korean conflict.

There are a number of hard lessons to be learned from the handling
of the press in Vietnam between 1961 and early 1964.

The most important is that despite all the motivations which exist to
the contrary the government can never expect success for a press policy
which does not rely on total candor. Thus, the government of the United
States, as a free democratic society, may be faced with an impossible
choice: that choice is between using any methods at its disposal, including
some secret operations, to defend the national interest and doing everything out in the open with the accepted drawbacks that such a policy
would produce.

I do not believe that such a choice should be forced on either government or press. It is at best an oversimplification and at worst unacceptable
to a great nation locked in struggle around the world.

It is why I have suggested frequently that instead of walking away from
a central problem of our time—and hoping that it will somehow go
away—it should now have the attention of the most knowledgeable and
creative people in both the government and the press.

There were numerous efforts during my tenure in the Kennedy administration to initiate such discussions. The most notable of these was the
President's own meeting with top press representatives after the Bay of
Pigs. All these efforts, however, met with failure. The failure rests on
both the press and the government with equal weight.

The recitation of the events in Vietnam during the years described
cries out for a new start to such an approach. The question is whether
the government and the press are content to limp through the rest of the
twentieth century on the basis of unfortunate policies based on improvi-
sation.

# XXIII

## AFTER KENNEDY

John F. Kennedy came back to the White House from Dallas at 4:25 A.M., Saturday, November 23, 1963.

Ken O'Donnell, Larry O'Brien, and I were among those waiting with Mrs. Kennedy when the casket was brought into the East Room. Candles were lit head and foot, a priest spoke his liturgy, and the widow knelt for a long moment by the black catafalque. Then, rising to leave, she saw Ken, Larry, and me.

"It's been a long day for all of us," she said, "and it's much too late for you to drive home. Why don't you all stay here?"

I had been asleep only an hour when the telephone rang at 8 A.M. in my third-floor bedroom.

"Mr. Salinger, the President is calling."

*The President?* But the President was dead. Then I heard the voice of Lyndon B. Johnson.

"Pierre, I know how much President Kennedy meant to you, and I know how you must feel now. But I want you to stay on the job. I need you more than he ever did."

I told him I would stay.

"Come over and see me as soon as you can," he said.

I dressed quickly and went down to my office, pausing in the East Room for another glimpse of the casket. The door to the President's office was ajar and I glanced inside. All of JFK's personal possessions had been taken away during the night—the rocking chair, the ship models, the marine paintings, the portraits of Caroline and John.

Lyndon Johnson was operating from his vice-presidential quarters in the Executive Office Building and did not move into the White House until several days after the funeral the following Monday. But the sight of that barren office, awaiting its new tenant, was for me the first realization that the transition had already begun.

Days later, when Mrs. Kennedy was sorting out her husband's belongings, she found something of special meaning for all of us on the staff. Her gift to me was the President's cigar holder with the initials JFK. She also sent me one of the flags that had hung in his office.

I saw the new President that first morning at 8:30, and we agreed that I should take personal charge of press arrangements for the funeral and that Malcolm Kilduff of my staff would move over to the Executive Office Building to assist George Reedy, who had been vice-presidential Press Secretary.

For the next four days, I found myself serving both a living and a dead President. My twice-daily press briefings were attended by the largest crowd of reporters in White House history. Each was split into two parts; the first dealing with the funeral plans and the second with the activities of President Johnson. The deep personal affection most of the correspondents felt for JFK was apparent at every briefing. Many of the newsmen wept openly. Others told me later they had to force themselves to take notes because they just couldn't believe they were reporting the funeral of John F. Kennedy. Quite often, not only during this period but in the months that followed, I would announce that "President Kennedy" had done this or that, but the press understood and not one correspondent reported my lapses.

After one of the briefings, I went to the outer office to check on a press release stencil. The girl who had been typing it was leaning against a filing cabinet and crying. Blue correction fluid was spilled on her desk and when I took the stencil out of her typewriter to give to another secretary, I saw the error she had been unable to correct: "President Kennedy today announced . . ."

On Monday, I marched with ten other staff members behind the gun carriage bearing JFK's body from the White House to St. Matthew's, and was a member of the honor guard accompanying the casket into the cathedral. After the burial at Arlington National Cemetery, I went back to my office—to the same chair, to the same clutter of newspapers on my desk, to the same chatter of news service teletypes. But for the first time in almost three years I felt that I didn't belong there. The memory of John F. Kennedy was too fresh and the scars would be too long healing.

Until then, no Press Secretary in history had served two Presidents. Steve Early did remain for a brief time with Harry S. Truman after the death of Franklin D. Roosevelt, but it was understood that he would leave as soon as his successor could be found. Traditionally, the relationship between a President and his Press Secretary is a highly sensitive one. The Press Secretary, speaking for the President, communicates his attitudes and actions, through the press, to hundreds of millions of readers and listeners a day. This demands a confidence born of long and congenial association, and it might be a very long time, if ever, before President Johnson and I could achieve that rapport.

I told him the first week that he ought to consider replacing me with his own man as soon as possible. I had two nominees—George Reedy, who had been with LBJ for many years and was held in high regard by the Washington press corps, and Carl Rowan, the former director of the U. S. Information Agency and then ambassador to Finland. LBJ and Rowan had made a trip to Southeast Asia together in 1961 when Rowan was with the State Department, and I knew that the new President had an extremely high opinion of his intelligence and abilities.

LBJ heard me out and said he understood my feelings. "But I want you to stay with me as long as you can."

The President's first objective was to hold JFK's Cabinet and staff intact. He knew that wholesale changes in top-level personnel would be damaging to the transition and to the nation's sense of continuity. Although he brought a number of his own men with him to the White House, they tried to be as unobtrusive as possible, undoubtedly on direct orders from him.

The ablest of the new staffers was Walter Jenkins, who had been with LBJ for twenty years and knew his man well. Jenkins had excellent judgment and the one asset that is vital to White House service—the ability to speak up to the President. His resignation in 1964 was a grievous loss to LBJ.

Two other key arrivals were Bill D. Moyers, now the White House Press Secretary, and Jack Valenti, a special assistant. Moyers, a former divinity student, had already demonstrated his competence as deputy director of the Peace Corps. He was both an able administrator and a gifted speech writer and became the most influential member of the staff.

Valenti, a short, dapper former Houston advertising and PR man, was indispensable to the President in those first days. He was at the White House twenty hours a day, transmitting LBJ's orders, welcoming dignitaries, approving speeches, and performing a hundred and one other chores. (He has since become president of the Motion Picture Association of America.)

I had certain advantages when I began my service with President Johnson. He had had a somewhat distant and cool relationship with certain members of JFK's staff. But I had tried to maintain the closest possible liaison with him and with Reedy. LBJ was always at President Kennedy's pre-press-conference briefings, and Reedy sat in on my weekly round-table for high-ranking public information officers. Still another factor was LBJ's knowledge that a number of key staffers had been violently against him for the vice-presidential nomination in Los Angeles. Although I had been for Stuart Symington, once JFK chose Lyndon Johnson I did all I could to assist him in recruiting his campaign staff and in coordinating JFK's operation with his.

As a result, the new President and I were on entirely friendly terms, and he went out of his way to make me feel at home in the rapidly changing atmosphere at the White House. He gave flat instructions to the new staffers he had brought with him that they were not to interfere with my duties. Reedy was given assignments outside the press office. Although he had had a right to expect he would succeed me when LBJ became President, Reedy accepted the new situation with unfailing good humor. I was also given full access to the President—the one staff member who could enter his office without asking permission. When I gave him advice, he generally took it, with the comment: "If you think it's the right thing to do, go ahead and do it."

But apart from our relationship in the White House, he was gracious to me in many other ways.

One Saturday morning, shortly after my wife and I had been the Johnsons' guests for dinner at the White House, I told him we would like to have him and Lady Bird spend an evening with us at Falls Church. He called me back minutes later.

"If you're free tonight, we would very much like to come to dinner."

I wasn't able to give my wife much notice that the President and Mrs. Johnson would be our guests, along with Judge and Mrs. Homer Thornberry, but the evening was one I will never forget. Both LBJ and his wife have a casual, unpretentious social manner that put my family totally at ease—despite the cordon of Secret Service agents outside the door.

Ceramics were my wife's hobby and she had made all the dishware on the table, including the demitasse cups.

The President took the first sip of his coffee and said, "You know, that is the first coffee cup I've ever had that didn't burn my lips."

"Then you must take it home as a present from us," my wife answered.

LBJ did and for weeks afterward he would comment to me that he drank from it every morning. Later that year, after I had left the White House, he met my wife again when he and I were campaigning together in California.

"I still have that cup," he told her, "and I'm still using it."

I discovered early in my relationship with President Johnson that he, like JFK, was not at all averse to personal diplomacy. One of my closest friends among the overseas Press Secretaries was Fabian Velarde, on the staff of President Roberto Chiari of Panama. Velarde telephoned me late in 1964, at the height of the student rioting against the U.S. in the Canal Zone, and said it was urgent that Presidents Johnson and Chiari discuss the Panama question personally. But there were diplomatic reasons, he said, why neither head of state should initiate a telephone call.

Velarde suggested to me that I be in President Johnson's office at a certain time and that he (Velarde) would call me from President Chiari's office. We would then hand the phones over to our principals. LBJ had no objection to the idea and it was carried out. It was in this conversation that President Johnson told the Panamanian leader that he understood the Latin nation's grievances and would be willing to renegotiate the canal treaty, but not at gunpoint. As soon as Chiari could restore order and put an end to the destruction of U.S. property, LBJ would be willing to talk. This brief conversation was the basis for the eventual settlement of the Panama dispute.

There was also another brief, but astounding, contact with the Russians.

One day, shortly after the death of President Kennedy, I received a call from a high official of the Soviet Embassy in Washington. It was urgent, he said, that we have lunch that day.

When we sat down at the table, he came right to the point.

"The Chairman [Khrushchev] has asked me to see you. He knows you and he trusts you, and he would like your estimate of the new President of the United States."

I was amazed by the audacity of the request! But I think I successfully masked my amazement as I told the Russian that I had every confidence that President Johnson was as interested in peace and good relations with the Soviet Union as President Kennedy had been.

The Russian thanked me profusely for this information and the luncheon went on to other subjects including a report of how Chairman Khrushchev had broken down and wept when he heard of the death of President Kennedy. "He just wandered around his office for several days, like he was in a daze," he told me.

One of the first trips I took with the new President was to the LBJ Ranch shortly before Christmas in 1963 when he was host to German Chancellor Ludwig Erhard. He took a dim view of my dude, city clothes and had his tailor come over from San Antonio to fit me for a Western outfit. But he was highly disappointed when the tailor delivered the clothes directly to me.

"I wanted to give them to you myself," he said.

When we were planning the trip to Texas, the President arranged special accommodations for me at the Driskill Hotel in Austin, which was headquarters for the press when LBJ was at his ranch.

I arrived to find a completely redecorated suite, including new carpets, new paint, new furniture, a television set, and a bountifully stocked liquor cabinet. As if this weren't enough, he also gave me a key to his own suite at the Driskill.

"If you ever want to get away from it all," he said, "just run upstairs and use my place." Later he told me: "When a man works for me, he's a member of my family."

We had a family lunch at the ranch every day, with the staff joining the President and his family at the same table. The President or Bill Moyers would say grace before we ate.

One of the events in honor of Chancellor Erhard was a barbecue in the gym of Stonewall High School, after which Texas-born pianist Van Cliburn entertained the crowd of six hundred with a number of extremely difficult works by Chopin.

When the applause died down, I heard the voice of the President boom over the PA system:

"Now, would Mr. Salinger please go to the piano?"

*Me follow Van Cliburn?*

With the same lump I had in my throat when JFK had me perform for Igor Stravinsky, I made my way to the baby grand and ran through the "No-name Sonata." This is a work of my own composition that I hold in reserve for such occasions because no other pianist in the world can play it, and an evaluation of my performance is clearly impossible.

When it was over, Erhard, who was no music critic, shook my hand enthusiastically. Then LBJ went back to the mike.

"I don't have to tell you," he said, "that Mr. Salinger was John F. Kennedy's Press Secretary . . . and I don't know what I would have done without him, night and day, over this past month."

It was a strange, almost incongruous, thing for him to do in the presence of a visiting head of state at a barbecue in Texas. But it was typical of the generous, if surprising, gestures toward me that he was capable of then and later.

I spent much more time with President Johnson at the White House than I had with JFK. I swam with him twice a day in the White House pool and our conversations were not only wide-ranging but extremely candid. President Johnson had the greatest admiration and respect for President and Mrs. Kennedy. He got highly emotional on occasion as he described their many kindnesses to him. "She always made me feel at home," he said. In fact, at one of these pool conversations, he talked seriously with me for more than an hour of his desire to name Mrs. Kennedy as an ambassador to a foreign country. Among the countries he had in mind were France and Mexico. While acknowledging the fact that Mrs. Kennedy would have been unbeatable as an ambassador, I told the President that I was sure Mrs. Kennedy would not accept such an offer and further that I thought he would be making an error in suggesting it. (To my knowledge, he never did.) His admiration for President Kennedy, however, did not extend to Attorney General Robert Kennedy who, he was convinced, attempted to sabotage his nomination for the vice-presidency in 1960. So vehement were his feelings on this matter that at one session I told him my understanding of the vice-presidential nomination as outlined earlier in this book. It was my feeling that the whole vice-presidential hassle was the result of a fatal misunderstanding, but I do not believe President Johnson was much persuaded by my story. He told me how Speaker Sam Rayburn and Senator Robert Kerr had insisted that he refuse the nomination, saying he would be "ruined" by running on the same ticket with "that Catholic." And he added that he finally convinced Rayburn and Kerr by pointing out to them what he and they considered the greater danger of Richard Nixon being elected President.

LBJ had always had fairly effective relations with the press and came into the White House with his own conceptions of how to portray his administration in the best possible light. But he did seek and take my advice on many aspects of his public relations, including a press conference format.

It was my feeling that he should experiment until he found the setting in which he felt most comfortable. JFK had chosen the mass press conference, open to live TV and radio, because he was convinced that he must go directly to the people to sell the innovations of the New Frontier. Also, he had great confidence in this format after his success against Richard Nixon in the debates.

Although I had no doubt of LBJ's ability to conduct himself admirably in this atmosphere, I was convinced that the same pressures did not apply. He could expect greater support from the Congress than JFK, not only because partisanship would not be as virulent during the presidential transition, but because of his own great skill in working with Congress.

We agreed that he should try a number of press conference formats, including live TV, but should start off in a more informal way. The first, held on December 7, 1963, was entirely impromptu. At the end of my own press briefing that morning, I announced that the President was in his office and would like to have the reporters in for a cup of coffee. The Q and A took place in an atmosphere reminiscent of Franklin D. Roosevelt's meetings with the press. There were only twenty or thirty reporters present—all White House regulars who were flattered by this special attention. There were howls, of course, from radio and TV, who didn't learn of it in time to set up their equipment, and from other reporters who were not at the White House that morning. But the conference was highly productive of news and LBJ was delighted with the coverage.

He was now eager to try his hand at live TV, but agreed with me that the setting should not be identical to JFK's in the new State Department auditorium. I chose the International Conference Room at State, where Secretary Rusk held his press conferences. It had four hundred seats against eight hundred in the main auditorium. But there was no reduction in capacity because we had always cut the larger auditorium in half with partitions. The only other change was that LBJ sat behind a desk while JFK had preferred to stand at a rostrum. This conference, held on February 29, 1964, was also extremely successful.

A third recommendation I made was that President Johnson go on television for an hour with leading network reporters in much the same way that President Kennedy had done in December 1962. I felt that such a program would help to establish the presidential image solidly around the nation. The President was much against this idea at the beginning, but after several weeks of persuasion, he finally agreed to the show. It went off on March 15, 1964, and was extremely well received. President Johnson's thoughtful responses to the questions did a great deal to underline the fact that he had the reins of government firmly in hand.

I feel on the basis of my service with Presidents Kennedy and Johnson that the press conference could be made an even more effective medium of public information than it has ever been in the past. Our Presidents and their Press Secretaries should, for example, consider an occasional one-subject press conference. All of the questions would deal with one specific area of overriding importance. Vietnam and fiscal policy would currently lend themselves to such in-depth questioning.

I believe, too, that press conferences could be split between written and oral questions. A reporter's purpose at a press conference is to elicit information from the President, not to catch him off-guard. The President could open the conference with four or five written questions on important matters which had been submitted in advance—questions he *wants* to answer because he believes it is important that the people have a greater knowledge of his position and intentions on a certain issue. This format would not rule out the tough or sensitive question, however. The reporter whose written question was not accepted by the President could ask it of him during the oral period.

I also think our Presidents should meet at least once a year with the editors of leading college newspapers. Our campuses are, very often, the most active centers of social and political unrest, and I believe students have the right to go directly to the President to ask for his views on matters of greatest concern to them. The President would, of course, have to field a lot of hot questions, but the improvement in communications with the younger generation would be worth it.

Like JFK, President Johnson had personal favorites in the press corps, among them Phil Potter of the Baltimore *Sun* and columnists William S. White and Max Freedman. Potter and White were long-time friends and Freedman had written speeches for him when he was Vice-President. But LBJ was highly accessible to all other White House correspondents. In fact, the only reporter for whom I tried to arrange an interview and was given a flat "no" was Theodore H. White.

Teddy, the author of *The Making of the President 1960* and its sequel in 1964, is one of the most brilliant political writers of our generation. He called me early in 1964 and said he was already at work on the new book and would like to spend an hour with LBJ, as he had with JFK four years earlier. I told him I was confident I could arrange it.

I was amazed, however, when the President said White had "done a job on me" in the 1960 book and he would have nothing to do with the sequel. I argued that even if his anger toward White was justified—and I did not feel it was—his best guarantee of objective treatment in the new book would be to answer White's questions. But he was adamant and White wrote *The Making of the President 1964* without once interviewing its principal character.

In general, however, President Johnson had excellent press relations his first weeks in office. The correspondents, of course, were not unaware of the national interest and tried to play a constructive role in restoring stability in Washington after the nightmare of Dallas. But no President's honeymoon with the press has ever lasted very long and LBJ's came to an end, too. Misunderstandings and resentments broke out on both sides. The President, accustomed to highly sympathetic treatment by the press in the weeks after the assassination, was incensed by the increasing frequency of tough questions at his press conferences and hostile editorials and columns. If the press had voluntarily become a partner of government in restoring national unity after Dallas, it was now clearly returning to its normal role.

In common with JFK, President Johnson would blow sky high over news leaks from the White House, particularly those involving presidential appointments. But he went further than President Kennedy in expressing his anger. A few of these hapless choices didn't get their appointments because of the premature announcements.

Gradually, the President became more secretive with the correspondents. And, because I was his direct contact with them, I began to get less information. I had always been able to enter his office at will, if he had no visitors, but one day his secretary said I would have to arrange an appointment in the future. This didn't offend me. I had always had to clear with Ken O'Donnell before calling on JFK and, until then, I had been the only member of LBJ's staff who had the run of his office.

A further source of friction between LBJ and the press corps was his frequent unwillingness to reveal his travel plans in advance. Once he notified me only ten minutes before climbing on a jet to spend the weekend in Texas. There are tremendous logistical problems in transporting fifty or sixty reporters and their luggage on such fast notice, and in this case, the follow-up press plane did not reach Texas until five hours after the President. This did little to improve an already worsening state of affairs.

Both Presidents Johnson and Kennedy frequently told me to call reporters to complain of unfair or inaccurate stories. With JFK I knew that in most cases it was just a passing irritation, and I wouldn't follow through. But I couldn't get away with that with LBJ. He not only expected me to make the call but to report back to him on the conversation.

Finally, Jack Valenti and Bill Moyers became concerned over the drift in press relations and met with me a number of times to discuss them. I suggested to Valenti that he might attend my press briefings to acquire a better understanding of the White House regulars and their problems. He did and this led to immediate charges by the press that Valenti was there to report to the President on the line of questioning and my responses. This, of course, was ridiculous. A full transcript of the briefings was always available to LBJ.

Another hassle, this one with the White House photographers, involved the activities of Yoichi R. Okamota, a first-rate photographer on the payroll of the U. S. Information Agency. Okamota had made a number of trips with Lyndon Johnson when he was Vice-President, and LBJ thought his work was outstanding. Early in 1964, the photographer began to spend most of his time around the President's office and the result was the most unusual and comprehensive picture history of the presidency that has ever been assembled—and one that should be published someday.

LBJ was so impressed with some of the pictures that he instructed me to give them to magazines and news services for publication. There was an immediate howl of rage from the regular White House photographers. While they had to admit that Okamota's pictures were highly dramatic, they protested that they were not given the same chance to take such exclusive and candid shots. Although their argument had some validity, it would have been impossible for such revealing pictures to be taken with a whole army of photographers hovering over the President. In any case, Okamota became a *cause célèbre* and the story of "President Johnson's private photographer" was played prominently in the newspapers and magazines. Then, one day, Okamota was gone—back to his old job at the USIA.

For me, all of this had become par for the course after three years in the White House, and had nothing to do with my decision that winter to resign as Press Secretary. I had then, and still have, a great affection and admiration for LBJ and a lasting debt of gratitude for his many kindnesses to me. The fact that it didn't work out for me in the White House after President Kennedy's death was my fault, not President Johnson's. I simply came to the realization that the memory of JFK was too overpowering, and that I wasn't functioning on all cylinders for LBJ.

But I was determined to leave (1) only when it would not inconvenience President Johnson, and (2) only for an occupation that would prove as challenging as my work in the White House had been.

The opportunity came in March of 1964.

# XXIV

## THE FLIGHT OF THE CARPETBAGGER

In August 1963, Democratic Senator Clair Engle of California underwent surgery in Washington for removal of a brain tumor. His response to post-operative therapy for partial paralysis was not encouraging, and President Kennedy was told by sources at Bethesda Naval Hospital that Engle would not be able to run for re-election in 1964.

The news came as a shock to me. The senator and I had been allies in California political wars dating back to the late 1940s, and I was his principal contact with the President on projects relating to our native state. Engle, who had spent fourteen years in the House before his election to the Senate in 1958, was one of the most colorful figures in Washington. A former cowhand from the valley town of Red Bluff in northern California, he had a genius for cutting complex issues—and his adversaries—down to size.

His Republican opponent in 1958 was Governor Goodwin J. Knight, an athletic six-footer who took offense at Engle's imposing billboard photograph. "That picture makes him look like a giant," complained Knight, "and he's just a little squirt."

"Where I come from," the five-foot-six Engle shot back, "they measure a man from the neck up."

The senator was a crusader for public power. Early in his Washington career, one of California's largest private utilities applied for the power-generating rights at a new federal dam on the Trinity River. "They want us to build the store and all they want is the cash register," he told his colleagues in the House and his argument won the day. But he later conceded he was fighting only for a principle. "There's more power in the fireflies on the Potomac than there is in the Trinity."

Engle had been almost certain of re-election and the probability that he would not be able to run was disturbing both to the President's political strategists and to Democratic Party leaders in California. The state, now the most populous in the nation, had not gone Democratic in a presidential year since Harry Truman's surprise victory over Thomas E. Dewey in 1948. JFK had lost it to Richard Nixon by a narrow margin in 1960, and the absence from the ticket of California's only Democratic senator—and a brilliant campaigner—was a discouraging prospect for 1964.

As the weeks went by and the seriousness of Engle's condition became more generally known, three names came to the fore in California as likely candidates to succeed him in the Democratic primary in June 1964 —Attorney General Stanley Mosk, State Controller Alan Cranston, and Congressman James Roosevelt, the oldest son of FDR.

Late in September 1963, the President flew to California to dedicate a dam at Whiskeytown. Governor Pat Brown was with us on *Air Force One*, and JFK told him of his concern that an intra-party fight over the nomination might cost us Engle's seat. The governor glanced at me. "What do you think, Pierre?"

"I think that if you guys don't stop fooling around, I might come out and run myself." The governor laughed.

At this point, I had never thought seriously of running for public office myself. In fact, I had twice declined opportunities to run for Congress from San Francisco. The first was in 1954 when friends tried to persuade me to run against Republican William S. Mailliard (who still holds the seat) and even put $10,000 in the bank to finance me. But I was with the San Francisco *Chronicle* at the time and saw journalism as a more exciting career than politics.

My second chance came in the summer of 1963 when Democratic Congressman John F. Shelley ran successfully for mayor of San Francisco. He came to see President Kennedy after declaring his candidacy and later told the White House press corps that I would be an "excellent candidate" to succeed him in Congress. When the correspondents came to me for a comment, I made a statement that was to haunt me night and day the following year: "My home's in Virginia. There's no way I could run for public office in California."

I had taken myself out of the political arena with an even more Sherman-like statement in the fall of 1962. The congressman from my district in Virginia was Republican Joel T. Broyhill, still one of the most reactionary and irascible legislators in Washington. When I threw a fund-raising party at my home for his Democratic opponent, Gus Johnson, Broyhill predictably accused the Kennedy administration of trying to purge him.

At his press conference later that week, the President was asked to reply to "the rather harsh things Congressman Broyhill had to say about you and your Press Secretary." JFK smiled. "I've never read as much about a congressman . . . and seen less legislative results."

Broyhill let fly with another blast at me, and my friends in the press corps said I could redeem my honor only by running against Broyhill myself the next time around. "You are looking at a fellow," I said, "who will never run for public office."

The sequence of events that was to reverse this decision actually began in the summer of 1963 in a most unlikely locale—Mexico City. I was there on vacation as a guest of President Adolfo Lopez Mateos and as the bearer of a proposal from JFK that the two Presidents confer on American soil the following year. Lopez Mateos readily agreed both to the visit and to my suggestion that it would have greater significance in Southern California, with its huge Mexican-American population, than in Washington.

I promptly began working out the arrangements with Ambassador Justo Sierra, Lopez Mateos' personal representative for press and public affairs. Jim Hagerty had told me when I took over his desk at the White House that "Justo is a great guy. You'll like working with him, as I have." Jim was right. Sierra was never devious in his relations with the American press or with me—a virtue often lacking in overseas press attachés—and we have since become the closest of friends.

Our negotiations came to a halt with the assassination of President Kennedy in November, but Lyndon Johnson told me to revive them late in December. It was finally agreed that the two Presidents would appear at a convocation at the University of California at Los Angeles on February 21, and then fly to Palm Springs for their formal discussions.

I came to California earlier that month to advance the presidential visit and to speak at a dinner honoring Attorney General Mosk for his services to the State of Israel. (At this point, only Cranston had thrown his hat in the ring for the Senate. Mosk and Roosevelt were still watching and waiting.) While we were sitting together at the head table, the Attorney General told me he had read my statement that I was ineligible to run for Shelley's seat in Congress. "You were wrong," he said. "You are eligible for federal office in California."

"Thanks for the information," I said. "I promise never to use it to run against you."

My decision to resign as Press Secretary was firming at that time. I simply had not been able to adjust to President Kennedy's death or to the persistent reminders of him around the White House. One of them was *A Tribute to John F. Kennedy*, a collection of memorials on which I was then collaborating with NBC correspondent Sander Vanocur. The book became a best-seller, with all profits going to the Kennedy Library. Although it was my intention to leave the White House in such a way as to not inconvenience President Johnson, I had given only passing thought to my future. I had had standing offers from a number of corporations to direct their press or government relations, and was leaning in that direction. Mosk's suggestion to me that I might return to California and run for public office was just another, and highly remote, possibility.

I did not consider it seriously until the day of my arrival in Los Angeles for the Johnson-Lopez Mateos "summit"—and only then because of an entirely unpredictable incident. After addressing the student convocation at UCLA, the two presidents went to the office of Chancellor Franklin Murphy in the Student Union Building for a cup of coffee. I left them there to rejoin the massive contingent of traveling press. As I came out the door of the Student Union, a crowd of undergraduates—waiting for a closer glimpse of the two heads of state—broke into applause.

I was taken completely off-guard. But then, and for the first time, it struck me that my service in the White House might prove to be an important political asset. The thought came to me that if I could arouse that spontaneous a reaction among university students, who are—and for good reason—highly suspicious of most politicians, I just might have voter appeal.

That same night in Palm Springs, friends of Attorney General Mosk told me he definitely would not run for the senatorial nomination. And, the very next day, Congressman Roosevelt withdrew after losing to Controller Cranston the pre-primary endorsement of the California Democratic Council (CDC), a statewide volunteer organization. That left only Cranston and Senator Engle officially in the race, and the latter's withdrawal was only a question of time.

I had known Cranston since 1957 when we were co-founders of the CDC. He had won the controller's office the following year in the same Democratic sweep that gave Pat Brown a million-vote victory over Senate Majority Leader William F. Knowland for the governorship. Alan and I had a cordial but not close relationship, and were occasionally on different sides of the political fence.

But the decision forming in my mind to oppose him for the Senate was not the result of past differences. Comparing his background with mine, I honestly felt that I could represent our state more effectively. In my more than three years at the White House, I had had a close working relationship with Senator Engle and with the California congressional delegation. JFK had sought my advice on both political and administrative matters affecting my native state, and I had flown to California many times to keep myself abreast of developments. I felt, too, that my association with Cabinet members and key administration and legislative leaders would give me far greater access to them in behalf of California than Cranston could hope to have. Still another factor was that Cranston was not acceptable to all factions of the California Democratic Party.

I made no move, however, until Mosk formally withdrew. Then, early in March, I sought the advice of Don L. Bradley, a long-time San Francisco friend and the executive secretary of the Democratic State Central Committee.

"If you've ever thought of running for elective office," he said, "you'll never have a better chance."

My next call was to Attorney General Mosk. "I'll be for you all the way," he said.

Jesse Unruh, the powerful speaker of the lower house of the California Legislature and a leader of the anti-Cranston element of the party, told me he was for Engle and would not back away from his commitment. "But if Clair withdraws, I'll be for you. In fact, I may be able to help you a little even if he doesn't."

I then spoke to Congressman Roosevelt (now one of our representatives to the UN) at the home of his brother Mayor Elliott Roosevelt of Palm Beach. He said he would do all he could for me but later went back on his promise and wrote a letter to his constituents urging them to vote for Cranston.

Earl (Squire) Behrens, the crusty political editor of the San Francisco *Chronicle*, was an ardent Republican with whom I had had many partisan arguments when I was also on the *Chronicle* staff. It was his opinion that I could defeat Cranston but he had doubts that I was legally eligible to file for the primary.

My last exploratory call was to a lawyer friend in California, an authority on election law. He agreed to research the question of my eligibility and said he would report back as quickly as possible. Time was running out. The deadline for filing nominating petitions for the primary was March 19—only ten days away.

On March 17, I told Attorney General Bob Kennedy and Ken O'Donnell that I was waiting only for the green light from the lawyer before resigning from the White House. Bob gave me a typical piece of Kennedy advice: "Run only if you can win." Ken thought it was "an interesting idea, but I don't think you've got the guts." That evening, I paid a visit to Jacqueline Kennedy at her Georgetown home. She was enthusiastic. "I know you'll win," she said, "and if there's some quiet way I can help, please let me know." Bob came by later for a drink. He wasn't at all convinced that I had time to put together a winning organization, but "you can count on my help." Five months later, he himself made the decision to run against Republican Senator Kenneth B. Keating of New York.

I was having lunch the next day with Bob Six, the president of Continental Air Lines, and his executive vice-president, Harding Lawrence, at the Sans Souci restaurant in Washington when the call came through from the California lawyer.

"You're entirely eligible to run. There's no question of it. I've got precedents coming out my ears."

16

"All right," I said, "I'm running."

On my way out of the restaurant, I saw Ken O'Donnell having lunch with his wife, Helen. "You said I didn't have the guts," I told Ken. "I just want you to know that I'm on my way to the President's office to resign." He almost fell out of his chair.

When I got back to the White House, President Johnson was hosting a delegation of publishers in the family dining room. I found Walter Jenkins and Bill Moyers together and said I had to see LBJ as quickly as possible—and I also told them why. They were almost as startled as O'Donnell, and Moyers promptly buzzed the President. Many acquaintances of mine, including Larry Fanning now of the Chicago *Daily News*, overheard LBJ's end of the conversation, but he said nothing to tip his luncheon guests that his Press Secretary was standing in the wings waiting to resign.

Moyers said the President would see me as soon as he was free. While waiting, I put in a call to my friend, Supreme Court Justice Arthur J. Goldberg. He was aghast at my decision. "I think you've had bad legal advice," he said. "It doesn't seem possible that a man who votes in Virginia can run for the Senate from California." But a half hour later he called me back. "I've had one of my clerks look into your case," he said, "and it appears you are eligible. But if your case ever comes before the Supreme Court, I'll have to disqualify myself."

The President sent for me at 3:30 P.M.

"You've been wonderful to me," I said, "and my decision is no reflection on you. But this is my chance to return to my own state for something I think is important."

"You don't have to explain it to me," he said. "Remember, I did the same thing myself once. When do you want to announce your resignation?"

"As soon as possible," I replied. "I will have to catch a plane for California tonight." He told me to draft a letter of resignation and said he would write one of his own accepting it.

I went back to my office, postponed what was to be my last press briefing from 4 to 6 P.M., and told the office staff of my plans. They were shaken. Ours had been a happy shop and now their own futures were up in the air. Most of the staff said they would be willing to come out to California and work in my headquarters and two of them—Sue Vogelsinger and Barbara Coleman—eventually did. The only staff member who was not at the White House that day was Andy Hatcher. The operator caught up with him at the Newark Airport.

"Announce my resignation at the same time you announce yours," he said. "I'm going back to California with you."

I gave the President my letter of resignation at 5 P.M. and he handed me his response to it. It's a letter I still treasure:

Dear Pierre:

I accept your resignation—but only with the greatest regret and with a reluctance that bows only to your strong personal desire to return to California.

You have served your country well in the past three years. I greatly appreciate the faithful and competent service you have given me since I became President. Your energy and talents have been indispensable, and they will be sorely missed.

I hate to see you go. I will always be grateful for the help and devotion you have shown me—but above all, for your friendship.

Sincerely,<br>*Lyndon Johnson*

I had given LBJ very little time to consider my successor. "Who do you think it should be," he asked me, "Reedy or Valenti?" I responded that Valenti was extremely able but that Reedy had a stronger news background and was held in high regard by the Washington press. In fact, before joining LBJ's staff in 1951, Reedy had been a Washington correspondent for one of the wire services.

The President then summoned Jenkins and O'Donnell for their opinion and they, too, voted for Reedy. George was then in a Washington hospital, where LBJ had sent him to lose fifty pounds. His stay there, where he was on practically a starvation diet, produced a story typical of his cryptic sense of humor. The President sent Reedy a bouquet of flowers on his fourth or fifth day, and George wired back: THANKS FOR THE FLOWERS. THEY WERE DELICIOUS.

But now LBJ told Jenkins to call Reedy at the hospital. "Tell him to jump into his clothes and get over here. He's the new Press Secretary as of now."

Then the President turned to me. "You know, of course, that I can't get mixed up in a Democratic primary, but there ought to be some way I can give you a hand. What's the filing fee out there in California?"

I said it was $450 but he must have heard $250. He took two hundred-dollar bills and a fifty out of his wallet and said: "Here's your first campaign contribution." I made the fast decision not to tell him he was $200 short.

We shook hands and that was that. I went back to my office where the press was waiting. I said only that I was resigning immediately to return to California, and would have an important decision to announce the following day. But the reporters all drew the obvious conclusion and the news that I would enter the Democratic senatorial primary was on the wires within minutes. The briefing itself was entirely impersonal, but afterwards many of the correspondents came into my office one by one to wish me luck. In the weeks to follow, twelve of them sent me campaign contributions ranging from $25 to $100.

New York *Times* correspondent Tom Wicker was at a Barrry Goldwater press conference in Los Angeles when he was summoned to the telephone by his Washington bureau and told of my resignation. He let out a whoop that was overheard by the senator, who was already campaigning in the California primary.

"What's that all about?" Goldwater asked.

"Pierre Salinger has just resigned and is coming out here to run for the Senate," Wicker replied.

"I think Pierre would make a good senator," Goldwater said. But that was the last boost he gave my candidacy.

It took me only forty-five minutes to clean out my desk and to place my last telephone call from the White House. It was to Governor Pat Brown, who had come out solidly for Cranston after Mosk's withdrawal. The governor was dead set against my entering the primary. He felt that I was coming in too late and that a primary fight would drain off Democratic dollars that could be put to better use in the run-off against the Republican nominee. He felt, too, that the party, after choosing sides in the primary, might not be able to unite fully behind the winner in the general election.

I replied that my decision was in no way a challenge to his leadership. It was my opinion then, and still is, that Brown is the most effective governor in the country. But I told him that Cranston certainly was not the consensus candidate—that I already had firm commitments of support from prominent Democrats, including many of the governor's own supporters. I said, too, that I was convinced that I had better qualifications than Cranston, and that the voters should be given the opportunity to choose between us.

When the governor reminded me of his commitment to Cranston, I said that he should, of course, honor it. "But I hope you will limit your activities to saying that you are for him and intend to vote for him. I don't think your commitment requires you to take an active part in the campaign." He disagreed. "If I'm for somebody, I'm not going to stand on the sidelines. I intend to do whatever I can for Cranston."

My family drove me to Washington's National Airport at ten o'clock that night to board a plane for San Francisco. It was then 7 P.M. in California—only twenty-two hours before I would have to present my nominating petition to the Registrar of Voters at San Francisco City Hall.

The one newspaperman waiting to say goodbye to me at the airport was Zygmunt Broniarek, the White House correspondent for *Trybuna Ludu*, a daily newspaper in Communist Poland.

"You should have come into the office earlier," I said. "You didn't have to come all the way out here."

"No," he said, "that was for your American friends. For me, it is better this way."

I landed in San Francisco at 4 A.M. Waiting for me on that cold and cheerless morning was the smallest delegation ever to welcome a candidate for a major political office—my brother Herbert, then assistant superintendent of schools in Napa, California; Don Bradley, who later agreed to manage my campaign; Melvin C. Tate, the owner of Hanno's Bar, my hangout in the old *Chronicle* days; and an old man who was a total stranger. He had heard that I was flying in and had been waiting since midnight.

"I was for John F. Kennedy and I'm for you," he said. "Here's a good luck piece. If you carry it with you all the time, you can't lose." He then gave me a new Kennedy half dollar. I had it made into a money clip and still carry it.

My brother, Bradley, and I went directly to a room at the Fairmont Hotel on Nob Hill. We then had less than twelve hours to qualify me as a candidate, to prepare for the certain legal test of my eligibility, and to start recruiting publicists, speech writers, advertising specialists, and a statewide Salinger for Senator Committee.

First, I had to round up sixty-five friends to sign my nominating petitions before 5 P.M. that first day. I kept the telephone humming with calls to newspaper friends and old classmates at the University of San Francisco. Among the latter was Rinaldo Carmazzi, a Republican who had to re-register Democratic before he could sign and circulate the petition.

On the legal front, two other friends—Alvin Goldstein and Quentin Kopp—agreed to represent me without fee, and promptly went to work researching precedents to support my eligibility.

The next essential was money. I called five wealthy acquaintances and asked each of them for a $5000 loan. "But I want you to understand," I said, "that not one penny is refundable if the court rules me off the track."

Walter Leftwich, a Los Angeles advertising and public relations man, flew to San Francisco early the first day to take over the media operation.

Within ten hours of my arrival, I had the sixty-five signatures for my nominating petition, $25,000 in the bank, and an order with an outdoor advertising company to print and post 7000 Salinger for Senator posters within the next forty-eight hours. That same day, we put together the nucleus of my campaign organization and began accepting speaking engagements. The first was three days later before a teachers' convention in Fresno. My brother wrote the draft of my first speech.

Our blitz took the Cranston forces by surprise. They, of course, had not foreseen major opposition in the primary and were still chugging along in low gear. Because of the speed and effectiveness with which we got our own operation rolling, they were convinced that my supporters had been secretly at work for weeks, plotting strategy, designing campaign materials, raising money, and recruiting a high-level professional staff.

Just one man, Bradley, was responsible for this impression. He had been Governor Brown's manager in his winning campaign against two Republican giants—William Knowland and Richard Nixon—and I put myself completely in his hands. He had to make most of the critical first decisions off the top of his head and in an environment that could not have been more hectic.

Through the first week, our only base of operations was the one room in the Fairmont. The sign on the door read SALLINGER H.Q.—a clue to the confusion that was to be found within. The room was jammed constantly with reporters, photographers, and well-wishers. The telephones never stopped ringing. The floor was a litter of newspapers. And every level surface was covered with coffeepots and the remnants of steak sandwiches and French fries. I would occasionally stagger to the bed to try to catch a five-minute nap, only to be jostled awake to give sleepy approval to a press release or to the appointment of a county chairman.

I was aroused from one such nap by an attractive blonde who was sitting next to me on the bed. She was wearing a red, white, and blue straw hat on which was printed SWEETHEARTS FOR SALINGER.

"I'm for you, Pierre," she murmured.

I mumbled something about being a married man and went back to sleep.

After Bradley, the man most responsible for launching my campaign with a splash was a Republican—Secretary of State Frank M. Jordan. Although the San Francisco Registrar of Voters took my nominating petition without question, Jordan refused to place my name on the ballot on the grounds that I had not been a member of the California Democratic Party for ninety days and therefore was not qualified to enter the primary.

I was clearly eligible under the U. S. Constitution, which requires only that a candidate for the Senate be an American citizen, at least thirty-five years of age, and an inhabitant of the state at the time of his election. The legal point at issue was whether a state could impose additional qualifications—in this case, the ninety-day party membership requirement.

Attorneys Goldstein and Kopp immediately went to the State Supreme Court for a writ of mandamus to force Jordan to accept my nominating petition. The crux of their argument was that the Democratic party is a national, not a state, party. And they were able to produce photostats of my party records from Virginia to prove that I had been a Democrat for far longer than ninety days.

While the lawyers argued, the reporters had a field day. The story was in banner headlines in all the metropolitan California newspapers and the lead story on radio and TV newscasts. Cranston was not a direct litigant in the suit, but supporters of his did prepare an amicus curiae brief supporting Jordan. The immediate reaction among many Democrats was that my opponent was trying to win in court a verdict he was afraid he could not win at the polls. This not only hurt Cranston but cast me in the role of the underdog.

But the publicity of my eleventh hour flight to California, and the challenge to my qualifications, had one important disadvantage. It dramatized what had to be Cranston's principal issue—that I was a carpetbagger, a Pierre-come-lately who had been away from California too long to understand its problems. To overcome this argument, it was necessary that I demonstrate a knowledge of California that was at least equal to Cranston's. And there was only one way I could do that—in a direct confrontation with him on statewide television. I began challenging him to a debate that first week and kept after him until he finally agreed.

On the eighth day, the Supreme Court ruled that I had complied "substantially" with the law and instructed Jordan to put my name on the ballot. The headlines, SALINGER WINS!, were prophetic of the eventual outcome. But Jordan wasn't through with me. He later refused to place the designation "Presidential Press Secretary" under my name on the ballot, claiming that I no longer held that position. It was sheer pique on his part but we didn't haul him back into court. One of the reasons was a public opinion poll taken the week after the Supreme Court decision, showing that 85 percent of the voters could identify my former occupation, and that only 35 percent knew who Cranston was. The same poll had me defeating him by a landslide margin of 16 percent of the vote, thanks, in part, to Jordan's challenge of my eligibility.

Cranston and I were never far apart on the basic issues. We were both supporters of the Kennedy-Johnson line on domestic policy, although I was more willing than he to criticize our actions abroad. I took issue, for example, with our recognition of a military coup d'état in Brazil, because it was an obvious encouragement to reactionary forces in other volatile Latin American countries to take up arms against democratic regimes. Cranston promptly accused me of shooting from the hip at President Johnson—a charge that brought angry mutterings from his progressive supporters in the California Democratic Council.

But his principal theme continued to be that I was a carpetbagger. Despite the Supreme Court ruling in my favor, he also reminded the voters ten times a day of my own inaccurate statement in Washington that my status as a voter in Virginia disqualified me from holding public office in California. A Salinger victory, he said, would give Virginia three senators and California only one.

Now I will admit to a strain of carpetbagger blood. My maternal grandfather, Pierre Bietry, was a member of the French Chamber of Deputies from 1906 to 1910, representing the district of Brest on the west coast. But his home was in the Territory of Belfort, only five miles from the Swiss border and as far away from Brest as one could live and still be in France. It was all perfectly legal. In France, a legislator does not have to be a resident of the district he represents.

In my case, however, I felt that Cranston was off base. I was born in California, as were my three children (and now my fourth). I was educated there, worked there, and had been active in the state's politics longer than my opponent. It was true that I had been in Washington for more than six years. But if I was a carpetbagger, the same charge could be made against Adlai Stevenson, who left the State Department to run for governor of Illinois, or Franklin Delano Roosevelt, who was an Under Secretary of the Navy before returning to New York to win its governorship.

My only direct conflict with Governor Brown was on the carpetbagger issue. He told a labor audience in Los Angeles that I was a "political rookie" who had no qualifications for returning to California to seek its highest federal office. I replied that he hadn't always thought of me as a "political rookie," and had been only too willing to use my services in his unsuccessful race against Estes Kefauver in the California presidential primary of 1952. But the governor was a good sport and after my victory over Cranston described me as "the rookie of the year."

Cranston had every right, of course, to exploit the charge that I had been away from California too long. But certain of his more zealous supporters went a step further by accusing me of misrepresenting both my relationship to John F. Kennedy and the importance of my duties at the White House. Mrs. Kennedy, who had been following the campaign closely in the Washington newspapers, was offended by the charge that I did not have JFK's confidence and was nothing more than a press agent. She set the record straight in an interview with Robert Thompson, a White House correspondent for the Los Angeles *Times*. Her statements were reprinted widely throughout the state, and the slander against me was not repeated.

But there was no question that the carpetbagger issue was hurting me. In every public opinion survey taken for me by Don Muchmore—the most accurate political pollster in the country—Cranston was gaining ground. I began to intensify my efforts to lure him into a TV debate in which I could match my knowledge of California problems against his in a direct confrontation. He finally agreed and we met in mid-May at NBC affiliate KOGO in San Diego. KOGO made the debate available to all other TV stations in California, and we drew a tremendous audience.

The moderator was Howard K. Smith, who also refereed the Kennedy-Nixon debates in 1960. I will confess now that the encounter produced more heat than light. One of my angles of attack against Cranston had been his solicitation of campaign contributions from the state's inheritance tax appraisers, who held their lucrative positions at his pleasure. Actually, he had made no greater political use of his appointees than his Republican predecessors. It was the system that was wrong, and Cranston later undertook major reforms on his own initiative. But the panel of reporters directing alternate questions to us was more concerned with developing the carpetbagger and tax appraiser issues than our respective stands on national and international affairs. Smith was obviously impatient with this provincial line of questioning and had little success in diverting the dialogue to more significant areas. When the debate did turn on state, national, and international affairs, I more than held my own. After that, much of the credibility was taken out of the carpetbagger attack.

But the major turning point came when Senator Engle—who had never left Washington—finally withdrew for reasons of health, without endorsing either Cranston or me. My opponent and I were now nip and tuck in the polls, and it was clear that the division of the Engle vote would decide the election. Until this time, I had not once approached either the senator or his gallant wife, Lucretia, for a commitment of support in the event of his withdrawal. But a day or two after his announcement, the late columnist George Dixon and his wife, Ymelda, daughter of Senator Dennis Chavez, spoke to Mrs. Engle on my behalf. Still another emissary was Jerry Waldie, one of my strongest backers and the Democratic majority leader of the California Assembly. Their arguments in my behalf were persuasive. Mrs. Engle went before the TV cameras and said that I was her choice to succeed her husband.

Two days before the election, pollster Muchmore told me I would win by between 150,000 and 200,000 votes. My final margin on June 2, 1964, was 174,000.

The Republican I would face in the November runoff was actor George Murphy, who won his party's nomination in a breeze from industrialist Leland Kaiser. But because of the 3 to 2 edge in Democratic voters in California, only two of the state's political observers gave him a chance to win. One was Murphy himself. The other was me.

# XXV

## CENTRAL CASTING WINS

When George Murphy won the Republican senatorial nomination, he was best known as the song-and-dance man who always lost the girl to his best friend in the late, late movies on television. He had not been active as a performer on the stage or screen for years, nor had he taken a leading role in Republican affairs. His political philosophy was a mystery, even to most members of his own party.

There were at least two significant clues, however. Most of his Hollywood intimates and financial backers were ardent Goldwaterites, and Murphy himself had been active for a time in Dr. Fred Schwarz's Christian Anti-Communism Crusade (Impeach Earl Warren, Get the US out of the UN). But in his listless primary against Leland Kaiser, Murphy was able to conceal his conservative associations and to dodge all direct questions on the vital issues with charming reminiscences of the old days in Hollywood.

I found myself facing a political neuter in the runoff—a candidate who was adept at expressing the concern that most Americans felt over civil rights or Vietnam, but who had no clear-cut opinions of his own on how we should deal with such questions.

My own advisers were convinced that Murphy could not win with such evasive tactics in the general election. With his friend and co-ideologist Barry Goldwater the almost certain Republican nominee for President, he would have no honorable choice but to speak out both for Goldwater and for their mutually held political convictions. Even in June, many weeks before the national conventions, the polls had President Lyndon B. Johnson a runaway victor over Goldwater in California, and my strategists were certain that Murphy would be buried in the landslide.

But I was dubious. Murphy, who had been careful to disassociate himself from Goldwater all through the primary, was reading the same polls. Principle to the contrary, why link himself now with a loser? And why reveal his own conservative convictions if his audiences were willing to settle for a smile and a handshake?

Another reason I never sold Murphy short was that he had come out of his own primary with no visible scars. The split between moderate and conservative Republicans over Goldwater did not affect him at all. He had taken no position that could offend either faction, and he was equally acceptable to conservative Democrats in a state that has a long history of voting for the man, not the party.

But my candidacy had left much ill feeling in Democratic ranks, particularly among the leaders of the liberal California Democratic Council, the largest precinct force in America. Alan Cranston, CDC's founding president, had been their candidate and his defeat had cost the organization much prestige. Although both Governor Pat Brown and Controller Cranston had given me their prompt endorsements after the primary, many in CDC were unwilling to forgive and forget. It wasn't likely that such Democrats would vote for Murphy, but they certainly weren't going to ring doorbells for me. Instead, they would concentrate their energies in the presidential race and in local contests for the State Legislature and the House of Representatives.

My activity on primary Election Day, when I was already certain of victory over Cranston, indicates that I had no such confidence in the coming race against Murphy. At five o'clock that morning, I was at a Los Angeles plant gate to ask the workers to support me against Cranston. I made eight additional appearances that day at rallies and shopping centers, and walked a precinct to get out the vote. I held a staff conference late that afternoon and went to my Los Angeles headquarters to hear the first returns. When the trend was apparent, I flew to a victory celebration in San Francisco. Two hours later, I was on a plane back to Los Angeles and at five the next morning was back at the same plant gate to thank the workers for their votes and to ask them to support me against Murphy.

It was my intention to run that hard and fast right up until Election Day in November. My only "vacation" was to be a three-week world tour for *Look* magazine, in which I was to write a series of articles describing overseas reaction to American foreign policy. I went first to Tokyo to interview Premier Hayato Ikeda, then to Manila for conversations with President Diosdado Macapagal and elder statesman Carlos P. Romulo. On August 3, I was in the office of Premier Nguyen Khanh in Saigon when a call came through for me from Washington. Senator Clair Engle was dead.

*Look* agreed to a brief interruption of the tour to enable me to attend Engle's funeral in Red Bluff. After the rites, I flew to the state capital in Sacramento with Governor Brown. He told me it was his intention to appoint me immediately as Engle's successor. There was a brief debate among my advisers over whether I should accept. Some were convinced that Murphy would promptly challenge my eligibility (which he did), thus reviving the carpetbagger issue. They felt, too, that Murphy would gain valuable ground at home while I was in Washington, and that my brief incumbency in the Senate would be of no material advantage. Their position had a certain validity, but the counterarguments were more persuasive. If the governor did not appoint me, it would suggest that he, too, questioned my eligibility to serve. It might also appear that his endorsement of me after the battle with Cranston was not exactly sincere.

But apart from such considerations, I was the obvious appointee. Engle was a Democrat and California's Democratic voters had chosen me as their nominee to succeed him. Further, my appointment would give me important seniority in committee assignments over new senators who would not take office until after the fall elections.

I told the governor I would accept and left California with him and more than one hundred prominent Democrats on a special charter flight at midnight, August 4. I went before the Senate the next day, after a sleepless night, to take the oath of office.

But a number of Republican senators, led by the redoubtable Everett M. Dirksen, challenged from the floor my legal right to take Engle's seat. Their objections were largely a re-hash of points raised before the California Supreme Court (and decided in my favor) more than three months earlier. They did, however, serve their obvious purpose—to assist Murphy by casting doubt on my qualifications and by resurrecting the carpetbagger image. The one Republican who spoke in my favor was Tom Kuchel of California. "My state is entitled to two senators, not one.") It took great courage for Kuchel to oppose his fellow Republicans, particularly in his position as minority whip. Finally, after more than two hours of debate, the Senate voted to seat me conditionally until a hearing could be held before the Senate Rules Committee (which voted the following week to seat me permanently). It was typical of Dirksen that after speaking at great length, and with much passion, against me, he was the first to shake my hand after I took the oath from Senator Carl Hayden of Arizona.

I was to serve in the Senate only 148 days. But in that time I was able to push through an amendment to the Social Security Act that would have meant $6,000,000 in additional benefits to elderly citizens of California had it not died in a Senate-House conference committee. I was a co-author with Kuchel of a regional water plan for the Pacific Southwest that is still a sound basis of negotiation for the long-standing dispute between California and Arizona over the division of the waters of the Colorado River. I was able to express my own great respect for Senator Engle by introducing legislation through which Trinity Dam in northern California is now known as Engle Dam. And, with White House approval, I answered in my first Senate speech the entirely baseless charge by Senator

Goldwater that John F. Kennedy had deliberately provoked the Cuban missile crisis to influence the fall elections in 1962. I also fell heir to one of the traditional duties of freshman senators—that of presiding when a quorum is not present. One night I spent more than two hours alone with Wayne Morse in the chamber while the Oregon senator read a hundred or more letters from constituents protesting our policy in Vietnam.

One afternoon, my youngest son, Stephen, was in the gallery to observe my performance in the chair. Later, while we were riding the Senate subway back to my office, (and in the presence of other senators) he said: "Gee, Dad, you've only been in the Senate a week and you're already running the joint!"

My duties in the Senate kept me hopping. In addition to quorum calls, committee hearings, and party caucuses, there was a mountain of mail to answer, a constant stream of visitors through my office, articles to be written for *Look* and other publications, and almost daily consultations with Senator Kuchel on legislation affecting California. Not once did he ever place partisan considerations above the state's interests, and my first weeks in the Senate would have been far more difficult without his counsel and friendship.

Even in the midst of this intense activity in Washington, I could not afford to ignore the contest with Murphy and tried to fly home at least once a week to honor commitments for appearances I had made before becoming senator. I would usually leave Washington on the last plane Friday night, and show up at my first appointment in California the next morning after little or no rest, and stay on the move until midnight Sunday, when I would catch the "red-eye special" back to Washington and arrive at my office Monday morning sleepless and haggard.

The Democratic National Convention in Atlantic City the last week in August was a welcome interruption of this killing routine. I could not be a delegate to the convention because I was not yet a qualified voter in California. But, at the request of President Johnson and Hubert H. Humphrey, it was my privilege to second the latter's nomination for Vice-President.

Under Humphrey's leadership, I was also active in working out the eventual compromise over seating the Mississippi Freedom Delegation. I argued in the California caucus against credentialing the full delegation on grounds it would provoke a mass walkout of white southern delegations. But I am still convinced that the compromise, calling for token seating of Negro delegates from Mississippi and an amendment to convention by-laws prohibiting all future delegate discrimination because of color, was the most significant victory that could be won.

I was not on the convention floor the night *A Thousand Days* was shown. Ken O'Donnell, Larry O'Brien, and I were going to watch the documentary film story of JFK's presidency on television in Ken's motel room. But Bob Kennedy's moving introduction left me in tears. I left the motel and was alone on the boardwalk when the picture was shown to the delegates and to an audience of millions on nation-wide TV.

With the adjournment of Congress on October 3, I flew back to California for the main event with George Murphy. The first poll taken after the primary had me defeating him by 16 percent of the vote. But he had cut that margin to 11 percent during the many weeks I had been in Washington. With only a weekend rival in the field, he had been able to soft-shoe around the issues, just as he had in the primary. Although no one knew exactly how he would vote on most national and international questions likely to come before the Senate, everyone found him attractive and affable.

Murphy's strategy was as transparent as it was effective. Certain of polling almost all of the Republican vote, he now must woo the one out of five Democrats he would need to win. And to accomplish that, he must detach himself absolutely from his own running mate.

Murphy did exactly that. He would not appear on the same platform with Goldwater and would disown certain of the Arizona senator's more inflammatory positions (although Murphy's own voting record in the Senate over the past two years has been equally conservative).

But I will have to admit that Murphy was too much for me. I found it impossible to lay a glove on a man who was for a more aggressive policy in Vietnam but against escalation of the war; who was for civil rights but against civil rights demonstrations, and who was for full employment of domestic farm workers but against a reduction in the importation of competing Mexican braceros. I can recall only two issues on which he took an unequivocal position—he was for desalinizing the Pacific and de-Salingerizing the Senate.

Yet his tactics were paying off. Each new poll had him closing the gap and I could find no way to stop him. But despite the increasing indications that I would lose, the campaign was not without its lighter moments.

At a reception for my Japanese-American Committee, I discovered that there are certain advantages to being five-foot-nine when your opponent is over six feet.

A Nisei gentleman shook my hand and said: "I didn't know who I was going to vote for until tonight. But now that I've seen you in person I'm for you 100 percent."

"That's wonderful."

"Don't you want to know why?" he persisted.

"Why?"

"Because you're our size."

An elderly woman came up to me at a rally in a supermarket parking lot one day and said she was going to vote for me "because I'm a taxpayer and I don't believe in wasting tax dollars."

"I'm glad you agree with my fiscal policies," I said.

"Your policies have nothing to do with it," she replied. "If Murphy's elected, we'll have to pay to move him and his whole family back to Washington. But you've already got a home there."

One of the most enjoyable of my campaign activities was the whistle-stop train tour through small communities. Hollywood celebrities often came along to entertain the crowds before I spoke.

But on one such tour through Orange County in Southern California —a stronghold of the John Birch Society—the audiences were hostile. Eggs and tomatoes were thrown at the train and placards were jabbed in the faces of the stars. Dick Van Dyke tried to calm the crowd down, but with no success. Angie Dickinson also faced the mob bravely for a time before retreating. But when massive Dan Blocker, "Hoss" in the *Bonanza* TV series, took over the microphone and told the rowdies to behave themselves, there was sudden and respectful silence.

Looking back on it now, my defeat was the result of many adverse factors, large and small. In the view of my strategists, one of them was television. California is the largest state in the nation in population and the third largest, after Alaska and Texas, in size. A candidate cannot hope to meet or speak personally to more than 2 or 3 percent of the state's more than 19,000,000 citizens and must rely on TV to project both his personality and his policies. There was general agreement that Murphy, with his many years of experience before the cameras, had the actor's advantage.

Our only face-to-face confrontation on television was in a statewide debate on the CBS network. It is not the best strategy, of course, for an incumbent to debate his opponent, but I felt I had no choice after pushing Cranston as hard as I had for a debate in the primary.

The one-hour direct confrontation with Murphy was just as frustrating as our long-range exchanges had been. I was never able to develop our differences on the issues. When it was all over, a studio technician told me: "You won the debate, Pierre, but George won the Oscar—and that's what counts on TV." His comment probably sums up the over-all impression voters had of us on television—an impression that was not to my advantage.

Many of my friends believe that Bob Kennedy's decision to run for the Senate in New York was a major reason for my defeat. I don't. Although it did keep the carpetbagger stew boiling, Murphy would have had it on the front burner with or without Bob's candidacy. My opponent's last week emphasis in full-page newspaper ads and in radio and TV spots was devastating: "Why vote for a man who can't vote for himself?"

There can also be no question that many conservative Democrats who found me preferable to Cranston in the primary because of his endorsement by the liberal CDC found Murphy closer than I to their philosophy in the runoff.

But I think now that perhaps the main factor in my defeat was Proposition 14—an issue on which I took an unpopular position and Murphy took no position at all.

Proposition 14 was an initiative on the fall ballot to amend the state constitution. Its effect was to nullify California's fair housing law by denying to all levels of government the right ever to legislate against a property owner's right to sell or rent to persons of his own choice. Or, to put it more directly, to give constitutional sanction to racial discrimination in California housing.

No other state—not even Georgia, Alabama, or Mississippi—had such a shameful clause in its constitution, and I felt that no candidate for public office could ignore its implications. But I was wrong. True to form, Murphy was neither for nor against Proposition 14—publicly, at least—although his off-guard statements left no doubt that he would vote for it. His "position" was that he had no obligation as a candidate for federal office to "influence the outcome of a state issue." This, of course, was ridiculous. Fair housing went to the very heart of civil rights, which was the most important national question in the 1964 elections.

Proposition 14 was a highly emotional issue. The California Real Estate Association spent a fortune to propagandize white property owners with the fear that fair housing would destroy property values. The White Citizens Council and the American Nazi Party took the even shriller line that freeing the Negro from his ghetto would turn white suburbia into a black belt of crime and violence.

It was apparent from the very outset that Proposition 14 would pass by a huge majority, and my own advisers told me I was being quixotic in speaking against it in every TV interview and public appearance.

Politically, it was unwise. Nothing I could do was likely to change the outcome. But morally I had no choice—not after sweating out Birmingham and Oxford with John F. Kennedy.

Ten days before the election, pollster Don Muchmore told me Murphy was ahead and that I was a certain loser unless I could capture almost all of the vote that was still up for grabs. But there wasn't much chance of that. The 5 percent of the voters who had not yet chosen between Murphy and me were 4 to 1 in favor of Proposition 14.

After that, I went through the motions, trying to appear happy and confident, but I knew I was dead.

I finally lost to Murphy by 216,643 votes while President Johnson was defeating Goldwater in California by 1,292,769. Proposition 14 carried by 2,130,713. It is impossible, of course, to weigh precisely the many elements of my defeat. But if only one in ten of those 2,130,713 Californians were against me because of my position on Proposition 14, that was the difference.

(In a poll taken the week before the election, the ticket-splitters—those who were voting for Democrat Johnson and Republican Murphy—were 9 to 1 in favor of Proposition 14.)

But it's long past the time for post-mortems. I'll settle for what a victorious Bob Kennedy said to me on the telephone from New York late on election night:

"My brother would have been proud of the way you lost."

The TV and radio coverage of the 1964 national elections raises what I believe to be a grave threat to the democratic process—the electronic forecasting of vote results. On the basis of first returns on the East Coast, the network computers had President Johnson a landslide winner when there was still an hour left to vote in the Midwest, two hours in the mountain states and three hours in California. In my own state, with the outcome of the national election already certain, 300,000 voters didn't bother to go to the polls.

This could not have made a difference in my own contest with Murphy. But it could have been the deciding factor in many close races for state and federal offices across the country.

I seriously question that the right to cover an election also includes the right to discourage voting by declaring that your vote or mine can't influence the outcome. Because of the bitter competitiveness among the news departments of the three major networks, it is unlikely that they would agree to voluntary restraints. The answer is to be found in a reorganization of our entire voting process.

I believe the states should agree to keep the polls open twenty-four hours a day, and close them at exactly the same time. For instance, voting would start on a Monday at 11 P.M. on the Eastern seaboard and end at 11 P.M. the following night. The polls in the Central Time zone would be open from 10 P.M. to 10 P.M., Mountain Standard Time from 9 P.M. to 9 P.M., Pacific Standard Time 8 P.M. to 8 P.M., Hawaiian and Alaskan time 6 P.M. to 6 P.M. By doing this through all the time zones, every polling place on the continent and in Hawaii and Alaska would close at exactly the same moment.

In this way, the computers would have to wait until every last vote was in before they could perform their wonders. There would still be vigorous enterprise among the networks to be first on the air with a projection of the first results available, but this competition could not possibly affect the result.

I am convinced that this system, or one like it, will become a part of our election process eventually. If it doesn't, we face the very real prospect that electronic disenfranchisement of millions of American voters may decide the outcome of a future presidential election.

I have never been lower emotionally than I was the day after the election. I was the only incumbent Democratic senator in the country to lose his seat, and the youngest ex-senator in American history. My friends and thousands of strangers I had never met had spent long days and nights stamping envelopes and walking precincts for me. In the primary and general elections, my supporters spent more than $1,300,000—and we were faced with a $300,000 deficit. And it was all for nothing.

My personal life was also at a difficult stage. Nancy, my wife of eight years, had never been able to adjust to the frenetic life we had led in Washington. An extremely artistic woman, she was determined to live a quieter life in which she could pursue her skills as a ceramicist. And we both knew that I could not be happy unless I was on the move. It was this difference in philosophies, not a lack of respect, that led to our decision to obtain a divorce.

But a vacation in Palm Springs, as Frank Sinatra's guest, did much to revive my spirits. Yul Brynner and Leo Durocher were also staying with him and we had a great time hacking around the golf courses and lounging around Frank's pool. Sinatra had lent his name and talents to the fight against Proposition 14, as he has to many liberal causes. We were having a drink one night when he asked his Negro house man, George Jacobs, how he had voted on Proposition 14.

George looked at Brynner, who is of Swiss-Mongolian extraction, and said: "I voted yes. Do you think I want that Oriental living next door to me?"

That first week after the election, I began to consider what I would do next. But before I could decide among a number of job opportunities, Bob and Ted Kennedy made it possible for me to go to Europe, with my son Marc, to open the John F. Kennedy Library exhibits in Zurich and Milan. Early in 1965, I accepted a position as vice-president of National General Corporation, whose home office is in Beverly Hills. My employer was Eugene Klein, who had been one of my principal supporters in the campaign. National General is a diversified corporation whose holdings range from theatre chains to savings and loan associations. My principal duties were in advertising and in pre-production planning and financing of motion pictures.

In September 1965, I became vice-president for International Affairs of Continental Air Lines, working with President Bob Six, the friend I was having lunch with at the Sans Souci restaurant the day I resigned from the White House. I still retain, however, my connection with National General as president of a subsidiary corporation involved in overseas theatre construction, and a consultant to the parent corporation.

Late in the campaign against George Murphy, I was in an elevator in a Hollywood office building when I heard an attractive young woman and her photographer companion speaking in French. When I turned toward them, she recognized me.

"Pierre Salinger! I've been trying to see you for days but your staff won't give me an appointment."

She then introduced herself as Nicole Gillmann, a correspondent for the French magazine *Réalités*, and said she had been assigned to interview me.

Now, a story in a French publication wasn't likely to produce many votes for me in California, but Miss Gillmann was too charming to resist and she rode in the car with me that afternoon to a series of rallies, shooting questions in rapid-fire French.

After the election, on my way to the Kennedy Library exhibit opening in Zurich and Milan, I met Miss Gillmann again, quite by accident, at a party in Paris.

Nicole is now my wife. Our first child, Gregory, was born on March 25, 1966. We live in a hillside home overlooking the Sunset Strip in Hollywood—a home that is always open to old friends in the Washington press corps and to my one-time colleagues on the White House staff.

I have continued my activity in politics as president of the California Golden Bear Club, a fund-raising organization for Democratic candidates, and as a member of Governor Brown's steering committee in his race for a third term.

But as my own brief but lively career in politics slips farther into the past, I am less and less inclined to think that I will ever run for public office again. But having issued irrevocable denials of political ambition in the past, only to back down on them, I will make none now.

Since leaving Washington, I have given as much of my time as I can speaking to student audiences. The question I receive most often is whether I believe John F. Kennedy will go down in history as a great President. The question is difficult to answer. He, certainly, was not at all satisfied with the record of his administration. He regarded the nuclear test ban treaty as his most important achievement, and Vietnam as the most frustrating of his foreign policy endeavors. In the domestic field, he was disappointed that he had not been able to push either Medicare or a comprehensive civil rights bill through the Congress. Yet there can be no question that the groundwork he laid for both was a factor in their eventual enactment under President Johnson.

I am, of course, a prejudiced witness. But I believe that future generations of Americans will rank him as one of our greatest Presidents—not because of his specific accomplishments, and there were many, but because he brought to a world, cynical after almost two decades of cold war, the hope that a better life was possible. Perhaps it was his youth, his eloquence, or his undeniable commitment to life and excellence. But whatever it was, it lit a new hope in the hearts of people everywhere in the world that the force of reason, not the force of arms, might finally prevail in the councils of man.

# EPILOGUE

What I have attempted to write down on these pages is a view of life at the center of power. The presidency of the United States is the ultimate in power as we know it in the world today.

Many have expressed amazement that any man would want to take on the burdens of the presidency. There have been different motives, of course, but those Presidents in our history who are remembered and will be remembered were men with ideas who knew that the presidency was the place where those ideas could be put into motion.

These men understood two things:

The first was the nature of power and an awareness of this nation's ultimate repository of power.

The second was more important—it was the concept that linked ideas and power and that to give force to ideas one had to know both how to launch them and from where they should be launched.

The twentieth-century world has given our Presidents a multiplicity of ways to disseminate their views. These same conduits of information have made it possible for a broader base of the American people to be informed, and therefore to have ideas of their own on the conduct of their country.

There are those who believe that one must always be guided by the other—either the people by the ideas of their President, or the President by the ideas of his people.

This is a fatal concept in our democratic system. For the people to abdicate their right to dissent and discussion with the decisions of their leaders is the ultimate destruction of democracy. It is equally destructive for a President to shape his decisions to conform with what he thinks the public wants. This is a complete abdication of his leadership responsibility.

Having said that, however, an American President cannot be successful unless there is a general acceptance and support for his position on a multiplicity of issues. Thus, the President may accept the public's views on some issues, and attempt to prod, cajole or, educate a change in the public's views on other issues.

The need for acceptance, the need, on occasion, to change the public viewpoint on great issues explain the importance of the American press —and its relationship with the American presidency.

I have noted an almost constant struggle between these two institutions but one should not be sorrowed by this struggle. It is inevitable and it will be continuing. The press (and I include all forms of communication) does more than transmit news. In a very real sense it reflects the questioning of the American people, a desire for more and more information on which to make an informed judgment. (One must wonder whether the deluge of information available in our democratic society sometimes confuses rather than informs.)

John F. Kennedy recognized this in one of his last speeches, at Amherst College on October 26, 1963, when he said: "The men who create power make an indispensable contribution to the nation's greatness, but the men who question power make a contribution just as indispensable, especially when that questioning is disinterested, for they determine whether we use power or power uses us. Our national strength matters, but the spirit which informs and controls our strength matters just as much."

The President has still another objective. He attempts to present the decisions and policies of his administration in the best possible light. He also feels the need for an orderly presentation of his views, which conflicts with the basic desire of the press, on occasion, to present what the President is going to do before he does it.

One cannot quarrel with the desires of the press or the desires of the President. One must understand them, however, because they are so basic to the conduct of the public's business in our country.

The history of our country suggests that where a President has fully and clearly explained his policies in a crisis situation, he has generally had the support of the people. When a President unintentionally or willfully does not fully or adequately explain his position, the result is invariably a divided and confused public opinion.

The press does not like to consider itself a propaganda arm for the presidency. At the same time it will generally faithfully transmit his viewpoint if given the opportunity to do so. The multiplicity of methods of communication have virtually set up a system of checks and balances within the press which presents the President with a number of options on how to communicate and clearly gives him the ability to communicate.

American television has unintentionally improved the standards of

American newspapers and widened the public's access to the type of background facts and information which used to be reserved for scholars and students. American television has also given a new dimension to the ability of American Presidents to communicate. A citizen seeing his President, live, on television, explaining his views can hardly be led astray by an incomplete account of what the President has said in his morning newspaper.

I have thus far talked only of American public opinion—but in reality it will be in the arena of international public opinion that the battle of men's minds will truly concentrate in the rest of this century.

The power of the American presidency goes far beyond the borders of our own country, and what he says is of vital importance to people everywhere. The advent of international television by satellite, not more than five years away from reality, will revolutionize the ability of American Presidents and other world leaders to communicate with the peoples of all nations. American Presidents of the past may have felt that what the peoples of other nations felt about their policies did not really matter. The Presidents of the future will not be permitted such a decision.

What I have said about American public opinion will also be true of international public opinion. American Presidents will not need to follow the view of peoples abroad, but they will have to be aware of those views, and in some instances will have to explain their policies in such a way as to have an impact on them. The American President who does not have a measure of support around the world will be as much a failure as the American President of today and yesterday who does not have a measure of support from the American people.

If I have been harsh on the American press from time to time in this book, it is not out of a dislike or distrust of the institution. The opposite is true. It is because I have such a high regard for the press when it lives up to its finest capabilities that I am disappointed when it does not. Nor have I used this book as an apologia for the government in its relations with the press. I have underlined the responsibilities of the government in a number of areas, and the errors of the government with a number of specifics. I do not believe that the press or the government is always right or always wrong. I certainly do not subscribe to the view that newsmen, on achieving a role in the government apparatus, suddenly become bitter adversaries of the press and part of a larger conspiracy to deprive the American people of the information to which they are rightfully entitled. Nor do I believe that the press is single-mindedly devoted to exposing the innermost secrets of the government to the advantage of its enemies.

What I do believe is that the government of the United States and the press of the United States need each other and must understand each other. Where communications between the two institutions break down, the public is the ultimate loser. In the kind of world we now live in, this is a loss we cannot afford.

I believe that in one critical area of the relationship between the press and the government, these communications have broken down. This is the area of how the government and the press work with each other in the time of national crisis short of a declared war.

We saw the problem at the time of the invasion at the Bay of Pigs, in the Cuban missile crisis of 1962, in the continuing struggle between the two institutions over information on the war in Vietnam.

What is needed now is an honest effort to come to grips with this problem. I would suggest an immediate conference, away from Washington, in a setting which would induce informal but incisive discussion of this subject. The participants at this conference should be the top news executives of our major networks and wire services, the editors of a half dozen to a dozen leading newspapers, and the top people in the government entrusted with the responsibility of information. Perhaps the Aspen Institute for Humanistic Studies, in Aspen, Colorado, would lend its splendid facilities for such a meeting. (I know that they would welcome such a meeting.) The central subject should be the dissemination of information by the government in the gray area of national security where the vital interests of our nation are at stake. The press representatives should be prepared to make a concrete contribution toward this discussion—without falling back on the usual cries of press censorship. And the government representatives should come to the meeting without the usual notion that the press is always the villain of the piece. Perhaps it would be well to include former Press Secretaries to American Presidents in this meeting, drawing on their experiences in the White House. Speaking for myself, I would welcome such an opportunity.

If this book stimulates such a discussion, then I will consider that it has served its purpose well.

# INDEX

64, 65–66, 216; and presidential campaign, 34–35, 49–50; and TV conferences, 56, 216

Sorensen, Thomas C., 220, 221, 222, 223, 233

Sotomayor, Antonio, 123

South America. *See* Latin America

Southeast Asia, 54, 68, 199, 210, 214, 255, 324. *See also* specific countries

South Vietnam. *See* Vietnam

Southwick, Paul, 10

Souvanna Phouma, Prince, 181, 194, 237

Soviet bloc, 54, 179, 192, 231, 269, 270. *See also* Communism; specific countries

Soviet Union, 134, 136, 158, 159, 191, 249–67 *passim*, 269–83 *passim*; and Bay of Pigs, 149, 154; communications with, 113, 134, 176–88, 189–96, 197–206, 208–17, 269–83 *passim*; correspondents from, 132, 183, 193, 195–96 (*see also* specific correspondents, news agencies); and Cuban missile crisis (*see under* Cuba); and disarmament (*see* Nuclear weapons); and Germany (*see* Berlin; East Germany; West Germany); and LBJ, 335; and nuclear testing (*see under* Nuclear weapons); press conferences in, 55, 191; and RB-47 incident, 136, 138, 140–41; Salinger in (*see under* Salinger, Pierre); security, news management in, 158, 159, 285–302 *passim*; and Vienna meeting, 133, 169, 175–82. *See also* Khrushchev, Nikita S.

*Soviet Union* (magazine), 211

Space flights, 178, 185

Spain, 309

Spalding, Charles, 94, 95, 98

Sparkman, John J., 71

Spaso House, 222, 233

Special Government Information Subcommittee of the House Committee on Government Operations, 152, 154

"Specials" (city daily newspapers), 116–19

Speeches, speech writing, 32, 66–67, 108–9, 113, 119, 155, 163, 164, 264, 357–58; JFK before UN, 190–91, 194–95. *See also* specific events, individuals, occasions

"Spirit of Camp David," 176, 232

Spivak, Al, 202

*Splendor in the Grass* (movie), 103

Spokane, Washington, 20

Sports Arena (Los Angeles), 36, 42, 43

Springfield, Ohio, 250

Squaw Island, 92

Staff, White House, 63–80, 88, 129, 316–17, 332, 333. *See also* specific individuals

Stalin, Joseph, 225, 226–27, 235, 236

Stanton, Frank, 215

Starlings, 101–2

State Department, U. S., 37–38, 53, 68, 120, 123, 172, 198, 202, 206, 210; and Bay of Pigs, 145, 154; and Cuban missile crisis, 249, 250, 251, 253, 257, 258, 260, 274–80, 293, 294, 295; and presidential travels, 164, 166, 168, 169; press and, 132, 133, 135, 137; and Salinger's trip to Russia, 219–20, 234; and Soviet newsmen, 193, 195–96; and Vietnam, 321–29. *See also* Rusk, Dean

State Department Building, 138, 140, 337

Statler Hotel (Los Angeles), 38

Stern, Isaac, 207, 309, 310

Steven, William P., 267

Stevens, George, 103

Stevens, George, Jr., 103

Stevenson, Adlai E., 1, 69, 352; and Bay of Pigs, 147; and Cuban missile crisis, 249, 250, 255, 259, 274, 280, 293, 295; and 1960 presidential campaign, 42–43; Salinger and political career of, 13, 29, 38, 42–43, 163; as UN Ambassador, 69

Stimson (Henry L.) papers, 67

Stockpile scandal, 118

Stockton, California, 16

Stone, Walker, 298–99